The Renaissance and Long Eighteenth Century

The Renaissance and Long Eighteenth Century is a pedagogical triumph. It is a wisely conceived, carefully structured, lucidly written and richly illustrated book. The activity sections anticipate, and deftly handle, some of the basic questions that always confront students encountering the literature of the Renaissance and the long eighteenth century – from literary terms and language, to historical contexts. At the same time, the volume also introduces students to the most challenging and exciting issues that have been raised by the best scholarship in the field. Students reading this book will develop skills of close-reading while also understanding the complex worlds in which these texts were produced.

Ania Loomba
Catherine Bryson Professor of English
University of Pennsylvania

Among the many anthologies designed for undergraduate course-work in the historical fields of English literature, this one stands out for its focus on the in-depth study of a few works organised according to genre and a coherent set of formal and thematic issues, as well as for the clarity of its editorial guidance. Representing the Renaissance, *Othello* and *The Duchess of Malfi* make for a dynamic pairing of tragedies of transgressive marriage, moral corruption and murder; while the focus on travel writing (over poetry or the novel) as exemplary genre of the long eighteenth century is positively inspired, attuning students to the global expansion of 'English' in the period. The volume will engage students in a broad range of approaches – formal and textual, historical and cultural – to the study of literature, equipping them with basic analytic tools and immersing them in live critical debates rather than settled conclusions. The editorial commentary is lucid, thorough and helpful without being overbearing.

Ian Duncan
Professor of English
University of California, Berkeley

Reading and Studying Literature

This book is part of the series *Reading and Studying Literature* published by Bloomsbury Academic in association with The Open University. The three books in the series are:

The Renaissance and Long Eighteenth Century (edited by Anita Pacheco and David Johnson)
   ISBN 978-1-84966-622-0 (hardback)
   ISBN 978-1-84966-614-5 (paperback)
   ISBN 978-1-84966-634-3 (ebook)

Romantics and Victorians (edited by Nicola J. Watson and Shafquat Towheed)
   ISBN 978-1-84966-623-7 (hardback)
   ISBN 978-1-84966-624-4 (paperback)
   ISBN 978-1-84966-637-4 (ebook)

The Twentieth Century (edited by Sara Haslam and Sue Asbee)
   ISBN 978-1-84966-620-6 (hardback)
   ISBN 978-1-84966-621-3 (paperback)
   ISBN 978-1-84966-640-4 (ebook)

This publication forms part of the Open University module A230 *Reading and studying literature*. Details of this and other Open University modules can be obtained from the Student Registration and Enquiry Service, The Open University, PO Box 197, Milton Keynes MK7 6BJ, United Kingdom (tel. +44 (0)845 300 60 90, email general-enquiries@open.ac.uk).

www.open.ac.uk

The Renaissance and Long Eighteenth Century

Edited by Anita Pacheco and David Johnson

The Open University

BLOOMSBURY ACADEMIC

Published by

Bloomsbury Academic
an imprint of Bloomsbury Publishing Plc
36 Soho Square
London W1D 3QY
United Kingdom
and
175 Fifth Avenue
New York
NY 10010
USA
www.bloomsburyacademic.com

In association with

The Open University
Walton Hall
Milton Keynes MK7 6AA
United Kingdom

First published 2012

Edited and designed by The Open University.

Printed and bound in the United Kingdom by Latimer Trend & Company, Estover Road, Plymouth PL6 7PY.

CIP records for this book are available from the British Library and the Library of Congress.

ISBN 978-1-84966-622-0 (hardback)
ISBN 978-1-84966-614-5 (paperback)
ISBN 978-1-84966-634-3 (ebook)

1.1

Contents

Preface

The Renaissance and Long Eighteenth Century is the first book in the three-volume series Reading and Studying Literature, which aims to provide a chronological overview of the major literary periods. The other two books in the series are *Romantics and Victorians* (edited by Nicola J. Watson and Shafquat Towheed) and *The Twentieth Century* (edited by Sara Haslam and Sue Asbee). Together, these three books form the core teaching material for the Open University undergraduate module *Reading and studying literature* (Open University module code A230).

Although the books should ideally be read together, *The Renaissance and Long Eighteenth Century* also stands on its own as a stimulating and innovative introduction to writing in English from the seventeenth and eighteenth centuries. The first part of this book, 'Love and death in the Renaissance', examines a period best known for its experiments in the writing of tragic drama. It looks at two major tragedies of the period, William Shakespeare's *Othello* and John Webster's *The Duchess of Malfi*. Both plays are about forbidden marriages for love which have catastrophic consequences. This part of the book explores how the two dramatists represent these love matches and invest them with tragic meaning. The focus is on the two related themes of love and death, but other important themes, like race, class and gender, also play a prominent role. The chapters are designed to develop skills of close reading while also giving due attention to the plays as texts written for performance.

The second part of the book, 'Journeys in the long eighteenth century', examines travel writing, both fictional and non-fictional, produced between the 1680s and the 1790s. It asks why travel writing should have been so popular a genre in this period and what uses its selected authors make of their journey narratives. The texts examined in this part are Aphra Behn's novel *Oroonoko, or The Royal Slave*, one of the earliest fictional representations of Atlantic slavery; Voltaire's *Candide*, which turns its hero's journeys into a meditation on contemporary philosophical problems; the autobiography of the ex-slave Ukawsaw Gronniosaw; and the documents produced in the aftermath of the mutiny on the ship the *Bounty* by Captain William Bligh and Fletcher Christian, among others. While the first part of this book focuses on the literary text, Part 2 considers the importance of context, and asks how the meanings of texts change when they are read in relation to the social, political, philosophical and literary currents of the period in which they were produced. Both parts of the book also explore what these texts mean to us today, examining the uses which the present makes of the past.

Open University modules and text books are the products of extensive collaboration and involve the labour of numerous people. Sincere thanks are due to members of the A230 module team who did not write for this volume but contributed generously to the discussions that helped to shape it: Richard Allen, Sue Asbee, Richard Danson Brown, Delia da Sousa Correa, Jessica Davies, Suman Gupta, Sara Haslam, Steve Padley, Clare Spencer, Shafquat Towheed and Nicola J. Watson; to the curriculum manager Rachel Pearce; the editors Hannah Parish and Richard Jones; and the external assessor Michael Baron.

List of contributors

Robert Fraser is Professor of English at The Open University. He is the author of books on Marcel Proust and the anthropologist Sir James Frazer, as well as full-length biographies of the twentieth-century British poet George Barker and the poet and translator David Gascoyne. A Fellow of the Royal Society of Literature, he is a co-author of the forthcoming official history of the Oxford University Press.

David Johnson is a Senior Lecturer in the Department of English at The Open University. His publications include *Shakespeare and South Africa* (1996) and *Jurisprudence: A South African Perspective* (2001). He co-edited *A Historical Companion to Postcolonial Literatures in English* (2005) and is series editor with Ania Loomba of the Edinburgh University Press series *Postcolonial Literary Studies*.

Anita Pacheco is a Senior Lecturer in the Department of English at The Open University and Chair of the Open University undergraduate module *Reading and studying literature*. She is the author of numerous articles and book chapters on Aphra Behn and the editor of *A Companion to Early Modern Women's Writing* (2002). Her book on Shakespeare's *Coriolanus* appeared in the 'Writers and their Work' series (2007).

Dennis Walder is Emeritus Professor of Literature in the English Department at The Open University. He is the author of *Dickens and Religion* (2007 [1987]). He published the first book on Athol Fugard in 1984, and has since edited Fugard's plays and produced a new study of the playwright (*Athol Fugard*, 2003). His other books include *Post-Colonial Literatures: History, Language, Theory* (1998) and *Postcolonial Nostalgias: Writing, Memory and Reputation* (2010).

Required reading

You will need to read the following texts in conjunction with this book:

Part 1

For Chapters 1 and 2: William Shakespeare (2008 [1622]) *Othello* (ed. Michael Neill), Oxford World's Classics, Oxford, Oxford University Press.

For Chapters 3 and 4: John Webster (2009 [1623]) *The Duchess of Malfi* (ed. Monical Kendall), Harlow, Pearson Longman.

Part 2

For Chapter 5: Aphra Behn (2003 [1688]) *Oroonoko* (ed. Janet Todd), London, Penguin Classics.

For Chapter 6: Voltaire (2005 [1759]) *Candide, or Optimism* (ed. and trans. Theo Cuffe, with an introduction by Michael Wood), London, Penguin Classics.

The required reading for Chapters 7 and 8 can be found in 'Readings for Part 2'.

Part 1
Love and death in the Renaissance

Aims

The first part of this book will:

- introduce you to the literature of the English Renaissance through the study of two tragedies of the period
- examine the representation of love and death in the plays
- consider the two plays as texts to be read, analysed and performed.

Introduction to Part 1

Anita Pacheco

Welcome to 'Love and death in the Renaissance', the first part of *The Renaissance and Long Eighteenth Century*. This part of the book will introduce you to the literature of the English Renaissance through the study of two plays of the period. Chapters 1 and 2 consider William Shakespeare's *Othello* (first performed in 1604), and Chapters 3 and 4 concentrate on John Webster's *The Duchess of Malfi* (first performed in 1613–14).

Let's start with a brief consideration of the literary period itself. The word 'Renaissance' means 'rebirth'; it refers to a cultural and educational movement which began in Italy in the fourteenth century and was dedicated to the revival in Europe of the art and culture of ancient Greece and Rome. The word 'Renaissance' refers both to this widespread movement and to the historical period in which it thrived, roughly 1500–1700 in England. However, many historians and literary critics prefer to use the term 'early modern' when writing about this era, on the grounds that it better highlights the period's transitional status between the Middle Ages and modernity. In the four chapters in this part, we will use both terms – Renaissance and early modern – though it's only fair to add that in its general usage, 'early modern' usually refers to a slightly longer block of time – from around 1500 to 1750 – than does the term 'Renaissance'.

We have chosen to concentrate on drama in this part of the book because the English Renaissance is a literary period still best known for its plays and especially, of course, for those written by Shakespeare. The Renaissance also produced many accomplished and innovative poets and writers of prose, but it is generally agreed that in England during the Renaissance the most remarkable outpouring of literary creativity took place in the theatre. One of the main reasons for this explosion of drama was the construction in London of the nation's first permanent, free-standing theatres in the second half of the sixteenth century. Drama, largely religious in nature, had flourished in England for many centuries but without a purpose-built playing space. Mystery plays were performed on pageant wagons that progressed through the streets during religious festivals, while the later morality plays were acted by troupes of travelling players in great halls of universities or aristocratic households. By the 1570s, theatre had its own unique space: the Theatre in Shoreditch was built in 1576 and was eventually replaced by a number of venues, including the Swan, the Rose and the Globe. The acting companies attached to these theatres depended for their survival on aristocratic or royal patronage, and the plays they performed were subject to the scrutiny of the government censor. The companies were also in competition with one another for the attendance of London theatre-goers. The necessity of appealing to the tastes and interests of this large and socially diverse group helped to inspire the writing and staging of a remarkable number of new plays in many different genres and styles.

Figure 1   A performance of Shakespeare's *Antony and Cleopatra* at the reconstructed Globe Theatre (London, 1999). Photo: Shakespeare's Globe.

Our interest in this part of the book is not just in Renaissance drama but, more specifically, in its treatment of love and death. We have opted to focus on these two themes on the grounds that they provide profitable angles from which to view the literature of the Renaissance. The two plays we will be looking at have several features in common. One is that they are both tragedies. Tragedy is a rather slippery literary term which tends to change its meaning in different historical periods. However, one thing we can say with a reasonable degree of accuracy is that tragedies end with the death of the protagonist, who in Renaissance drama is usually a man of high birth and exceptional abilities. In this they obviously contrast with comedies, which in all literary periods are characterised by their happy endings. The death of the tragic protagonist is brought about by a conflict which can take many forms, but we can perhaps risk a generalisation here: tragedies stage a conflict between a remarkable individual – the tragic hero – and some powerful shaping force – fate, God, established authority – which limits his aspirations and finally destroys him. Yet even this loose definition fails to accommodate *The Duchess of Malfi*, which places at its centre a tragic heroine rather than a hero.

Tragic drama thrived on the English stage from the 1580s through to the 1620s. What kind of conditions might have encouraged such a flowering of tragedy in this period? Elizabethans and Jacobeans lived in a society that was highly stratified, where political power was concentrated in the hands of the monarch and a small ruling elite, and where authorities liked to preach the virtues of 'knowing your place' in the social hierarchy. Yet what if the ruler or any member of the governing class proved to be incompetent, corrupt or even criminal? In what was unquestionably the most popular form of tragedy in Renaissance England – the revenge tragedy – this intractable social problem is rehearsed time and again, as the stage revenger struggles to find justice in a dramatic world in which the privileged few abuse their power and fail to govern with fairness or justice. These plays suggest that tragedies in general fulfilled an important social and political function in late sixteenth- and early seventeenth-century England, staging widespread communal tensions and anxieties generated by the society in which they were written. This claim for the social utility of tragic drama accords with what the ancient Greek philosopher Aristotle, in his *Poetics* (fourth century BCE), saw as the chief aim of the tragic dramatist: to create 'catharsis', or a purging of powerful emotions, in spectators, who leave the theatre feeling relieved, even elated, despite having just spent several hours watching dramatic representations of suffering and death.

Both of the plays examined in this part of the book, especially *The Duchess of Malfi*, are shaped by the conventions of revenge tragedy. Yet they also have an affinity with another subgenre, the domestic tragedy, so-called because its focus is the domestic sphere, the realm of the family and marriage. This brings us to our second theme of love. If *Othello* and *The Duchess of Malfi* are both tragedies, they are also centrally concerned with love. As a theme, love is ubiquitous in English Renaissance literature, which examines love in its many guises. Much of the love poetry of the period depicts a man's love for a woman (or, in some cases, for another man) as spiritually uplifting. But this does not mean that Elizabethans and Jacobeans were in any way shy of confronting the sexual element in love. The two plays we are studying in this part of the book are concerned with married love, in which sexual desire plays a crucial part. On the stage, this type of love was the central theme of comedies of the time, many of which dealt with the courtship of young lovers who end up defying parental disapproval and marrying for love. This could with some justice be called the classic comic plot, and in a comedy the conflict between young love and parental (especially paternal) authority is resolved in the lovers' favour, allowing for the happy ending that distinguishes comedy from tragedy, and which in Renaissance comedy more often than not takes the form of marriage.

This standard comic plot suggests one reason why marriage for love could be fruitful material for tragedy in this period: there were clearly opposing notions of what a marriage ought to be. Was it a strategic alliance between families best arranged by the heads of those families, or an institution whose principal end was the happiness and fulfilment, including the sexual fulfilment, of husband and wife? We have seen that tragedies in this period focus on the upper classes, and it was this social group that was most preoccupied with marriage as an economic and political transaction between families, in which the wishes and feelings of the bride and groom meant little. But by the sixteenth century, this idea had to compete with other powerful cultural trends, such as the Protestant view that marriage constituted the fount of human happiness and so needed to be based upon mutual affection and desire if it was to fulfil its exalted purpose. Yet, if the freedom to choose one's marriage partner came to seem desirable to most people in this period, on what basis ought a young man or woman choose? Many Renaissance writers, including Shakespeare and Webster, were alert to the powerfully destabilising and unpredictable properties of sexual passion. Was it therefore prudent to build a marriage on such an unstable foundation?

Othello and *The Duchess of Malfi* are informed by such contemporary questions and debates about the nature and function of marriage. Marriage for love in these plays involves not just defying familial authority but marrying outside one's race or class. These love matches, with their bold challenges to social norms and expectations, prove to be desperately fragile, either because of their own internal weaknesses or because of external pressures. Unable to trigger the happy resolution of comedies, they mark instead the start of a tragic cycle of decline culminating in death.

In addition to introducing you to the treatment of the themes of love and death in two Renaissance tragedies, this part will examine a concept central to literary studies – the concept of the 'text'. This is a term which has figured especially prominently in literary criticism over the last forty years or so. Indeed, what used to be called 'literary works' are much more likely nowadays to be called 'literary texts'. This change of vocabulary reflects a desire to place a certain distance between a piece of writing and its author – a desire which resulted from a growing sense that authors are not necessarily entirely in control of the writings they produce, due to such factors as the slipperiness of language, the power of culture to shape human consciousness and the complex workings of the human psyche. The word 'work' has been supplanted with the more impersonal term 'text' in an effort to foreground the view that a literary text can end up meaning things that the author never consciously intended.

We will be considering 'texts' in a more straightforward way – as words on the page, the printed version of the play, or the play text. This will be the principal object of study in this part of the book. There are certainly other ways to read and study literary texts. For example, many literary critics prefer to read them historically; that is, by placing the text in its historical contexts, looking at how its meanings are shaped by the period in which it was produced. We will certainly be considering some of the contexts of *Othello* and *The Duchess of Malfi* in the chapters that follow, but the main focus will be on how meaning is created by the words on the page. In each chapter, there are a number of activities. Many of these activities aim to hone your skills of textual analysis by engaging in close reading of particular passages of the play texts. Through detailed examination of the distinctive features of the language, these activities attempt to uncover the techniques and strategies that enable a passage of the dramatic text to convey particular meanings to the reader or spectator. We strongly suggest that you attempt these activities before reading the discussions that follow them. You may also find it useful to consult the glossary at the end of the book, which contains definitions of literary terms key to the study of literature. Terms in the glossary are **emboldened** on their first occurrence.

Because we are studying plays, we will also give some attention to the question of how the words on the page might be translated into performance. Plays are, above all, performance texts, so that analysis of the way the language works can also provide clues as to how an actor might deliver the particular speech or passage – in what tone and with what emphasis and accompanying movements. This can then be expanded into a consideration of other aspects of performance, such as lighting, sound and costume.

Renaissance play texts are often quite unstable entities. Several of Shakespeare's major plays, for example, have survived in two or more significantly different printed versions. How do we decide which one is authoritative? And how do we define 'authoritative'? Does it mean the version that best preserves what Shakespeare actually wrote, or the play as it was acted on the stage of the Globe, which perhaps was considerably shorter than the original manuscript? These are complex questions that it is the job of textual scholars and editors to try to answer. But it is worth bearing in mind as you read *Othello* and *The Duchess of Malfi* that they were produced in a period when plays were the property not of the dramatist but of the theatre company for which he wrote, and when plays were often (though not always) seen primarily as working scripts written for the stage rather than finished works of art destined for the publisher.

Let's turn now to the plays themselves and their rich and complex portrayals of love and death.

Chapter 1
William Shakespeare, *Othello*: impediments to love

Dennis Walder

Aims

This chapter will:

- introduce you to reading a Shakespeare play text closely, attending to the language, dramatic techniques and performance possibilities
- introduce you to the techniques of characterisation in *Othello*
- introduce you to the treatment of the theme of love in *Othello*, focusing on Act 1
- introduce related themes and concerns of the play, such as those of race or 'difference'.

Introduction

One of William Shakespeare's (*c*.1564–1616) most well-known **sonnets** begins 'Let me not to the marriage of true minds / Admit impediments' (Kerrigan, 1986, p. 134). Love, and the impediments to love, make up one of the great themes of literature. In the Renaissance, it was a theme that provided endless scope for poets and dramatists, and Shakespeare developed it in plays as various as *Romeo and Juliet*, *A Midsummer Night's Dream*, *As You Like It* and *Othello*. In comedies like *A Midsummer Night's Dream*, love triumphs over adversity, and the conclusion is marriage. But in the play that concerns us here, *Othello* (first performed in 1604), the love of the two characters at its centre is met by jealousy, hate, treachery and finally death. It is a play that feels very close to us in its focus on feelings with which we are familiar; in fact, in the theatre the intensity with which it depicts those feelings has led audience members sometimes to cry out to the characters in fear or warning.

This reminds us how important it is to think about how a play comes across in performance. A willingness to use our imagination to look for the meanings in the extraordinarily rich yet sometimes also obscure words of the text can take us a good way towards understanding and enjoying what we are seeing, on the page as well as on the stage. Stage directions and explanations can be a help, although you may not find very many of these in Shakespeare's texts, and some you do find will have been added later by editors. So you must watch out for indications of the 'Look, who comes here?' type when reading the text.

This connects with the way in which the concept of the 'text' is dealt with in this chapter, and indeed throughout this part of the book, not only as a matter of close scrutiny of the words on the page, but also as a recognition that a text is not necessarily fixed, despite appearing in print. A play text is a script for a performance, which is always a group product, the result of decisions about the text taken by all those involved in a production, to a greater or lesser degree. This may well lead to revisions, excisions and other alterations – even apart from the fact that in any given performance, actors may add or delete things. In the theatre, a play will run for just an evening, lasting a few hours; our journey as readers will be longer, since we will be pausing frequently, to read and reread the text and to think about what we are reading, and working out how to express our views about its concerns. Understanding this distinction should mean that when you come across this play – and others by Shakespeare – you will enjoy it with greater understanding and insight than before.

It's often said that you must see a Shakespeare play before you read it. Like other playwrights of his time, Shakespeare wrote his plays principally for the stage, with the intention that actors would speak his words in front of audiences, rather than for readers to read them in book form. However, he may well have expected his plays to be published together after his death, and indeed roughly half of his plays were published during his lifetime. Initially, these were in a kind of paperback known as a 'quarto', so-called because they were made from paper folded twice to make four leaves, 22 × 16 cm in size. When *Othello* was first published in 1622, it was as a quarto. A year later, in 1623, it was published in a collection of his plays in a more prestigious format, a folio, in which the paper is folded only once, making a large book about 45 × 32 cm in size. This was the First Folio, or F1. There are some important differences between these two published texts, which I will refer to later. The important point here is that we cannot always be certain exactly what Shakespeare wrote or which version of the play text was performed in the early seventeenth century.

Reading the play

The edition of the play that is referred to in Chapters 1 and 2 is the Oxford World's Classics (2008) edition, edited by Michael Neill. This was a choice determined not only by quality and availability, but by the extensive introductory remarks on staging and performance history, including production photographs and related artwork. You are not expected to read Neill's introduction unless you wish to do so, but rather to begin your reading of the play text.

This chapter will concentrate on the first act of the play, and Chapter 2 will consider Acts 2–5. You should ensure that you have read the relevant parts of the play before starting the chapters.

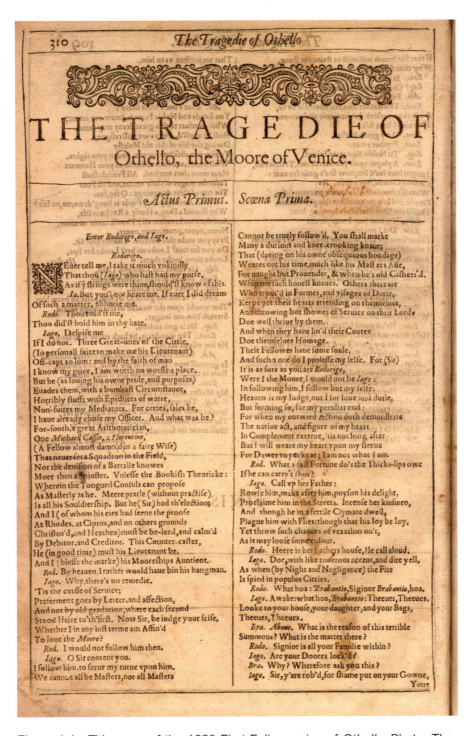

Figure 1.1 Title page of the 1623 First Folio version of *Othello*. Photo: The Folger Shakespeare Library, Washington, D.C.

Act 1, Scene 1: making a start

As you can see in Figure 1.1, the play's full title is *The Tragedie of Othello, the Moore of Venice*. This title gives a few clues about the nature and content of the play. A contemporary audience would know what to expect from its being called a **tragedy**: the term signified a play involving the death of a great or noble person. Second, the main character, or tragic hero, is called Othello, who is a Moor. The Moors were the Muslim inhabitants of North Africa, mainly Morocco and Algeria. In the eighth century, they conquered much of present-day Spain, which was not re-conquered until the fifteenth century. Moors were considered heathens, although some became Christians after the re-conquest.

By the time that *Othello* appeared on the stage, there was a **tradition** of African characters being called Moors, and the term 'blackamoor' came to be used derogatorily of any person considered black-skinned. There were villainous Moors, such as the character Aaron in Shakespeare's earlier play *Titus Andronicus* (1592–3). There were also white or 'tawny' Moors whose blackness was not emphasised, and who were usually portrayed as dignified oriental rulers, like the character Morocco in Shakespeare's *The Merchant of Venice* (1596). The original audience would no doubt have waited with interest to see what kind of Moor Othello is.

The play *Othello* begins like this:

Enter Roderigo and Iago

RODERIGO   Tush, never tell me! I take it much unkindly
              That thou, Iago, who hast had my purse
              As if the strings were thine, shouldst know of this.

IAGO   'Sblood, but you'll not hear me! If ever I
              Did dream of such a matter, abhor me.

RODERIGO   Thou told'st me thou didst hold him in thy hate.

IAGO   Despise me if I do not.

(1.1.1–7)

I have always found these opening lines a bit of a puzzle in the theatre – the actors rattling them off before I have settled down to listen properly. Furthermore, expressions like 'Tush' and 'never tell me' sound like something from another world, and of course in a sense they are, having been written some 400 years ago. But do not be put off. 'Tush' is glossed by Michael Neill as a 'mild expletive', and together the opening sentences mean something like 'Rubbish, don't give me that!' What they refer to is only made clear later. If it all seems somewhat puzzling, well that is the point. We are expected to want to know what is going on, who these characters are and, even more significantly, to whom and what they are referring. Our curiosity is stirred as we overhear a conversation that has apparently been going on for a bit – an opening ploy typical of many plays before and since.

Until you get used to it, the language of the play may well seem strange, such as the expression ''Sblood', which is short for 'God's blood', an oath considered so strong it was cut from later published texts of the play (as were other oaths). Then there are all those 'thou' and 'thine' forms in use at the time (I will come back to this). But the overall sense seems clear enough, doesn't it? To be sure you can agree, try the following activity.

Activity 1

Reread Act 1, Scene 1, from the beginning through to line 81 and the entry of Brabantio, not paying too much attention to any difficult words or phrases or the editorial notes, but simply trying to get the gist of what is going on. Try to summarise where the play has got to by the end of the dialogue between Iago and Roderigo by answering the following questions in a sentence or two for each:

1   What have we learned about the relationship between Iago and Roderigo from these opening lines?

2   What is Iago apparently most concerned about in this opening section of the play?

3   What do you make of Iago's tone when he refers to Othello as 'his Moorship' in line 32? Respectful? Mocking? Consider the **context** carefully.

4   How far are we prepared for what happens next in the play?

Discussion

Below are my responses. Don't worry if they differ somewhat from your own.

1   Roderigo is dependent on Iago, who has been using his money for some purpose not yet made clear. Iago also appears to rely on Roderigo in some way.

2   Iago has been passed over for promotion ('election' (l. 26)), and consequently feels both angry and humiliated. This is perhaps the most obviously important thing to emerge from the opening moments of the play.

3   Iago's tone is sarcastic or mocking, and hardly respectful. When you think that he is apparently referring to his army superior as 'his Moorship', a **pun** on 'his worship', you can see that he is undermining the conventional sense of the term for someone of higher status.

4   We have been prepared for some kind of conspiracy and disruption – we gather one has already been set afoot – as Iago eggs Roderigo on to 'incense' Brabantio (l. 69), who is 'her' father (we do not know who 'she' is yet).

You may have noticed that Roderigo addresses Iago as 'thou', while Iago uses the 'you' form of the personal pronoun to Roderigo. That is, Iago addresses Roderigo in the polite form, as someone of an inferior rank should (he also calls him 'sir'), while at the same time it becomes clear that Iago is actually the dominant force in these exchanges, which have to do with some kind of betrayal regarding Roderigo's money. We do not know who the 'him' is in line 9, though by the end of Iago's first speech we guess that the person referred to several times thereafter is 'his Moorship'. In fact, it is not until Othello's entry in Act 1, Scene 3 that he is dignified with a personal name. This is a process repeated throughout the play: we hear people's views of Othello as a kind of build-up before we see or hear him in person.

What is being established at this point in the play is Iago's behaviour and character traits, and to a lesser extent those of Roderigo. Iago seems to be adept at manipulating those around him, and his expression of resentment at being passed over by 'his Moorship' highlights his disdain, as well as his verbal inventiveness. Shakespeare shows this by contrasting Iago's quickness with Roderigo's brief and rather dim responses.

From the start, then, Iago seems to be presented to us as a bluff and somewhat cynical soldier, who sets up the duffer Roderigo to play a prank on old Brabantio. If we did not know the play was going to be a tragedy, we might take it as a comedy at this stage. We are also led by the opening speeches to appreciate Iago's alertness, and his readiness to attack those who he believes have been given preference over him – notably Cassio. Cassio is referred to as an 'arithmetician' (l. 18), meaning someone who knows about the abstract theory of war rather than the practicalities of soldiering – which Iago suggests he himself is skilled in, and therefore more deserving of advancement. The dismissive, **alliterative** phrase 'Mere prattle without practice' (l. 25) is memorable, sounding like a cleverly damning remark about Cassio, the Florentine (citizen of Florence).

Another point worth making here, since Iago's language is at times quite complex and obscure, is that this obscurity in itself seems to be an aspect of Shakespeare's **characterisation** of him. Iago teases and baffles others by speaking in a way that appears at first to be impressively sensible, but which on closer inspection seems empty, or to reflect badly on the speaker. An example is the speech beginning 'We cannot all be masters …', which ends with the sinister 'I am not what I am' (ll. 43–65). Well, what *is* he, then? He is someone who seems to be saying he will not show everyone who and what he is, thereby pursuing his 'peculiar end' (l. 60), that is, his own specific aims and ambitions ('peculiar' in early modern English is not the same as the modern 'odd' or 'weird'). 'I am not what I am' is a key remark, coming at the end of a speech in which, through a variety of expressions, Iago has effectively announced the kind of person he is: by his wit and energy he invites us to admire him before we realise what the outcome of his behaviour might be. If Roderigo is being turned into Iago's audience, so are we. And, as you will see, Iago increasingly turns to the audience to let us know what he is thinking.

It is important to notice that, as usual with Shakespeare, such speeches do much more than simply engage us with the **plot** which, up to this point, has barely begun. Read these words of Iago's again:

> Were I the Moor, I would not be Iago:
> In following him, I follow but myself –
> Heaven is my judge, not I for love and duty,
> But seeming so for my peculiar end;
> For when my outward action doth demonstrate
> The native act and figure of my heart
> In compliment extern, 'tis not long after
> But I will wear my heart upon my sleeve
> For daws to peck at: I am not what I am.

(1.1.57–65)

In trying to follow his thought, you become aware of how devious Iago is, and also how cleverly he manages to project himself and to dominate Roderigo. Only when you look closely at his tortuous syntax, or word order (do all those 'buts' really make an argument?), and grasp the emptiness of some of his phrases, do you realise – as will be confirmed later – how manipulative he is.

What is Iago saying when he opposes the 'native act and figure of my heart' to 'outward action' (ll. 62, 61)? Simply put, he is saying that if his outward behaviour were to become a reflection of his innermost feelings and intentions, then he would in effect be wearing his heart on his sleeve, 'For daws to peck at' (l. 65); that is, dangerously exposing his inner self to everyone. The familiar proverbial expression 'wearing your heart on your sleeve' is itself a figurative or metaphorical way of putting it. **Figurative language** is language used in a non-literal way. No one ever really wears their heart on their sleeve; what the expression conveys is how it can feel to open one's heart to others unreservedly. The familiarity of such a phrase helps us to understand what's being said here. Shakespeare uses a proverbial expression at this point in the play to convey to his audience an important feature of Iago's character: that he is intent on hiding his inner self from others.

Let's think now about the fact that Shakespeare is creating Iago's character in verse, specifically in lines of unrhymed **iambic pentameter**, or **blank verse**, the favoured medium of drama of the time. Here follows a brief technical digression, containing ideas with which you may already be familiar. The rhythm of a line of verse is provided by the repetition of stressed and unstressed syllables, and an iambic line contains a pattern of rhythmic units in which an unstressed or weak syllable is followed by a stressed or strong syllable: like the word reSTRICT (overemphasised to make the point). To define the rhythm of a line, the syllables are divided into measures, 'feet' or 'meters'. A line of ten syllables can be divided into five feet: the technical term is 'pentameter', from the Greek 'penta' for five and 'meter' for measure. So an iambic pentameter is a line of ten syllables that fall into five measures of two syllables each, in which one unstressed syllable is followed by one stressed syllable. Thus, from Iago's speech, line 62

> The native act and figure of my heart

can be rendered like this, marked with capitals and slashes to bring out the rhythm:

> The NA/tive ACT/ and FIG/ure OF/ my HEART

This is overdoing it, but I hope you can see what I mean. Notice that the rhythmic divisions do not necessarily coincide with the words. This is a standard iambic pentameter line. What you will quickly realise when you look for this pattern in other lines is that many lines vary from this basic beat – they have to, or our ears would quickly become bored. But the variation is always upon this basic rhythm.

There were two main reasons why blank verse was used by Shakespeare and his contemporaries: first, it is easy to say a line like this so that it sounds natural, because the rhythm is based on the rhythm of everyday English speech (the absence of rhyme intensifies this effect); second, an iambic pentameter line is easier to memorise than a longer line or more complicated rhythm. This would have been very helpful to actors who at the time had to perform prodigious feats of memory, performing as they did six or seven plays a week. Shakespeare would also have had to perform such feats since, somewhat unusually, he was an actor as well as a playwright. In 1594, he was a founding member of a theatre company called the Lord Chamberlain's Men (after their noble patron) which in 1603, after the accession of James I, changed its name to the King's Men, thus signalling its dominant position in the theatre of the time.

But to return to the opening, or **exposition** of the play. As you might have noticed, there is a racist element in Iago's repeated references to Othello not by name but as 'the Moor', the negative undertones of which are immediately picked up by Roderigo when he refers coarsely to 'the thick-lips' (l. 66), a remark that we find Brabantio repeating later in the scene. I will come back to this issue, but note that these are hints of what will become increasingly evident: that 'the Moor' is being identified as an outsider by these Venetians, as someone different in ways that will be exploited later.

Now, what immediately follows these opening exchanges? We have certainly been set up by the plotting of Iago and Roderigo and their noisy shouts to expect something dramatic to happen. You might also notice that 'Awake!', 'put on your gown!' and 'Arise, arise!' (ll. 79, 86, 89) all tell us that the opening scene takes place at night. In a modern production, lighting effects would already have indicated as much, heightening the air of suspense and uncertainty with which the play has begun, and confirming that Iago and Roderigo are behaving like a pair of conspirators. In the open-air Globe Theatre, that darkness would have had to be imagined (though the actors may well have carried torches); an indoor theatre like the Blackfriars would have had dimmed lights. *Othello* was performed by the King's Men at both the outdoor Globe and the indoor Blackfriars. The Globe was a 'public' theatre, shaped like a 'wooden O' (as described by the opening **Chorus** in *Henry V*) and built south of the Thames in Southwark. Performances were in the afternoons, since there was no artificial illumination, unlike the 'private' Blackfriars, which was basically a large room with a roof and a stage at one end. The stages of the two theatres were not entirely bare, but audiences were expected to use their imagination. All the actors were male, with boys playing the female characters.

It is not until later in the opening scene that the audience discovers what the important 'something' is that Iago has not passed on to Roderigo: Othello's secret marriage to Desdemona. The whole love plot is about to surface.

The entrance of Othello

As Act 1 proceeds, we learn the full story behind the opening scene and, with the entry of Othello himself, we finally get to see the kind of man who has been the focus of so much anticipatory comment. We also begin to gather a sense of what might be called the symbolic geography of the play: that is, the importance of the place in which it is set and from which it moves. The play starts in Venice, the great centre of civilisation of the time in Europe, and a city state at the heart of a vast commercial empire reliant on military strength drawn where necessary from outsiders and mercenaries like Othello. In Act 2, the action moves to Cyprus, an outpost of that empire, under threat from another empire, the Turkish or Ottoman, and it is in Cyprus that the rest of the play takes place.

But the private dimension of the story is where we are as the first scene continues – and it is where we will stay, despite the potential for the world of war and empires to interfere. Indeed, the last scene of the play is set entirely in a bedroom. *Othello* is called a domestic tragedy precisely because its action remains strictly within this domestic sphere.

With Brabantio's arousal, the full background to the opening scene emerges: Roderigo has been suitor to Brabantio's daughter, Desdemona, who has eloped with 'the Moor' (Othello is still not named at this point). Iago has prompted Roderigo into stirring up Brabantio with a 'dire yell' of the kind usually heard when a fire is 'spied' in the city (1.1.75–7). The near silence and darkness of the opening is split by their cries in the street, followed by the commotion when Brabantio appears 'at a window above', as the stage direction puts it (1.1.81), and which can be thought of as the balcony on the tiring house wall at the back of the stage at the Globe. For the Blackfriars, or our own darkened theatres, imagine a shaft of light suddenly piercing the gloom below when he opens the window.

Activity 2

Do you notice anything remarkable about the language used by Iago and Roderigo as they try to provoke Brabantio? Look closely at the **imagery** in lines 86–116 and consider if there is a particular current of associations driving it, and what purpose that might serve. Check the notes by Neill for any terms you do not understand.

Discussion

The imagery and figurative language is extremely unpleasant; a **register** of animalistic sexual activity which, you may have observed, is first introduced by Iago and then picked up by Roderigo. Iago suggests to Brabantio that 'an old black ram / Is tupping your white ewe' (1.1.88–9). As Neill points out in the note for line 88, the ram was associated with lust and sexual potency, its blackness here additionally associating it with a traditional image of the devil. You might also have noted the allusion to Othello as 'old' – the first of several hints to the effect that he is substantially older than his wife.

Othello's race, then, is being connected – through Shakespeare's use of a **metaphor** – with rampant sexuality, darkness and evil. Metaphors establish an identity between two apparently dissimilar things: here, Othello is identified with an 'old black ram', Desdemona with a 'white ewe' and the sexual act with 'tupping', or animal intercourse (1.1.88, 89). Iago uses language to suggest that Brabantio's daughter is being sexually defiled and worse: she has not simply been stolen or abducted; rather, she is, according to his fevered imagination, being 'covered' by a 'Barbary horse' (1.1.111), the word 'Barbary' referring to North Africa. Like 'tupping', 'covered' associates sex with animality. Iago makes a bad joke out of these implications by remarking (his language so coarse now that it is in the lower key of prose rather than verse) that the resulting progeny will be 'nephews [who] neigh to you' (1.1.112).

This thread of inflammatory suggestion is then picked up by Roderigo, who exclaims that Brabantio's daughter is subject to 'the gross clasps of a lascivious Moor' (1.1.125). This of course further incites the old man who is, it seems, all too ready to rise to the bait and allow his mind to be filled with the suggestions of abduction and worse. You might notice the **alliteration** in Roderigo's phrasing here: the 's' sounds adding to the resonance of his utterance, encouraging the actor almost to spit the words out in disgust. This emphasises the unpleasantness of 'lascivious' in particular, a word which reinforces the association of Moors with unbridled sexuality. Interestingly, none of these lines exists in the earliest (Q1) printed text, which may (we do not know for certain) reflect an attempt to tone down these stereotypical slurs for one of the play's earliest performances (Marcus, 2007, pp. 24–5).

But the text as we receive it nowadays explicitly introduces the theme of sexual love in terms of bestiality, racism and evil. As we will see, this is consistently Iago's way of representing love: love for him *means* animal lust, and when it combines with the idea of racial difference, the standard imagery of racial hatred taken to an extreme, to violence, is very near the surface. This is the case even with Roderigo or Brabantio, who are represented as ordinary Venetians, that is, as members of a wealthy and secure city state. If they feel threatened, the threat is of their own making, prompted by Iago.

For Brabantio, 'This is Venice: / My house is not a grange' (1.1.105–6). A grange, here, is an isolated farmhouse, far from the amenities of civilisation, and where perhaps daughters may be expected to be more vulnerable to the predations of strangers. He even thinks that some kind of witchcraft must have robbed him of his daughter. In some ways, Brabantio here resembles the traditional figure of comedy: the father robbed of his daughter, rushing about in his nightshirt with exaggerated fears. But – and this is where the larger, more public dimension momentarily comes in – we are led to understand that he is nonetheless an important figure in the city, while 'the Moor' is vital to the security of the state, and is about to be sent abroad to Cyprus in its defence. That Brabantio should have been robbed – as he thinks – of his daughter by witchcraft says a great deal about his attitude to Desdemona and to women generally: he sees his daughter as his possession, something that can be stolen from him, which in turn suggests that it is his right to choose the man she marries. Brabantio's reading of the situation also assumes that a black man like Othello could have secured Desdemona's consent to marriage only by using witchcraft on her. It is worth mentioning that at the time, in Jacobean

England, as in Scotland, witchcraft was taken very seriously by many people. King James I himself wrote a tract on the subject.

The potential for violence and intrigue generated by Iago and Roderigo at the start of the play is contrasted with and opposed by the order and control invoked by the older Venetian. Yet this control is clearly fragile,

Figure 1.2   Paul Robeson as Othello and Uta Hagen as Desdemona in *Othello*, dir. Margaret Webster (Theatre Guild Production, Broadway, 1943–4). Photo: Library of Congress Prints and Photographs, Washington, D.C.

and it is not until Scene 3, and the entrance of the Senators, that calm is established after the rather frenzied opening.

What about Othello himself? The glimpses that we have been given by the characters who precede him begin to be developed by his first

Figure 1.3 Lenny Henry as Othello in *Othello*, dir. Barrie Rutter (West Yorkshire Playhouse, Leeds, February 2009). Photo: Geraint Lewis/Rex Features.

appearance in Act 1, Scene 2. What do you make of the way in which he is represented? Clearly, how Othello is dressed and bears himself on his first entrance here matters a lot, and can affect how we view him, his speech and his actions from this point on. Is he to wear modern military officer's dress, as in some productions, such as the 2009 West Yorkshire Playhouse Production with Lenny Henry (see Figure 1.3)? Or in flowing robes and a turban, to look like a Moor of earlier times? Does he bear himself as an arrogant black general, or a noble, and even aloof, heroic figure? There are other possibilities too, of course. In the 1964 National Theatre production, a blacked-up Laurence Olivier appeared at the start in a loose tunic with a cross dangling on his chest, to signal Othello's conversion to Christianity, while sniffing a rose to indicate his new interest in love. This was possibly one of the last great performances in which Othello was *not* played by a black actor. (You might like to look at pp. 44–71 of Michael Neill's introduction in your edition of the play for more about the casting of the role of Othello.)

We will look later at the critical debate about Shakespeare's representation of Othello, but you should start off thinking about the play and its hero for yourself. Let's take a stab at the way Othello's character is depicted at this point in the play.

Activity 3

Have a go at answering the following questions about Othello:

1 Do you have a positive impression of Othello, despite all that has been said about him so far?
2 If so, what makes you feel favourably disposed towards him?
3 Consider Othello's first appearance, especially the words he uses. Do any of them strike you in particular?

You should try to define his manner through what the words of the text imply. Consider especially 1.2.6–32.

Discussion

Here are my answers to these questions, though yours may be quite different:

1 I would say yes, I do get a favourable impression of Othello.
2 Presented by Iago with Brabantio's complaint against him, Othello calmly states 'Let him do his spite', adding that his reputation or 'services' with the state are too solid to allow such trivia to count against him (1.2.17–19).

3   You might have selected several words as standing out from the others, but among the most striking for me was 'unhousèd' (l. 26). I'll discuss this further below.

As with the opening of the play, Scene 2 begins apparently casually, the audience overhearing two men conversing as they enter, with Iago giving Othello his version of what has just happened. If we hadn't already seen and heard Iago, we might well take him at face value here and accept what he says, as Othello does. Othello's opening words are brief, but eloquent, suggesting a man of seriousness, dignity, authority and weight; not at all the 'gross' or 'lascivious' animal of Iago's and Roderigo's talk, or the black magician conjured up in Brabantio's overheated imagination. We have been tempted by them into seeing him through prejudiced eyes; now we see the man himself.

Othello's language

Othello says that his services 'Shall out-tongue his complaints' (1.2.19). This is a striking metaphor that conveys in a vivid and compact way that his known virtues and achievements shall speak more loudly than Brabantio's accusations. His origins, he says, are 'royal' (1.2.22). Notice how Othello mentions this: ''Tis yet to know' suggests that those around him are unaware of his exalted ancestry (1.2.19); 'when I know that boasting is an honour', then he will 'provulgate', or advertise, the fact (1.2.20–1). In other words, he says it would be boasting to announce his royal status publicly, yet it is a part of what counteracts the accusations that might be made against him. And he has already boasted anyway, hasn't he, if only to Iago? Does this indicate something fundamental about the way in which his character is being depicted, revealing a tendency to present himself to others as if he is not sure how they will receive him, perhaps with good reason considering the kind of remarks we have been hearing Venetians make of him?

The love theme is introduced at this point, as we learn of Othello's love for Desdemona, who is also now named for the first time. We have the first intimation of what will soon become a more marked feature of his language: the high-flown, daring comparisons that signal a man of large scope and imagination, beyond those smaller beings around him, and in particular the petty, low-minded cynicism of Iago, with which we can compare Othello's words:

> For know, Iago,
> But that I love the gentle Desdemona,
> I would not my unhousèd free condition
> Put into circumscription and confine
> For the seas' worth.
>
> (1.2.24–8)

In other words, if it were not for his love for Desdemona, he would not exchange his freedom for the confinement of marriage, no, not for all the seas of the world. Later, in Act 1, Scene 3, we realise what a contemporary audience might well have assumed anyway – that he has been a slave, and knows very well the difference between being 'confined' and 'free'. Neill's note to line 26 suggests further that it was a belief of the time that 'barbarians' from beyond the 'civilised' Christian world had an enviable but dangerous freedom from the constraints within which civilised people had to live.

It becomes even clearer as the play proceeds that Othello's language has a rhythm and **idiom** that contrasts sharply with those of many of the characters around him, not merely with Iago. His characteristic **rhetoric** gives an impression of space and vastness; this is conveyed here by the use of pairs of joined nouns or adjectives which are variations on the same meaning, such as 'circumscription and confine' (1.2.27). Soon you will come across 'very noble and approved good masters' (1.3.78) and 'the flinty and steel couch' (1.3.229).

I mentioned in the discussion to Activity 3 the word 'unhousèd'. Why is this so striking? It has an accented 'e' to indicate that the last syllable is pronounced, which draws out the unusual word and adds to its resonance. As Neill notes, this word describing Othello's 'condition' reflects the fact that he is not a citizen of Venice, unlike the firmly 'housed' Brabantio: he is a soldier employed by the state. The main characters in this play are all to a greater or lesser extent loosed from the ties of property, being soldiers, mercenaries or their womenfolk; and all will move further away from 'home' as the setting changes to Cyprus.

What Othello's speech also begins to reveal is how his sense of who he is comes from a profound sense of his *difference* from those around him, in a number of ways: as we have just seen, 'free' is a hint of his awareness that he was once a slave. It feels quite natural that he should use the imagery of the sea: it is, after all, a sea-bound republic that he serves, and he will soon be upon the seas again. But when you go on to consider later speeches in the play, you will find that it is characteristic of Othello to create an image of himself as linked to the forces of nature – sea and sky and deserts and mountains – rather than to the order and manners of the city and civilisation. It certainly suggests a certain power and majesty, doesn't it?

The impression of largeness, grandeur even, is confirmed by Othello's response to Iago's suggestion that he go in and hide himself as the stage fills with the arrival of officers with torches, whom we might (with Iago) have assumed would be Brabantio and his search party. Instead of 'going in' at his ensign's urging, Othello calmly remarks 'Not I – I must be found' (1.2.30). No hole-in-the-corner man, he. And when it looks as if fighting will break out, he utters the classic line 'Keep up your bright swords, for the dew will rust them' (1.2.59). Othello comes across as dignified, witty and superior: an utter contrast to the violence of Brabantio's breathless accusations that he 'stole' his daughter.

Othello agrees to accompany his accusers, which opens the way to Scene 3, at the Signiory or council chamber in the Doge's (Duke's) palace. Here, the haste and dramatic confusion of the preceding scenes shifts to the quieter atmosphere of the seat of power and justice, although the threat of the 'Ottomites' maintains a sense of danger while Othello faces the accusations against him.

Act 1, Scene 3: a lover's 'music'?

I have already referred to Othello's calm and majestic appearance, and the way in which Shakespeare sets us up in the packed opening sequence of the play to share the prejudices of Iago, Roderigo and Brabantio, before contrasting them with the appearance of the **protagonist**, and his noble manner of speech and action. In performance, this can be and has been altered: Othello can be played as mannered and self-regarding, or foolish, almost petty. If, as I have been suggesting, Shakespeare is making a point in contrasting the prejudice expressed by Iago, Roderigo and Brabantio with Othello's appearance as a commanding and impressive figure, then I think we can accept that the race issue is an important part of this play – though not all directors or performers have agreed.

It is important to notice that in his defence against Brabantio's charges, Othello launches into a powerful and dignified speech that, if anything, amplifies our growing sense of the importance of the position he holds in the Venetian republic. At the same time, we are introduced to what has been aptly called 'the Othello music' – a phrase first introduced by the Shakespearean critic G. Wilson Knight as a way of describing Othello's characteristically heroic mode of speech (Wilson Knight, 1930).

'Most potent, grave, and reverend signors' (1.3.77) begins the first of Othello's truly grand speeches, followed by his account of wooing Desdemona, referred to already (1.3.128–70). The claim that he lacks eloquence ('Rude am I in my speech' (1.3.82)) is the conventional modest disclaimer, but also a reminder that he is a soldier, not accustomed to matters of domestic interest such as love and marriage – a lack of experience that we may feel turns out to have fatal consequences. Then he launches into his defence against Brabantio's repeated charge of abduction through witchcraft or magic.

Activity 4

Read 1.3.128–70 (up to Desdemona's entrance) carefully. What emerges about the presentation of Othello's character from his defence (which is also his life story)? What would you say is especially noticeable about it, compared with what we know about the other characters? And what clues do we have about the nature of Desdemona? Consider both her father's and her husband's remarks about her in this part of the scene.

Discussion

What I notice is the suggestion of how much deeper and broader is Othello's life experience and history than that of the Venetians around him, including Iago. He has passed a lifetime of action in the field and had wild adventures in strange and unknown regions. What he says about his earlier life of adventure in 'deserts idle' and of 'hair-breadth scapes' from battle (1.3.140, 136) gives us glimpses of a life led far away, subject to circumstances the Venetians around him would not know of, including of course Desdemona, whom it has so impressed.

The sheer richness of Othello's language is surely something that impacts upon us – not only the wonders of his exotic life story, but such phrases as 'She'd ... with a greedy ear / Devour up my discourse' (1.3.149–50). Some soldier, this, and hardly an 'unvarnished' tale that he tells (as he claimed in line 91), either about himself or about how he impressed Desdemona.

Desdemona, in her father's eyes, is a 'maiden never bold' (1.3.95), the epitome of feminine modesty. To Othello, she seemed somewhat more forward than her father's view, giving him hints, he says, of her willingness to be wooed.

You might also have noticed the contrast between Othello's grand oration, with its sweeping rhythms and global, even cosmic comparisons, and the more prosaic language of those around him; the Duke and Brabantio are both briefer and plainer (the Duke turns to prose later in the scene (1.3.220–7)), while Iago's later exchange with Roderigo is entirely in prose, as he works on his gull ('Virtue? A fig! 'Tis in ourselves that we are thus, or thus' 1.3.315–16). Wilson Knight's 'Othello music' refers to the note struck by this kind of poetry, which is not to say Shakespeare is representing a poet, but that he is conveying through the kind of poetry Othello utters the romantic glamour that, for Othello himself and for those around him, invests him and what he stands for.

Is it Othello's glamour that has entranced Desdemona, then? Has she fallen in love with the man or the wonderful story he tells about himself? At the very least, his account of his life, and the range of wonderful, exotic creatures he has come across, from cannibals to 'Anthropophagi' (1.3.144), seem designed to intrigue his listeners, if not bewitch Desdemona. As he recounts:

> She swore 'in faith 'twas strange, 'twas passing strange,
> 'Twas pitiful, 'twas wondrous pitiful!'
> She wished she had not heard it, yet she wished
> That heaven had made her such a man …

(1.3.160–3)

It feels both moving and natural that a young woman who, we can assume, has been kept closely confined by her father, and certainly has had the limited life experience of a patrician female, should love Othello 'for the dangers' he 'had passed', and for him to love her 'that she did pity them' (1.3.167–8). As the Duke remarks wryly, emphasising the power of Othello's language, 'this tale would win my daughter too' (1.3.171).

And what of Desdemona herself? She has been ventriloquised by Othello at the end of his long speech, but she can and does speak for herself too, rather crucially, in this early scene. Her speech in response to the Duke's somewhat ham-fisted attempts to reconcile the parties creates for her a space in the audience's feelings, and one she begins to occupy with increasing strength. Here is a woman in love, who has been fascinated by the exotic stranger, whom she will follow to Cyprus whatever her father or the Duke may say.

Desdemona's responses in Act 1, Scene 3 are unquestionably powerful – responses often missed by those post-Jacobean, pre-feminist productions which stressed her frailty and innocence rather than her challenging quality. Notice her words here:

> That I did love the Moor to live with him,
> My downright violence and scorn of fortunes
> May trumpet to the world. ...
> > Let me go with him.

> (1.3.246–8, 257)

This is defiant compared with her more careful, and carefully judged, reaction to her father's call on her loyalties, when she explains that the duty she owed him she now must, like her mother before her, transfer to her chosen husband (1.3.180–8). Furthermore, it is striking how she insists publicly that she does not wish to be 'bereft' of the 'rites' for which she loves Othello (1.3.255): since we can hear the word 'rites' as 'rights', too, there is more than a hint that sexual fulfilment is part of what she expects, as well as the usual rituals associated with love and marriage. And this is despite her insistence (as if to meet any racist implications) that she saw Othello's 'visage in his mind' (1.3.250). This wife wants to be with her husband, in every sense. Desdemona, in other words, has her own characteristic music too, it seems, even if it will be overwhelmed, as she is overwhelmed, by that of Othello in what follows.

As if he understands the drift of implication, Othello adds that he desires Desdemona to be with him:

> not
> To please the palate of my appetite,
> Nor to comply with heat the young affects
> In my defunct and proper satisfaction,
> But to be free and bounteous to her mind ...

> (1.3.259–63)

In other words, he is declaring that it is not the hot sexual appetites of the young that drive him to request that Desdemona be allowed to join him in Cyprus. Remember these are public declarations, before the Duke, senators and Desdemona's father, hence their emphasis on the 'mind' or spiritual side of love, even as they suggest the need for physical fulfilment, too.

There is an interesting ambiguity about these declarations: is Othello being presented here as the older man in a potential mismatch? Or is he the outsider trying to show that his love is as pure as anybody could wish, in the society to which he has adhered himself by marriage? Marrying Desdemona takes him into intimate connection with Venice, whereas before he was their admired mercenary – quite a different relationship.

Discordance: Iago's first soliloquy

As the major characters have been introduced, and their interaction developed, we have also been introduced to the variety of perceptions and significances that enrich the theme of love in the play. That death is to follow is anticipated by the final exchanges of Act 1, Scene 3 between Roderigo and Iago, which set in motion the counter-movement leading in the final fatal direction of the tragedy. Brabantio's warning to Othello will echo throughout what follows: 'She has deceived her father, and may thee' (1.3.291).

Iago's language in this final section of Act 1 represents a major contrast to what I referred to earlier as the Othello music. It expresses a different kind of egotism from the hero's: more colloquial (hence often in prose), less grandiose, and viewing love in terms as gross and basic as before; 'merely a lust of the blood and a permission of the will', as he puts it to Roderigo (1.3.329–30). In many of Shakespeare's plays, there is an opposing voice, acting as a kind of foil to the hero. In *Othello*, this role is played by Iago. Iago is not interested in how anybody else sees love, reducing even Desdemona's love for Othello to the level of simple physical gratification: 'when she is sated with his body she will find the errors of her choice' (1.3.343–4). The belief that there is something more than bodily satisfaction in love presents a challenge to the brutal view of life he endorses, which is, we presume, one reason why he must undermine the idea of love as more than merely a matter of physical attraction whenever he can.

Act 1 ends as it began: in darkness, with Iago almost playing with Roderigo's pathetic desires – 'Put money in thy purse', he tells him repeatedly (1.3.333–54) – so as to further their plotting against Othello. Repeating the phrase until it seems almost ridiculous is part of his strategy, and any actor worth his salt will vary it with relish. In the final speech of the scene, Iago is on his own, and we are made party to his thoughts by a **soliloquy** – one of the most important techniques of the early modern theatre.

Activity 5

Let's consider the function of Iago's soliloquy here (1.3.372–93). Whom does it address? What do you think the speech serves to reveal? Does it draw you into sympathising with Iago's viewpoint, or are you simply repelled by him? Or, perhaps you feel something in between?

Discussion

On one level, the function of the speech is fairly obvious: it reveals to us Iago's motivation and his plan to use Cassio to bring Othello down. Iago exposes his hatred for Othello, and the fact that he thinks Othello has cuckolded him (that is, slept with his wife Emilia). His plan is to use Othello's 'free and open nature' (1.3.388) and Cassio's smooth appearance and manners against them.

Iago seems to be addressing the audience, although evidently the speech can be performed in different ways. We may not sympathise with him, but we are surely drawn into sharing his viewpoint and inner thoughts, maybe even to feeling complicit with his plotting.

Soliloquies and **asides** – when a character speaks so that we in the audience, but not the other characters onstage, can overhear – encourage us to share that character's viewpoint, potentially to sympathise with them, but not necessarily to agree with what they say. Iago's soliloquy certainly seems aimed at making us co-conspirators. That is how Ian McKellen played it in the televised version of Trevor Nunn's intelligent 1989 Royal Shakespeare Company (RSC) production, in which he turns to the camera in close-up as he reveals his evil thoughts and plans.

Here, we already know that Iago resents Othello's choice of Cassio for his lieutenant; now he appears to find another motive for hating him – his fear that Othello has cuckolded him. Yet he isn't sure about this; it's a widespread rumour. Does this suggest that he is actually searching for reasons to injure Othello? One of the earlier critics of the play, the Romantic poet Samuel Taylor Coleridge (1772–1834), was prompted by this soliloquy in particular to invent a phrase for Iago's behaviour which has had a considerable influence on interpretations since: 'the motive-hunting of a motiveless malignity' was what Iago was doing, he said (quoted in Wain, 1994, p. 53). According to Coleridge, Iago was driven by his 'malignity', or pure destructive wickedness, rather than by any clear, comprehensible motive. As the play progresses and he shares his thoughts with us in subsequent soliloquies, there appear to pop into Iago's head, only to leave it again, suspicions and ideas he uses to justify his purposes. Later, he says it is Cassio's 'daily beauty' that makes him want to have him murdered (5.1.19). The sheer force of his hatred or 'malignity' – not only towards Othello – becomes plain to the audience now, although not to any of the other characters.

Notice the pause in rhythm in line 391: to complete the iambic pentameter would require at least another three 'feet'. This is an indication to the actor to pause at that point, after 'As asses are', so that there is a silence while we watch him thinking – until his plan is 'engendered' (1.3.392). The movement of Iago's mind itself is thus dramatised, as the plot to undermine Othello and Cassio, which will lead to the lovers' deaths, is set in motion.

We can now see Iago for what he is: a devious 'machiavel', or manipulator (after the Florentine political philosopher Niccolò Machiavelli (1469–1527), thought to espouse dangerously immoral political ideas). Iago constructs plots by knowing others better than they know themselves. His words also serve to underline the contrast between himself and Othello, whose 'free and open nature' will, he says, lead him to think men 'honest that but seem to be so' (1.3.388–9). 'Honest' is particularly interesting, as a word that had numerous connotations at the time somewhat different from our own. Here it picks up and ironically echoes Othello's earlier use of it to describe Iago as a man of 'honesty and trust' to whom he will give the job of conducting Desdemona to Cyprus (1.3.282), a judgement we already know to be mistaken. The word is then repeated many times through the play, each time with a slightly different twist, working on our minds as an echoing reminder of the opening contrast between Iago and Othello. The word was used to mean honourable, trustworthy or faithful, worthy, forthright and, regarding women, chaste. Playing with the meanings of a word, often in a **punning** though not necessarily comic way, was much in favour at the time, especially when the word might have sexual overtones. But I will return to 'honest', as the play does, later.

Conclusion

In this chapter, I have taken you through the first act of *Othello* in detail. We have looked at how Shakespeare sets up the plot and introduces the major characters and concerns of the play. You have also been made aware of the importance of attending to the detail of how the language of the text works, through words, phrases, 'figures' or metaphors, and the rhythmic patterns or effects. I have also discussed the importance of trying to visualise what is happening onstage from moment to moment, scene to scene, to understand and appreciate the action more fully. And finally, you have learned about the presence of the theme of love in the play, and the ways in which the different characters are shown to understand or deal with the idea of love.

In the next chapter, I will develop these aspects of our study of the play further, being more selective about the scenes we look at, while introducing you to some of the influential critical perspectives that have affected how it is understood and performed.

References

Kerrigan, J. (ed.) (1986) *The Sonnets and a Lover's Complaint*, London, Penguin.

Marcus, L. (2007) 'The two texts of *Othello* and early modern constructions of race' in Erne, L. and Kidnie, M.J. (eds) *Textual Performances: The Modern Reproduction of Shakespeare's Drama*, Cambridge, Cambridge University Press, pp. 21–36.

Shakespeare, W. (2008 [1622]) *Othello* (ed. M. Neill), Oxford World's Classics, Oxford, Oxford University Press.

Wain, J. (ed.) (1994) *Shakespeare:* Othello*: A Selection of Critical Essays* (rev. edn), Casebook Series, Basingstoke, Palgrave Macmillan.

Wilson Knight, G. (1930) *The Wheel of Fire: Interpretations of Shakespearian Tragedy*, Oxford, Oxford University Press.

Further reading

Briggs, J. (1997) *This Stage-Play World: Texts and Contexts 1580–1625* (new edn), Oxford, Oxford University Press.

Fiedler, L.A. (1973) *The Stranger in Shakespeare*, St Albans, Paladin.

Garber, M. (2004) *Shakespeare After All*, New York, Anchor Books.

Gordon, M. (2010) *Theatre and the Mind*, London, Oberon Books.

Hankey, J. (ed.) (2005) *Othello* (2nd edn), Shakespeare in Production Series, Cambridge, Cambridge University Press.

Hindle, M. (2007) *Studying Shakespeare on Film*, Basingstoke, Palgrave Macmillan.

Kott, J. (1967) *Shakespeare Our Contemporary* (2nd edn), London, Methuen.

Leggatt, A. (2005) *Shakespeare's Tragedies: Violation and Identity*, Cambridge, Cambridge University Press.

Loomba, A. (2002) *Shakespeare, Race, and Colonialism*, Oxford, Oxford University Press.

Maus, K.E. (1995) *Inwardness and Theater in the English Renaissance*, Chicago, University of Chicago Press.

Potter, N. (ed.) (2000) *Shakespeare:* Othello*: A Reader's Guide to Essential Criticism*, Basingstoke, Palgrave Macmillan.

Wells, S. (2010) *Shakespeare, Sex and Love*, Oxford, Oxford University Press.

Chapter 2

William Shakespeare, *Othello*: honesty and difference, men and women

Dennis Walder

Aims

This chapter will:

- continue the study of *Othello* as a play text through discussion of the themes of love and death and their dramatic embodiment in a selection of key scenes or moments
- introduce you to some of the most influential critical debates about the play
- develop further the discussion of 'difference' in terms of race and gender
- discuss the genre of the play.

Introduction

What is a 'theme'? In any play, certain actions, turns of plot and expressions are repeated and revealed as important. I have mentioned love, and in Chapter 1 you saw how this theme is introduced in terms of characters' different views of it: high-minded and romantic in the case of Othello and Desdemona; physical and cynically reductive according to Iago and Roderigo. Roderigo comes across more as the desperate young suitor willing to be led, Cassio as the courtly lieutenant, while Iago is the source of the most basic, even obscene version of this human passion. The word 'love' itself is used and reflected upon differently by different characters, adding to the richness of the text and its meanings in performance. Key words like this are repeated, often at turning points in the play, which is how the thematic patterning works on us, often subliminally in the theatre, but more obviously when we read the text. The theme becomes almost an independent part of what is happening, to the extent that it becomes a system of connected meanings, which may be analysed as such.

In order to reflect upon the play's thematic patterns, then, it is important to familiarise yourself thoroughly with the play. This does not mean working through every line of the text looking as closely at the language as we did in the preceding chapter. What it does mean is that you need to have read through to the end of the play, pausing when you come across moments of interest or difficulty in order to think about what appears to be happening and whether any words recur – as, typically in Shakespeare, they do. In this chapter, I will look at the development of theme as an aspect of character, plot and language, and the dramatic techniques Shakespeare uses to achieve his ends. I will also introduce you to some of the significant critical debates the play has stimulated.

Before reading this chapter, you should ensure that you have read through to the end of the play. You should then return to and reread the sections I discuss in more detail in the chapter.

Act 2: a soldier's (love) life?

It's important to notice that, as we move on from Act 1, we also move in geographical setting (as in many of Shakespeare's plays) from a place symbolic of order and control, to a place of confusion and uncertainty. As we saw in the preceding chapter, the Venetians represent Renaissance civilisation and discipline, evident when the Duke and senators arrive in Scene 3, exerting authority over the turbulence threatening to break out. But this is not entirely true: Iago's soliloquy that concludes Act 1 reminds us of the continuing threat of disorder. As he exclaims in his last words as he departs the stage: 'Hell and Night' will soon bring the dark, 'monstrous' idea he has engendered into 'the world's light' (1.3.392–3). The staging will reflect this; the light of the council chamber scene having driven out the conspiratorial darkness of the opening sequence, only for the threat of darkness to return.

Depending on the production, the transition from Act 1 to Act 2 can be suggested by lighting effects; Iago's departure being immediately followed by the darkness of a storm, with lightning and thunder, and the sounds of wind and rain. As soon as we arrive in Cyprus – where the rest of the play is set – we sense that we have moved beyond the civilised and civilising sway of Venice, to a place where the forces of nature are less controlled, and therefore where Iago's sinister plotting has more scope.

If one of the main things that defines Othello is being good at waging war, then the arrival in Cyprus with the news that war has been averted suggests that, like the other soldiers, he is left with nothing to do – perhaps a dangerous thing for any soldier. As the famous essayist Francis Bacon (1561–1626) observed, in a 'slothful peace', 'courages will effeminate and manners corrupt' (1985 [1612], p. 153). Even more important in the context of this play, the trust and loyalty or honour developed between soldiers in the field becomes a potential weakness, which may be exploited by a character like Iago.

Activity 1

Try summarising the action of Act 2, Scene 1. How does the change of setting reinforce developments?

Discussion

All is alarm and confusion as the engagement with the Turkish fleet is awaited, and then dispelled. Othello, Desdemona and Iago arrive safely in Cyprus and, once again, Iago ensnares Roderigo in a plot against Othello – but this time through discrediting Cassio, whose gallantry towards Desdemona has suggested to Iago how he can use him. You might also have noted that Desdemona arrives before Othello, and while they wait for him she distracts herself through a bantering, bawdy exchange with Iago about the nature of women. Desdemona cleverly matches his suggestiveness without descending to his level. (The exchange contributes interestingly to the characterisation of Desdemona and the play's interest in men's attitudes to women.)

The storm with which Act 2 opens represents – as in other Shakespeare plays – a premonition as well as a sign: of the instability of the world the characters now inhabit. For the Venetians, as for the English at the time, the sea was both the source of power and of danger. As if to confirm this, there is a current of sea imagery running through the language of the play. The concern of all the characters at the opening of Act 2 is whether or not the battle with the Turks has taken place, and the outcome. The realisation that there will after all be no threat from outside leaves everyone, including the audience, to focus on the domestic world of the love plot for the rest of the play.

This shift in focus is neatly signalled by Othello's greeting to Desdemona when he lands: 'O, my fair warrior!' (2.1.177). This is a deeply affectionate moment which recalls the love poetry of the period, much of which was addressed to lovers or mistresses and drew on well-established traditions and conventions of courtly love and romance which insisted on the woman's power over the man. The differences between Othello's and Iago's views of love become more sharply evident as Act 2 proceeds. For Othello, 'If it were now to die, / 'Twere now to be most happy' (2.1.184–5), and he prattles happily to Desdemona in anticipation of the delayed consummation of their marriage. 'To die' carried a sexual resonance at the time, meaning to orgasm, and was a popular pun in early modern drama and poetry, including in Shakespeare's sonnets. So although Othello's main meaning seems obvious, on another level we might think that he is becoming impatient for the pleasures of the marriage bed.

Married love, however, is far from Iago's thoughts as he once more poisons the concept with his insinuations – not only to Roderigo (2.1.209–76) but, crucially for the development of the plot, to Cassio (2.3.12–43). It is as if, being away from Venice, Iago can give free rein to his narrow, cynical view of human relations, something others find difficult to combat. Why? Not only because of his energy and inventiveness, but perhaps because on some level they partially share his views? As for Cassio, he may appear as the smooth libertine, an aspect of his character underscored by his relationship with Bianca, but there is an exchange with Iago which carefully clarifies the difference between their views of love and sex, in Act 2, Scene 3. Iago says his general has left early to be with Desdemona and make 'wanton the night with her' (2.3.16). 'She's a most exquisite lady' responds Cassio, going on to reply in courtly terms to Iago's mounting attempt to pull his superior down to his level of coarseness (2.3.18–25).

It is easy to be so absorbed by Iago's performance in Act 2 that one loses sight of Othello, the object of his hatred and envy, and many critics and theatre directors have moved in this direction – most notably perhaps in the RSC production filmed in 1990, in which Ian McKellen's Iago is so powerful and manipulative from the start that even the imposing presence of opera star Willard White's Othello can hardly compete (see Figure 2.1). This is not to say that the production is 'wrong', just that the balance between the two major characters is crucial, for how it is managed goes a long way towards determining the meaning of the play in performance.

Activity 2

A simple fact about Act 2 is that for much of the time Othello is absent from the stage. Do you therefore feel the balance of the play at this point is shifting towards Iago? Look especially at Act 2, Scene 3, comparing and contrasting Othello's and Iago's speeches, and looking out for key words and phrases that seem to suggest how we are to understand their characters.

Discussion

I would say yes, the balance is shifting towards Iago, despite the references to Othello in his absence. For here is where we see Iago's technique of exploiting the weaknesses of those to whom he pretends loyalty coming into its own, as he uses Cassio's drunken rage to destroy the man's position and reputation.

Figure 2.1   Willard White as Othello and Ian McKellen as Iago in *Othello*, dir. Trevor Nunn (Royal Shakespeare Company, Young Vic, London, 1990). Photo: Alastair Muir/Rex Features.

But when Othello first comes in, we notice how forceful and commanding he is, shaming his brawling men by exclaiming 'Are we turned Turks' (2.3.161) – ironic, considering he is accused in the play of being a heathen. He orders them to 'put by' their behaviour, or die on the spot (2.3.163–5). After all, this is an island only just escaped from the threat of war. 'Silence that dreadful bell' he orders (2.3.166), to prevent further disturbance. To locate those responsible, Othello quite naturally turns to 'Honest Iago' for a report (2.3.168). This is, of course, deeply ironic: that he should turn to the very man whom we in the audience know is behind it all. But before he does so, Othello reveals a little more of himself, as we will have cause to remember later in the play. Notice how, in the speech beginning 'Now, by heaven' (2.3.195–208), his impartiality is touched by passion, even rage. The next few lines suggest he can be overtaken or ruled by his 'blood', his 'best judgement' darkened or 'collied' by passion (2.3.196–8).

Perhaps not even the most balanced judgement could withstand Iago's account of the preceding events, as he expresses regret and appears to try to excuse Cassio while omitting entirely his own role. Once Iago's brilliantly devious rhetoric has done its work, and Cassio – whose name Iago keeps mentioning, even while excusing him – is assumed to be at fault, Othello immediately demotes his lieutenant, who goes on to bewail his loss of soldierly honour or 'reputation' (2.3.253–6).

Iago's ascendancy is, if anything, confirmed by the exchanges with Cassio that follow, in which, as if from nowhere, the idea arrives in his head that he should prompt the disgraced soldier to approach Desdemona to plead to Othello on his behalf. Cassio swallows the bait and departs, as Iago turns and addresses us directly: 'And what's he then that says I play the villain' (2.3.321), he asks. He then goes on to justify himself in another tour de force soliloquy in which the word Othello uses about him, 'honest', is twisted until it means simply foolish or naive. (When Othello again uses it repeatedly in Act 3, Scene 3, it seems almost to have been drained of meaning.)

We can see from this section of the play that Iago, the bluff and confident soldier, is shown also to be a consummate actor, devious and controlling towards us, his audience, as well as towards the other characters. Othello is becoming his victim, although we cannot yet see how the hero's love for Desdemona is going to bring him down and, crucially, our sympathies are being moved towards Othello and then away from him by what we hear and see.

Many audiences find themselves enjoying Iago's energy, and feel complicit in his plotting at this point, while the increasingly distant figure of Othello commands respect rather than fellow feeling. How you interpret the rest of the play depends very much on your response to the whole complex of feelings evoked by what has happened up to the opening of Act 3 (often preceded by an interval).

Act 3: temptation

As we have seen, *Othello* is a domestic tragedy, in the sense that while matters of state, such as the war with the Turks, are present, especially in the first act, they are marginal to the play's central concern with love, and the deaths which overtake it towards the end. Moreover, the play has a relatively simple plot, and no **sub-plot**; that is to say, no shift of attention away from the central characters, and hardly any 'comic relief'. The drinking sequence in Act 2 can be and often is played as comedy, but it has a dark undercurrent, as we know all along that it is part of Iago's plan to undermine Cassio. The opening of Act 3 in the text is often omitted in the theatre; it is in any case little more than a momentary relief from the onward surge of the plot. Nor is there, as in other Shakespeare tragedies, some onstage character a little outside the action – like Horatio in *Hamlet* – enabling us to watch what happens with a certain sympathetic detachment. I have already mentioned how Iago lets us know what he is up to, which only makes us more concerned with what is about to happen to the principal characters, the lovers. *Othello* is so intensely focused on Othello and Desdemona and Iago's plot to deceive and entrap them, that it is no wonder that many audience members have in the past shouted out warnings to them.

All the more reason, then, for us to reflect deeply upon how we understand the characterisation of Othello and Desdemona, and how we judge their actions. I would like now to consider some of the key scenes that should enable you to develop your opinions on this score, using the view of an influential twentieth-century critic, F.R. Leavis, as a starting point. Leavis's interpretation has had an impact not only on other critics and readers, but also on the way in which the play came to be directed and performed. This is most notable in the 1964 National Theatre production, directed by John Dexter, with Laurence Olivier as Othello, Frank Finlay as Iago and Maggie Smith as Desdemona (see Figure 2.2). This production was subsequently made into a film by director Stuart Burge.

Othello's love for Desdemona may well seem to be the centre of the play, as he himself is. This is how many critics have understood *Othello*. A.C. Bradley, the author of an influential though very early critical study,

Figure 2.2   Laurence Olivier as Othello and Frank Finlay as Iago in *Othello*, dir. John Dexter (BHE Films, 1965). Photo: © SNAP/Rex Features.

Shakespearean Tragedy (1904), saw Othello as open and passionate, a lover the strength of whose passion inspired the love not only of Desdemona but the audience, who were swayed by his grandiloquence and pitied him when he fell – despite his murder of his wife. The newness of Othello's marriage made his jealousy credible. But, as so often, there was a reaction against this pro-Othello view, led by the poet and critic T.S. Eliot, who picked up what he saw as Othello's tendency to self-dramatise, especially in his final speeches. A more extreme and influential view was expressed by Leavis in a famous essay attacking Bradley, entitled 'Diabolic intellect and the noble hero' (1952).

The importance of the Leavis view is that it challenges us to think about how we understand the role of Othello and the play as a tragedy: in particular, how far what happens is the product of the hero's nobility being brought low by the devilish machinations of Iago (which shifts the focus somewhat onto Iago), and how far he is himself unwittingly responsible for the tragedy. Either way, for many years Leavis's account of the play dominated thinking about how to play the character of Othello. You have to make up your own mind. But the point of literary criticism is to engage you in a conversation with other informed readers, directors and play-goers in order that you may come to a view of your own.

According to Leavis, the view of the play elaborated by A.C. Bradley (and implicitly by those who follow him) is that the tragedy is 'the undoing of the noble Moor by the devilish cunning of Iago' (1963 [1952], p. 137). The Bradley view was, according to Leavis, that it was 'external evil, the malice of the demi-devil, that turned a happy story of romantic love – of romantic lovers who were qualified to live happily ever after, so to speak – into a tragedy' (p. 137). For Leavis, this is to 'sentimentalise Shakespeare's tragedy and to displace its centre' (p. 137). You will recall how I suggested above that the balance between Othello and Iago in Act 2 is an issue for debate. Too much attention, according to Leavis, tends to be paid to the character of Iago and his 'diabolic intellect'. 'The plain fact', continues Leavis, 'is that in Shakespeare's tragedy of *Othello* Othello is the chief personage – the chief personage in such a sense that the tragedy may fairly be said to be Othello's character in action. Iago is subordinate and merely ancillary' (p. 138). This is his first point. Leavis then goes on to suggest that Wilson Knight's view of the grand 'Othello music', which I discussed in Chapter 1, should be understood in a more critical way, as an indication of 'a habit of self-approving self-dramatization' that is 'an essential element in Othello's make-up, and remains so at the very end' (p. 142). What's more, Iago's 'prompt success' in persuading Othello of Desdemona's alleged treachery is not so much the result of Iago's 'diabolic intellect' as of 'Othello's readiness to respond' (p. 140). This is central to the Leavis argument: 'Iago's power, in fact, in the temptation-scene is that he represents something that is in Othello – in Othello the husband of Desdemona: the essential traitor is within the gates' (pp. 140–1). Iago is simply 'a mechanism necessary for precipitating tragedy in a dramatic action' (p. 141).

Whether we agree or disagree with this depends on how we read the whole play, and how we interpret Shakespeare's characterisation of Othello and Iago throughout. But Leavis's focus on 'the temptation scene' is helpful, since that is the real turning point of the action. It is the longest scene in the play, as well as standing at the structural centre – Act 3, Scene 3, which I will turn to now.

Act 3, Scene 3: the temptation scene

Activity 3

Every line in this scene requires careful attention. For now, try reading it through with the following questions in mind, prompted by Leavis's interpretation.

1   What or who is the bait with which Iago catches Othello? Notice Iago's aside in line 33: what does it indicate is happening onstage?

2   How does Iago tempt or manipulate Othello so as to enrage him against Cassio and Desdemona?

Having thought about your answers to 1 and 2, try responding to this question:

3   Is Iago just a dramatic 'mechanism', as Leavis suggests, whereby Othello's deeper fantasies are brought out? Or is Othello really noble, while lacking the necessary defences against the diabolic mind that defeats him here?

Discussion

1   Cassio is the bait, as Iago's pretended aside 'Ha? I like not that' (intended to be overheard) indicates, at the moment when, we assume, Cassio takes an exaggerated or even intimate farewell of Desdemona. But the bait is also, surely, Othello's own suspicious fantasies and insecurities, which eventually allow something as trifling as the handkerchief to become firm proof of Desdemona's alleged deceit, as Iago points out (3.3.323–6).

2   By his pretended perplexity at and poisonous interpretation of Cassio's and Desdemona's innocent behaviour, Iago insinuates the idea into Othello's mind that they are cheating or, in the language of the time, cuckolding him.

3   Surely there is some truth in both views? If so, then where would you put the emphasis? On Othello's or Iago's responsibility? I leave it to you to decide. But here are some further thoughts to consider.

It has been suggested by the critic Marjorie Garber that one of the ways Iago manages or tempts Othello is by being an 'echo', turning the meaning of his words against themselves (2004, p. 607). Certainly, Iago's apparently innocent repetition of Othello's 'indeed', 'honest' and 'think' is typical of his technique, of pretending to avoid speaking the awful truth so as to protect his master from it, while at the same time ensuring it filters into Othello's mind. So we have this dramatic line-by-line exchange, when Iago asks whether Cassio knew from early on that Othello was in love with Desdemona:

OTHELLO	O yes, and went between us very oft.
IAGO	Indeed?
OTHELLO	Indeed? Ay, indeed. Discern'st thou aught in that? Is he not honest?
IAGO	Honest, my lord?
OTHELLO	Honest? Ay, honest.
IAGO	My lord, for aught I know.
OTHELLO	What dost thou think?
IAGO	Think, my lord?
OTHELLO	'Think, my lord'? By heaven, thou echo'st me, As if there were some monster in thy thought …

(3.3.102–10)

Yet the question remains: why is Othello so ready to accept Iago's insinuations? Shakespeare suggests that it is Othello's own insecurity that gives Iago the opportunity to work on his feelings. Why should the protagonist be insecure? Remember he is the outsider, the 'extravagant and wheeling stranger' (1.1.135) in this community of Venetians, and, as one critic put it, 'portrayed as forever homeless, uprooted, and on the move, incapable – or at least so his enemies contend – of ever being naturalized' (Fiedler, 1973, p. 146). And he is ethnically different, too. In Act 1, Scene 1, Iago, Roderigo and Brabantio take it for granted that the marriage between a black African and a white Venetian woman is deeply unnatural; Brabantio, as we have seen, assumes that the only way his daughter could have found Othello attractive is if she had been bewitched by black magic. These are the humiliating charges that Othello has to defend himself and his marriage against in Act 1, Scene 3. If we add to this climate of racism the fact that Othello is a middle-aged soldier accustomed to the exclusively male world of military life and quite unaccustomed to the company of women, then it is not hard to see why he seems predisposed to believe his ensign over his wife. When Iago tells Othello that Desdemona 'did deceive her father, marrying you; / And when she seemed to shake and fear your looks, / She loved them most' (3.3.209–11), he echoes Brabantio's warning at the end of Act 1, Scene 3, while subtly reinforcing Othello's insecurities about his sexual attractiveness. He also taps into a rich vein of misogyny and masculine anxieties about women, who are portrayed in these lines as deeply untrustworthy and duplicitous. These views are common in the Venetian world of the play: as I discussed in Chapter 1, Brabantio, in his disappointment that his daughter proved to be a human being with a will of her own rather than his obedient possession, voices them; and Iago too is seized with a fear of female deception, as we recognise when on three separate occasions in his soliloquies he expresses his anxiety that Emilia has been unfaithful to him. Othello shows himself to be all too susceptible to such ideas, his insecurities about his race and age and lack of experience with women intensifying a tendency to expect the worst of the opposite sex. This is not to excuse Othello's collapse into homicidal sexual jealousy, but to seek to explain it. Looked at in this light, Othello does appear to some extent as the victim of Iago's cunning. But Shakespeare also makes it clear how much the hero resembles Iago and the other male Venetians in his masculine pride and suspicious distrust of women.

This last point is underscored by showing how his usual grandiloquence is twisted into an expression of horror at the thought of being deceived by Desdemona, revealing his decline to the level of Iago's pornographic imagination: 'I had been happy if the general camp, / Pioneers and all, had tasted her sweet body, / So I had nothing known' (3.3.347–9). The soldier's base view of women surfaces here – the other side of the 'Pride, pomp, and circumstance of glorious war' (3.3.356) to which he now bids farewell (look at the rest of his speech from 3.3.349 onwards). Is this what the 'Othello music' has become? As the Polish critic and theatre director Jan Kott remarks:

> There is enchanting poetry here, but at the same time a decaying set of values … Not only shall Othello crawl at Iago's feet [when he has his fit, in 4.1.41]; he shall talk his language [and] take over from Iago all his obsessions, as if he were unable to break away from the images of monkeys and goats, mongrels and lewd bitches.
>
> (Kott, 1967, pp. 88, 90)

We cannot understand Othello without addressing this aspect of his 'character in action'. It becomes 'action' in the way he behaves towards

Desdemona, leading him to the point when, in the opening scene of Act 4, he strikes her (4.1.232), to the shocked astonishment of the characters onstage – and us. The effect in the theatre is always profound, and the blow anticipates his more extreme action at the end of the play.

Moment after moment in this play, we sense the downward slide into violence and death. Othello seems to have been right when, earlier in Act 3, Scene 3, as Desdemona departed the stage, he remarked, as if in a final expression of his love:

> Excellent wretch, perdition catch my soul
> But I do love thee! and when I love thee not,
> Chaos is come again.

> (3.3.91–3)

This is a typically grand, **hyperbolic** (or exaggerated) utterance. There is a significant ambiguity in these words: does he mean 'I love you at the risk of perdition, or damnation' (i.e. for preferring earthly love to divine); or does he mean 'I am damned if I do not love you'? However we interpret his words, Othello's tendency to link his own emotions to large, even cosmic forces remains striking.

The other side of Othello's grand self-image is represented by Iago's lust for destruction. The question remains: is the deception of Othello a matter of Iago's manipulation of his fears and insecurities, and thus on one level it represents some emanation of Othello's unconscious? Or is Iago after all a 'diabolic intellect', a consummate machiavel, or villain? And how far are our sympathies swayed by these different readings towards one character or the other? You have to make up your own mind, based on the evidence you can muster. The Leavis view relies on his interpretation of the temptation scene, which we have discussed above, but also on Act 5, which I will come to later in this chapter.

Act 4: men and women

We all bring ourselves to Shakespeare: who we are, what we know and the worlds we live in at the moment. That is true of critics too, of course. Critical texts, just like authorial texts (in this case *Othello*), arise in particular contexts. During the 1980s and 1990s, a wave of 'new theory' emerged which generated a whole new language of Shakespeare criticism, based on the assumption that earlier critics, brilliant though some were, underestimated the power of historical and cultural processes to shape literary texts (Hawkes, 1996, p. 7). This new theoretical movement advocated seeing early modern culture as less stable and more contradictory than hitherto, renegotiating the relationship between text and context so as not always to see the former simply reflecting the latter. It also meant placing critics as well as texts and authors in relation to their contexts.

These thoughts are prompted by noting that in F.R. Leavis's attack on the interpretation of Othello as a heroic figure, rather than a flawed and egotistical one, he suggests 'the cult of T.E. Lawrence has some relevance here' (1963 [1952], p. 152). Better known as Lawrence of Arabia, Lawrence (1888–1935) was a British army officer renowned for his role in the Arab revolt against the Turkish Empire during the First World War, and could be described as a flawed military genius. The parallels with Othello are intriguing and could be pursued further. Apart from anything else, this reminds us of the importance of seeing Othello and Iago as soldiers, and hence of the importance of that bond which separates them from the civilians in the play. But the point here is that Leavis was writing at a time (his original essay appeared in the influential journal *Scrutiny* in 1937) when the role of the professional soldier had lost its glamour following the First World War. Do you think that your own view of soldiering, or of military heroes, might influence how you see Othello, or how theatre directors might interpret the role for a production today? I leave that for you to ponder, though I will return to the issue in relation to masculinity and 'difference' later.

It is not until the end of the play that the larger public dimension of Othello's role returns, as the Venetians return to Cyprus, imposing order upon chaos. Until then, the drama feels increasingly claustrophobic, as we watch Othello's disintegration due to his belief in Desdemona's infidelity. In Act 4, the handkerchief she is supposed to have given Cassio becomes a symbol of guilt and betrayal, as Othello's half-crazed condition leads him further and further into incoherence and rage under the masterful direction of Iago (like a theatre director himself at times).

Just as Iago earlier on in the play was eavesdropping on Cassio and Desdemona, so Othello is now reduced to doing the same thing, secretly watching Iago and Cassio and misinterpreting what he sees, and going on to will himself into believing the worst of Desdemona. If we believe in his love for her, it is because her presence continues to evoke it in him, even while Iago's poison turns him against her.

Yet there is one moment in Act 4 when this onward rush of action seems to halt, and we see Desdemona isolated, represented in a sympathetic, yet pathetic light: Scene 3.

Act 4, Scene 3: the 'willow song'

Activity 4

Act 4, Scene 3 does not seem to propel the action forward, and so what do you think might be its point, or dramatic function? Does it look ahead to the end? What does it depict?

Discussion

Act 4, Scene 3 is the melancholy scene in which Emilia, Iago's wife and Desdemona's maidservant, helps Desdemona prepare for bed. Perhaps the most surprising thing about it is how far it anticipates the end and Desdemona's death scene. It is one of many moments of **proleptic irony** (or foreshadowing) in the play – a poignant harbinger of doom. Dramatically, it is a moment of rest, before the headlong rush of Act 5 begins. What it depicts is an intimate moment between women, contrasting sharply with all the scenes between men, or of women surrounded by and dominated by men. That the men are all soldiers, courtiers or senators, that is, active in public life, makes the contrast between male and female characters all the stronger.

Yet this is a moment of heightened tension, too, because of its content. It relates the story of Barbary, Desdemona's mother's maid (see Neill's note, in which it is suggested that she was possibly black), whose lover 'proved mad, / And did forsake her', and who died singing a 'Song of Willow' (4.3.25–6). The song expresses female despair and longing, and passive acceptance towards the lover: 'Let nobody blame him, his scorn I approve' (4.3.47). Is this the Desdemona who could resist her father's pleas, marry in secret, and depart from her home city for a foreign shore? Apparently so. Desdemona cannot get the song out of her mind, she says, and she proceeds to sing it, while Emilia helps her undress. The words and context of the song make us more aware of Desdemona's own tragic situation, in which her lover too has gone 'mad', and she has become the apparently passive victim of his lunacy.

Notice, too, how the language of the play has changed once again here, giving us those extraordinarily evocative, individual touches – as

Desdemona wonders if the wind is someone knocking and feels her eyes itching, the effect of which is to bring home her human reality (4.3.48–9, 53–4). These touches also make her death scene, when it comes, all the more moving, generating an even stronger sense of waste. You should also have noticed what the conversation between the two women is about; in particular Emilia's last speech, which is a plea for recognition of women's equal humanity. It is comparable to the famous speech by Shylock in *The Merchant of Venice* on the equal humanity of Jews (with the well-known line 'if you prick us, do we not bleed'), and challenges the anti-woman sentiments expressed by so many of the male characters.

The shift in perspective from soldierly honour as a matter of concern to the subjects of women's fidelity and attitude to marriage deepens our sense of the moral richness of the play. Love and marriage, for Emilia, are matters of everyday reality, which brings out just how unworldly Desdemona now seems – and, ironically, how much closer her moral position is to Othello's. 'Wouldst thou do such a deed for all the world?' (i.e. sleep with another man), Desdemona asks Emilia (4.3.59), whose response undercuts the largeness of implication in Desdemona's (and Othello's) language: 'The world's a huge thing: it is a great price / For a small vice' (4.3.64–5). Their difference in outlook towards love and marriage, and love in marriage, is transparently clear. Emilia's forthright, unromantic view provides a crucial variation, not only on Desdemona's and Othello's views of love, but also Iago's – she, too, can be blunt and down to earth, opposing the lovers' naive idealism with her own realism. However, unlike her husband, she does not envy or despise them for it.

Further, Emilia's lengthy defence of the rights of wives (4.3.81–98) opens up the whole question of how women were treated at the time and later. As you may recall from my introduction to Chapter 1, *Othello* exists in two crucially different early printed versions – Q1 and F1. Interestingly, as Neill points out in his note, Emilia's speech did not appear in the first published text of the play – the Q1 of 1622 – but was reinstated in the F1 edition of 1623. (Appendix B of your edition of *Othello* goes into the whole matter of these different texts in detail.) We cannot know for certain why this is the case, and different editors offer different explanations for it. But this is a good example of just how unstable early modern play texts can be, and of how the meaning of the play alters depending on which version of it you read. For example, the critic and historian Lisa Jardine argues that without

Emilia's speech, Desdemona's song of a lover abandoned 'becomes a stylised, emblematic representation of female passivity and culpability'; whereas with the inclusion of Emilia's 'assertive counterpoint' the scene becomes 'one which struggles with female and male responsibility and its limitations and negotiations' (quoted in Dunant, 1995, p. 103). You might also like to read what Neill has to say about Emilia's role in this scene in pp. 174–5 of the introduction to your edition.

Act 5: 'It is the cause': death, difference and tragedy

Perhaps we all learn to define ourselves by what we are not. In early modern drama, including Shakespeare's plays, Italians, Jews, Indians and Africans appear as figures who may be admired, but are more often stigmatised. During the preceding (sixteenth) century, improving trade links and increasing travel meant a general awareness of the presence of people from continents, races and religions beyond England, Britain and Europe. But when a people become more open on one level, they can become more closed on another. The critic Ania Loomba argues that as Europeans 'became increasingly aware of the power, wealth, and learning of other peoples … this awareness often only intensified expressions of European and Christian superiority' (2002, p. 4). Questions of difference had long been central to the literature of the Crusades, and to the encounters between Christians, Jews and Muslims in Europe. And as the search for new markets and colonies grew, so too did debates about difference.

What, then, were the likely racial attitudes of the first audiences of *Othello*? More specifically, how would the fact that Shakespeare's hero Othello was a black man have influenced these audiences? Queen Elizabeth I herself had 'ordered the deportation of "Negroes and blackamoors" from England on the grounds that they were depriving her own "Christian people" of jobs' (Loomba and Burton, 2007, p. 16). Such intolerance was the product of centuries of accumulated ideas about racial hierarchy, but it also overlapped with and was reinforced by ideas of class and gender difference. Loomba emphasises that with regard to class differences, '[a]ll over Europe, the nobility were often understood as a "race" distinct from ordinary folk', and that with regard to gender differences, Europeans distinguished themselves from other races in terms of 'an inversion or distortion of "normal" gender roles and sexual behaviour – Jewish men were said to menstruate, Muslim men to be sodomites, Egyptian women to stand up while urinating, and witches and Amazons to be kin to cannibals' (2002, p. 7). What Loomba concludes is that '[p]atriarchal domination and gender inequality provided a model for establishing (and were themselves reinforced by) racial hierarchies and colonial domination' (2002, p. 7). While we might wrestle with precisely how these various forms of difference and hierarchy were articulated in Shakespeare's society, by simply registering that there were significant racial, class and gender hierarchies, we are alerted to the need to look at how the language of *Othello* expresses racial, class and gender differences.

I hope you will start by thinking about the many signs in *Othello* of stereotyping language and behaviour, and about how these are challenged, undermined or confirmed. The extent to which questions of difference are raised in the play is part of what makes it both rich and satisfying as a theatrical experience, as well as leaving in our minds matter for serious reflection. As we have seen, men's perceptions of women, and women's of men, are as much at issue in this play as considerations of race or colour, prompted by the interracial marriage at its centre. Indeed, they are as intimately bound up with each other as the lovers themselves. According to the Nigerian writer Ben Okri, every age presents *Othello* 'in relation to how they perceive *the other*', and the 'emotional explosiveness' of the play 'depends utterly on seeing it on stage. Othello's colour is not real on the page' (2002, pp. 72–3). After witnessing the closing image of the black Othello lying beside (or, as in some productions, on top of) the fair Desdemona, dead on their wedding bed, we surely leave the theatre stunned, if also reflective.

Discussing questions of gender and race in relation to the play may seem particularly up to date, but they have been present for a very long time, if not from the beginning of the play's performance history. This is precisely because *Othello* as it has come down to us is so centrally about how such questions affect love and, in this play, bring about death. Thus, the first known systematic analysis of the play, Thomas Rymer's *Short View of Tragedy* (1693), argued that its 'Moral' was: first, a 'caution to all Maidens of Quality' who might consider running away with 'Blackamoors' without their parents' consent; second, 'a warning to all good Wives, that they look well to their Linnen'; and finally, a 'lesson to Husbands, that before their Jealousie be Tragical, the proofs may be Mathematical' (quoted in Potter, 2000, p. 15).

Rymer saw *Othello* as little more than a sorry farce, but he clearly touches on issues of race and gender, as well as class and **genre**. Even the allusion to wives' 'Linnen' (linen) is apt: he means Desdemona's handkerchief, the apparently trivial object that becomes the fatal focus of Othello's jealousy, presented to his mother by an Egyptian 'charmer' (3.4.56), a figure suggestive of the exotic qualities that attracted Desdemona to Othello in the first place.

The view of tragedy in Rymer's time was that it should be above all 'classical', that is, follow the rules of the genre set down by classical authorities such as, mainly, the ancient Greek philosopher Aristotle. According to Aristotle's *Poetics*, the tragic hero is a great man who falls from prosperity to misery and death through an 'error' of judgement (from the Greek *hamartia*, often translated as 'flaw'), and the audience experiences 'catharsis', or a release of feeling, from the pity or fear that this fall has aroused. We might feel that this is pretty close to the effect of *Othello* on us, especially the final scene. But if, like Rymer (and others of the time), you felt that a 'blackamoor' was an inappropriate hero, on the grounds of race or class, and his error of judgement a matter apparently so trivial as that of misinterpreting the whereabouts of his wife's handkerchief, then you might indeed have felt neither pity nor fear at the outcome. This is all part of what makes the play a *domestic* tragedy; it also touches on the question raised by Leavis and others of whether Othello is heroic or admirable enough for his fall to be truly tragic.

Moreover, if we emerge from the theatre with a sense of having had our emotions aroused to a high pitch, I would suggest we feel the same about our thoughts. A recent playwright has pointed out that in the 'safe' environment of the theatre, our minds are temporarily released from their usual concerns with day-to-day survival: 'And so in the theatre our minds can be radicals … it is precisely because our experience of theatre does not have to lead to action or change in our normal lives that our minds have a wonderful freedom … to safely consider the creative possibilities of deviance' (Gordon, 2010, pp. 14–15). Our response can be one of identification or empathy. So what we have to consider in contemplating *Othello* is what it would be like to be different, or radically other than what we are – in terms of gender, race or class.

Act 5 is the key. Here, the issues of genre as well as of difference come to fruition, although without being totally resolved by the deaths that follow. A tense and dramatic opening scene, in which Cassio is wounded by Roderigo, who is stabbed and killed by Iago, leaves the audience in a state of high expectation. It parallels the opening of the play, revealing the mortal end of the intrigue set in motion then. The next and final scene seems at first to move unbearably slowly, as the climax arrives and the tragedy is played out in multiple deaths. Again, every line of the text bears close consideration, but let us look at a few moments of this last scene, with issues of 'difference' primarily in mind.

Act 5, Scene 2: endings

The first time we see Othello in Act 5 is at the opening of Scene 2, when he enters Desdemona's sleeping chamber '*with a light*' (a lantern), and utters these memorable, and yet strange, almost incoherent words:

> It is the cause, it is the cause, my soul –
> Let me not name it to you, you chaste stars:
> It is the cause. Yet I'll not shed her blood,
> Nor scar that whiter skin of hers than snow
> And smooth as monumental alabaster –
> Yet she must die … .

(5.2.1–6)

He already imagines his wife resembling one of those marble figures of deceased aristocrats one can see in churches, anticipating not just her death, but the time thereafter. His stature as tragic hero is at issue here; Othello addresses a larger world beyond the one in which he is at the moment, but we might well feel that this is to the detriment of any remaining sense of the human reality of his wife.

Contemporary audiences were used to hearing speeches from the scaffold, in which the dying put off their guilt, and as the scene proceeds we see Othello doing so too, although in words of great resonance. I assume Othello is here referring to the 'cause' or reason for what he is about to do, his wife's alleged infidelity, which he cannot bring himself to name (hence 'chaste' stars), although some productions have emphasised the specifically racial aspect of the play by having him put Desdemona's white hand beside his as he says 'It is the cause' (see Hankey, 2005, p. 270).

Figure 2.3   Orson Welles as Othello and Suzanne Cloutier as Desdemona in *Othello*, dir. Orson Welles (Marceau Films/United Artists, 1952). Photo: © Everett Collection/Rex Features.

As Michael Neill notes, the meaning of 'cause' has a legal sense as well, referring to the charge or accusation in a case. That Othello addresses his soul suggests he is referring his 'case' to a higher authority, a divine court, where he expects the act he is contemplating to be judged. It also implies that he sees his role in relation to his wife as that of both judge and executioner. The contrast between the image of himself he is creating, and what he goes on to do when he smothers Desdemona, is dramatically shocking, and various productions have attempted to represent this in different ways – for example, by making the murder of Desdemona simultaneously an act of love and death, with Othello rolling off her prone body 'almost post-coitally' (Hankey, 2005, p. 276). This highlights once more the paradox of Othello's character: is he a deluded, self-important fool, or a noble hero brought down by circumstance?

The Leavis view, as we have seen, leans towards the former interpretation. For those that accept it, Othello's apparent concern for justice as the play moves towards the end – what Leavis calls Othello's 'noble self-bracing to a sacrifice' – appears as self-deception (1963 [1952], p. 150). This view might be confirmed by his last great speeches which, despite their magnificence, create, according to Leavis, the 'curious and characteristic effect of self-preoccupation, of preoccupation with his emotions rather than with Desdemona in her own right' (p. 150). So his last speech before stabbing himself (beginning 'Soft you, a word or two before you go ...' (5.2.337–54)) becomes, as Leavis suggests, 'unmistakably self-dramatization – self-dramatization as un-self-comprehending as before' (p. 152).

Do you accept this? Or do you prefer the interpretation that emphasises his nobility – 'An honourable murderer, if you will, / For naught I did in hate, but all in honour' (5.2.292–3), words that might suggest a level of self-awareness, while highlighting the central paradox of his character? It is worthwhile reading Othello's final speech in relation to historians' and critics' current views of the early modern period. For Marjorie Garber, 'Shakespeare's time – like ours – was one of great historical changes and social anomalies', including the presence of black men and women living in London, and women of all social ranks arguing for greater independence. *Othello*, she argues, 'records and responds to a world in crisis, a crisis figured in part through emergent categories like race, class, gender – and sexuality' (2004, p. 589). This world is represented in the play in terms of a symbolic geography (which I discussed in Chapter 1), contrasting the Christian, 'civilised' and ordered world of the city of Venice, and the disorderly world of Cyprus, itself a kind of borderland beyond which may be found the cannibals and sorcerers Othello refers to in his speeches.

Activity 5

With these ideas and perspectives in mind, reread 5.2.337–54. What does the speech tell us about Othello and his position as a black man in white Venetian society?

Discussion

What is perhaps most striking about his last speech is that in it Othello presents himself as simultaneously a hero and a villain. How can this be? Because, in effect having internalised the negative attitudes of those Venetians who see him as radically different and unchristian, while also having been honoured by them as noble and Christian, he has become the place where these contradictions cancel each other out in the only way possible – through his suicide:

OTHELLO   Set you down this;
          And say besides that in Aleppo once,
          Where a malignant and a turbaned Turk
          Beat a Venetian and traduced the state,
          I took by th' throat the circumcisèd dog
          And smote him – thus.

               He stabs himself

                                        (5.2.350–5)

Othello's final gesture means he kills himself just as he once killed a Muslim on behalf of Venice and 'civilisation'; a profoundly ironic gesture, reminding us of his outsider status, while dramatising the contradictions of a society in which identities are shifting and unstable, and doing so more than any other play of the time dealing with differences of race and religion. Thus, the hero's death by suicide, the end towards which the play has been moving, encapsulates all the contradictions of his position within Venetian society which have in large part contributed to his demise. As he kills the alien within himself, Othello enacts his role as the outsider striving to belong to a society that will always exclude him.

Where *Othello* is truly remarkable is in the way it associates these differences with gender issues as well. It is clear from the repetition of the 'willow song' in the final scene that we are to recall the end of the previous act and the exchange between Desdemona and Emilia, contrasting the former's passive acceptance of her role as the suffering wife with her maid's forthright insistence on women's claims to equality. Neither of the women will survive, however. The tragic **irony** continues: Iago's murder of his wife mirrors Othello's murder of his, their actions summed up by Othello's pathetic line 'why should Honour outlive Honesty?' (*that* word again), as he gives up all resistance – 'Let it go all' (5.2.244–5). With these lines, Othello seems to retain a certain dignity. Or is this still part of his self-excusing rant – if that is how you see his last lines?

There are further considerations. For all the differences in class and race as well as behaviour and character between Othello and Iago, their physical closeness can be suggestive. You might like to think about how you would react to Iago's behaviour when he is confronted by the final tableau of Othello and Desdemona. Ian McKellen's Iago in the 1989 production remains standing, apparently cold and unmoved by the sight. David Suchet, in Stratford in 1985, by contrast, threw himself on Othello's dying body. What do you think was the point of this?

It is always important when thinking of a play in performance to consider not only what the principals would be doing, but also the reactions of other characters. Iago, of course, may also be thought of as a principal in the play, although by the final scene his power has gone. Suchet himself said that he threw himself on Othello's body to express shock and surprise at the suicide, and to follow the love–hate theme through to the end (Hankey, 2005, pp. 293–4).

But whose love is he thinking of? Iago's for Othello, perhaps? There is a line of reasoning about Iago's motivation that detects a hidden homoerotic compulsion, a frustrated love for his manly superior that he must hide from himself, and which therefore generates his rage against the innocent Desdemona, and terrible manipulation of Othello. As Stanley Wells suggests in *Shakespeare, Sex and Love*, 'Iago speaks the most homoerotically charged lines in the whole of Shakespeare' (2010, p. 177) when, to substantiate his insinuation of Cassio's adultery with Desdemona, he claims to have shared Cassio's bed, describing in sensuous detail how Cassio threw his leg over his, sighed and kissed him, crying 'Cursèd fate that gave thee to the Moor!' (3.3.420–7).

Of course, on one level, it *is* fate or destiny that has put Iago in Othello's way, with disastrous consequences for them all. How far you wish to pursue other levels of meaning is up to you. For myself, I find that although this is an entirely feasible explanation for Iago's behaviour, which can be acted out convincingly in performance and which suggests another level on which issues of race, gender and sexuality circulate within the play, there remains a residue of uncertainty about Iago, just as there remains an uncertainty about the source(s) of evil in the world. And this, to me, is part of what makes the play an authentic tragedy: it involves a profound moral conflict which draws us in, yet leaves us without any certain resolution to the dilemmas it poses.

If the play has really worked in the theatre, then it is what we might call the image of the universe that we are left with, a tragic world that we would like to close our eyes to, but cannot. That is certainly how I feel during and after Act 5. Evil and suffering have been presented, perhaps even defeated, but without leaving me with a sense that there is a social or divine order arranging things for any happy outcome. As Iago is led off to be tortured at the end, do we feel that justice is satisfied, at least on the level of Venetian society? I do not think so – but I leave it to you to decide for yourself.

Conclusion

In this chapter, I have taken you through *Othello* as a play text in terms of the themes of love, death and 'difference', focusing on a selection of key scenes to illustrate how a close textual reading of a Shakespeare play operates, and how this also and inevitably engages us in considering the play's contexts – then and now – from time to time. I have also introduced you to a few of the critical debates about the play.

To give you an idea of how helpful insightful criticism can be, I have described some of the most influential critical views, especially those that focus on Othello as a 'self-dramatiser' (Leavis) which, although expressed some time ago, still underlie more recent productions and approaches despite apparently having been superseded by our more current concerns with the politics of race and gender (Jardine, Garber, Loomba). Calling the play a tragedy means that it should end in the death of its central figure or figures and so on, but it also invites us to think about what it means in terms of the kind of moral vision the play proposes.

References

Bacon, F. (1985 [1612]) 'Of the true greatness of kingdom and estates' in Pitcher, J. (ed.) *The Essays*, London, Penguin, pp. 147–55.

Bradley, A.C. (1904) *Shakespearean Tragedy: Lectures on* Hamlet*,* Othello*,* King Lear*,* Macbeth, London, Macmillan.

Fiedler, L.A. (1973) *The Stranger in Shakespeare*, St Albans, Paladin.

Garber, M. (2004) *Shakespeare After All*, New York, Anchor.

Gordon, M. (2010) *Theatre and the Mind*, London, Oberon.

Hankey, J. (ed.) (2005) *Othello* (2nd edn), Shakespeare in Production Series, Cambridge, Cambridge University Press.

Hawkes, T. (ed.) (1996) *Alternative Shakespeares*, vol. 2, London and New York, Routledge.

Jardine, L. (1995) 'Canon to left of them, canon to right of them' in Dunant, S. (ed.) *The War of the Words: The Political Correctness Debate*, London, Virago, pp. 97–115.

Kott, J. (1967) *Shakespeare Our Contemporary* (2nd edn), London, Methuen.

Leavis, F.R. (1963 [1952]) 'Diabolic intellect and the noble hero' in *The Common Pursuit*, Harmondsworth, Penguin, pp. 136–59.

Loomba, A. (2002) *Shakespeare, Race, and Colonialism*, Oxford, Oxford University Press.

Loomba, A. and Burton, J. (2007) *Race in Early Modern England: A Documentary Companion*, Basingstoke, Palgrave Macmillan.

Okri, B. (2002) *A Way of Being Free*, London, Phoenix.

Potter, N. (ed.) (2000) *Shakespeare:* Othello*: A Reader's Guide to Essential Criticism*, Basingstoke, Palgrave Macmillan.

Shakespeare, W. (2008 [1622]) *Othello* (ed. M. Neill), Oxford World's Classics, Oxford, Oxford University Press.

Wells, S. (2010) *Shakespeare, Sex and Love*, Oxford, Oxford University Press.

Further reading

Briggs, J. (1997) *This Stage-Play World: Texts and Contexts 1580–1625* (2nd edn), Oxford, Oxford University Press.

Danson, L. (2002) 'England, Islam, and the Mediterranean drama: *Othello* and others', *Journal for Early Modern Cultural Studies*, vol. 2, pp. 1–25.

Greenblatt, S. (1980*) Renaissance Self-Fashioning: From More to Shakespeare*, Chicago, University of Chicago Press.

Orlin, L.C. (ed.) (2004) *Othello*, New York, Palgrave Macmillan.

Chapter 3

John Webster, *The Duchess of Malfi*: love and marriage in the Malfi court

Anita Pacheco

Aims

This chapter will:

- introduce you to the treatment of the theme of love in Acts 1 and 2 of John Webster's play *The Duchess of Malfi*, along with some consideration of the theme of death
- examine other related themes and concerns of Acts 1 and 2
- provide you with practice in textual analysis
- consider some of the historical contexts of the play.

Introduction

John Webster (*c*.1580–*c*.1634) was Shakespeare's contemporary, though sixteen years younger. He makes a brief appearance in the 1998 film *Shakespeare in Love* as a boy who tortures mice, spies on Shakespeare's love-making, and feels inspired to take up the pen himself after seeing Shakespeare's blood-soaked revenge tragedy, *Titus Andronicus*. 'Plenty of blood. That's the only writing', he asserts. This affectionate but crude caricature testifies to Webster's reputation for writing dark and violent plays. Yet it also testifies to the enduring popularity of those plays. Shakespeare had many gifted colleagues in the play-writing business, but only two – Webster and Christopher Marlowe (1564–1593) – are graced with roles in this enormously popular mainstream movie about the late sixteenth-century theatre scene. Chapters 3 and 4 of this book will look at Webster's most well-known play, *The Duchess of Malfi*, and in the course of our studies we will consider some possible reasons for the play's continued prominence in the twenty-first-century theatre repertoire.

The Duchess of Malfi does indeed have 'plenty of blood', but, as you will have discovered from your reading of *Othello*, this is nothing unusual in Renaissance tragedies. Like *Othello*, Webster's play is a tragedy about a forbidden love, more specifically a forbidden marriage, which leads ultimately to the deaths of the lovers and many others. While Shakespeare's focus in his tragedy of love is race, Webster's is class, or rank, to use a more authentically early modern term. (Historians of the period often prefer the term 'rank' on the grounds that it better captures relationships in a highly stratified society where the vertical ties of patronage and deference were strong and class consciousness poorly developed in social groups below the level of the ruling elite.) Both terms will be used in this and the following chapter. At the centre of *The Duchess of Malfi* stands a heroine rather than a hero, which is fairly unusual in Renaissance tragedy. The play also contains a villain every bit as enigmatic and sinister as Iago. This chapter will examine how Webster represents his heroine's marriage for love, which goes against the wishes of her aristocratic family with disastrous consequences.

The Duchess of Malfi was first performed in 1613 or 1614 by the King's Men, the acting company to which Shakespeare belonged. The play was not printed until around ten years later in 1623, in quarto, a smaller and less expensive edition than the larger folio size used for the first edition of Shakespeare's complete works. The title page of this edition (shown in Figure 3.1) tells us that the play 'was presented privately, at the Blackfriers and publicly at the Globe'; that is, the play opened at the Blackfriars, the company's indoor theatre, and then played at the open-air Globe. The title page also informs potential readers that the text of the play is the 'perfect and exact Coppy, with diverse things Printed, that the length of the Play would not beare in the Presentment'; in other words, the play text includes numerous passages that were cut for performance. The publisher, then, appears to be trying to tempt buyers with the prospect of a longer, fuller version of the play than had ever been seen in the theatre. This is testament to Webster's fame and reputation as a dramatic poet, as is the announcement of the author's name in the next line, in larger type. The 1623 quarto is the only substantive text of the play that we have, and modern editions and productions are based on it. We have no way of knowing what *The Duchess of Malfi* looked like in its first performances, beyond assuming that it was shorter than the text that has descended to us. What is interesting is that the title page of the 1623 quarto draws such a clear distinction between the play in performance and the play as a text to be read and savoured in the study.

The edition of the play that is referred to in Chapters 3 and 4 is the Pearson Longman (2009) edition, edited by Monica Kendall.

Over the course of the next two chapters, we will work our way through the play in a roughly linear fashion. Chapter 3 focuses mainly on Acts 1 and 2, and Chapter 4 on Acts 3 to 5. You should make sure that you have read the relevant parts of the play before reading the teaching material.

Act 1: setting the scene

The representation of love in *The Duchess of Malfi* begins in earnest with the Duchess's courtship of and marriage to her steward Antonio. This is also a major dramatic climax, the event which drives the action of the rest of the play. Yet it does not take place until the end of Act 1. Indeed, the Duchess's wooing of Antonio does not even begin until we are 365 lines into the play. Why do we have to wait such a long time for this crucial episode? What is achieved by structuring the scene in this way? Clearly, by the time the marriage unfolds onstage, we are in possession of a good deal of information about the dramatic world in which it is taking place. Webster, it seems, is providing us with a dramatic context against which to respond to his representation of love

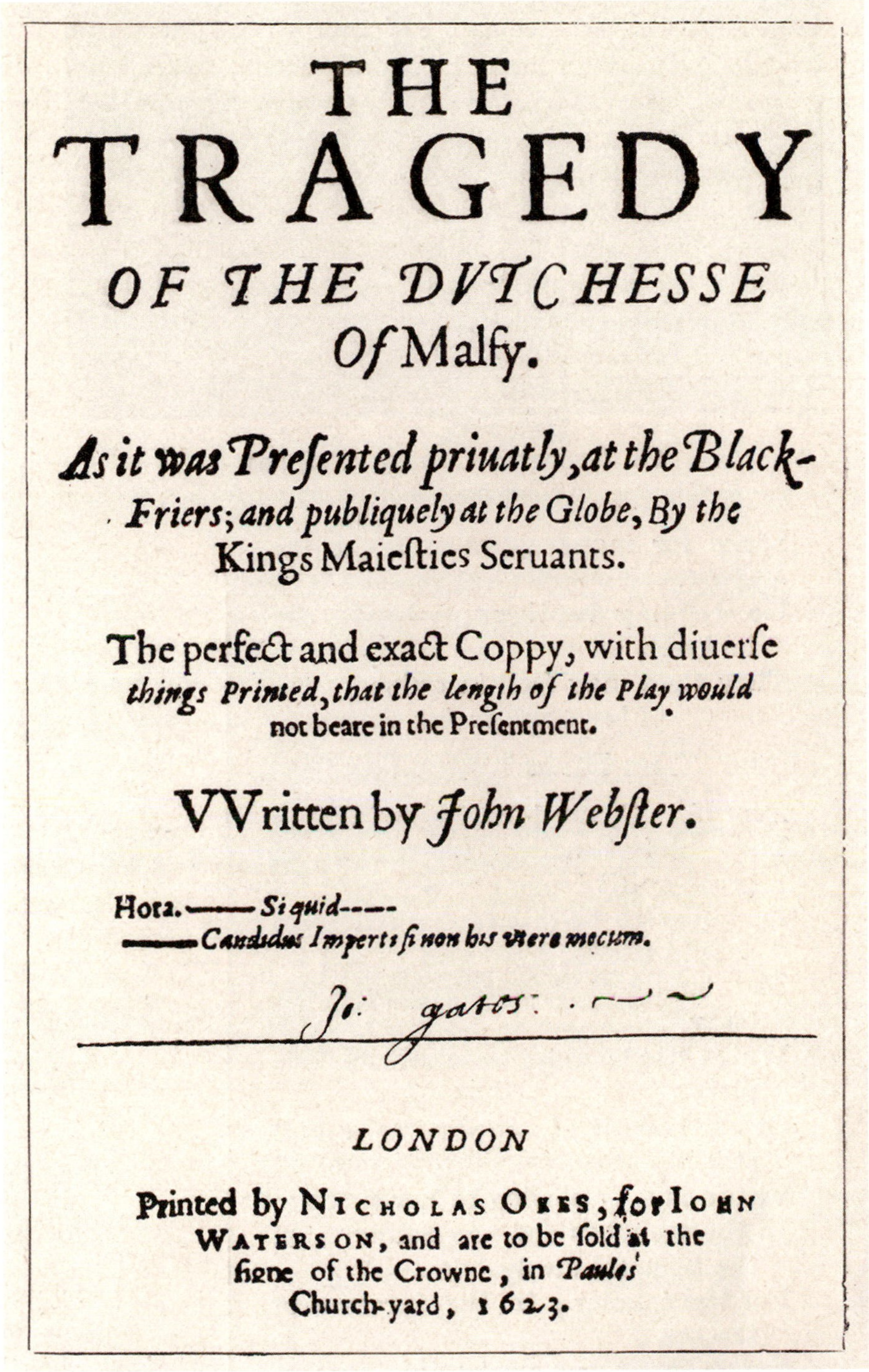

THE
TRAGEDY

OF THE DVTCHESSE
Of Malfy.

As it was Presented priuatly, at the Black-
. Friers; and publiquely at the Globe, By the
Kings Maiesties Seruants.

The perfect and exact Coppy, with diuerse
things Printed, that the length of the Play would
not beare in the Presentment.

VVritten by *John Webster.*

Hora.———— *Si quid*————
————*Candidus Imperti si non his vtere mecum.*

Jo: gatos.

LONDON

Printed by NICHOLAS OKES, for IOHN
WATERSON, and are to be sold at the
signe of the Crowne, in *Paules*
Church-yard, 1623.

Figure 3.1   Title page of the 1623 quarto version of *The Duchess of Malfi*.
Photo: Lebrecht Authors.

and marriage. In the first section of this chapter, I will consider how Webster sets the scene for the Duchess's forbidden marriage, before going on to examine his depiction of this important moment in the play.

Courts ideal and real

The play opens with an exchange between Antonio and his friend Delio. Antonio has been away in France and Delio asks him what he thought of the court of the French king.

Activity 1

How does Antonio reply to his friend's question? Reread his speech (1.1.4–22) and then try to summarise it in no more than five sentences.

Discussion

Here is my response:

1   Antonio admires the French court for its lack of corruption, the 'judicious' or wise king having banished all flatterers and people of bad character or reputation.

2   The king considers this cleansing of his court to be divinely inspired; God's work rather than his own.

3   This is because of the enormous influence the royal court has on the entire country – the court that is healthy has a benign influence, while the corrupt one infects 'the whole land'.

4   Antonio then asks what the source is of this 'blessed government' that he found in France and answers that it is the king's wise and truthful counsellors who, rather than flattering the king, give him candid and truthful advice about the state of the nation.

Antonio, then, opens the play with a statement of how important the royal court is to the well-being of the nation as a whole. That is what he says, but we need to think as well about the way he says it. What is distinctive about the language of Antonio's description of the French court? Perhaps the most striking part of the speech is the long analogy he makes between royal courts generally and 'a common fountain'. The appearance of the word 'like' in line 12 tells us that this analogy is a **simile**, a comparison of two apparently dissimilar things that uses either 'like' or 'as' to enforce the comparison. Antonio's simile is an extended one, as he goes on to develop it in the course of the next four lines: the 'common fountain' from which everyone drinks should be pure, but if it is poisoned (i.e. corrupt), it spreads its contagion throughout the land.

In the main, the passage is typical blank verse, which, as you saw in Chapter 1, means unrhymed lines of iambic pentameter. That is, the lines of verse in general do not rhyme and have ten syllables each, five stressed (in bold) and five unstressed, arranged in the following pattern: de **dum**, de **dum**, de **dum**, de **dum**, de **dum**. One of the effects of employing this fairly regular metre is that deviations from it tend to stand out. Look, for example, at the following passage:

> but if't chance
> Some cursed example poison't near the head,
> Death and diseases through the whole land spread.

> (1.1.13–15)

Line 14 is metrically quite even, but line 15 is a bit different: it would be hard to read it without placing a fairly strong stress on the first word, 'death'. After that, the metre returns to iambic, but the brief deviation serves to draw the spectator's attention to the word 'death'. In this way, Webster underlines the dire consequences of a degenerate court. The point is highlighted further by the sudden appearance of a rhyme between 'head' and 'spread' in lines 14 and 15, which makes the lines stand out even more.

There is a stark contrast in the speech between the image of 'pure silver drops' and the language of poison, disease and death, as there is between pejorative terms like 'flatt'ring sycophants' (l. 6) and Antonio's religious register: 'the work of heaven' (l. 10), 'blessed government' (l. 16). In literary studies, a register is a particular type or style of language; you can refer to a character employing a formal or informal register, for example, or to his or her use of vocabulary associated with a particular profession or sphere of activity. The fact that Antonio speaks about a royal court in a religious register reminds us that in early modern England doctrines like the divine right of kings, which claimed that kings were God's representatives on earth, invested the monarchy with a religious significance.

So what happens next? First, Bosola enters, followed by the Cardinal. Their conversation at the very least makes us suspect that what Antonio observed in France is conspicuously lacking in Italy, in particular when Bosola reminds the Cardinal that he 'fell into the galleys in your service' (1.1.34). A few lines later, any doubts we might have had about Bosola's meaning vanish, as Delio informs Antonio: 'I knew this fellow seven years in the galleys / For a notorious murder, and 'twas thought / The Cardinal suborned it' (1.1.72–4). We quickly grasp that in this drama, the powerful, far from surrounding themselves with wise and candid counsellors, hire men to commit crimes on their behalf. Moving from text to performance, in the theatre this point would be reinforced visually by the Cardinal's religious costume, which tells us that even churchmen use their power for criminal ends. The enormous gap separating the French ideal from the Italian reality is driven home a bit later in the scene, when Ferdinand, the Cardinal's brother and Duke of Calabria, reproaches two of his assembled courtiers for laughing:

> Why do you laugh? Methinks you that are courtiers should be my touchwood, take fire when I give fire, that is, laugh when I laugh, were the subject never so witty.

> (1.1.127–30)

We could hardly have a clearer indication of how far the Italian courts fall short of the 'fixed order' described by Antonio: in place of a rational prince advised and guided by honest advisors, we have a prince who surrounds himself with courtiers whose sole purpose is to flatter his ego with their obsequious behaviour.

So Webster begins his play with a description of an ideal court only then to show onstage a court that fails in every respect to live up to that ideal. This is a crucial part of his construction of the play's dramatic world, but most critics have assumed that this portrayal of courtly decadence and corruption in the play text also gains from being viewed in the context of the court of King James I, who had been on the English throne for around ten years when *The Duchess of Malfi* was first performed. James would wholeheartedly have endorsed the sentiments expressed in Antonio's opening speech; indeed, he had himself produced a comparable description of the ideal royal court in his book on kingship, *Basilikon Doron* (Greek for *Royal Gift*) (1599). The book is addressed to his eldest son and heir Prince Henry, and advises him to take great care in choosing his chief courtiers:

> see that they bee of a good fame and without blemish: otherwise, what can the people thinke? but that yee have chosen a companie unto you according to your owne humour, and so have preferred these men for the love of their vices and crimes that ye know them to be guyltie of … And nexte, see that they be indued with such honest qualities, as are meete for such offices as yee ordayne

them to serve in, that your judgement may be knowne in imploying every man according to his gifts … Make your Court and companie to bee a paterne of godlinesse and all honeste vertues to all the reste of the people.

(James I, 1599, pp. 76–7, 83)

Yet in reality, James's court was infamous for its profligacy and corruption. He himself showered his favourites with money, offices and privileges, and those same favourites spared no expense in displaying their prestige to the world through their own lavish spending. James's extravagance contributed to a constant need for money that he satisfied in part by selling titles of honour like knighthoods and peerages. Traditionally thought of as indicators of distinguished ancestry or rewards for loyal service, such titles in James's court were up for grabs by anyone with sufficient money to pay for them. It is not hard to see how a court dominated by the king's powerful favourites which funded its taste for extravagance through the unabashed sale of honours worked to point out the discrepancy between James's theory of kingship and the actual practice. This was no doubt reinforced by the Jacobean court's reputation for graft – James's treasurers were notoriously corrupt – and for the sexual licentiousness that will be embodied in Webster's play by Julia and the Cardinal. Later in the opening scene of *The Duchess*, when Ferdinand secures Bosola the post of the Duchess's Provisorship of Horse on condition that he spies on his employer, the play enacts another feature of James's court: its status as a hotbed of plotting and intrigue.

Bosola the malcontent

In placing the action of his play within a corrupt courtly setting, Webster is also adhering to one of the main conventions of the dramatic genre to which *The Duchess of Malfi* is usually thought to belong: revenge tragedy, an enormously popular genre in sixteenth- and seventeenth-century England. From Thomas Kyd's *The Spanish Tragedy* (*c.*1587), one of the earliest and most influential of this group of plays, through Shakespeare's *Hamlet* (1601), the most famous of all revenge tragedies, to a later example of the genre like Thomas Middleton's *The Revenger's Tragedy* (1606), revenge tragedies consistently present their audience with the spectacle of decadent courts and irresponsible, often criminal, rulers. The deficiencies of the status quo create a logical space for a particular character type: the malcontent, a character who is

Figure 3.2   Attributed to William Larkin, *George Villiers*, *c*.1616, oil on canvas, 206 × 119 cm. National Portrait Gallery, London. Photo: © National Portrait Gallery. George Villiers, the First Duke of Buckingham, was one of James I's powerful favourites.

consumed with disgust at the corruption and stupidity of courtly society and who vents his spleen by railing against it. Hamlet plays this role in Shakespeare's revenge tragedy, and in *The Duchess of Malfi* it is filled by Bosola. When Antonio refers to Bosola as the 'only court-gall' (1.1.23), he is using a metaphor, which, like a simile, makes a comparison between two things – in this case between Bosola and a 'gall', or a sore produced by rubbing – but without the presence of 'like' or 'as'. Metaphors, then, establish a much closer relationship between the two items being associated than similes do. Antonio is alluding to Bosola's fondness for railing at the court, harassing and tormenting it with his verbal abuse. ('Gall' also means 'bile', the bitter substance secreted by the liver; a secondary sense which intensifies the force of Antonio's metaphor.)

Activity 2

A few lines later, when the Cardinal has left the stage, Bosola complains to Antonio and Delio about the Cardinal and his brother Ferdinand. Look at his speech at lines 50–64. What point is he making about the Duchess's brothers, and how do his similes and metaphors help to drive his meaning home?

Discussion

Bosola attacks the Cardinal and Ferdinand for presiding over a courtly environment where loyal service reaps no reward, where only 'flatt'ring panders' prosper (1.1.54). His language is extraordinarily colourful and energetic, due in large part to the similes and metaphors he uses. He begins by likening the brothers to 'plum trees that grow crooked over standing pools' (1.1.50–1) and then goes on to explain the simile: however 'rich' and 'o'erladen with fruit' they are, the fact that they stand over stagnant water means that only 'crows, pies and caterpillars feed on them' (1.1.52–3). The 'standing pool' presents an obvious contrast to Antonio's clear and flowing courtly fountain, while the 'crows, pies and caterpillars' are metaphors for the kind of courtly parasites that flourish under the Cardinal and Ferdinand. By identifying them with scavengers and insects, Bosola manages to convey both their contemptibility and their voracious appetite for the rewards that come with princely favour. This type of imagery continues in his next simile: 'Could I be one of their flatt'ring panders, I would hang on their ears like a horse-leech till I were full, and then drop off' (1.1.53–5). Bosola's similes and metaphors vividly capture the brothers' enormous power and wealth, along with the greedy ambition of courtly suppliants. His speech is in prose not verse, but that in no way diminishes its linguistic richness. Any actor playing the part of Bosola would need to let the character's linguistic energy and bitterness guide his delivery of the lines.

Like Antonio, Bosola is low-born, and therefore entirely dependent for material success on the patronage of his social betters. His role thus contributes significantly to an important aspect of the play: its examination of class relations in a highly stratified society. Bosola's wit and satirical edge are throughout the play levelled at a patronage system that rewards toadying rather than merit. Yet the play makes clear the invidious position he is in. Indeed, Antonio has already given us his opinion of Bosola:

> yet I observe his railing
> Is not for simple love of piety,
> Indeed he rails at those things which he wants,
> Would be as lecherous, covetous, or proud,
> Bloody, or envious, as any man,
> If he had means to be so.

(1.1.23–8)

Bosola is torn between an acute awareness of the social and moral deficiencies of the patronage system and a longing for social advancement that binds him to it. His vision of himself as a horse-leech, greedily sucking the brothers' blood until he drops off, captures something of this doubleness: he may despise the yes-men who thrive in the courtly milieu, but at the same time he wants to share in the material prosperity they enjoy. Bosola has in common with Iago his status as a disgruntled servant, though Webster invests his version of this character type with a level of moral awareness absent from Shakespeare's viciously resentful ensign.

Marriage for love: family opposition

Having alerted us to the autocratic and criminal propensities of the Cardinal and Ferdinand, Webster goes on to inform us in the opening scene of their opposition to the idea of their widowed sister's remarrying.

Activity 3

Have another look at lines 298–344. Try to identify two reasons for the Cardinal's and Ferdinand's hostility to the prospect of their sister's marrying a second time.

Discussion

Here's what I've come up with:

1 Both brothers seem to be worried that their widowed sister will succumb to temptation and undertake a marriage that damages the family honour.

2 They also appear to be afraid that because she is a widow she is more likely to want to marry a second time.

This is another aspect of the play that is worthwhile examining in its historical and cultural context. The brothers' attitudes tell us a great deal about early modern ideas about women and family honour. Their fears are in large part fuelled by anxieties about female sexuality in general and of widows in particular. Women in early modern England were widely thought to have a much stronger sexual appetite than men, which is one of the main reasons they were often feared as untrustworthy and why chastity was so insistently invoked as the cardinal feminine virtue. This is the anxiety voiced so poignantly by Othello when he exclaims: 'O curse of marriage, / That we can call these delicate creatures ours, / And not their appetites' (Shakespeare, 2008 [1622], 3.3.271–3). Ferdinand expresses this misogynistic commonplace when he says to the Duchess: 'And women like that part which, like the lamprey, / Hath ne'er a bone in't (1.1.340–1), his reference to the lamprey, a type of eel, containing a bawdy suggestion of 'penis'. Widows, as sexually experienced women, were thought to be especially susceptible to this feminine vice. As the writer Joseph Swetnam put it in his work *The Arraignment of Lewd, Froward and Unconstant Women* (1615), 'it is more easy for a young man or maid to forbear carnal acts than it is for a widow' (quoted in Henderson and MacManus, 1985, p. 239). So we find the Cardinal telling his sister that widows' vows never to remarry commonly last 'no longer / Than the turning of an hourglass' (1.1.309–10), while Ferdinand harps on about this theme with particular urgency, declaring that to marry twice is 'luxurious' (lascivious) (1.1.303), that those who do so have 'spotted' livers (1.1.304) – the liver was seen as the seat of passion – and calling his sister 'lusty widow' before leaving the stage (1.1.344).

The fact that widows were not firmly under the control of their male relations intensified their ability to arouse masculine anxieties. In this period, when a woman married she moved from a position of legal subservience to her father to being legally subject to her husband. A widow, then, especially if she inherited wealth from her dead husband, could claim an alarming degree of independence. She might, as a result, presume to choose her second husband herself, rather than marrying in accordance with her family's wishes. This is a prospect that clearly worries the Cardinal, who warns his sister not to 'take your own choice' (1.1.322). The Duchess's position as a female ruler only exacerbates her brothers' concerns about her capacity to act independently of their wishes. Their repeated references to the dangerous temptations of the courtly life – 'You live in a rank pasture here, i'th'court' (1.1.312) and 'I would have you to give o'er these chargeable revels' (1.1.337) – disclose their unease with the power she wields as a duchess who presides over her own court.

Both brothers are concerned about family honour, but what precisely would make a second marriage dishonourable? Neither Ferdinand nor the Cardinal says outright that what they fear is that their sister will marry 'beneath her', but this uneasiness about rank is strongly implied in the advice they give her:

FERDINAND   You are a widow:
        You know already what man is, and therefore
        Let not youth, high promotion, eloquence –
CARDINAL   No, nor any thing without the addition, honour,
        Sway your high blood.

(1.1.299–303)

The Cardinal's reference to the Duchess's 'high blood' in particular smacks of class insecurity: he is afraid that she will fall into the arms of a lower-class man. Later in the play, when the brothers learn that their sister has indeed remarried, they leap to the conclusion that her second husband is of humble birth. So the Cardinal cries 'Shall our blood, / The royal blood of Aragon and Castile, / Be thus attainted?' (2.5.21–3), confirming his belief that a cross-class marriage constitutes a tainting or corruption of the family's pure noble blood. The fact that at this stage they do not even know the identity of their sister's new husband demonstrates just how insecure and under threat they feel, as though the privileges and power they inherited by virtue of their exalted birth are now being put under pressure by interlopers from lower down the social scale.

The brothers' jitteriness about rank reflects the unprecedented levels of social mobility that characterised early modern England. Those in power were fond of claiming that a fixed and rigid social hierarchy was divinely ordained, but the reality was restless movement up and down the social scale, as land and wealth flowed away from old, established families into the hands of 'new' men – lawyers, merchants, administrators, yeomen – who were eager to step into their predecessors' shoes. Not surprisingly, this erosion of the social hierarchy was accompanied by a heated debate about whether noble blood or personal merit was more deserving of honour. Webster, the son of a wealthy coach-maker, contributed to this debate throughout his theatrical career. According to literary critic Elli Abraham Shellist (2004), it is 'the source of cultural conflict that is most frequently and intensely enacted' in his plays. In *The Duchess of Malfi*, Webster signals that the play's dominant aristocratic order is in a state of crisis, threatened by men like Antonio, an able administrator who, as we will soon learn, captures the heart of a high-born woman more impressed by merit than rank.

So the brothers' attitude to the Duchess's marrying again is determined not just by their ideas about women but also by their ideas about class boundaries and the nature of marriage. They share misogynistic views of the sexuality of widows and the patriarchal assumption that they have the right to dictate their sister's sexual destiny. But these attitudes are all bound up with their belief that marriage is a union between a man and a woman which should be chosen not by the individual but by the family, and not for reasons of love but with a view to enhancing family power and maintaining elite exclusivity. By the time Webster wrote *The Duchess*, this conception of marriage was very much associated with the upper classes. It is important to recognise that there was an alternative view available, often called the companionate ideal of marriage, which (as its name suggests) placed love and compatibility above the demands of family honour. This very different notion of marriage derived from the Protestant belief that marriage was an essential ingredient of human happiness and, as such, had to be built on a foundation of mutual love and respect. As an early seventeenth-century commentator put it: 'As for love, it is the life and soul of marriage, without which it is no more itself than a carcass is a man; yea, it is uncomfortable, miserable and a living death' (William Whately (1617) quoted in Keeble, 1994, p. 150).

While the aristocracy clung to its desire for dynastic unions, other sections of early modern English society adhered to an idea of marriage as a partnership based on reciprocal affection.

Love and marriage: Antonio the steward

The brothers, of course, turn out to be right about their sister, who is indeed planning a second marriage to a commoner. Like Desdemona, she chooses for herself rather than deferring to the wishes of her male relations. How does the play encourage us to feel about the Duchess's defiant second marriage? It is important that by the time her intentions towards Antonio are made clear, we have become well acquainted with the object of her affections. We have already seen that Antonio and Delio begin the scene alone onstage, when Antonio is depicted in terms of his well-developed and credible political ideas. As the other main characters enter and exit, the two characters stand apart and discuss them, Antonio providing detailed descriptions of Bosola, the Cardinal and Ferdinand, and finally of the Duchess. The fact that it is he who is selected to provide the audience with this information endows this character of humble birth with a considerable amount of authority. It has often been remarked that in this opening scene Antonio and Delio serve as a kind of Chorus, guiding the spectators' responses in the manner of the Choruses of the tragedies of ancient Greece.

As the Duchess's steward, Antonio occupies the same position as Malvolio in Shakespeare's comedy *Twelfth Night* (1601). It is a measure of the difference between the two plays that while Malvolio is ridiculed and humiliated as a social-climbing kill-joy, Antonio is treated with considerable respect. Not only is he allowed to enlighten the spectators as to the natures of the play's main characters; his merit is emphasised when he is announced as the winner of the joust (1.1.90–3). Malvolio is tricked into revealing his deep-seated longing for the social advancement that marriage to his employer, the Countess Olivia, would bring. Antonio, by contrast, discovers in this scene that he really is the object of his employer's desire. By investing the figure of the steward with so much authority, Webster is presenting a direct challenge to the elitism and caste pride represented by the Duchess's brothers.

Antonio's descriptions of the Cardinal and Ferdinand serve to enhance our understanding of the kind of social and political rottenness the brothers embody. What he stresses is the gap between their inner and outer selves. According to Antonio, while the Cardinal may play the role of 'brave fellow' when in company (1.1.159), underneath he is 'a melancholy churchman' (1.1.164) given to inveterate plotting against his enemies and not averse to bribing his way to the top of his profession. Ferdinand, in a similar fashion, acts the part of suave Renaissance prince, but beneath the surface lies a 'most perverse and turbulent nature' (1.1.176). In his role as judge, he pretends 'to sleep o'th'bench / Only to entrap offenders in their answers' (1.1.182–3). Through Antonio, then, the play identifies both brothers with a talent for dissimulation; they are actors who use performance to control and dominate others.

Activity 4

Look now at lines 195–217 of Act 1, Scene 1 and try to answer these two questions:

1   What does Antonio say about his employer, the Duchess?

2   What strikes you as distinctive about his language?

Discussion

1   Antonio describes the Duchess as a paragon of womanhood, as different from her corrupt brothers as it is possible to be. Her speech, he says, is enchanting without being in any way sinister, and her countenance is so lovely that it could cure paralysis! Antonio stresses the Duchess's virtue as well, specifically her chastity: she may attract men through her beauty and eloquence, but these are coupled with a 'divine' 'continence' that 'cuts off' lustful thoughts and that endows even her dreams with a purity that other women, including those who have just been to confession, fail to match. Like the Duchess's brothers, Antonio sees chastity as the quintessential feminine virtue, but while the Cardinal and Ferdinand take for granted their sister's moral frailty, Antonio pays her the compliment of claiming she entirely lives up to the ideal. He concludes that the Duchess ought to be a model for other women to emulate.

2   This summary makes it clear how exaggerated, how hyperbolic, Antonio's praise of the Duchess is. When he says that her speech and sweet look combined could enable a man crippled with paralysis to dance a galliard, a dance that required considerable speed and strength, he does not mean his words to be taken literally; he is using **hyperbole**, or extravagant overstatement, to convey the power of the Duchess's charms.

Webster is drawing here on a particular kind of love poetry of the period, often termed Petrarchan, from its originator, the Italian poet Francesco Petrarca (1304–1374). Petrarchan love poetry usually took the form of the sonnet – a 14-line poem in iambic pentameter with a complex rhyme scheme – and had numerous conventions, one of which was a strong tendency to idealise the loved object. Look at this fairly typical example by Edmund Spenser (*c*.1552–1599), which is sonnet 3 from his sonnet sequence *Amoretti*:

> The soverayne beauty which I doo admyre,
>   witnesse the world how worthy to be prayzed;
>   the light wherof hath kindled heavenly fyre
>   in my fraile spirit by her from baseness raysed:
> That being now with her huge brightnesse dazed,   5
>   base thing I can no more endure to view,
>   but looking still on her I stand amazed
>   at wondrous sight of so celestiall hew.
> So when my toung would speake her praises dew,
>   it stopped is with thought's astonishment;   10
>   and when my pen would write her titles true,
>   it ravisht is with fancie's wonderment:
> Yet in my hart I then both speake and write
>   the wonder that my wit cannot endite [put into words].

(Evans, 1977, p. 115)

Like Antonio's speech, Spenser's poem is concerned with the power of female beauty, which is associated with monarchy in the word 'soverayne' (sovereign) (l. 1) and with divinity in words like 'heavenly' (l. 3) and 'celestiall' (l. 8). Antonio too invests the Duchess's appearance with a spiritual potency, and both the sonnet and the speech see this as capable of strengthening and ennobling the onlooker: like Antonio's man lying in 'a dead palsy', the speaker of Spenser's poem is raised from baseness by the woman's beauty, his 'fraile' spirit revived and renewed.

By the time of the first performance of *The Duchess* in 1613–14, this kind of love poetry, with its idealised picture of the woman, was fairly old-fashioned, and this is reflected in Delio's amused response to his friend's rapturous speech: 'Fie, Antonio, / You play the wire-drawer with her commendations' (1.1.213–14). By identifying Antonio with a man who stretches metal to make wire, Delio's metaphor suggests that his praise of the Duchess was both long-winded and a trifle excessive. But Antonio sticks to his guns, closing his description of the Duchess with a memorable **couplet**: 'All her particular worth grows to this sum, / She stains the time past, lights the time to come' (1.1.216–17). In other words, she leaves an indelible mark on the past (or possibly makes it look dark by comparison with herself) and casts a light upon the future. Thus, by the time the Duchess begins her courtship of Antonio, we know that he is in love with her, and Webster's representation of that love in Petrarchan terms identifies it as intensely romantic, as a form of adoration that, in Antonio's circumstances, defines the social distance separating him from his aristocratic employer.

Love and marriage: the Duchess

What of the Duchess herself? According to Clifford Leech and James L. Calderwood, in studies of the play produced in the 1950s and 1960s, she is portrayed in accordance with the stereotypes of the highly sexed widow voiced by her brothers, and her marriage to Antonio is depicted as wilful, wanton and irresponsible (Rabkin, 1968, pp. 75–9, 93). Do you agree? We will address this question by looking at Webster's representation of the Duchess's courtship of her steward, but before we do that, it is worth remembering that by the time we meet the play's protagonist, her brothers have been revealed unambiguously as villains. It seems unlikely, then, that the play would invite us to endorse their views. A more credible argument would be that the play is seeking to discredit misogynistic attitudes to women by putting them in the mouths of its least appealing characters.

The Duchess is certainly violating norms of femininity in the final episode of Act 1, as she adopts the active role in the marriage, courting and effectively proposing marriage to Antonio. She is thus even bolder than Desdemona, who only 'hints' to Othello that she would welcome his courtship (Shakespeare, 2008 [1622], 1.3.166). Yet, I would argue that the Duchess's seizing of the initiative is not presented as the result of an overactive libido. Indeed, the Duchess speaks of her own sexuality with admirable common sense, saying to Antonio: 'This is flesh and blood, sir, / 'Tis not the figure cut in alabaster / Kneels at my husband's tomb' (1.1.457–9). This is refreshing, not only after the brothers' misogyny, but also after Antonio's own desexualised portrait of the Duchess. Later in the play, in a moment of great danger, she asks Ferdinand: 'Why should only I / Of all the other princes of the world / Be cased up like a holy relic? I have youth, / And a little beauty' (3.2.137–9). Both these passages stress the difference between nature and artifice, between the naturalness of a woman's flesh, blood, youth and beauty and the way patriarchal society seeks to transform women into decorative, precious objects that can be locked away and safely controlled. This contrast between nature and representation suggests that the Duchess is neither lascivious, as her brothers would have it, nor the inhuman paragon of loyalty and chastity – the alabaster figure, the holy relic – that men would like her, and women generally, to be. She expresses her own sexuality in a manner that makes it sound healthy and natural, in opposition to a patriarchal mindset predisposed to see women in terms of the binary oppositions of angel and whore.

Webster, then, appears to have no qualms about stressing the sexual dimension of the Duchess's love for Antonio. What else can we say about his portrayal of the lovers' relationship in the final courtship section of the play's long opening scene? The expression of love and desire is necessarily muted at the start, as the Duchess keeps up the pretence that she has sent for Antonio to help her in the preparation of her will. There are moments when her nerves seem to get the better of her, as when she forgets what she just asked Antonio to do and needs to be reminded (1.1.365–8). But their mutual attraction is evident throughout, and in the theatre a director would need to decide just how openly flirtatious or guarded their initial interaction should be. The Duchess takes more pleasure in Antonio's compliment – 'So please your beauteous excellence' (1.1.372) – than seems strictly compatible with her position as his employer. And both parties waste no time in bringing the discussion around to the topic of marriage, Antonio revealing, when pressed, a touching desire for parenthood:

> Say a man never marry, nor have children,
> What takes that from him? Only the bare name
> Of being a father, or the weak delight
> To see the little wanton ride a-cock-horse
> Upon a painted stick, or hear him chatter
> Like a taught starling.

(1.1.402–7)

Slowly, the Duchess builds up to a more open expression of her feelings, declaring her love – 'Go, go brag / You have left me heartless, mine is in your bosom' (1.1.452–3) – and revealing that it is rooted in her perception and appreciation of Antonio's virtues:

Figure 3.3   Helen Mirren as the Duchess in *The Duchess of Malfi*, dir. Adrian Noble (Manchester Royal Exchange, 1980). Photo: Photostage.

> If you will know where breathes a complete man –
> I speak it without flattery – turn your eyes
> And progress through yourself.

$$(1.1.439{-}41)$$

The marriage itself is represented in terms of harmony and mutuality. Both characters kneel and speak lines that evoke strongly companionate ideas of marriage: the 'sacred Gordian' knot that cannot be untied (1.1.482); the music of the 'spheres' (1.1.483); the 'loving palms' that 'ne'er bore fruit divided' (1.1.485, 487). The delivery of the lines, the fact that they are performed as a kind of duet with the Duchess and Antonio echoing and completing one another's images, reinforces the couple's mutual affection.

Figure 3.4   Emblem of loving palms as a symbol of a good marriage, in Cats, J. (1657) *Emblemata Moralia et Oeconomica*, in *Alle de Werken van Jakob Cats*, Amsterdam. Photo: By permission of the Folger Shakespeare Library, Washington, D.C.

It seems highly likely that Webster's original Protestant audience would have responded favourably to this depiction of a marriage based on shared admiration and the desire to raise a family. Would it have been a problem that the marriage was clandestine? Early modern marriage law is too complex a topic to deal with in any depth here; suffice it to say that a valid and binding marriage required only that the couple declare their mutual consent in the present tense – what the Duchess refers to as 'a contract in a chamber, / *Per verba de presenti*' (1.1.480–1). But in 1604, James I sought 'to clarify the definition of marriage by taking it out of private hands and requiring it to be validated by ecclesiastical ceremony' (Marcus, 2009, p. 36), a move opposed by large segments of English society who saw this as an encroachment by church and state on a time-honoured tradition. When the Duchess declares 'We now are man and wife, and 'tis the Church / That must but echo this' (1.1.492–3), she is giving priority to an idea of marriage as a private contract outside the direct control of the ecclesiastical authorities – an idea with which many of the play's original spectators would no doubt have sympathised.

To portray the relationship between the Duchess and Antonio as devoid of affection, as some productions do, is to ignore the copious textual evidence that Webster depicts it as a love match. It is certainly true, however, that Webster never lets us forget the power differential between the bride and groom. The staging of the courtship stresses how much this marriage turns conventional gender roles on their heads. Not only does the Duchess instigate the wooing; it is she who places the ring on Antonio's finger, and when he kneels in response, she raises him up again. Visually, this underscores her powerful position. Webster's use of **dramatic irony** strengthens our sense of this; not to be confused with **verbal irony**, when a text means something quite different from what it says, dramatic irony involves a situation in which an audience or reader knows more than one or more characters. The fact that we know what the Duchess is up to, while Antonio remains in the dark until the Duchess slips the ring onto his finger, intensifies our awareness of his inferior position.

Webster also makes it clear that for Antonio part of the attraction of the Duchess's proposal is the self-advancement it promises, hence his initial response when she gives him her wedding ring and her amorous intentions become clear: 'There is a saucy and ambitious devil / Is dancing in this circle' (1.1.416–17). The metaphor of the wedding ring as a magic circle inside of which a 'saucy and ambitious devil' is dancing conveys not only Antonio's desire for upward social mobility, but also his conviction that that desire is a dangerous temptation. Webster is hardly cynical about this: we have already heard Antonio's fulsome speech of praise for the Duchess, as well as his deeply felt evocation of the joys of fatherhood. The point is not that Antonio feels no love for the Duchess, but that his motives for marrying are mixed.

He is also frightened of the Duchess's brothers, and Webster encourages us to share his fear. We have just heard both Ferdinand and the Cardinal make thinly veiled threats to their sister, the language of which suggests that a secret, unauthorised second marriage will be met with severe punishment. So Ferdinand declares: 'Such weddings may more properly be said / To be executed than celebrated' (1.1.327–8); the Cardinal adding: 'The marriage night / Is the entrance into some prison' (1.1.328–9). These statements serve as prolepses gesturing towards the violent treatment awaiting the Duchess and setting up strong verbal links between marriage for love on the one hand and suffering and death on the other. Webster continues to provide verbal clues as to the fate of this forbidden union during the courtship and marriage. We have seen that the Duchess is forced to dissemble her intentions at the start of the wooing, but her pretence that she is making her will seems a desperately ominous start to the courtship, and the language at this point, with its talk of the 'deep groans and terrible ghastly looks' of the dying, and the 'winding sheet' in which a corpse was wrapped (1.1.383, 393), underlines just how ill-fated this marriage for love will prove. Webster's language subtly yokes love and death, alerting the spectators to the dangers awaiting the lovers, even if the heroine herself chooses to dismiss them.

Activity 5

Read the Duchess's speech that follows Ferdinand's exit at line 345 and precedes Cariola's entry at 353. How would you characterise the mood of this passage?

Discussion

I would say that the mood of the speech is extraordinarily defiant. We have just heard Ferdinand and the Cardinal threaten to punish a second marriage, but as soon as the Duchess is alone onstage, she dismisses them with withering contempt:

> If all my royal kindred
> Lay in my way unto this marriage
> I'd make them my low foot-steps ...

> (1.1.345–7)

The lines imagine her royal kindred as a literal obstacle blocking her path to 'this marriage', an obstacle she simply turns to her advantage, using them as 'low foot-steps' to the altar. The Duchess's sentence carries on for another six lines, most of which are taken up with an extended simile in which she makes an analogy between herself and 'men in some great battles' who '[b]y apprehending danger have achieved / Almost impossible actions' (1.1.348, 349–50). As in the opening lines of the speech, the Duchess acknowledges the problem but determines to use it to her advantage, just as men in battle sometimes do, facing danger and thereby transforming their fear into courage and valour.

The Duchess is entering imaginatively into a masculine world of military heroism that she has only heard about: 'I have heard soldiers say so' (1.1.350). Her sex may exclude her from this world, but her high rank connects her to it, for war had traditionally been the chief vocation of the male aristocrat, as Ferdinand indicates earlier in the scene when he asks impatiently 'When shall we leave this sportive action and fall to action indeed?' (1.1.93–4). We can hear the note of class pride in the Duchess's speech: the easy sense of superiority that fuels the metaphor of her 'royal kindred' as nothing more than 'low foot-steps'; the self-assertiveness of her declaration 'So I, through frights and threat'nings will assay / This dangerous venture' (1.1.351–2). When Antonio, later in the scene, asks 'But for your brothers?' (1.1.472), the Duchess replies:

> Do not think of them.
> All discord, without this circumference,
> Is only to be pitied and not feared.

> (1.1.472–4)

This is a pattern that will be repeated throughout Acts 2 and 3 in moments of danger, as the Duchess seeks to reassure her husband, who consistently feels helpless and overwhelmed by the course of events. Antonio seems to recognise the gender confusion when he says to his new wife: 'These words should be mine' (1.1.476).

So the play, while staging a cross-class marriage, never loses sight of the class differences of the couple and the way this skews traditional gender roles. The Duchess may marry the steward she admires as 'a complete man' (1.1.439), but she remains very much an aristocrat. This brings us to the vexed question of why she places Cariola behind the arras prior to wooing Antonio. It seems that Cariola emerges from her hiding place in order to act as witness of the couple's marriage vows, but numerous critics, including Clifford Leech and Frank Whigham, have felt that there is something duplicitous and coercive in the Duchess's treatment of her prospective husband in this episode; the wary steward is enticed with promises of vast wealth (1.1.432–4) and ultimately trapped in wedlock by the Duchess's own spy behind the arras (Leech in Rabkin, 1968, p. 93; Whigham, 1985, p. 173). Does Webster, then, reveal in his heroine traces of the kind of manipulative bullying we see as well in her brothers, suggesting that using people is part and parcel of being a member of the ruling class? Perhaps, but other critics have argued for a reading of this episode that is more flattering to the Duchess. For example, William Empson suggests that she hides Cariola precisely in order to leave Antonio free to decline her proposal, an insult he may have felt disinclined to deliver in the presence of her waiting woman (Rabkin, 1968, p. 93).

This long opening scene draws to a close with Cariola's choric commentary:

> Whether the spirit of greatness or of woman
> Reign most in her, I know not, but it shows
> A fearful madness. I owe her much of pity.

> (1.1.504–6)

Cariola is uncertain whether to see the Duchess's bid for self-determination as evidence of her 'greatness' of spirit or her feminine wilfulness. It is important that 'greatness' is offered here as a possibility. Whigham calls the Duchess 'a cultural voyager' who 'arrogates to herself a new role, that of female hero' (1985, p. 172). She does this not only in the speech we considered earlier but also when she says to Cariola: 'Wish me good speed, / For I am going into a wilderness / Where I shall find nor path, nor friendly clew / To be my guide' (1.1.362–5). She is moving knowingly into uncharted waters, beyond the bounds of socially accepted behaviour where there will be no clear path to guide her. It is in the absence of models to imitate that she identifies herself with the notion of masculine heroism so integral to her class. Cariola, too, is uncertain how to describe an aristocratic woman who is flouting the requirements of her rank and gender.

In Act 1, Webster constructs a dramatic world dominated by a morally impoverished aristocratic elite obsessed with controlling their sister's sexuality and policing the class boundary that sets them apart from those lower down the social scale. It is against the backdrop of this poisonous courtly milieu that the marriage between the Duchess and Antonio takes on such positive meanings, and becomes a vehicle for upholding a view of marriage based on mutual love and compatibility and the right of a woman to determine her own sexual destiny, independently of her male relations. There is nothing glib or sentimental in Webster's endorsement of these values; the play does not pretend that love provides a simple solution to disparities of rank, for example. Yet to a very real extent, Webster draws on the conventions of stage comedy in Act 1 of *The Duchess*, presenting us with an obstacle to true love, in the form of familial disapproval, and inviting sympathy for the lovers who defy that authority. Yet the play is too dark and its authority figures too sinister to sustain much hope of a comic **denouement**, and Webster's language steadily reminds us that in this play love and death are inextricable.

Act 2: discovery

Nine months elapse between Acts 1 and 2, and the bulk of the second act is taken up with Bosola's attempt to determine whether or not the Duchess is pregnant. On this level, the play stresses her femaleness: we see her pregnant onstage, devouring apricots, watch her go into labour and then hear, at the close of Act 2, Scene 2, that she has given birth to a son. The play, then, highlights not only her role as duchess, but also her roles as wife and mother, emphasising the fertility of the marriage.

The danger of the couple's position is conveyed through the desperate and ultimately futile attempts to keep the birth of the child a secret. By the end of the act, Ferdinand and the Cardinal have received Bosola's letter informing them of the birth of the Duchess's son.

Ferdinand

Both brothers are clearly furious at the news, making explicit the kind of rank-based disquiet I discussed earlier. Both give vent to misogynist commonplaces, such as the following:

> Foolish men,
> That e'er will trust their honour in a bark
> Made of so slight weak bullrush as is woman,
> Apt every minute to sink it!

(2.5.33–6)

Yet, Ferdinand's anger seems different in kind from the Cardinal's. Indeed, the Cardinal is as shocked by his brother's ravings as any member of the audience, and his alarmed responses confirm that Ferdinand's attitude to the Duchess is obsessive and pathological: 'Speak lower' (2.5.4); 'Why do you make yourself / So wild a tempest?' (2.5.16–17); 'You fly beyond your reason' (2.5.46); 'Are you stark mad?' (2.5.66).

Activity 6

How did you respond to Ferdinand's conduct in this scene? Did it surprise you, or do you think that Webster's characterisation of the Duke of Calabria in Act 1 lays the foundations for his conduct here? Go back through Act 1 and see if you can find any suggestions of the kind of mental instability represented in this scene.

Discussion

In Act 1, before the brothers gang up on their sister in an effort to bully her into submission, Ferdinand tells Bosola that he 'would not have her marry again' (1.1.262). This blanket hostility to a second marriage goes beyond anything voiced by the Cardinal, who is much more concerned about the prospect of an inappropriate union. In reply, Bosola says only 'No, sir?' (1.1.262), yet this unchallenging response is enough to spark the highly defensive 'Do not you ask the reason, but be satisfied / I say I would not' (1.1.263–4). Webster seems to be deliberately arousing our curiosity about Ferdinand's motives here, giving us a glance of the turbulent, unstable personality Antonio mentioned earlier in the scene. Later, when the brothers confront the Duchess, it is Ferdinand whose language is compulsively sexual, culminating in the dirty joke about the lamprey we considered earlier. He goes on to brandish their father's dagger at her – a gesture many critics have interpreted in phallic terms.

It is these suggestions of an intensely sexualised attitude towards his sister that burst into the open in Act 2, Scene 5. Ferdinand is gripped by fevered, voyeuristic visions of his sister having sex with working-class men characterised by their physical vigour and attractiveness:

> Happily with some strong-thighed bargeman;
> Or one o'th'woodyard that can quoit the sledge
> Or toss the bar; or else some lovely squire
> That carries coals up to her privy lodgings.

(2.5.42–5)

The lines register a fear of encroachment by men whose lower rank is compensated for by their superior masculinity. But what the verse chiefly conveys is Ferdinand's loss of control: he cannot stop himself from visualising the Duchess 'in the shameful act of sin' (2.5.41). He asks his brother 'Talk to me somewhat quickly' (2.5.39), in a futile attempt to shut down an imagination that immediately goes on to enumerate a selection of possible low-class sexual partners. When he shouts ''Tis not your whore's milk that shall quench my wild-fire, / But your whore's blood!' (2.5.47–8), his words are so deranged as to be unintelligible, though his obsession with his sister's body remains clear, as does his powerful urge to do violence to her.

It is probably fair to say that nowadays most critics of the play agree that what underlies Ferdinand's relationship with his sister is unconscious incestuous desire. Indeed, the German playwright Bertolt Brecht, when he adapted *The Duchess of Malfi* in 1946, appended a prologue in which Ferdinand confesses his incestuous passion for his sister. What seems to drive Ferdinand's collapse into hysteria in Act 2, Scene 5 is a ferocious sexual jealousy that seems bent not just on the destruction but the obliteration of the loved object. So he imagines 'hewing' the Duchess 'to pieces' (2.5.31) and, in the following passage, rehearses with demented relish different ways of annihilating her and her family:

> I would have their bodies
> Burnt in a coal pit with the ventage stopped,
> That their cursed smoke might not ascend to heaven;
> Or dip the sheets they lie in, in pitch or sulphur,
> Wrap them in't and then light them like a match;
> Or else to boil their bastard to a cullis

> And give't his lecherous father to renew
> The sin of his back.

(2.5.66–73)

There is a longing here for a revenge so total that the offending physical selves will cease to exist. There is also a desire to punish the father for his lechery by making him eat his child – a form of retribution Webster would have known from Shakespeare's early revenge tragedy *Titus Andronicus*, in which the protagonist avenges himself on his enemy Tamora by killing her two sons and baking them in a pie which he feeds to her at a dinner party.

By this point in the play there can be no doubt in our minds that Ferdinand is the play's principal villain, albeit a fascinating one. Yet even here, Webster injects a moral dimension, suggesting that the Duke of Calabria's furious desire for vengeance stems in part from guilt:

> I could kill her now
> In you, or in myself, for I do think
> It is some sin in us heaven doth revenge
> By her.

(2.5.63–6)

These cryptic lines imply that Ferdinand's savagery derives in part from a self-loathing which he projects onto his sister. As with Bosola and Antonio, Webster seems keen to endow Ferdinand with a degree of psychological complexity.

Conclusion

In *Othello*, Shakespeare explores the link between love and a violent sexual jealousy that ultimately turns murderous. Webster is interested in exploring the same connection, though by locating the homicidal jealousy in a brother's yearning for his sister he compounds our awareness of the dark side of sexual desire, the potential for certain species of love to explode into violence. In Ferdinand, Webster presents us with another form of forbidden love and allows us to explore the relationship between love and death from the perspective of the villain.

Brecht's particular interest in Ferdinand's illicit sexual desires points to one of the reasons for our continued fascination with this play.

The establishment of Freudian psychoanalysis in the course of the twentieth century brought with it a model of the human psyche which sees unruly repressed desires and impulses as exerting a powerful influence on human behaviour. Webster's characterisation of the Duke of Calabria as a man in the grip of unconscious and taboo erotic longings meshes with a modern conception of the instability and irreducible complexity of the human personality. Having said that, there is every indication that Webster's contemporaries found Ferdinand equally compelling; the role was originally played by Richard Burbage, the great tragic actor of the King's Men who had created the roles of Shakespeare's tragic heroes Hamlet, King Lear and Othello. That Burbage played Ferdinand as well suggests that the character was seen as the principal male role in the first productions of the play.

We have looked in this chapter at how Webster situates his forbidden cross-class marriage within a very particular dramatic context, thereby stimulating a sympathetic response towards the lovers who flout the dictates of the arbitrary aristocratic power embodied by the Cardinal and Ferdinand. In the next chapter, we will concentrate on Acts 3 to 5, examining the representation of love and death as the Duchess and her family face the full force of the brothers' retaliation and the play's tragic conflict comes increasingly to the fore.

References

Evans, M. (ed.) (1977) *Elizabethan Sonnets*, London, J.M. Dent and Sons.

Henderson, K.U. and MacManus, B. (1985) *Half Humankind: Contexts and Texts of the Controversy about Women in England 1540–1640*, Urbana, IL, University of Illinois Press.

James I (1599) *Basilikon Doron Devided into Three Bookes*, Edinburgh.

Keeble, N.H. (ed.) (1994) *The Cultural Identity of Seventeenth-Century Woman*, London, Routledge.

Marcus, L.S. (ed.) (2009) *The Duchess of Malfi*, Arden Early Modern Drama, London, Methuen.

Rabkin, N. (ed.) (1968) *Twentieth Century Interpretations of* The Duchess of Malfi, Englewood Cliffs, NJ, Prentice-Hall.

Shakespeare, W. (2008 [1622]) *Othello* (ed. M. Neill), Oxford World's Classics, Oxford, Oxford University Press.

Shellist, E.A. (2004) 'John Webster' in Kinney, A.F. (ed.) *A Companion to Renaissance Drama*, Oxford, Blackwell, also available online at http//www.blackwellreference.com/subscriber/tocnode?id=g9781405121798_chunk_g978140512179839 (Accessed 21 September 2009).

Webster, J. (2009 [1623]) *The Duchess of Malfi* (ed. M. Kendall), Harlow, Pearson Longman.

Whigham, F. (1985) 'Sexual and social mobility in *The Duchess of Malfi*', *Publications of the Modern Language Association*, vol. 100, no. 2, pp. 167–86.

Further reading

Aughterson, K. (2001) *Webster: The Tragedies*, Basingstoke, Palgrave.

Belsey, C. (1980) 'Emblem and antithesis in *The Duchess of Malfi*', *Renaissance Drama*, vol. 11, pp. 115–34.

Ekeblad, I.S. (1958) 'The impure art of John Webster', *Review of English Studies*, vol. 9, pp. 253–67.

Maus, K.E. (ed.) (1995) *Four Revenge Tragedies*, Oxford World's Classics, Oxford, Oxford University Press.

Neill, M. (1997) *Issues of Death: Mortality and Identity in English Renaissance Tragedy*, Oxford, Clarendon Press.

Chapter 4
John Webster, *The Duchess of Malfi*: tragic conflict

Anita Pacheco

Aims

This chapter will:

- examine the treatment of the themes of love and death in Acts 3–5 of *The Duchess of Malfi*
- provide you with further practice in textual analysis
- discuss some of the theatrical devices and techniques Webster employs in the play
- consider the play as a performance text.

Introduction

The conflict set up in Acts 1 and 2 intensifies in Acts 3–5, as the play's tragic conventions take centre stage. Not surprisingly then, we will focus in this chapter more on the representation of death than love. We will look first at the mounting danger facing the Duchess and her family in Act 3 and then go on to examine how the tragic crisis of Act 4 is staged. We will also consider the dramatic function of Act 5, viewed by many as the least successful part of the play. Throughout this chapter, we will continue to analyse the language of the text, while also attending to Webster's stagecraft and the performance possibilities of particular episodes.

Act 3: reversal of fortune

The discussion between Antonio and Delio that opens Act 3, Scene 1 alerts us to the fact that a considerable amount of time has elapsed since Ferdinand's vow of revenge – enough time for the Duchess to give birth to two more children, a son and a daughter. So in part, the function of this scene is to inform us of the passage of time. The scene also lets us know that Ferdinand has returned to the Duchess's court.

When the Duchess and Antonio exit, leaving Ferdinand and Bosola alone onstage, Ferdinand immediately reveals his real state of mind – 'Her guilt treads on / Hot burning coulters' (3.1.56–7) – along with his determination to 'force confession from her' '[t]his night' (3.1.79, 78). He then asks Bosola for a key to the Duchess's bedchamber.

Act 3, Scene 2: the turning point

Act 3, Scene 1 clearly colours our response to the next scene, which is set in the Duchess's bedchamber, and which we watch with the strong suspicion that Ferdinand is waiting in the wings. This works to create an almost unbearable level of suspense. The film director Alfred Hitchcock, a master of suspense, was once asked in an interview how he went about stimulating suspense in an audience. He gave the following reply:

> Let us suppose that there is a bomb underneath this table between us. Nothing happens, and then all of a sudden, 'Boom!' There is an explosion. The public is surprised, but prior to this surprise, it

has seen an absolutely ordinary scene, of no special consequence. Now, let us take a suspense situation. The bomb is underneath the table and the public knows it … . The public is aware that the bomb is going to explode at one o'clock and there is a clock in the decor. The public can see that it is a quarter to one. … The audience is longing to warn the characters … . In the first case we have given the public fifteen seconds of surprise at the moment of the explosion. In the second case we have provided them with fifteen minutes of suspense.

(Hitchcock in Truffaut, 1967, p. 52)

Hitchcock was talking here about film rather than drama, but the principle is the same. Webster generates suspense in his readers and spectators by making them aware of the presence of a threat of which the characters onstage are oblivious. So in Act 3, Scene 2, we are shown that rarity in early modern tragedy – a happy and loving marriage. This is all the more remarkable given the numerous pressures it has had to endure: the discrepancy in rank and authority between wife and husband; the years of enforced secrecy accompanied by the constant risk of discovery; the fact that the couple have now had three children together and thus are far from being in the first throes of passion. Antonio and the Duchess are getting ready for bed, teasing one another and joking, looking forward to sleeping together. Their mutual affection is expressed not in sentimental platitudes of true love but in an erotic playfulness that is all the more affecting because we know or suspect that this moment of domestic happiness is about to be shattered. As in the courtship episode of Act 1, Webster is happy to acknowledge sexual desire as an integral ingredient in a successful marriage. Yet here too his language intensifies our sense of the fragility of the mutual love and attraction being enacted. As Frank Whigham explains:

Antonio says he rises early after a night with his wife because he is glad his wearisome night's work is over. The affectionate inversion displaces the real reason for early rising: the oppressive need for secrecy, typical of adultery rather than of marriage.
Lightheartedness is simultaneously present and painfully absent.

(Whigham, 1985, p. 174)

It is when Antonio and Cariola decide to play an affectionate joke on the Duchess that she is left alone in her bedchamber and Ferdinand enters. In the theatre, then, the scene would provide visual signals of her isolation and vulnerability. There is, moreover, a telling substitution for Ferdinand as, for a moment, the Duchess chatters on and he stands in her husband's place.

This is a major turning point in the play; the moment when a tragic outcome seems inevitable. The dramatic change of tone is signalled visually, by the stage business, but also linguistically, by a change in language. The easy, informal banter of the first section of the scene gives way to a very different brand of speech as Ferdinand dominates the proceedings, speaking the majority of lines and twice ordering his sister to be silent. While not quite as frenzied as in Act 2, Scene 5, Ferdinand's language still manages to suggest the depth of the character's anger and agitation. It abounds in rhetorical questions, such as 'Virtue, where art thou hid?' (3.2.71), and this hectoring, self-righteous tone alternates with more overtly violent reproaches: 'Die then, quickly!' (3.2.70) and 'The howling of a wolf / Is music to thee, screech owl' (3.2.88–9). The last quotation shows his habitual fondness for likening human beings to the most negative aspects of the animal world. He addresses his longest speech to Antonio, though he declines the Duchess's invitation to meet her new husband, on the grounds that it would provoke 'such violent effects / As would damn us both' (3.2.94–5). Although his angry and long-winded preaching at his sister is alienating, his language does point to a genuine moral anxiety about his

Figure 4.1 Harriet Walter as the Duchess and Bruce Alexander as Ferdinand in *The Duchess of Malfi*, dir. Bill Alexander (Royal Shakespeare Company, Swan Theatre, Stratford-Upon-Avon, 1989). Photo: Photostage.

own conduct; as before, in Act 2, Scene 5, Webster seems intent on endowing his principal villain with moral and psychological complexity. In the end, Ferdinand leaves the stage still ignorant of the identity of the Duchess's new husband, though he assures her that she is 'undone' (3.2.111), or ruined, and (twice) that he will never see her again.

Activity 1

Let's consider now how this crucial moment in the play – Ferdinand's appearance in the Duchess's bedchamber – might look onstage. In doing this, we need to think about any clues the play text gives us about performance possibilities. Reread Act 3, Scene 2 from the start up to the point when Ferdinand first speaks (line 70) and try to answer these questions:

1   What is the Duchess doing when Ferdinand enters?

2   What does Ferdinand do when he appears in the bedchamber?

3   How does the Duchess react to her brother?

Discussion

Here are my answers to the questions:

1   At the start of the scene, the Duchess requests a mirror and a jewellery box, and later makes several comments on her hair: 'My hair tangles' (3.2.52) and 'Doth not the colour of my hair 'gin to change?' (3.2.57). These are textual clues which suggest that in performance the actress playing the Duchess would be sitting in front of the mirror, brushing her hair, still chatting to her now absent husband when Ferdinand silently enters. Her half-line 'Have you lost your tongue?' (3.2.67) is a cue for her either to turn around and discover her brother standing behind her, or to see his reflection in the mirror.

2   The stage direction tells us that Ferdinand '*gives her a poniard*', or dagger, perhaps the same one he appeared to threaten her with in Act 1, Scene 1. Stage directions are obviously one of the principal ways in which dramatists indicate how the text of the play should be performed. But in early modern drama, they are often few and far between and lacking in detail, leaving directors with many performance-related decisions to make.

3   Here are the first lines the Duchess speaks after discovering her brother's presence:

> 'Tis welcome:
> For know, whether I am doomed to live, or die,
> I can do both like a prince.

(3.2.68–70)

The first, very short line requires there to be a pause before the next one begins if the metre is to be sustained; in performance, this may indicate the Duchess's shocked silence, or her reaching out and taking of the dagger. If the former, her recovery is swift, as she adopts again the heroic idiom we heard at the end of Act 1 when she was venturing into the 'wilderness' of her clandestine marriage. What strikes me most about the Duchess's reaction to her brother's very threatening appearance is her astonishing self-possession. The actress playing the Duchess would need to convey this through her voice and posture.

The text also provides us with information about the set and the costumes in this scene. The fact that it takes place in the Duchess's bedchamber means that in most productions there is a bed onstage, which often adds to the scene's sexual charge. The Duchess is usually wearing a nightgown, which can increase the sense of her vulnerability here.

The Duchess's language in this part of the play contrasts sharply with her brother's. She meets Ferdinand's anger with clear, straightforward statements and questions: 'I pray sir, hear me: I am married' (3.2.82) and 'Will you see my husband?' (3.2.86). She also objects to his tone of moral outrage:

> Why might not I marry?
> I have not gone about in this to create
> Any new world or custom.

> (3.2.109–11)

On one level, this seems disingenuous; as her earlier speeches in Act 1, Scene 1 make clear, she knows full well how radical and unprecedented her second marriage is. Yet on another level, her simplicity of expression captures the irrationality of the brothers' prohibition and so invites our sympathy: to marry a second time is indeed not 'to create / Any new world'.

The Duchess's conduct in this scene also contrasts with that of her husband, who remains offstage throughout her ordeal and re-enters, carrying a pistol and making threats, only once Ferdinand is safely out of the way. The Duchess, by contrast, has already come up with a plan for dealing with the situation, which she immediately puts into action when Bosola turns up on the scene a few lines later. This final section of Act 3, Scene 2, involving Antonio's flight to Ancona under cover of the Duchess's trumped-up charge of embezzlement, opens a space for further **satire** on the royal court and explicit consideration of the debate about the relative claims of birth and merit, as Bosola, with his usual linguistic creativity, presents an extended defence of the now disgraced Antonio.

This brings us to the difficult question of whether Bosola means what he says here. At the end of the scene, he is left alone onstage to deliver a soliloquy in which he discloses to the audience that he is going to tell Ferdinand everything he has just learned. Moreover, when he enters at the close of Act 3, Scene 5 to arrest the Duchess, he contradicts everything he has said here on the merit versus birth debate. His inconsistency provides us with a good example of just how ambiguous early modern play texts can be. We have in these two chapters on *The Duchess of Malfi* repeatedly attempted to interpret the text of the play, considering, for example, whether the Duchess is represented critically or sympathetically, and how we should read Ferdinand's extreme reaction to the birth of his sister's first child. Bosola's conduct in Act 3 is a particularly glaring instance of a moment when a play text appears to be crying out for its audience to engage in the act of interpretation. There is no single right answer to the question of whether or not Bosola is sincere in his defence of Antonio, and each reader and spectator will need to decide where he or she stands on this question. A director of the play would have to come to a similar decision. This does not mean that every reading or staging is as good as every other; any interpretation that can explain itself by reference to the text of the play, the actual words on the page, will obviously be more convincing than one that cannot.

Activity 2

Pretend that you are directing a production of *The Duchess of Malfi*. How would you instruct the actor playing Bosola to play Act 3, Scene 2? How would you justify your reading of his character? Remember that you need to anchor your interpretation in the text of the play.

Discussion

This is how I would direct the actor playing Bosola (and remember, this is only one possible response). I would stress the importance of trying to convey to the audience the essential ambiguity of Bosola's character. From the start, Webster has told us that his malcontent character despises courtly corruption at the same time that he is hopelessly implicated in it. He wants social advancement but loathes the servility that is the only way to rise in the world of the court. There is little reason to believe that Bosola admires Antonio as much as he says he does in his speeches to the Duchess; the play has made it clear there is little love lost between these two characters. But he has watched as a courtly official, low-born like himself, has been dismissed from his office, apparently on the whim of the Duchess, and castigated by other officers who yesterday fawned on him. It would be strange if Bosola did not feel a certain amount of indignation at these events.

I would further justify this way of playing the role of Bosola by reference to his speeches in this part of the play, which are full of the self-loathing that characterises him throughout, especially in relation to his role as Ferdinand's 'intelligencer'. When Bosola wants to describe the kind of degrading toadying for favour in which court officers engage, he imagines their being willing even to make their eldest sons court spies (3.2.230). In his soliloquy, he characterises the politician, or political schemer, as 'the devil's quilted anvil' (3.2.319) – a metaphor which figures the devil as a demonic blacksmith silently bringing sin into the world courtesy of the 'politician's' cunning and dissimulation. The ingenuity of the metaphor is typical of Bosola's linguistic flamboyance, and it bespeaks a certain amount of self-congratulation. But Bosola is no Iago, revelling in his own destructive powers. To describe oneself as the devil's servant is less than entirely flattering and the self-criticism surfaces, albeit briefly, in the exclamation 'Oh, this base quality / Of intelligencer!' (3.2.323–4) – a pang of conscience which he brushes aside by telling himself that a spy, like any other professional person, naturally desires to be rewarded and praised for a job well done. The concluding couplet drives the point home: Bosola wants preferment and he will, for the time being at least, remain the servant of forces he knows are wicked. But Webster stresses the inner division that makes his court satirist so ambiguous and complex a figure.

So how would an actor convey this kind of ambivalence to the audience? It would be a good deal easier on film, where the close-up would provide ample opportunities for a good actor to show through facial expressions the kind of rapid fluctuation in mood, from self-disgust to self-congratulation and back again, that is signalled by the language of the soliloquy. On a stage, an actor would be more reliant on tone and pace of delivery, using his voice to convey these mood changes, with gestures and body movements contributing to the overall effect, helping to communicate to the audience the combination of self-criticism and self-satisfaction which the language of the speech suggests.

Act 3, Scene 4: the dumb show

In Act 3, Scene 4, Ferdinand and the Cardinal learn from Bosola the identity of their sister's husband and that her family is seeking sanctuary in the state of Ancona. The Cardinal, about to resume his profession as a soldier, determines to have the family banished. Webster chose to enact these two events – the Cardinal's return to soldiership and the banishment of the Duchess and her family from Ancona – in the form of a **dumb show**, a performance employing gestures and body movements without words. Why? By removing speech and focusing instead on mimed action, the dumb show achieves a highly symbolic, pictorial style of theatrical representation. Because meaning is conveyed through spectacle rather than words, we are distanced from the action; rather than encouraging us to get caught up in the emotions of the characters, the visual tableau asks us instead to step back and evaluate the moral implications of what is happening onstage. It is important that the action takes place at a religious shrine, and that the stage direction calls for '*solemn music*' sung '*by divers Churchmen*' (though when the play was published Webster disowned the lyrics of the 'ditty' they sing). We watch as the Cardinal sheds the symbols of his religious vocation – '*cross, hat, robes and ring*' – and takes on the trappings of a soldier – '*sword, helmet, shield and spurs*'. This gives vivid visual confirmation of the superficiality of his religious vocation and the ecclesiastical corruption he has consistently represented. The mimed action of the Duchess's banishment gives a central place to another symbol: her wedding ring, which her brother removes from her finger with violence (3.4.35–6). As the family is ejected from a place of sanctuary, the visual tableau stresses its extreme vulnerability, as well as the brothers' successful assault on the Duchess's marriage.

The dumb show is framed by the dialogue of two pilgrims, who begin by anticipating a 'noble ceremony' (3.4.6) and end in a state of some distress, exchanging anxious questions and judgements about the ceremonies they have just witnessed. While they do not entirely exonerate the Duchess – 'who would have thought / So great a lady would have matched herself / Unto so mean a person?' (3.4.23–5) – their strongest disapproval is reserved for the brothers and the powers-that-be who have acted unjustly in banishing a 'free prince' solely on 'her brother's instigation' (3.4.28, 34). As the critic Kate Aughterson points out, the fact that the pilgrims lack individual identity, remain unnamed and never appear again establishes 'a physical bond with the audience, which encourages us to believe in their objectivity: they observe and depart, as we do. Their anonymity and function are choral: like the choruses of Greek tragedy, they objectify and comment on the action, distancing and interpreting' (2001, p. 171). The pilgrims' commentary invites us to grasp the moral and political significance of the Duchess's banishment rather than her own experience of it; it presents her and her family as the victims of an institutional conspiracy.

Many of the dramatic devices Webster employs in *The Duchess of Malfi* are ones we would tend to describe as 'realistic': his insistence on the complexity of his characters' personalities, his attempts to involve us in the dramatic action unfolding onstage, not least through the creation of suspense. Yet he also uses other dramatic techniques, often inherited from medieval drama, that are less concerned to provide a plausible depiction of human motivation or to draw the audience into the action; instead these older techniques, like the dumb show in Act 3, Scene 4, seek to distance us from the action unfolding onstage in order to promote our understanding of the larger meanings being conveyed. This mixture of medieval and more modern theatrical devices is not at all unusual in early modern drama. Marlowe does something similar in his play *Doctor Faustus* (1604), which has characters like a Good and Bad Angel borrowed from medieval **morality plays** and at the same time uses soliloquy to endow its protagonist with what the audience experiences as a complex inner life. In *The Duchess of Malfi*, the combination of realist and non-realist theatrical devices suggests that Webster wanted his audience to think as well as feel, to identify strongly with the heroine and her family but also to step back and analyse the moral and political implications of their persecution. He was clearly writing with the theatre and performance very much in mind, using the resources of the stage to elicit a quite complex response from a live audience.

Act 4: torture and death

Act 4, comprised of two scenes, enacts the Duchess's torture and death – the punishment meted out to her for her forbidden love and marriage. The scenes are arguably among the most memorable in early modern tragedy, yet they contain theatrical devices that can seem alien to a modern-day reader or spectator. Imprisoned in her palace, the Duchess is exposed to a dead man's hand, complete with wedding ring, a wax tableau of her husband and children presented to her as their dead bodies, and finally a dance of madmen. Why did Webster choose to stage the Duchess's suffering and death in this way, using these (to us) rather puzzling dramatic devices?

There are many possible answers to that question, and literary critics are not in agreement about the meaning or the effectiveness of Webster's stagecraft in these scenes. But it might help at this point to consider the play text in relation to its contemporary contexts, specifically in relation to early modern revenge tragedy in general. In the first major revenge tragedy of the period, Thomas Kyd's *The Spanish Tragedy*, the climactic revenge takes the form of an onstage play presented by the hero Hieronimo and starring his enemies, all of whom are murdered as they perform his play-within-a-play. Afterwards, Hieronimo explains to the shocked onstage audience the meaning of his violent actions. Something rather similar takes place in Act 4 of *The Duchess*. Just as Kyd has his revenger–hero present a play that is really the culmination of his quest for vengeance, so Webster has his revenger–villain stage a play for his victim complete with props – the dead man's hand, the wax effigies of Antonio and the children – and an onstage entertainment by madmen which the critic Inga-Stina Ekeblad identifies as a kind of masque, an elaborate courtly extravaganza, with music and dance and allegorical tableaux, much favoured by the court of James I (1958, pp. 256–67). Just as Kyd's Hieronimo interprets his play for the onstage audience, so Bosola, after the revelation of the wax figures, explains to the Duchess the meaning of what she has just witnessed:

> He [Ferdinand] doth present you this sad spectacle,
> That now you know directly they are dead.
> Hereafter you may, wisely, cease to grieve
> For that which cannot be recovered.

> (4.1.56–9)

In early modern revenge tragedies, then, revenge often takes the form of a theatrical spectacle, a play-within-a-play. The critic Katharine Eisaman Maus speculates that the intimate relation between revenge and theatre in Renaissance revenge tragedies stems in part from the highly theatrical nature of judicial punishment in the period:

> Legally prescribed punishments were themselves popular spectacles throughout Renaissance Europe. Beheadings, hangings, whippings, and pilloryings occurred on raised platforms before large crowds. Many such penalties had symbolic dimensions. Adulterers were paraded in bedsheets; traitors disembowelled to signify the exposure of their secret malice. The revenger's methods, in other

words, do not deviate as markedly as a modern audience might assume from the normal routines of Renaissance justice.

(Maus, 1995, pp. xvi–xvii)

Ferdinand, though, is putting on a play for his sister that he pretends is reality not theatre. Readers know this, as the stage direction informs them that the figures of Antonio and the children are not corpses but effigies. But a theatre audience, at least those who don't know the play, spends most of Act 4, Scene 1 sharing the Duchess's belief that Antonio and the children have been murdered. They thereby participate in the heroine's anguish and grief as she laments the loss of her family and longs for death: 'There is not between heaven and earth one wish / I stay for after this' (4.1.60–1). Then, towards the end of the scene, spectators become privy to information denied the Duchess: that the figures are made of wax, literal theatrical props, in a play written and directed by Ferdinand with the intention of driving his sister to despair. Why does Webster stage Act 4, Scene 1 in this way? This is a good example of the way in which he seeks to involve us in the action and then to distance us from it, as the pathos of the scene is succeeded by a renewed awareness of Ferdinand's duplicity. You will recall that Ferdinand and the Cardinal have from the start been identified as accomplished actors who use their gift for dissembling to manipulate and dominate other people. In Act 4, Scene 1, we are reminded of this as Ferdinand is revealed as a kind of playwright who wants his sister to follow the script he has written for her. Once again, Webster shows us that his aristocratic villain uses theatre as an instrument of control.

The play devotes an entire act to the torture and murder of its protagonist and, as a result, the Duchess's death takes on an enormous significance. On one level, death is a straightforward evil in the world of the play, part of the sickness and poison which the Cardinal and Ferdinand have been made to represent, from Antonio's line on the destructive impact of corrupt courts ('Death and diseases through the whole land spread' (1.1.15)), through Ferdinand's deranged revenge fantasies, to the counterfeit dead bodies produced in Act 4, Scene 1. Yet Ferdinand's aim is not merely to murder his sister but to 'bring her to despair' (4.1.113), to break her spirit.

Ultimately, his plan fails miserably, but it focuses our attention on the inner resources that enable the Duchess to endure her torments and meet her death with so much courage and dignity. To some extent, her fortitude stems from her religious faith. She first expresses Christian attitudes to death and suffering at the end of Act 3. Facing imminent separation from Antonio and their eldest son, she says to him: 'In the eternal Church, sir, / I do hope we shall not part thus' (3.5.68–9). Antonio counsels patient forbearance, and the Duchess replies:

> Must I like to a slave-born Russian
> Account it praise to suffer tyranny?
> And yet, oh heaven, thy heavy hand is in't.
> I have seen my little boy oft scourge his top
> And compared myself to't: nought made me e'er
> Go right but heaven's scourge-stick.

(3.5.73–8)

There is a tension in the lines between her class pride, which bristles at subjection to 'tyranny', and a Christian belief in divine providence which sees God's hand at work in all human suffering. The Duchess makes her own simile here, comparing her relationship to God to that between her little boy and his top – a startling image which reminds us of her maternal role and is not wholly flattering to the 'heavy handed' deity she imagines to be scourging her. When she courted and married Antonio, she thought their mutual consent more important than the validation of the Church. Here, in Act 3, Scene 5, she expresses her faith not with the schooled responses of the regular and obedient church-goer but in a deeply personal, almost idiosyncratic, fashion.

The Duchess hopes but is not sure that she will be reunited with Antonio after death, and later, in Act 4, Scene 2, she asks Cariola: 'Dost thou think we shall know one another / In th'other world?' (4.2.18–19). Cariola replies 'Yes, out of question' (4.2.19), but the Duchess sounds more sceptical: 'Oh that it were possible we might / But hold some two days' conference with the dead' (4.2.20–1). When Bosola enters disguised as an old man, she is far from fully receptive to the Christian contempt for the body which he voices:

> Thou art a box of worm-seed, at best but a salvatory of green
> mummy. What's this flesh? A little cruded milk, fantastical puff
> paste: our bodies are weaker than those paper prisons boys use to
> keep flies in – more contemptible, since ours is to preserve
> earthworms.

(4.2.122–7)

This kind of language, designed to instil disgust with what is mortal and corruptible and to focus the eyes of the dying on the eternal life to come, elicits from the Duchess what is probably the most famous line of the play – 'I am Duchess of Malfi still' (4.2.141) – which is an affirmation of identity clearly resistant to Bosola's assault on human pride. Yet, when her executioners enter the stage carrying a coffin, cords and a bell, and Bosola asks her 'Doth not death fright you?' (4.2.210), she musters a confidence about the afterlife that earlier eluded her: 'Who would be afraid on't, / Knowing to meet such excellent company / In th'other world?' (4.2.210–12). Her final speech, as the executioners prepare to strangle her, offers another strikingly personal 'take' on Christian doctrine: in place of the traditional concept of the soul's flight up to heaven, she imagines her murderers pulling heaven down upon her; and when finally she kneels, it is in a very last-minute acknowledgement that 'heaven gates are not so highly arched / As princes' palaces' (4.2.231–2). But the play makes it clear that religion is not the only source of the Duchess's strength of character. Her outburst of annoyance at the 'whispering' jailers (4.2.222) from whom she clearly longs to escape tells us that to a considerable extent the Duchess simply welcomes death as a release from intolerable suffering.

The Duchess's courage, then, is not defined solely or even chiefly in terms of her piety. Indeed, Cariola, who is presented much more clearly as a devout Christian, is shown to confront death with a very human fearfulness that is obviously intended to enhance our admiration for the Duchess. Webster goes to great lengths to convey the full horror of his heroine's death: the executioners are present onstage for a full seventy lines before the murder takes place. We are also made to listen to a discussion of the chosen method of execution – strangling – and then to watch it as it takes place onstage. This can be devastating for an audience, but it serves to communicate the core meaning of death in this play: that how you meet this terrifying end is the ultimate test of your character. This is hardly a novel idea; it is fundamental to several philosophical systems and lies at the heart of the aristocratic concept of honour, which makes the capacity to face the terror of death without flinching the measure of individual heroism. What *is* novel is that Webster applies what had traditionally been masculine, often martial, conceptions of heroism to his heroine, creating in the process a character who has been called 'the first fully tragic woman in Renaissance drama' (Whigham, 1985, p. 174).

Activity 3

Webster devotes a substantial part of this scene to the reactions of Bosola and Ferdinand to the Duchess's death. Why do you think he does this? Have another look at the final section of Act 4, Scene 2 (line 237 onwards) and then try to identify at least three dramatic functions of this episode.

Discussion

This is what I came up with:

1   This section of the scene is important in that it indicates the enormous impact the Duchess's death will have on the rest of the play.

2   It marks the first stage of Bosola's repentance.

3   It also marks the first clear signs of Ferdinand's impending madness.

All three of these functions look forward to Act 5. Webster, then, is preparing the ground for the last act at the close of Act 4.

Figure 4.2   Elisabeth Bergner as the Duchess in *The Duchess of Malfi*, dir. George Rylands (Ethel Barrymore Theatre, Broadway, 1946). Photo: Eileen Darby/Time Life Pictures/Getty Images.

Bosola's repentance at the end of this scene is obviously a crucial element in the action to come. Yet what strikes me most about its portrayal at this point in the play is that it is far from straightforward; it has all the ambiguity that characterises Bosola throughout. He seems genuinely moved by the Duchess's death, and at the very end of the scene, when she stirs briefly back to life (rather like Desdemona in *Othello*), he comforts her with a truth – that Antonio is alive – and a lie – that he has been reconciled to her brothers. He also fulfils her last wish that her body should be bestowed upon her women. Yet his assertion that he would not change his 'peace of conscience / For all the wealth of Europe' (4.2.339–40) comes only after Ferdinand resolutely refuses to reward him for murdering his sister. As ever with Bosola, moral impulses are hopelessly entangled with his dependence on the ruling elite that habitually employs him to do its dirty work only then to deny him the promised payment.

Ferdinand's refusal to recompense Bosola stems from a comparably powerful sense of the horror of the deed, coupled with a denial of any responsibility for it. The ruler who blames the servant for committing the murder he suborned presents a grotesque distortion of the courtly ideal elaborated at the start of the play. Ferdinand's extreme reaction to the Duchess's death also testifies to his mounting mental instability. His obsession with his sister's sexuality emerges once again in Act 4 when Bosola asks him to give the Duchess 'a penitential garment to put on / Next to her delicate skin' (4.1.115–16), and the mere mention of his sister's flesh is enough to send Ferdinand reeling:

> Damn her, that body of hers,
> While that my blood ran pure in't, was more worth
> Than that which thou wouldst comfort, called a soul.

> (4.1.117–19)

The lines suggest how deeply entangled are Ferdinand's fixations on aristocratic purity of blood and his sister's body, perhaps implying that his incestuous desire stems from a class pride so extreme that only his own sister appears an appropriate sexual partner. Intriguingly, he tells us in Act 4, Scene 2 that the two of them were twins, which reinforces the closeness of the family tie. At any rate, by this stage of the play, we are unlikely to feel convinced by Ferdinand's claim that he opposed the Duchess's remarriage because he was hoping to gain an 'infinite mass of treasure by her death' (4.2.284) had she remained a widow. He reveals to Bosola that he and the Duchess were twins immediately after seeing his sister's dead body for the first time. His one-line response to the sight – 'Cover her face. Mine eyes dazzle. She died young.' (4.2.263) – has often been admired for the glimpse it seems to give us of a state of acute psychological distress. The punctuation varies from edition to edition; the original quarto prefers semi-colons to full stops. Yet regardless of the punctuation used, what is unusual and striking about the line is that it seems so full, with its three sentences or clauses of three words each packed into eleven syllables. It is in fact hard for actors to deliver in the theatre without placing significant pauses between each clause or sentence. But this crowded, highly condensed line seems to point to a world of pain and loss as Ferdinand sees his dead sister and grasps the enormity of what he has done. By the close of the scene, he is falling apart, deteriorating into the lunacy that will characterise him in Act 5: 'I'll go hunt the badger by owl-light: / 'Tis a deed of darkness' (4.2.333–4).

Act 5: the play without the Duchess

Act 5 has, more than any other aspect of the play, raised the hackles of critics. Webster has often been rebuked, especially by feminist critics, for killing off his heroine at the end of Act 4 rather than at the end of the play, as is normally the fate of tragic heroes. Many critics have been frankly baffled by the tone of Act 5, which seems to be aiming not for the high seriousness one expects of a tragedy but for a kind of black comedy. What do you think Webster was trying to achieve in Act 5? Why write a tragedy with a tragic heroine who is absent from the entire last act? We can begin trying to answer those questions by looking at one of the most famous scenes in the play – Act 5, Scene 3 – known as the echo scene.

Act 5, Scene 3: the echo scene

Activity 4

Reread this scene now. What in your view is the point of this scene? What meanings does it convey to a reader/spectator?

Discussion

I would say that one of the main points of this scene is to convey to readers and spectators the Duchess's continued presence in the world of the play. The previous scene draws to a close with Bosola's words 'Still methinks the Duchess / Haunts me!' (5.2.344–5), and the echo scene is in a very real sense another haunting. The audience, aware that the Duchess is dead, quickly grasps the supernatural significance of the voice which sounds to Antonio so much like the voice of his wife and which tries to warn him of impending danger: '*O fly your fate*' (5.3.35). It's not surprising that in many productions of the play, the Duchess appears onstage during the scene.

This is another scene worth considering in relation to the conventions of revenge tragedy. If you are familiar with *Hamlet* you will know that ghosts often haunt revenge tragedies, bringing messages to the living from beyond the grave. Webster, though, makes his ghost an echo in a ruined abbey. For Antonio, unaware of what has happened to his wife, the echo is just an echo, and much of the scene's sadness derives from the fact that the Duchess's warning does not get through, that she is unable to protect her husband. Yet the scene is perhaps ultimately not as bleak as this suggests. It is set in a ruined abbey which, on one level, presents change, decay and death as the condition of the world; Antonio comments that the men buried there must have imagined the abbey would shelter them for all time, when in fact 'all things have their end' (5.3.17). Yet, in Antonio's view, something potent remains of the 'ancient ruins' (5.3.9): its 'reverend history' (5.3.11). In much the same way, the Duchess, though also ruined, survives in the form of 'a clear light' that reveals momentarily to Antonio 'a face folded in sorrow' (5.3.43, 44) (Belsey, 1980, p. 115). The scene ends with three lines that, unbeknown to Antonio, could serve as the Duchess's epitaph and sum up her heroism:

> Though in our miseries Fortune hath a part,
> Yet in our noble suff'rings she hath none.
> Contempt of pain – that we may call our own.

> (5.3.54–6)

The Aragonian brethren

Ferdinand's lycanthropy, his belief that he has been transformed into a wolf whose skin is hairy on the inside rather than the outside, clearly manifests a mental collapse attendant on the murder of the Duchess – he is driven mad by guilt and a self-revulsion that convicts him of being no better than the most vicious of animals. His lycanthropy is at once a judgement on his appalling cruelty, and a reminder of the flickering moral awareness that has always been part of his character. He is convinced not only that he has turned into a wolf but that he is damned (5.2.40–3).

Figure 4.3   A fifteenth-century werewolf from 'Monsters born from the Deluge', after the wood engravings in the *Chronique de Nuremberg* (1493), illustration from Lacroix, P. (1878) *Science and Literature in the Middle Ages and at the Period of the Renaissance*, London. Photo: The Bridgeman Art Library.

The Cardinal too is shown to be consumed with guilt. Not that he has stopped plotting and murdering: he despatches Bosola to assassinate Antonio, and he murders Julia, the mistress of whom he has grown weary, by having her kiss a poisoned Bible. In this episode, Webster is working well within the conventions of revenge tragedy, a genre which revels in inventing and staging ever more ingenious ways of killing people, particularly with poison: poisoned skulls, poisoned shirts and poisoned showers of gold, along with the Cardinal's poisoned Bible, are all instruments of murder in Renaissance revenge tragedies. Yet despite the Cardinal's continued crimes, the play makes it clear that he has a bad conscience. In Act 5, Webster gives him two brief soliloquies; the first, in Scene 4, shows him wanting to pray but lacking any real confidence in its efficacy (5.4.26–8). This is not an indication of his lack of faith, as his second soliloquy, which opens Scene 5, demonstrates. The Cardinal enters carrying a book, the argument of which is that some people destined for the fires of hell will suffer more than others: like Ferdinand, then, the Cardinal fully expects to go to hell. Although he is not in the grip of a full-blown mental illness, his soliloquy makes clear the extent of his mental disturbance: when he looks in the fishponds in his garden, he hallucinates: 'Methinks I see a thing armed with a rake / That seems to strike at me' (5.5.6–7). The Cardinal is haunted by visions of the retribution awaiting him for his crimes.

A savage farce?

We have seen that Bosola too is haunted by his part in the Duchess's death, though in his case this leads to a desire to repent, to ally himself unambiguously with the forces of good by protecting Antonio from the Cardinal's homicidal intentions. But he ends up inadvertently doing the Cardinal's bidding: he kills Antonio by mistake. This looks like a comment on Bosola's quest for redemption, an enactment of the sad fact that he is just too tainted by his past actions to renounce his role as hired assassin. However, we also need to consider this accidental killing within the context of the fifth act as a whole. After the seriousness of Act 4 and the Duchess's torture and death, we find ourselves suddenly in a very different dramatic world, which we might be inclined to call a 'savage farce', adapting the poet T.S. Eliot's description of Christopher Marlowe's bitterly satiric play *The Jew of Malta* (*c*.1589–90) (Eliot, 1932, p. 105). There is certainly grim humour in the staging of Ferdinand's lunacy, particularly in his attempt to throttle his own shadow in Scene 2, and his altercations with the Doctor who fails miserably to control him. The wild comedy escalates in Scene 5, as Bosola, bent on vengeance, closes in on the Cardinal, whose screams for help are ignored by the courtiers who believe they come from the mad Ferdinand. Ferdinand then enters, mad as a hatter, thinking he is on a noisy battlefield and his brother is an enemy soldier. He ends up stabbing his brother and Bosola in an undignified scuffle, having no idea where he is or what he is doing. Bosola then stabs and kills Ferdinand.

What are we to make of all this? By the end of the play, the stage is littered with corpses. This is nothing unusual in a Renaissance tragedy, but the dark comedy that runs through the entire last act seems designed to deprive these deaths of the dignity accorded the Duchess in her final moments. The stage action evokes chaos and disorder, a group of men running headlong to their destruction. To Bosola, this bespeaks grim truths about the nature of earthly existence. As he observes bitterly after accidentally giving Antonio his death wound: 'We are merely the stars' tennis balls, struck and banded / Which way please them' (5.4.54–5). In other words, human beings have no free will and no real significance; we are simply the playthings of probably malevolent cosmic forces. Ferdinand says something similar in his dying moments:

> My sister! Oh my sister, there's the cause on't!
> 'Whether we fall by ambition, blood, or lust,
> Like diamonds we are cut with our own dust.'

(5.5.71–3)

The inverted commas around the couplet signal that Ferdinand's dying words had a proverbial status: he is applying to himself an entirely appropriate saying about human beings' capacity for self-destruction; we are prisoners of our own temperaments, driven by forces, passions and instincts over which we have minimum control. Ferdinand's focus is the human personality, Bosola's the cosmos, but the two characters agree that human beings exert precious little control over what they do. Even Antonio dies convinced of the vanity of his own ambitions:

> in all our quest of greatness,
> Like wanton boys whose pastime is their care,
> We follow after bubbles blown in the air.

(5.4.64–6)

The search for self-advancement is ultimately futile in Antonio's eyes. His dying wish is that his eldest son should 'fly the courts of princes' and thereby avoid the trap into which his father fell (5.4.72). The Cardinal dies thinking not of the hellfire that preoccupied him earlier but of his own insignificance: 'And now, I pray, let me / Be laid by, and never thought of' (5.5.89–90).

In the absence of the Duchess, the principal male characters stumble and stagger towards death persuaded of the vanity and meaninglessness of their lives. This would seem to be Webster's point, as the critic Leah Marcus explains:

> The Duchess is not flawless, but she carries with her a capacity for light, joy and love that enlivens an otherwise festering world. By showing how the play is emptied of light and reduced to madness and chaos once she is gone, Webster makes large claims for the power of virtue in general.

(Marcus, 2009, p. 55)

Thus, the grim humour of Act 5 can be seen as an integral part of Webster's overall design; the sign of a dramatic world deprived of the positive values the Duchess came to represent.

It is clear, moreover, that of the many deaths that have occurred by the end of the play, the Duchess's alone appears both heroic in its self-possession and tragic in the sense of loss it engenders. Her brothers die expressing a degree of clarity and self-knowledge conspicuously lacking in their lives, and their deaths are memorable, thanks to the striking lines given them by their creator. But Webster imparts to those deaths a very different meaning from that accorded the Duchess's, summed up in the Cardinal's dying words and by Delio in the closing speech of the play:

> These wretched eminent things
> Leave no more fame behind 'em than should one
> Fall in a frost and leave his print in snow:
> As soon as the sun shines, it ever melts,
> Both form and matter.

(5.5.113–17)

Delio's analogy between the 'wretched eminent things' lying dead on the stage and a footprint in snow condemns Ferdinand and the Cardinal to obscurity and oblivion. Death for them means erasure from the historical record – a dreadful fate for members of the ruling elite who traditionally expected their status and power to leave its mark on the world and to guarantee them an afterlife in the memory of the community.

We often expect, or at least want, the endings of plays to offer us some kind of consolation – an expectation that may well be intensified by the Duchess's death at the end of Act 4 and the enormous sense of loss it creates. While Ferdinand and the Cardinal may fear damnation, the play is not interested in speculating on the divine judgements that might await them in the next world. Instead, it keeps its eyes firmly on this world, presenting us with the spectacle of its two principal villains falling apart, cracking under the strain of their own guilt and remorse. The contrast with the sister they tormented and murdered is obvious. The second consolation the play proffers is equally secular – the promise that great men who use their power to wicked ends will be forgotten after death. Again, there is a marked contrast with the Duchess, who lives on so vividly in the memories of the characters who survive her. Delio's closing couplet – 'Integrity of life is fame's best friend, / Which nobly, beyond death, shall crown the end' (5.5.120–1) – envisages only one form of eternal life: the lasting fame and noble reputation that greet 'integrity of life'. This reward the play clearly bestows on its heroine and conspicuously denies its villains.

We may also derive some comfort from the fact that Delio appears onstage in the closing moments of the play with the eldest son of Antonio and the Duchess and proposes that the survivors 'join all our force / To establish this young hopeful gentleman / In's mother's right' (5.5.111–13).

Activity 5

How should we respond to the prospect of the eldest child of the Duchess's forbidden marriage inheriting his mother's dukedom? A good way to start answering this question is to go back through the play and remind yourself of all the information provided to us about this child. Does this encourage us to feel optimistic or pessimistic about the future? Is there another claimant to the title?

Discussion

The first thing we learn about the child is that his horoscope predicts a '*short life*' and '*a violent death*' (2.3.63, 65) – hardly a hopeful sign. Later, in Act 3, Scene 3 (lines 69–71), we are told that the Duchess had a son with her first husband, whose claim on the dukedom her brothers are supporting: Ferdinand refers to him in this scene as the Duke of Malfi. And of course we can hardly help but remember Antonio's dying words: 'And let my son fly the courts of princes' (5.4.72).

None of this seems designed to instil much confidence in the child's chances of securing and holding on to the dukedom of Malfi; the likelihood of his succeeding in the cut-throat world of Italian politics seems slim. But we should consider as well what the play's final moments look like in the theatre; the visual signs they give an audience. There are six dead bodies on the stage, and six living characters: Delio, the boy and four courtiers. As Antonio's loyal friend, Delio invites our trust (though in this instance he is unwittingly violating his friend's final request). Yet the courtiers, apart from Pescara, have been Ferdinand's lackeys, which does not necessarily augur well for the birth of a new social order. The child is young and vulnerable. In productions, he is often dressed in white, which may signal innocence and purity but also weakness (Aughterson, 2001, pp. 43–4).

Ultimately, it is up to directors to decide whether to stage the play's final moments in a hopeful or pessimistic fashion.

What kind of tragedy is *The Duchess of Malfi*?

The critics I mentioned in Chapter 3 who have argued for the Duchess's culpability, her own responsibility for the disastrous consequences of a marriage entered into out of lust and a lamentable feminine wilfulness, were partly indulging their own negative views of women and partly working on the assumption that all Renaissance tragic protagonists have a 'tragic flaw', a serious character failing that propels them towards disaster. This notion of the tragic flaw comes from a misreading of Aristotle, the fourth century BCE Greek philosopher who, in his *Poetics*, came to general conclusions about the characteristics of tragedy on the basis of the tragic drama he had watched in Athens. In describing the tragic hero, Aristotle used the word '*hamartia*', which is better translated as 'error of judgement' or 'mistake' than 'character flaw' (Hutton, 1982, p. 57). But this has not stopped twentieth-century literary critics from expending a good deal of energy identifying and dissecting the fatal flaws of Renaissance tragic heroes, including Webster's Duchess.

Having spent the last two chapters reading and studying *The Duchess of Malfi*, we should perhaps conclude by asking ourselves whether Webster's conception of tragedy in the play has much if anything to do with Aristotle or with what we conceive Aristotle to have said about tragic plays. Certainly, as Leah Marcus observes, the Duchess is not portrayed as blameless; we have seen that there are murmurs of criticism levelled at her by credible characters like Cariola and the pilgrims, and the play unquestionably leaves room for us to recognise her rashness in defying her brothers. But it would, I think, be hard to argue persuasively that it blames her for the tragic course of events. On the contrary, as Act 5 makes abundantly clear, she is the sole source of light and love in a gloomy, claustrophobic dramatic world. The tragedy of *The Duchess of Malfi* is that she is destroyed, her bid for self-determination crushed by a brutal and corrupt aristocratic order. Webster, then, seems to be much less interested in fatal flaws than in flawed social and political systems and the havoc they wreak in decent people's lives. His tragic world shows us the individual trapped by destructive social and political ideas and practices, yet powerful in so far as she can affirm her integrity and human dignity even in defeat.

Conclusion

The Duchess of Malfi has been performed more often in the twentieth and twenty-first centuries than any other non-Shakespearean play of the early modern period (Marcus, 2009, p. 1). Between 1934 and 1989, there were no fewer than forty commercial productions. It has been revived with particular frequency since 1945 and the end of the Second World War. Marcus argues that this peak in popularity attests to 'the frequent correlation between a public taste for Webster and broader social trauma', that the 'cumulative cultural rupture of two world wars and the Holocaust resonated with Webster's dramatic emphasis on horror, disjunction and extreme suffering' (2009, pp. 104, 101). I would argue that the play's continued appeal for twentieth- and twenty-first-century audiences also has much to do with the way in which Webster finds tragic meaning in the struggle against an oppressive patriarchal elite. Unlike Shakespeare, who concentrates so much of his imaginative energies on dramatising the experiences and suffering of 'great men', Webster is interested in what it feels like to be a woman, even one of noble birth, in a world dominated by ruling-class men, and to be a man of lower rank entirely dependent on one's social superiors for advancement. His highly politicised understanding of tragedy produced, as we have seen, the first fully tragic heroine in English drama, a role which has attracted some of the finest British actresses of recent years, including Judi Dench, Helen Mirren, Harriet Walter and Janet McTeer. It might be fitting to close this chapter with the words of the Irish poet Derek Mahon, who in 1998 wrote a poem, called 'Dirge', about the infectious power of Webster's play and his heroine:

> Even so we revel in the infection, flirt
> with the corruption of a provincial court,
> seduced by scheming web and flowery skull
> and dazzled by 'I am Duchess of Malfi still'.

(Mahon, 2000, p. 196)

His wish as a poet, Mahon says, is 'to do homage in our own violent time / to one who lights time past and time to come' (2000, p. 197).

References

Aughterson, K. (2001) *Webster: The Tragedies*, Basingstoke, Palgrave.

Belsey, C. (1980) 'Emblem and antithesis in *The Duchess of Malfi*', *Renaissance Drama*, vol. 11, pp. 115–34.

Ekeblad, I.S. (1958) 'The impure art of John Webster', *Review of English Studies*, vol. 9, pp. 253–67.

Eliot, T.S. (1932) *Selected Essays 1917–1932*, New York, Harcourt, Brace and Company.

Hutton, J. (trans.) (1982) *Aristotle's Poetics*, New York, Norton.

Mahon, D. (2000) *Selected Poems*, London, Penguin.

Marcus, L.S. (ed.) (2009) *The Duchess of Malfi*, Arden Early Modern Drama, London, Methuen.

Maus, K.E. (ed.) (1995) *Four Revenge Tragedies*, Oxford World's Classics, Oxford, Oxford University Press.

Truffaut, F. (1967) *Hitchcock*, New York, Simon and Schuster.

Webster, J. (2009 [1623]) *The Duchess of Malfi* (ed. M. Kendall), Harlow, Pearson Longman.

Whigham, F. (1985) 'Sexual and social mobility in *The Duchess of Malfi*', *Publications of the Modern Language Association*, vol. 100, no. 2, pp. 167–86.

Further reading

Henderson, K.U. and MacManus, B. (1985) *Half Humankind: Contexts and Texts of the Controversy about Women in England 1540–1640*, Urbana, IL, University of Illinois Press.

Keeble, N.H. (ed.) (1994) *The Cultural Identity of Seventeenth-Century Woman*, London, Routledge.

Luckyj, C. (ed.) (2011) The Duchess of Malfi: *A Critical Guide*, London, Continuum.

Neill, M. (1997) *Issues of Death: Mortality and Identity in English Renaissance Tragedy*, Oxford, Clarendon Press.

Rabkin, N. (ed.) (1968) *Twentieth Century Interpretations of* The Duchess of Malfi, Englewood Cliffs, NJ, Prentice Hall.

Shellist, E.A. (2004) 'John Webster' in Kinney, A.F. (ed.) *A Companion to Renaissance Drama*, Oxford, Blackwell, also available online at http//www.blackwellreference.com/subscriber/tocnode?id=g9781405121798_chunk_g978140512179839 (Accessed 21 September 2009).

Conclusion to Part 1

Anita Pacheco

This part of the book has illustrated how central the themes of love and death are to the writing of the English Renaissance. *Othello* is, to a very real extent, a play concerned with exploring the meaning of the word 'love', as its characters repeatedly analyse and debate its nature. If Iago's cynical reduction of love to lust does not invite our endorsement, is Othello's expansive idealism any better? Did Desdemona fall in love with Othello, or with the glamorous and inflated image some critics think he habitually projects of himself? Is Emilia right when she counters her mistress's vision of absolute marital fidelity with a more worldly, realistic view of a wife's marital obligations? As is often the case with Shakespeare, the play seems more interested in asking such questions than in providing hard and fast answers to them, inviting us to evaluate the strengths and weaknesses of its characters' contrasting attitudes to the subjects of love and marriage. *The Duchess of Malfi* stages its characters' competing notions of the nature of marriage; what for the Duchess is a union that should be freely chosen on the basis of mutual liking is in her brothers' eyes a patriarchal institution designed to serve the interests of the male heads of a family. There is little doubt as to which view the play encourages us to support in its opening scene, pitting its heroine's desire to marry a commoner against her corrupt brothers' desire to control her marital destiny. Both plays present marriages for love which flout established authority and turn conventional models of acceptable marriage partners on their heads. Both plays also invest these love matches with tragic meaning, disclosing how unstable and insecure they are, how vulnerable to erosion from within and to attack by hostile external forces.

As tragedies, the two plays attach great significance to the deaths they dramatise in their later acts. In *Othello*, the murder of Desdemona marks the hero's nadir, showing us how far he has fallen. His own subsequent suicide is open to different interpretations, but there is little doubt that it constitutes an economical staging of his own ambivalent role as the Moor of Venice, simultaneously the state's loyal servant and the dangerous outsider who threatens it. The death of the play's tragic protagonist thus has enormous explanatory power as well as poignancy, exposing the deep insecurities and unstable sense of identity that have helped to make him vulnerable to Iago's machinations. The death of

Othello reminds us that the play is in a real sense the tragedy of a black African in a white Christian society to which he can never entirely belong.

For Webster, death is the ultimate test of character, that which separates the wheat from the chaff, the good from the merely powerful. His decision to locate tragic heroism in a female character who marries beneath her and is savagely punished for it produces a searing indictment of the corrupt royal court and patriarchal power structures of Jacobean England. Although we have focused on the texts of the plays, both on the page and in performance, we have also seen how *Othello* and *The Duchess* can profitably be read in relation to their own historical period – a period characterised by expanding trade and exposure to non-European peoples, by increasing social mobility that brought in its wake both an interrogation of social hierarchy and reactionary defences of it, and by a widespread debate over the proper meaning and conduct of marriage. Having honed your skills of textual analysis and discovered the pleasures and insights to be had by reading literary texts with an eye to their contexts, you are now well equipped to move on to the next part of the book, which concentrates on early prose works, both fictional and non-fictional, and the interesting and illuminating ways they interact with the period in which they were written.

Part 2
Journeys in the long eighteenth century

Aims

The second part of this book will:

- introduce you to the literature of the long eighteenth century through the study of travel narratives of the period
- examine how journeys are described in both fictional and non-fictional texts
- consider the many different contexts of eighteenth-century travel writing.

Introduction to Part 2

David Johnson

Welcome to 'Journeys in the long eighteenth century', the second part of *The Renaissance and Long Eighteenth Century*. In this part of the book, you will study a variety of texts describing journeys undertaken between the 1680s and the 1790s. We start with two well-known fictional journeys: *Oroonoko, or The Royal Slave* (1688) by Aphra Behn (*c.*1640–1689) and *Candide, or Optimism* (1759) by Voltaire (1694–1778). We then move on to non-fictional travel narratives, analysing the slave autobiography (*c.*1770) of Ukawsaw Gronniosaw (born *c.*1710), as well as several further accounts of the 'middle passage' undertaken by African slaves to the Americas. We conclude with the competing non-fictional and fictional versions of the famous mutiny on the ship the *Bounty*, which took place on 28 April 1789. The journeys of Oroonoko, Candide, Gronniosaw and the *Bounty* are traced on the world map in Figure 1.

The long eighteenth century was bracketed by two major upheavals in European history: the so-called 'Glorious Revolution' in England of 1688 and the French Revolution of 1789. This period was characterised by the rapid expansion of European power around the globe. A number of major historical events and trends contributed to Europe's ascendancy: the collapse or decline of other competing empires (the Safavid regime in Iran after 1722; the Mughal Empire in India after 1739; and, more gradually, the Ottoman Empire from the 1760s); the improvements in European modes of warfare and military technology (notably the flintlock rifle); the increase in the number of African slaves transported to the Americas (two-thirds of the overall total of fourteen million slaves undertook this enforced journey between 1700 and 1808); the European discovery and commercial exploitation of new lands in the Indian and Pacific Oceans (Tahiti in 1767; Australia in 1788); the consolidation and expansion of East India Company rule in India after the Battle of Plassey in 1757; and the accelerated economic penetration of North America following the Seven Years War (1756–63) between Britain and France (but also involving Austria, Russia and Prussia). In 1688, European consciousness of the world was bounded by the Mediterranean Sea; by 1789, these seismic events in the Middle and Far East, the Indian and Pacific Oceans, Africa, India and the Americas, had opened European eyes to many more worlds beyond their own. For the many peoples outside Europe, their lives were permanently

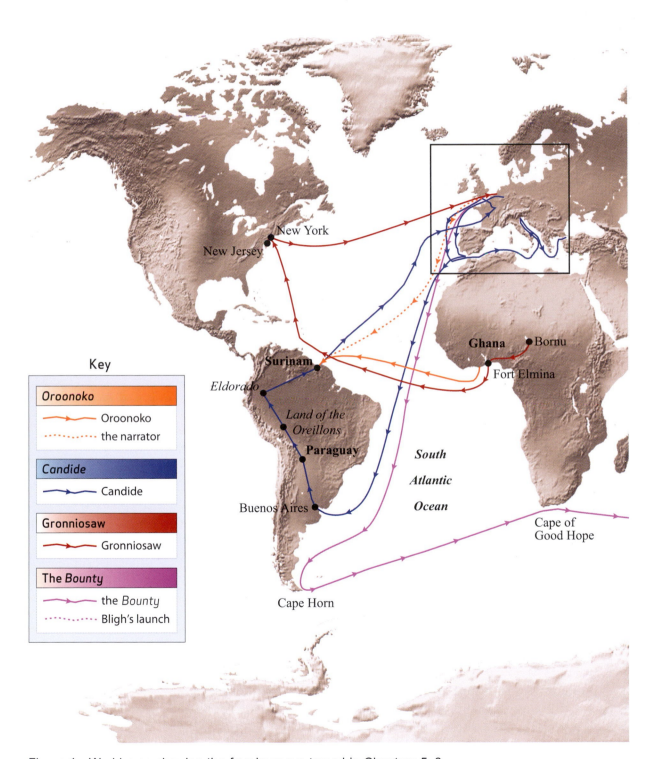

Figure 1   World map showing the four journeys traced in Chapters 5–8.

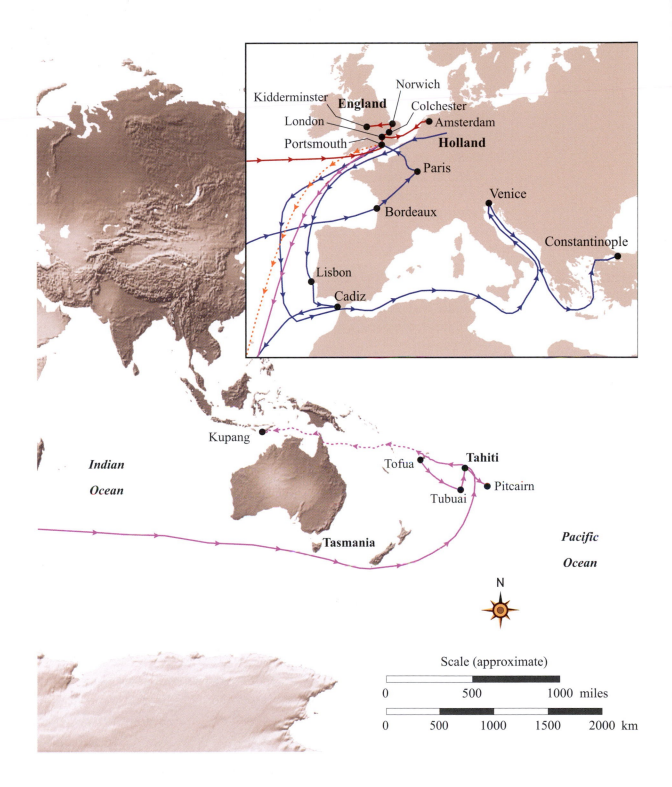

Kidderminster
Norwich
England
Colchester
London
Amsterdam
Portsmouth
Holland
Paris
Venice
Bordeaux
Constantinople
Lisbon
Cadiz

Kupang
Tofua
Tahiti
Indian
Ocean
Tubuai
Pitcairn
Tasmania
Pacific
Ocean

N

Scale (approximate)

| 0 | 500 | 1000 miles |

| 0 | 500 | 1000 | 1500 | 2000 km |

changed (or even abruptly ended) by the arrival, colonisation or settlement on their lands of ever increasing numbers of European travellers.

This global expansion of European power was accompanied by a proliferation of writing on journeys and travel. Before the eighteenth century, there had, of course, been many texts about journeys and travel in a variety of different genres. Journeys are fundamental to two of the founding texts of European literature: Homer's epic *The Odyssey* (*c.*880 BCE) involves the hero Odysseus travelling great distances and overcoming myriad obstacles on his journey home, and Herodotus' *Histories* (*c.*450 BCE–*c.*420 BCE) digresses frequently from the history of the Greco-Persian War to recount half-factual, half-mythic travellers' tales. A third variety of ancient Greek travel writing with a lengthy afterlife is the tourist guidebook. Initiated in the second century CE, Pausanius' ten-book compilation, *A Guide to Greece*, introduced Roman visitors to Greek sites like the Acropolis and the Oracle at Delphi. During the European Middle Ages, descriptions of journeys were central in other genres of writing, most notably Christian accounts of pilgrimages and crusades, but also in factual travelogues like the late thirteenth-century *Travels of Marco Polo* and the writings of the North African traveller Ibn Battuta (1304–*c.*1368). Less easy to categorise are the *Travels* (1356) of John Mandeville, which combined serious observations of peoples and their customs with fanciful tales of giants, headless men and pygmies. In the Renaissance, travellers' tales were appropriated for yet another use by Thomas More (1478–1535) in his *Utopia* (1516), which filtered his critique of early sixteenth-century England through the traveller-narrator Raphael Hythloday's descriptions of the imaginary island 'Utopia'. Subsequent utopian fictions, such as *New Atlantis* (1627) by Francis Bacon (1561–1626) and *The Isle of Pines* (1688) by Henry Neville (1620–1694), in like manner travelled imaginatively to distant lands in order to criticise British society. In the same period, the motif of journeying was used by Miguel de Cervantes (1547–1616) in his picaresque novel tale *Don Quixote* (1605, 1615), in order both to mock, and (in the second part) to critique in more serious mode the conventions and values associated with the chivalric romance. Another flourishing literary-religious genre of the seventeenth century, which drew heavily upon descriptions of journeys both real and metaphorical, was the fictional spiritual autobiography, exemplified by *The Pilgrim's Progress* (1678) of John Bunyan (1628–1688).

By 1688, it was therefore possible to write about journeys in a wide variety of different genres: epic, history writing, tourist guide, religious quest, non-fictional travel narrative, utopia, picaresque tale, spiritual autobiography, or, indeed, in mixed and difficult-to-define genres like Mandeville's *Travels*. In addition to these well-known genres, many other kinds of writing associated with travel were published, circulated and consumed in the eighteenth century: the personal letters and diaries of travellers; the accounts of wealthy young men or their tutors on the 'Grand Tour' to the classical sites of Italy; the reports of merchants and missionaries to their superiors based in Europe; the captain's log-books and ships' journals from long voyages; and the collected observations of travelling doctors, botanists and cartographers.

The proliferation of travel-related writings occurred in the context of a steady rise in the sheer quantity of prose published in the long eighteenth century. In Britain, the emergent middle class's appetite for reading was met by a rapid increase in the numbers of books, magazines, periodicals and newspapers published: the number of master printers in London rose from about 60 in 1660, to 75 in 1724, to 124 in 1785, and to 216 in 1808; the number of periodicals in Britain increased from 66 in 1711 to 265 in 1800; and the number of printed items published annually in Britain rose from about 2,000 per year in 1685 to well in excess of 8,000 per year in 1800. The majority of publications were religious and political tracts, but there were also increasing numbers of fictional and non-fictional travel narratives (some in serialised form). Both of these genres were immensely popular, and they flourished in part by borrowing heavily from each other's conventions. The emerging fictional genre of the novel borrowed from the non-fictional travel narrative in order to simulate historical verisimilitude, and many novels addressed readers in the same form and language as factual travelogues. For example, in the case of *Oroonoko*, the novel defines itself as 'A True History', and *Candide* gives an impression of historical authenticity by claiming to have been translated from the German text of 'Doctor Ralph'. Recourse to such narrative strategies was widespread, and is abundantly evident in some of the best-known prose works of the century, notably *Robinson Crusoe* (1719) by Daniel Defoe (1659–1731), *Gulliver's Travels* (1726) by Jonathan Swift (1667–1745), *The History of Rasselas, Prince of Abissinia* (1759) by Samuel Johnson (1709–1784) and *A Sentimental Journey through France and Italy* (1768) by Lawrence Sterne (1713–1768).

The process of novels borrowing from factual travel narratives, however, was not one-way; non-fiction travel narratives, in turn, drew extensively from the novel and other fictional genres. For example, the ex-slave Gronniosaw's factual account of his life was powerfully influenced by the pressure to observe the conventions of the literary-religious genre of the spiritual autobiography, and William Bligh's factual account of the journey of the *Bounty*'s launch to Timor manipulates reader sympathies by adopting narrative techniques associated with fictional genres like the novel. In other words, we challenge the strict distinction between 'the fictional' and 'the factual' by studying how fictional texts like *Oroonoko* and *Candide* borrow from factual genres, and how non-fictional texts like those of Gronniosaw and Bligh use fictional techniques to tell their own travel stories and to try to win arguments.

Supplementing the close analysis of each of these set texts is an extended consideration of their respective contexts, and further, of the relation between each text and its context(s). Literary critics have not always been interested in the contexts of literary texts; indeed, up until the 1970s, the dominant literary-critical orthodoxy dictated that the meanings of literary works should be determined exclusively by the formal analysis of the words on the page, with no reference to extra-textual evidence. Known in Britain as 'practical criticism' and in the United States as 'New Criticism', this de-contextualised method of reading and studying literature came under assault when the post-1968 generation of readers and critics brought their quite distinct political and cultural sensibilities to bear upon the criticism of literature. In the decades since, literary criticism has been transformed by its adoption of the critical vocabularies of adjacent disciplines (philosophy, psychoanalysis, history, linguistics, sociology, political theory, economics) and by its explicit engagement with politics (feminism, Marxism, gay rights, green or eco-politics). Of particular relevance for our purposes here has been literary criticism's engagement with history: 'cultural materialist' critics in Britain and 'new historicist' critics in the United States have argued persuasively that literary texts can only be understood in relation to the contexts of their production and reception. In the past two decades, this critical and methodological axiom has become widely accepted, and very few critics now dispute the relevance of 'context' (broadly conceived) in the reading and studying of literary texts. Instead, most critics today study the multiple contexts of literary texts with the same close attention they dedicate to the literary texts themselves.

Our focus on the theoretical concept of 'context' in Part 2 of this book builds upon the discussions of the contexts of *Othello* and *The Duchess of Malfi* in Part 1. You may recall that in order to analyse the texts of the two plays, you were referred to specific aspects of their respective contexts: for *Othello*, Renaissance ideas about race were outlined to explain the character of Othello, and for *The Duchess of Malfi*, Jacobean marriage conventions were summarised to explain the love affair between Antonio and the Duchess. In Part 2, our attention to the contexts of the texts discussed is developed further by distinguishing between the many different kinds of contexts: the historical, the economic, the political, the cultural, the literary, the religious, and the philosophical. For example, in analysing *Oroonoko*, you will consider the contexts of European colonisation, African slavery and the political events in England in 1688; in analysing *Candide*, you will relate the literary text to Voltaire's philosophical context; in reading Gronniosaw's autobiography, you will foreground the contexts of his pre-colonial West African childhood, his experiences of slavery, and the Christian doctrines he encountered in North America and England; and, in analysing the competing narratives of the mutiny on the *Bounty*, you will take account of the contexts of British maritime exploration in the South Pacific, the personal histories of the main protagonists, and the political events in post-1789 Europe. By paying sustained attention to the diverse eighteenth-century contexts of these selected travellers' tales, we demonstrate more generally how the formal analysis of a text can be enhanced by the simultaneous engagement with its context(s).

One final context we consider throughout is that of the present, as we pose the question: what do writings on the journeys of the long eighteenth century mean for us today? A substantial part of the answer resides in the fact that these texts from over two hundred years ago dramatise social tensions which continue to trouble us today. *Oroonoko* and Gronniosaw's *Narrative* wrestle with issues of racial identity and economic exploitation; Voltaire's *Candide* poses questions about finding faith and hope in an unforgiving universe; and the competing *Bounty* narratives lay bare unresolved class conflicts. This is not to say that we will find satisfying answers to our twenty-first century questions in these eighteenth-century texts. But we will discover fascinating examples of how our contemporary questions have been addressed, narrated, dramatised, evaded and (temporarily) resolved in a variety of texts from different but related worlds.

Chapter 5
Aphra Behn, *Oroonoko, or The Royal Slave*

Anita Pacheco

Aims

This chapter will:

- introduce you to Aphra Behn's *Oroonoko*, concentrating on its representation of travel
- encourage you to read literary texts with an awareness of their contexts and the way this affects the meanings they offer
- introduce you to reading prose fiction, with an emphasis on the role of narrators.

Introduction

Aphra Behn (*c*.1640–1689) was probably the first woman in England to earn her living by writing. She lived and worked during the historical period we call the Restoration, which began in 1660 when the monarchy was restored after its abolition in 1649 by the victorious Parliamentarian side in the English Civil War. Behn's closest literary tie was to the Restoration theatre, for which she wrote at least nineteen plays. She also wrote poetry, worked as a translator and is thought of nowadays as a pioneer of prose fiction who made a significant contribution to the early development of the novel. We know little about her life, though evidence suggests she was born in Kent, the daughter of Bartholomew Johnson, a barber, and his wife, Elizabeth, a midwife. Most of her biographers think that in 1663–4, she visited the English colony of Surinam (in north-eastern South America), the setting of her late prose work *Oroonoko, or The Royal Slave* (1688). By 1666, she was using the surname Behn; if this was her married name, as seems likely, neither the marriage nor the husband has left traces in the historical record. We do know that she worked as a government spy in the Netherlands in 1666; when she returned to England a year later, she was destitute and may have spent some time in a debtors' prison. In 1670, her first play was staged, and she went on to live independently and work as a professional writer at a time when writing and especially publishing were widely thought to be activities unsuitable for women. Behn doubly flouted such prevailing ideologies of gender by producing numerous, highly bawdy, comedies. Yet she was, in general, well respected during her lifetime and had cordial relations with many of her famous male colleagues, such as John Dryden (1631–1700) and Thomas Otway (1652–1685).

When Behn wrote *Oroonoko*, travel writing, both fictional and non-fictional, was enormously popular, due no doubt to the increasing exposure to non-European territories and peoples that went along with England's participation in the European colonial enterprise. Early modern travel narratives often recount the traveller's journey from home to a particular foreign destination. Yet more often than not, they are just as interested in what happens after the journey is over, when the traveller encounters cultures radically different from his or her own. It is this latter subject that interests Behn in *Oroonoko*, which offers an early fictional representation of encounters between Europeans, Africans and Native Americans (the Arawaks and Caribs of Surinam).

Figure 5.1   Mary Beale, portrait of Aphra Behn, seventeenth century, oil on panel, 25 × 20 cm. St. Hilda's College, Oxford. Photo: St Hilda's College, Oxford/The Bridgeman Art Library.

This chapter will look at *Oroonoko* in relation to three important contemporary **contexts**: European colonisation, African slavery and the tumultuous political events unfolding in England in 1688. It will consider how reading the novel in relation to each of these contexts reveals different layers of meaning in the text. But we will also examine *Oroonoko* as a literary text, in particular as a work of prose fiction whose meaning is determined, in large part, by the author's use of literary devices such as **narrators**.

We have referred throughout to the Penguin Classics (2003) edition of *Oronooko*, edited by Janet Todd. You should make sure you have read the entire text before starting work on this chapter.

The narrator

Before we begin to examine *Oroonoko* in relation to its relevant contexts, it is important to be clear about how Behn chooses to tell us her story. We need, that is, to think about what kind of narrator she employs in the novel. We discover early on that the narrator is a woman writer connected to London theatrical society, when she tells us that the English colonists used to trade for feathers with the native Surinamese: 'I had a set of these presented to me, and I gave them to the King's Theatre, and it was the dress of the *Indian Queen*, infinitely admired by persons of quality, and were inimitable' (p. 10). Behn seems to be inviting her readers to identify writer and narrator and to see the text of *Oroonoko* not as fictional at all, but as a factual travel narrative. A glance at the title page in your edition reminds us that she calls her text '*A True History*'. As I discussed in the introduction to this chapter, in general Behn's biographers accept that she travelled to Surinam as a young woman and so is writing a story that, while not necessarily true, might well be based on first-hand knowledge of the colony. There is, however, no hard evidence to support this view and, in the absence of such evidence, it seems only prudent to treat *Oroonoko* as a work of fiction and its narrator not as an autobiographical self-portrait but as a fictional character. We need to remember as well that many early modern fictional travel narratives purport to be works of non-fiction, Defoe's *Robinson Crusoe* (1719) being a case in point. In claiming that her novel is a 'true history' and establishing an identity between herself and the narrator, Behn may simply have been conforming to this convention of the genre.

What other characteristics does Behn's narrator have?

Activity 1

Below are the openings of two novels, both of them fictional travel narratives. Please read them, paying attention to the narrators and how they differ. Can you identify the main characteristics of each?

Passage 1

I was born in the year 1632, in the city of *York*, of a good family, tho' not of that country, my father being a foreigner of *Bremen*, who settled first at Hull: He got a good estate by merchandise, and leaving off his trade, lived afterwards at *York*, from whence he had married my mother, whose relations were call'd *Robinson*, a very good family in that country, and from whom I was call'd *Robinson Kreutznaer*; but by the usual corruption of words in *England*, we are now call'd, nay we call our selves, and write our name *Crusoe*, and so my companions have always call'd me.

(Daniel Defoe, *Robinson Crusoe*, 2001 [1719], p. 5)

Passage 2

The family of Francisco Manoel da Silva had assembled at Ouidah to honour his memory with a Requiem Mass and dinner. It was the usual suffocating afternoon in March. He had been dead a hundred and seventeen years.

(Bruce Chatwin, *The Viceroy of Ouidah*, 1980, p. 1)

Discussion

Chatwin's narrator refers to the characters in the third-person: 'the family', 'Francisco Manoel da Silva', 'He'. This is the case throughout the novel; the characters are invariably referred to either by their names, their social roles, or as 'she', 'he' or 'they'. Defoe's narrator is very different in this regard. He speaks to us as 'I', and we can tell from the book's opening that he is going to be a character in the story he is narrating.

In *The Viceroy of Ouidah*, then, Chatwin uses what we call a **third-person narrator**, someone who is 'outside' the story. Defoe, in *Robinson Crusoe*, employs a **first-person narrator**, who speaks to us in the first person ('I') and takes part in the story he is telling.

If we return to *Oroonoko*, it shouldn't have taken you long to figure out that, like Defoe, Behn chose to use a first-person narrator. Indeed, both novels begin with the word 'I'. Behn's narrator wastes no time telling us that 'I was myself an eye-witness to a great part of what you will find here set down; and what I could not be witness of I received from the mouth of the chief actor in this history, the hero himself, who gave us the whole transactions of his youth' (p. 9). So the narrator does two things: she tells us about events that she witnessed, and also relates to us stories which Oroonoko, 'the chief actor … the hero himself', told her. In the section of the novel set in Coramantien (generally thought to be on the Gold Coast, in modern-day Ghana), the narrator tells the story mainly (though not solely) from Oroonoko's **point of view**. She operates here virtually as a **third-person narrator**, apart from the odd comment she makes in the first person. In the Surinam half of the narrative, she continues to privilege Oroonoko's point of view, but her own perspective comes much more to the fore.

Behn's decision to employ this kind of first-person narration has a fundamental and complex effect on the way we respond to the story. In the first place, it means that the story is told overwhelmingly from the narrator's and Oroonoko's points of view. This, of course, means that their perspectives dominate, so that we are encouraged to adopt their attitudes to the events being recounted. Think how different our response to the novel would be if it were written mainly from the point of view of Imoinda or Deputy Governor Byam. However, if the prominence of the narrator's voice gives her authority with readers, her status as a first-person narrator may well place limits on that authority. The presence of a first-person narrator in a work of prose fiction always requires that we ask: 'are they reliable?' This is because, as actors within the narrative, their own perspective may well be limited or blinkered. In this respect, first-person narrators are often quite unlike third-person narrators, who are frequently (though not always) endowed with omniscience; that is to say, they know everything about the story they are telling. The question of the reliability of Behn's narrator is one to which we will return in the course of this chapter, as we examine what she has to tell us about the English colony of Surinam and her own relationship with the enslaved prince Oroonoko.

Contexts

European colonisation

Let's turn now to the first of our three contexts. When Behn wrote *Oroonoko*, the English project to colonise the Americas was well underway. During the sixteenth century the English had been busy consolidating their conquest and settlement of Ireland, and had regarded North America principally as a profitable base for piracy and harassment of the Spanish, who were already in possession of a sizeable part of what we now call Latin America. By the end of the century, however, the English government had begun to appreciate the advantages of colonisation as a source of valuable raw materials, a market for English goods, and as a convenient repository for the nation's poor. In 1607, Jamestown, the first permanent English settlement in America, was established in the swamplands along the James River in what is now southern Virginia. Later, in the 1620s and 1630s, the English occupied Barbados, the first step in a gradual expansion of their colonial influence in the Caribbean. It was the governor of Barbados, Lord Willoughby, who founded the English colony in Surinam in the 1650s.

So what does Behn's narrator tell us about Surinam? We learn little about her journey there but a great deal about her experience of the colony once she has arrived. She starts off giving us a rapturous account of the abundant natural resources which Surinam affords. We are only four paragraphs into the novel when the narrator begins a detailed description of the myriad wonderful objects the colonists gain through trade with the native Surinamese:

> trading with them for their fish, venison, buffaloes, skins and little rarities, as marmosets, a sort of monkey, as big as a rat or weasel, but of a marvellous and delicate shape, and has face and hands like an human creature … Then for little parakeets, great parrots, macaw, and a thousand other birds and beasts of wonderful and surprising forms, shapes and colours. For skins of prodigious snakes, of which there are some three-score yards in length, as is the skin of one that may be seen at his Majesty's Antiquaries, where are also some rare flies of amazing forms and colours, presented to them by myself, some as big as my fist, some less, and all of various excellencies, such as art cannot imitate.

(pp. 9–10)

The critic Laura Brown observes of this passage: 'Behn's enumeration of these goods is typical of the age's economic and literary language, where the mere act of listing, the evocation of brilliant colors, and the sense of an incalculable numerousness express the period's fascination with imperialist accumulation' (Brown, 1998, p. 208). Behn is, in fact, borrowing one of the principal conventions of early modern travel writing here, and her narrator will continue to detail the benefits of the colonial project throughout the text. In 1667, the English lost Surinam to the Dutch and, in *Oroonoko*, the narrator laments that the late King Charles II had 'parted so easily' with such a hugely profitable colony that 'affords all things both for beauty and use' (p. 51).

Travel writing of this period typically takes an interest not only in the commodities and natural wonders of the 'New World', but also in its native inhabitants (Sherman, 2006, p. 26). Behn adopts this convention as well, having her narrator describe the indigenous peoples of Surinam in some detail.

Activity 2

Read the following passage from *Oroonoko* and then answer these three questions:

1 What does Behn's narrator mean when she associates the Surinamese Indians with 'the first state of innocence'?

2 What is the role of nature in the passage?

3 How does she depict 'white men' in the passage?

> And these people represented to me an absolute idea of the first state of innocence, before man knew how to sin; and it is most evident and plain that simple Nature is the most harmless, inoffensive and virtuous mistress. It is she alone, if she were permitted, that better instructs the world than all the inventions of man; religion would here but destroy that tranquillity they possess by ignorance, and laws would but teach them to know offence, of which now they have no notion. ... They have a native justice, which knows no fraud; and they understand no vice or cunning, but when they are taught by the white men.
>
> (p. 11)

Discussion

Here are my answers to the questions:

1 By 'the first state of innocence', Behn's narrator is referring to the state of Adam and Eve in the Garden of Eden before they ate from the tree of the knowledge of good and evil (Genesis 3:1–24). According to Christian theology, this act, known as the original sin, brought sin into the world. Thus Behn's narrator sees the natives of Surinam as inhabiting a paradise.

2   Nature is enormously important in the passage. It is what Europeans ought to be living in harmony with but no longer are. According to the narrator, nature teaches us better than 'all the inventions of men'. There is a strong opposition in the passage between nature, which is healthy and beneficial, and aspects of 'civilisation' like religion and law, which are portrayed in a negative light.

3   'White men' are associated with 'vice' and 'cunning' in the passage. The narrator is strongly implying that contact with Europeans will corrupt the natural virtues of the indigenous way of life.

Now let's look at another, earlier, European description of native peoples: an extract from the essay 'Of Cannibals' by the French philosopher and essayist Michel de Montaigne (1533–1592). In 1562, Montaigne met a Native American cannibal (from the area now known as Brazil), who had been brought to France by a French explorer. Some fifteen years later, he composed 'Of Cannibals', which reflects on the common European view of such peoples as 'barbarians', lacking the benefits of European civilisation.

Activity 3

Read the extract from 'Of Cannibals' below and then answer the following two questions:

1   How does Montaigne's account of indigenous culture compare with Behn's account, quoted in the previous activity?

2   What do we learn about Behn's description of the native Surinamese by reading it in the context of other early modern representations of indigenous peoples?

> These people are wild in the same way as we say that fruits are wild, when nature has produced them by herself and in her ordinary way ... They are still governed by natural laws and very little corrupted by our own. They are in such a state of purity that it sometimes saddens me to think that we did not learn of them earlier, at a time when there were men who were better able to appreciate them than we ... This is a nation ... in which there is no kind of commerce, no knowledge of letters, no science of numbers, no title of magistrate or of political superiority, no habit of service, riches or poverty, no contracts, no inheritance, no divisions of property, only leisurely occupations, no respect for any kinship but the

common ties, no clothes, no agriculture, no metals, no use of corn or wine. The very words denoting lying, treason, deceit, greed, envy, slander, and forgiveness have never been heard.

(Montaigne, 1958 [1580], pp. 109–10)

Discussion

Here are my answers to the questions:

1   The two passages are very similar. Like Behn's narrator, Montaigne associates indigenous peoples with a life lived in accordance with nature. Montaigne believes that the native peoples live according to natural laws and display natural virtues – a condition he perceives as a state of purity which Europeans have long since lost. The people live without the many facets of Western 'civilisation', such as commerce, a social hierarchy and private property, and they have no words for vices common among European people, such as 'lying' and 'greed'. Like Behn's narrator, Montaigne seems to believe that contact with Europeans will corrupt the natives' pure and natural way of life.

2   Reading Behn's account of the native inhabitants of Surinam in conjunction with Montaigne's essay helps to clarify that there is nothing particularly novel or strange about her critique of European culture. In fact, she was writing about the indigenous peoples of the colony in a recognisable way.

Behn may well have known Montaigne's essay, as it was famous and had already influenced Shakespeare's writing of *The Tempest* (1611). But even if she did not, she would have been familiar with the kind of **tradition**, or long-standing literary practice, within which Montaigne was writing. The practice of criticising civilisation as far inferior to a life lived in natural surroundings was very well-established by the sixteenth century. It formed the foundation of a particular literary tradition, called **pastoral**, which originated in ancient Greece and Rome and, typically, praised the virtues of a life lived in harmony with nature, far away from the complexities and stresses of urban life. When Europeans began to come into contact with the native peoples of the Americas, the pastoral tradition was easily adapted by authors who wished to challenge European assumptions of superiority over such 'barbarians'.

Figure 5.2   Sebastien le Clerc, engraving showing native people in a pastoral setting from Jean Baptiste Du Tertre's *Histoire Générale des Antilles Habitées par les Français*, Paris, 1667. Photo: Courtesy of the John Carter Brown Library at Brown University.

It is interesting, though, that on occasion Behn's narrator expresses far less positive judgements of the native Surinamese. Her long opening account of the Indians, which is so complimentary and so critical of the West, ends on a rather different note:

> So that they being, on all occasions very useful to us, we find it absolutely necessary to caress them as friends, and not to treat them as slaves; nor dare we do other, their numbers so far surpassing ours in that continent.
>
> (p. 12)

After heaping praise on their innocence and purity, the narrator finishes by describing the colonists' warm relations with the Indians as entirely pragmatic, based on a cool appraisal of their usefulness and of the threat their superior numbers pose to the survival of the colony. Later in the novel, she tells us that conflict has indeed broken out between the English and the Indians (p. 56). When she and Oroonoko and a few others visit an Indian village, her account of the war captains, who mutilate themselves in a competition for the office of general, elicits a considerably less enthusiastic response from the narrator, who takes them 'for hobgoblins, or fiends, rather than men' and reports Oroonoko's view that this sort of courage was 'too brutal to be applauded' (p. 59). Thus, the narrator's idealised portrait of the Indians as the perfect embodiment of nature sits alongside quite different views which register suspicion, anxiety and hostility in the face of alien cultures. The novel thus signals to its readers that its English narrator holds contradictory attitudes to the indigenous peoples she encounters in the colony of Surinam.

African slavery

This leads to the second of our three contexts. The narrator's journey to Surinam brings her into contact with the institution of slavery as it supported European colonisation. She sums up the situation near the start of the novel: 'Those then whom we make use of to work in our plantations of sugar are Negroes, black slaves altogether' (p. 12). Devoted principally to the cultivation of sugar, Surinam was a colony of large plantations at the centre of the growing slave trade. In the 1660s, there were probably around 3,000 African slaves in the colony; by the end of the century, the number of slaves in English colonies in the Caribbean as a whole had swollen to a quarter of a million, and would soon be ten times that.

The representation of slavery and black Africans is almost certainly the most contentious aspect of *Oroonoko*. On the one hand, the text has been praised for its ability to arouse strong anti-slavery feelings, even though it was written many years before the creation of the abolitionist movement in the eighteenth century (Goreau, 1980, p. 289); on the other hand, it has been criticised for peddling views of Africans that helped to justify slavery (Starr, 1990, pp. 364–6). How can one fairly short literary work accommodate such diametrically opposed readings? Let's have a look now at one of the most controversial passages in the novel to see if we can start to answer that question: the narrator's description of the enslaved prince Oroonoko.

Activity 4

Read the following passage from *Oroonoko*. What does the narrator have to say about Oroonoko's appearance? What does she say about his character? What relationship does she set up between Europeans and Africans?

> He had nothing of barbarity in his nature, but in all points addressed himself as if his education had been in some European court. ... His face was not of that brown, rusty black which most of that nation are, but a perfect ebony or polished jet. ... His nose was rising and Roman instead of African and flat. His mouth, the finest shaped that could be seen, far from those great turned lips which are so natural to the rest of the Negroes. The whole proportion and air of his face was so noble and exactly formed that, bating [excepting] his colour, there could be nothing in nature more beautiful, agreeable and handsome. ... Nor did the perfections of his mind come short of those of his person; for his discourse was admirable upon almost any subject, and whoever had heard him speak would have been convinced of their errors that all fine wit is confined to the white men, especially to those of Christendom ...
>
> (p. 15)

Discussion

The narrator tells us that Oroonoko is beautiful, but his physical beauty depends on its difference from other Africans and its similarity to European ideals. When it comes to Oroonoko's character, the narrator states that he has 'nothing of barbarity in his nature'. Like Montaigne, then, she denies that non-European peoples are by definition barbaric.

She then goes on to say that Oroonoko is admirable insofar as he embodies European standards of civility. In fact, just prior to this passage, the narrator accounts for the prince's nobility and refinement at least in part by telling us he has been educated by a French tutor 'of wit and learning' and has spent a lot of time in the company of the English gentlemen involved in trade in Coramantien (p. 14). Thus, his education may not have taken place in a European court, but it is, nonetheless, to all intents and purposes, European.

It is not hard to see why many readers and critics have found the physical description of Oroonoko objectionable. The account of his character is more complex: it rejects arguments for the inherent barbarity of Africans, and for Europeans' exclusive claim on 'fine wit'. At the same time it seems unable to see nobility except in recognisably European terms, while the description of the prince's education is, arguably, informed by a belief in the ennobling properties of European culture. Then again, perhaps the stress on education suggests that it is culture that makes us what we are, and that, as a consequence, the differences between Europeans and other races are what Derek Hughes calls the 'potentially reversible ones of education' (2002, p. 7).

Let's try to historicise this passage, that is, look at it in the context of other contemporary representations of Africans. According to the critic Joanna Lipking, Behn depicts Oroonoko as the 'marvellous exception', as the African who meets European standards of beauty and courtly refinement (2004, p. 170). This is a figure who turns up fairly regularly in early modern travel literature. Thus, in his four-volume collection of travel writings, first published in 1625, Samuel Purchas describes a king in the Portuguese Congo as 'magnificall, and wittie … wise in counsell … besides very liberal and courteous' (1905–7 [1625], vol. 6, p. 485), while the French traveller Nicholas Villault de Bellefond found a Sierra Leone prince, in spite of his 'complexion', 'a very handsome man', with a 'courteous and majestick' air (1670, p. 133).

Behn may have had this concept of the Europeanised upper-class African in mind when constructing her protagonist. There were certainly much worse views of Africans available. In his work *The Negro's & Indians Advocate* (1680), the Anglican minister Morgan Godwyn, who served in Virginia and Barbados in the late seventeenth century, wrote angrily about planters in both colonies who argue that 'the *Negro's*, though in their Figure they carry some resemblances of Manhood, yet are indeed *no Men*', and attempt to use scripture to bolster their claims (1680, p. 3). According to Godwyn, the same denial of humanity 'was some time since invented by the *Spaniards*, to justifie *their murthering the Americans*' (by Americans, Godwyn means Native Americans) (Godwyn, 1680, p. 3). Godwyn undertakes a vigorous defence of the common humanity of African slaves and the indigenous peoples of America, not in order to undermine the institution of slavery, but rather to establish the right of both groups to be instructed and baptised in the Christian faith. His work demonstrates the existence in the seventeenth century both of arguments for the innate inferiority of Africans and of spirited opposition to such arguments. Nowadays, many readers and critics find Behn's portrait of Oroonoko both Eurocentric, in its apparent inability to measure the value of other peoples and cultures except by specifically European criteria, and unjustifiably complacent, in its assumption of the superiority and redeeming benefits of Western culture. Godwyn too, with his passionate desire to bring Christianity to Africans and Native Americans, is implicated in such assumptions. But we can see how far Behn's description of her hero is from endorsing claims for the essential inferiority of Africans: it is not 'racist', in that sense. Godwyn grasps more firmly than Behn that perceptions of physical beauty are culturally constructed, observing that black Africans think themselves beautiful and Europeans ugly (Godwyn, 1680, p. 21). He also argues that it is education that makes us what we are, and that differences between Africans and Europeans are consequently superficial (1680, p. 36), a conviction that Behn's focus on her hero's education may well endorse.

It is important to recognise as well that the kind of Europeanised African we find in *Oroonoko* was a crucial element in eighteenth-century anti-slavery literature, much of which sought to humanise Africans by portraying them as capable of living up to an exacting standard of European refinement (Brown, 1998, p. 204; Pacheco, 1994, p. 492). We can see then why Behn's description of her protagonist, which on the one hand has sparked accusations of racism, has on the other contributed to the novel's reputation as a text that might be pressed into the service of an emancipationist agenda.

Is there other evidence within the text to support the claim that *Oroonoko* is capable of stimulating anti-slavery sentiments? Oroonoko's abduction by the English sea captain associates the slave trade with treachery and betrayal, while the captain's repeated breaking of his promises to the prince, at the same time that he refuses to trust 'a heathen … upon his parole' (p. 39), is just one of many occasions in the novel when Christian slave traders and owners are depicted as hypocrites and liars. In the Surinam half of the narrative, we find Oroonoko's speech to the slaves, whom he seeks to inspire to join him in his escape attempt. The narrator tells us that Caesar (Oroonoko's slave name) 'made a harangue' to the slaves 'of the miseries and ignominies of slavery; counting up all their toils and sufferings under such loads, burdens and drudgeries as were fitter for beasts than men; senseless brutes, than human souls' (p. 61). She carries on:

> He told them, it was not for days, months or years, but for eternity; there was no end to be of their misfortunes. They suffered not like men who might find a glory and fortitude in oppression, but like dogs that loved the whip and bell, and fawned the more they were beaten. That they had lost the divine quality of men and were become insensible asses, fit only to bear.
>
> (p. 61)

This is stirring **rhetoric** that attacks slavery as a violation of human dignity capable of transforming human beings into beasts of burden. When the slave escape fails and Oroonoko is captured, we are given a painfully graphic account of the physical punishments to which he is subjected. First, he is savagely whipped, then placed in irons while pepper is rubbed into his wounds. Later, he is horribly mutilated: his nose, ears and arm hacked off, before his dead body is cut into quarters and dispersed 'to several of the chief plantations' (p. 76). Here the novel testifies to the kind of brutal punishments inflicted upon recalcitrant slaves in the colonies, much as Godwyn had done a few years earlier when he wrote scathingly about the colonists 'Emasculating and Beheading' slaves: '*croping off their Ears* … their *Amputations of Legs*, and even Dissecting them alive' (1680, p. 41). All of these aspects of the novel can be seen as encouraging the condemnation of slavery.

Yet we need to ask ourselves whether this is the whole story. Are there other areas of the text that are less easy to reconcile with a humanitarian reading? It seems significant in this regard that Oroonoko is the prince of a people who entirely accept the existence of slavery and the slave trade, at least for those lower-class men unfortunate enough to be taken prisoner in battle. We are told that the Coramantine upper classes, constantly at war with their neighbours, make a handsome profit by selling all their low-born prisoners of war to European slave traders. Before he was abducted by the English sea captain, Oroonoko was himself an enthusiastic slave holder and trader.

Figure 5.3   William Blake, after John Gabriel Stedman, 'A Negro hung alive by the Ribs to a Gallows', engraving from *Narrative of a Five Years' Expedition against the Revolted Negroes of Surinam, in Guiana, on the Wild Coast of South America, from the year 1772, to 1777*, published by Joseph Johnson, London, 1796. Photo: Private Collection/Archives Charmet/The Bridgeman Art Library.

Indeed, when he arrives in Surinam, he discovers that most of the slaves in the colony are there because he sold them into slavery. Far from welcoming the prince's enslavement as a well-deserved retribution, they fall at his feet 'crying out in their language, *Live, O King! Long live, O King!* And kissing his feet, paid him even divine homage' (p. 44). When the slave escape collapses because the other slaves are persuaded to abandon him, Oroonoko reflects bitterly on his foolishness 'in endeavouring to make those free, who were by nature slaves' (p. 66).

What should we make of all this? There are certainly significant sections of the novel that appear to be entirely uncritical of the institution of slavery except when it is imposed on a man of high, in this case royal, birth.

Activity 5

Read the following passage describing Oroonoko's journey upriver in Surinam just after he has been sold into slavery. What do you think is the point of this passage? Why does it occur at this particular point in the text, and what response is it inviting?

> In their passage up the river they put in at several houses for refreshment, and ever when they landed, numbers of people would flock to behold this man; ... the fame of Oroonoko was gone before him, and all people were in admiration of his beauty. Besides, he had a rich habit on, in which he was taken, so different from the rest ... When he found his habit made him liable, as he thought, to be gazed at the more, he begged Trefry to give him something more befitting a slave ... Nevertheless, he shone through all ... The royal youth appeared in spite of the slave, and people could not help treating him after a different manner without designing it; as soon as they approached him, they venerated and esteemed him; his eyes insensibly commanded respect, and his behaviour insinuated it into every soul.
>
> (pp. 42–3)

Discussion

Oroonoko puts on clothes befitting a slave, but still his royalty shines through. He simply cannot hide his superiority over the other slaves, and the people in turn cannot help treating him with veneration and respect. This is classic royalist language, which peddles the myth that people with royal blood really are better than other people, and that the blue blood that runs in their veins gives them an aura of royalty which frustrates any attempt to disguise it. The point of the passage, then, is to reaffirm Oroonoko's royal stature at the moment when it seems most endangered. He has just been sold into slavery, in every respect the antithesis of princely status. It is at this point then that the text stresses that his royal identity defies effacement.

Passages like this suggest that what matters about Oroonoko is less his skin colour than his rank: that the sense of outrage which the novel conveys is directed not at slavery per se but at the enslavement of a prince. We have already seen that the other slaves, who unlike the colonists know full well who Oroonoko is, fall at his feet when they see him and worship him as a god. This reinforces the argument that the problem the novel is exploring is not slavery as such, but an assault on a legitimate royal line – hence its subtitle *The Royal Slave*.

Royalty and the politics of 1688

We turn now to our final context. Behn lived and wrote during a period characterised by sustained conflict between Parliament and the king, which began in the late 1670s and reached its climax in 1688. The conflict stemmed in large part from religion: Charles II, who had no legitimate children, named as his heir his brother James, Duke of York, who was a Catholic, a religion viewed with intense suspicion and hostility by many of Charles's Protestant subjects. But religion and politics in early modern England were pretty much inseparable: for many English Protestants, Catholicism had an intimate connection with absolute monarchy, and they had only to look across the Channel to France to find living proof of this in the person of Louis XIV, the Catholic king of France, who did indeed wield something approaching absolute power. So what James's opponents in Parliament feared was that he would try, if he became king, to return England (a Protestant country since the early sixteenth century) to the Roman Catholic Church and that he would rule with a despotic hand. After his accession to the throne in 1685, he began a concerted campaign to remove legal restrictions on his fellow English Catholics, who were prohibited by law from worshipping freely and holding public office. This required him to use his royal powers in a fashion many felt was reckless, offensive and dubiously legal. In 1688, a group of James's most powerful subjects invited the Dutch prince William of Orange, who was married to

James's Protestant daughter Mary, to come to England and help restore what they saw as the threatened laws and liberties of England. James fled in the face of the invasion, and William and Mary were eventually crowned king and queen. This is the regime change known as the Glorious Revolution.

Figure 5.4   Jan Wyck, *William III Landing at Brixham, Torbay 5 November, 1688*, 1688, oil on canvas, 158 x 132 cm, National Maritime Museum, Greenwich, London. Photo: National Maritime Museum, Greenwich, London.

When the conflict over James's accession broke out in the late 1670s, it gave rise to the first stirrings of the two-party system in England. Tories, broadly speaking, were royalists, loyal to the crown and determined that the legitimate heir to the throne should become king despite his unfortunate taste in religion. The Whigs, by contrast, advocated excluding James from the throne; they also tended to foreground the role of Parliament in governing the nation and to endorse a limited conception of monarchical power. Both parties developed propaganda machines in which writers played a vital role. The theatre was particularly deeply involved in the political struggles of the time, with most dramatists producing plays in support of either the Tories or the Whigs, though poetry and prose fiction were also employed as vehicles of party political messages. As a result, contemporary audiences and readers grew accustomed to finding political meaning in a range of different genres and narratives.

Behn was a loyal Tory writer who, in her plays and her prose fiction, engaged energetically in the political crisis surrounding James's accession to the throne. Might *Oroonoko, or The Royal Slave* be a coded political narrative, providing a commentary on the crisis of 1688 from the Tory perspective? Does it use the story of an enslaved African prince to register the sense of outrage with which loyalists faced the impending collapse of James's kingship? Looked at from this angle, Oroonoko's enslavement becomes a **metaphor** for what Tories loyal to James would have seen as the violation of royal authority taking place in England in 1688. We can never know for certain what Behn's intentions were, but awareness of the political context of the novel, in particular of its author's political sympathies, allows us at least to recognise the strong possibility that Behn employed a travel narrative not primarily to examine foreign lands and peoples, but as a way of confronting problems back home.

If we read *Oroonoko* as a political text about the Glorious Revolution, it sheds new light on several aspects of the narrative. Behn's stress on the protagonist's European education and appearance looks less like an intervention in contemporary debates about Africans than a clue to the novel's underlying political meaning, its covert support for another European prince. Oroonoko's slave name of Caesar emerges as another coded reference to the text's loyalist allegiances, as does the fact that after he is sold into slavery, the protagonist never actually engages in slave labour: that would presumably be a degradation too far for the author to inflict upon her royal hero. The royalist mythology we discussed a moment ago emerges as a tool to affirm the rightness of the royal power under assault in England, while the text's curious mixture of indignation and indifference to slavery makes sense within the context of a defence of the legitimate king of England, which objects to slavery only when it is visited on royals born and brought up to rule over others.

However, even if Behn did write *Oroonoko* as an intervention in the political crisis of 1688 from the loyalist side, we should not therefore conclude that the novel is not about slavery and the early English colonial project after all. By couching her political text within two journey narratives, each integrally connected to slavery in Surinam, Behn could hardly avoid representing, and so making comments on, those subjects as well. This is a good example of the way in which narratives take on a life of their own, not quite independent of their authors but not fully under their control either.

Oroonoko and the narrator

Behn's narrator has figured prominently in this chapter. We have seen how contradictory she can be in her responses to non-European peoples and in her attitude to Western culture, which strongly suggests that, like many first-person narrators, she is less than entirely reliable. In the second half of the novel, she presents herself very much as Oroonoko's devoted ally and defender. Is her relationship with him as clear cut as she would have it?

Activity 6

Look at the following passage from *Oroonoko*, which occurs after Imoinda's pregnancy makes Oroonoko 'more impatient of liberty' (p. 48). What effect does this passage have on your assessment of the narrator's reliability?

> They fed him from day to day with promises, and delayed him till the Lord Governor should come, so that he began to suspect them of falsehood, and that they would delay him till the time of his wife's delivery, and make a slave of that too, for all the breed is theirs to whom the parents belong. This thought made him very uneasy, and his sullenness gave them some jealousies of him, so that I was obliged, by some persons who feared a mutiny (which is very fatal sometimes in

those colonies that abound so with slaves that they exceed the whites in vast numbers), to discourse with Caesar, and to give him all the satisfaction I possibly could ...

After this, I neither thought it convenient to trust him much out of our view, nor did the country who feared him; but with one accord it was advised to treat him fairly, and oblige him to remain within such a compass, and that he should be permitted, as seldom as could be, to go up to the plantations of the Negroes; or, if he did, to be accompanied by some that should be rather in appearance attendants than spies.

(pp. 48, 50)

Discussion

I would say that this passage underscores the tensions in the narrator's relationship with Oroonoko. She starts off talking about an unidentified 'they' who 'feed' Oroonoko with promises of liberty that are, by implication, false. The use of 'they' differentiates the narrator from the colonists who are lying to the prince and serves to emphasise her status as Oroonoko's ally. In the second sentence, the alliances start to shift. We are told that she was 'obliged, by some persons who feared a mutiny' to reassure Oroonoko of the colonists' good faith in order to prevent a potentially disastrous slave uprising (there is an echo here of the same anxiety expressed earlier in relation to the Surinam Indians). So it turns out that the narrator has no choice but to do these people's bidding. They remain an unidentified group ('some persons') whom she serves involuntarily – though the passage in brackets, about the danger of slave mutinies, sounds like an attempt at exoneration. By the time we reach the final sentence in the passage, the narrator's loyalties have completely changed. Now it is she who does not trust Oroonoko, and in this lack of trust she is at one with 'the country': the colonists are united in their fear and distrust of the prince. She asserts that a unanimous decision was taken to treat Oroonoko 'fairly', and then tells us that this involves curtailing his freedom of movement and surrounding him with attendants who are in reality spies. Behn's narrator here seems to be trying to erase or at least to minimise her complicity in the colonists' duplicitous and self-interested treatment of Oroonoko. She wants to pretend that she can reconcile her loyalty to the prince with her allegiance to the English colony. However, we see what she does not want to admit: that she cannot reconcile them, and that, ultimately, her loyalty to the colony wins out.

It is clear, then, that in this section of the narrative Behn's narrator appears deeply unreliable, and that this produces **irony** in the text, moments when we, as readers, perceive more about the situation than the fallible narrator does. Consider, as well, the following passage recounting the narrator's response to the slaves' attempt at escape:

> You must know, that when the news was brought on Monday morning, that Caesar had betaken himself to the woods and carried with him all the Negroes, we were possessed with extreme fear, which no persuasions could dissipate, that he would secure himself till night, and then, that he would come down and cut all our throats. This apprehension made all the females of us fly down the river to be secured, and while we were away, they acted this cruelty. For I suppose I had authority and interest enough there, had I suspected any such thing, to have prevented it, but we had not gone many leagues but the news overtook us that Caesar was taken and whipped like a common slave.
>
> (p. 68)

It would be hard to imagine a clearer indication of the strains in the narrator's allegiance to Oroonoko. On the one hand, he is the leader of a band of runaway slaves whom she and the other women in the colony regard with terror, fully expecting him to 'come down and cut all our throats'. On the other, he is a prince whose capture and whipping 'as a common slave' she condemns out of hand. The narrator is also keen to provide herself with an alibi: she could not prevent the whipping because she was absent, having fled down the river with the other women. Once again, she appears to be making excuses for her failure to protect Oroonoko. We may also be inclined to feel sceptical about her claim that, had she been present, her 'authority and interest' in the colony would have prevented the whipping, as this jars with her earlier statement that she had been 'obliged' by 'some persons' in the colony to calm Oroonoko's restiveness. Is she really as powerful as she makes out? Once again, Behn is using her narrator to engender irony, allowing our understanding of her relationship to Oroonoko and her position in the colony to exceed her own.

As Oroonoko's suffering intensifies, the narrator's outrage mounts but so does her distance from the protagonist. After his horrible ordeal in the woods, where he beheads Imoinda (to protect her from rape at the hands of the colonists) and then disembowels himself, a group of well-disposed colonists rescue him and return him to Parham.

The narrator is struck most by the loss of his beauty: 'he was now so altered that his face was like a death's head blacked over, nothing but teeth and eye-holes' (p. 75). She finds that 'the earthy smell about him was so strong' that she had to leave the sick room, being 'but sickly' herself, and 'very apt to fall into fits of dangerous illness upon any extraordinary melancholy' (p. 75). So she is absent from the scene of execution. Her mother and sister are present but are 'not suffered to save him' (p. 76). There is more than a little physical disgust in the narrator's description of Oroonoko's demise, reminiscent of that which emerges on the trip to the native Surinamese village.

Activity 7

How does Behn's construction of this difficult friendship between her narrator and her protagonist contribute to the meaning of the novel? Below is a passage from Jane Spencer's book, *The Rise of the Woman Novelist* (1986). Spencer discusses the point in the novel when the narrator flees from the slave uprising and so fails to protect Oroonoko. Please read her comments and then try to answer these two questions:

1   According to Spencer, what meanings emerge from this episode?

2   How plausible do you find her reading of this part of the novel?

> The trust between the royal slave and his 'Great Mistress' has been shattered by their racial differences, and yet her ignominious flight reveals similarities in the positions of the European woman and the enslaved African man. Like Oroonoko, who is given the outward respect due to a prince but kept from real power, the narrator is under the illusion that she has high status in the colony; but when it comes to a crisis the men are the real rulers, and being the daughter of a man who would have governed Surinam if he had lived does not help her. Ironically, she still seems to believe in her 'Authority and Interest' as she tells a story which reveals how illusory these were ....In *Oroonoko* the narrator's femininity is especially important because the similarities between the slave's and the woman's positions allow her her sympathetic insight into the hero's feelings at the same time as she creates a full sense of the difference of his race and culture.
>
> (Spencer, 1986, pp. 50–1)

Discussion

Here are my answers to the questions:

1   According to Spencer, the conduct of Behn's unreliable narrator serves to uncover the similar positions of the European woman and the enslaved African man in English colonial society. In Spencer's view, it is the female narrator's marginal position within colonial society that enables her to sympathise with the royal slave and which also allows Behn to disclose links between European women and African slaves. Although Oroonoko and the narrator share elite status, both are in reality powerless within a white, male-dominated colony which defines them ultimately in terms of related forms of inferiority: his race and her gender.

2   Spencer's reading considers the relationship between gender and race in the novel – another relevant context which we have not really explored in this chapter. But I would argue that its attempt to find textual traces of the shared experience of different oppressed groups tends to minimise the tensions that destabilise the narrator's friendship with the royal slave. I also find it hard to agree with the assertion that it is the narrator's femininity which fosters her sympathy for Oroonoko, as the text makes it clear that the prince has numerous male supporters as well. It is more persuasive to claim that the two characters are linked by their high rank, but this reveals little if anything about the way ordinary slaves and ordinary women experienced oppression in this period.

We have seen that Behn's narrator enthusiastically supports English colonisation, which ultimately takes priority over her loyalty to Oroonoko. In this way, she embodies a rather less optimistic relationship between European women and African slaves than Spencer suggests. Behn invites us to see her narrator as an upper-class Englishwoman who is, in many ways, well-meaning, painfully aware of how flawed and hypocritical Christian culture can be and more than capable of seeing nobility in colonial 'others'. Yet the author also repeatedly signals to her readers just how deep European identity goes; that is, the way in which economic self-interest, prejudice and unexamined assumptions about European culture work to undermine the narrator's efforts to establish bonds with non-Europeans. To focus on Behn's use of a first-person fallible narrator while reading *Oroonoko* is to recognise the extent to which the novel sheds light on European women's complicity and active participation in the colonial project.

Oroonoko's afterlife

Oroonoko's importance as an early modern travel narrative is attested to by its long and full afterlife. In 1696, Behn's colleague Thomas Southerne (1660–1746) adapted *Oroonoko* for the stage. His African prince is as Europeanised as Behn's, but in dramatising the novel he changed it in significant ways. Perhaps most notably, his Imoinda is white, and his representation of slavery and the slave trade is considerably more complacent than his predecessor's. Yet this complacency did not stop Southerne's *Oroonoko* from becoming an influential text in the eighteenth-century anti-slavery movement. The nineteenth-century abolitionist movement returned to Behn's original tale, enlisting it as a text whose capacity to foster emancipationist outrage rivalled Harriet Beecher Stowe's abolitionist novel *Uncle Tom's Cabin* (1852).

Behn's *Oroonoko* figured in the growing number of histories of slavery and the slave trade that appeared in the twentieth century, but it was in the 1980s that an explosion of interest in the novel took place. This was due in part to the feminist project of recovering women's writing which had been excluded from or marginalised by the literary canon – a project in which Behn figured prominently, early modern women writers having suffered the most thoroughgoing erasure from the literary record. The emergence of postcolonial criticism, with its interest in analysing the systems of values that supported colonialism and slavery, intensified interest in the novel and helped to guarantee it a central place in early modern literary studies. Outside the academy, *Oroonoko* continues to be enlisted into humanitarian causes. In 1999, the Royal Shakespeare Company commissioned the Nigerian novelist and playwright Biyi Bandele to produce a new dramatic version of the Oroonoko story. Bandele's play takes Behn's novel and Southerne's drama and makes them more palatable to a modern audience, stripping the protagonist of the European attributes with which both Behn and Southerne endowed him, foregrounding his African origins, and transforming the story of the royal slave into an unambiguous attack on slavery and racism.

Conclusion

In this chapter, we have been more interested in examining the rough edges of Behn's novel than in smoothing them out. We have looked at her contribution to early modern travel writing in terms of its treatment of the English female narrator's colonial encounter with African slaves and indigenous peoples. We have historicised the novel's depictions of both groups by looking at them in the context of other contemporary representations, a process that allowed us better to understand their conventionality and their distance from more negative models. The novel's portrayal of slavery emerged as profoundly ambiguous, as both critical and complacent. We found that one way of explaining this ambiguity was by reading *Oroonoko* in relation to its political contexts, considering the possibility that it is more concerned with the fall from power of James II than with colonisation and slavery. Throughout the chapter, we analysed the role of Behn's first-person narrator, who generates so many of the text's complexities and provides us with such a sobering portrait of the European woman's involvement in colonialism. All in all, we have discovered that this important early fictional representation of slavery and English colonial expansion, written by a woman who was also a royalist during a period of political crisis, looks subtly different when read in relation to different historical contexts.

References

Behn, A. (2003 [1688]) *Oroonoko* (ed. Janet Todd), London, Penguin.

Bellefond, N.V. de (1670) *A Relation of the Coasts of Africk called Guinee*, London, p. 133.

Brown, L. (1998) 'The romance of empire: Oroonoko and the trade in slaves' in Pacheco, A. (ed.) *Early Women Writers: 1600–1720*, Harlow, Longman, pp. 197–221.

Chatwin, B. (1980) *The Viceroy of Ouidah*, London, Jonathan Cape.

Defoe, D. (2001 [1719]) *Robinson Crusoe* (ed. J. Richetti), London, Penguin.

Godwyn, M. (1680) *The Negro's & Indians Advocate, Suing for their Submission to the Church*, London.

Goreau, A. (1980) *Reconstructing Aphra: A Social Biography of Aphra Behn*, New York, Dial Press.

Hughes, D. (2002) 'Race, gender, and scholarly practice: Aphra Behn's *Oroonoko*', *Essays in Criticism*, vol. 52, pp. 1–22.

Lipking, J. (2004) '"Others", slaves, and colonists in *Oroonoko*' in Hughes, D. and Todd, J. (eds) *The Cambridge Companion to Aphra Behn*, Cambridge, Cambridge University Press, pp. 166–87.

Montaigne, M. de (1958 [1580]) *Essays* (trans. and ed. J.M. Cohen), Harmondsworth, Penguin.

Pacheco, A. (1994) 'Royalism and honor in Aphra Behn's *Oroonoko*', *Studies in English Literature*, vol. 34, no. 3, pp. 491–506.

Purchas, S. (1905–7 [1625]) *Hakluytus Posthumus or Purchas His Pilgrimes*, 20 vols, Glasgow, J. MacLehose and Sons, vol. 6, p. 485.

Sherman, W.H. (2006) 'Stirrings and searchings (1500–1720)' in Hulme, P. and Youngs T. (eds) *The Cambridge Companion to Travel Writing*, Cambridge, Cambridge University Press, pp. 17–36.

Southerne, T. (1988 [1695]) *Oroonoko* in Jordan, R. and Love, H. (eds) *The Works of Thomas Southerne*, 2 vols, Oxford, Clarendon Press, vol. 2.

Spencer, J. (1986) *The Rise of the Woman Novelist: From Aphra Behn to Jane Austen*, Oxford, Basil Blackwell.

Starr, G.A. (1990) 'Aphra Behn and the genealogy of the man of feeling', *Modern Philology*, vol. 87, no. 4, pp. 362–72.

Further reading

Harris, T. (2007) *Revolution: The Great Crisis of the British Monarchy, 1685–1720*, London, Penguin.

Pincus, S. (2009) *1688: The First Modern Revolution*, New Haven and London, Yale University Press.

Rosenthal, L.J. (2004) '*Oroonoko*: reception, ideology and narrative strategy' in Hughes, D. and Todd, J. (eds) *The Cambridge Companion to Aphra Behn*, Cambridge, Cambridge University Press, pp. 151–65.

Spengemann, W.G. (1984) 'The earliest American novel: Aphra Behn's *Oroonoko*', *Nineteenth-Century Fiction*, vol. 32, no. 4, pp. 384–414.

Todd, J. (2000) *The Secret Life of Aphra Behn*, London, Pandora.

Chapter 6
Voltaire, *Candide, or Optimism*

Robert Fraser

Aims

This chapter will:

- undertake a close literary analysis of Voltaire's prose work *Candide*
- examine the function of both real and metaphorical travels in *Candide*
- explore the relationship between *Candide* and its literary and philosophical contexts.

Introduction

Two Parisian buildings encapsulate the life history and reputation of François-Marie Arouet (1694–1778), known to literature as 'Voltaire'. The first building, on the right bank of the River Seine, is the Bastille prison, the stoutest and most fearful jail maintained by what we now call the *ancien régime* in France. Demolished by a mob of rioters on the eve of the French Revolution in 1789, it had for centuries epitomised the social repression and power of a royalist church and state. The second building, on the left bank of the Seine, is the Pantheon, converted at the Revolution from a church to a secular temple to house the remains of France's most revered authors. Voltaire is notable for being an occupant of both buildings: he was briefly imprisoned in the first for his outspokenness in 1717–18, and his body was finally transferred to the second with great pomp and ceremony in 1791. Voltaire's progress from the one building to the other, and the resulting dramatic change in his national status, tells us much about him, and about France.

In this chapter, we will consider Voltaire's best-known text, *Candide, or Optimism* (1759). Voltaire was a remarkably prolific writer, and *Candide* appeared late in his career. He sometimes spoke of his '*rage d'écrire*', his mania for writing, and a legend exists to the effect that he dashed off *Candide* in three short days. But *Candide* was in fact a work of quite long gestation, lasting at least a year, during which its author responded to public events by tinkering extensively with his wording and structure.

In this chapter, we will study the physical and philosophical journeys of the main characters in *Candide* in the contexts of Voltaire's own life and intellectual world. We have referred throughout to the Penguin Classics (2005) edition, translated and edited by Theo Cuffe. You may want to read the entire text now, before starting work on this chapter.

Voltaire, his world and his book

Before we turn to the text of *Candide*, it is important to think about its place in Voltaire's life and career.

Activity 1

1   Read through the chronology of Voltaire's life at the beginning of your edition of *Candide* (pp. vii–x). Note down the most significant events in Voltaire's life, paying particular attention to those that made him so controversial in his day.

2   Read through 'A Note on the Text' in your edition of *Candide* (pp. xxxiv–xxxv) and summarise *Candide*'s publication history and its initial impact.

Discussion

I noted the following points:

1   Voltaire was born into an affluent family in 1694 and educated by the Jesuits at the Collège Louis-le-Grand. Voltaire became a reluctant law student to please his notary father, and was briefly a diplomat, but from 1715 he occupied himself exclusively with his writing, earning his first brief spell of imprisonment in 1717–18 for writing a **satire** against the Regent. After his release, he was sufficiently in favour to have three of his plays performed at King Louis XV's wedding (in 1725), but by 1726 he was in trouble again and had to flee to England. In England, he met King George I and many members of the literary and scientific elite. For much of the 1730s, Voltaire was in official disfavour and living in exile, but by the 1740s his fortunes recovered, and he became a major figure on the European stage: friend to Frederick of Prussia, protégé of Madame de Pompadour (a mistress of Louis XV), Royal Historiographer, and Member of the Academie Française.

By 1754, however, his star had plummeted again. He quarrelled with Frederick, was refused entry back into France, and was forced to wander around central Europe in a condition of virtual statelessness. He settled in Switzerland, and in 1756 published the first edition of his *Essai sur l'histoire générale et sur les moeurs et l'esprit de nations* (*Essay on General History and on the Manners and Spirit of the Nations*). He continued to participate in political intrigues: in 1757 he was involved in secret peace negotiations between Frederick of Prussia and Louis XV. In early 1759, *Candide* was published, and the French parliament impounded the loose sheets; even sympathetic Geneva briefly banned the book. Voltaire stayed in the relative safety of Switzerland for most of the rest of his life, producing literary works well into his eighties, notably his *Dictionnaire Philosophique Portatif* (*Philosophical Dictionary*) (1764). Never afraid of contention, he risked notoriety yet again in 1762–3 by challenging the French government over its treatment of Jean Calas, a Huguenot (French Protestant) merchant falsely accused of murdering his son for wanting to convert to Catholicism. He had one last triumph, when in 1778 he returned to Paris for the first time in twenty years to see his last play, the **tragedy** *Irène*, performed. While he was there he fell ill and died with the words 'For God's sake leave me in peace'. The words were somewhat typical of him, at the same time irreverent and strangely reverend, impatient yet longing for tranquillity.

2 *Candide* first appeared in late January 1759 when it was issued in three simultaneous editions of a thousand copies each in Paris, Geneva and Amsterdam. This strategy was motivated by the desire to sell as many copies as possible before it was pirated and by the fear of censorship. Both of these considerations were justified: over twenty further editions (including translations) were published in 1759 alone, and, in February 1759, authorities in Paris and Geneva seized copies of *Candide* in an attempt to suppress it. The title page bore the inscription 'from the German of Doctor Ralph', and Voltaire's name did not in fact appear. The authorship of the book, however, was an open secret; Voltaire only publicly admitted to being the author in 1768. A new edition was published in 1761, incorporating some rewriting and new passages, and it is this edition that we study in this chapter.

Voltaire was a writer of great comic gifts, with a vivid sense of pace. He would have wanted you to relish his wicked story, because he believed that literature should be entertaining, and also because his almost farcical effects are often part of his message. Indeed, it was for these reasons that in 1956 an acclaimed musical version of *Candide* was produced on Broadway, with lyrics by Lillian Hellman, Stephen Sondheim and others, and a score by Leonard Bernstein.

Activity 2

If you have not already done so, you should read *Candide* now. Read it through in one go, not pausing unduly over details or references you do not recognise. Most will become clear as we go along. What are the different ways in which the idea of journeying operates throughout the text?

Discussion

Several kinds of travel are implicated, either directly or indirectly, in this versatile book. Among them are the personal itineraries of Candide and Cunégonde (traced for you in Figure 1 in the 'Introduction to Part 2') and in your edition of *Candide*, pp. xxxviii–xxxix), as well as the digressions from the main track taken by minor figures such as Candide's servant Cacambo. Another less literal kind of journey is the intellectual journey that follows the succession of challenges to Pangloss's ideal of 'optimism'.

The routes and destinations of all of these interconnected travels constitute an absorbing mix of ideas and debate and I shall deal with each of the different journeys the text recounts. First, though, I will consider the literary and philosophical precursors available for Voltaire to emulate and/or satirise.

Literary and philosophical antecedents

The group of wanderers in *Candide* is spurred on by more than idle curiosity. Partly they seem to be driven by some sort of philosophical quest. If this is 'travel writing', then, it is travel writing in a particular tradition. To contextualise this, it is helpful to look at different ways in which travel writing has been used. Superficially, travel writing may seem to constitute a genre that is primarily descriptive and narrative. It tells the story – real or imagined – of a person or a group of persons voyaging from place to place. In practice, as you saw in the previous chapter on *Oroonoko*, no such writing is ever neutral, since travellers inevitably compare the worlds they are travelling through to their own world. Sometimes, this can lead travellers to make negative and even racist judgements; at other times, it can lead them to recognise flaws in their own society; and on yet other occasions, it can lead them to reflect upon 'the universality of the human condition'.

A marked philosophical strand thus runs through much early travel writing. Fifth-century BCE Greek historian Herodotus, for example, was much interested in the religion and morals of the countries through which he passed, and Pausanias' second-century CE account of his travels through Greece dwells on the belief systems and cults of every community he visits. In the early modern period, it was a comparatively straightforward development for writers schooled in such ancient travel accounts to turn the focus back to front. Instead of deriving insights into customs and beliefs from observations of different peoples and places, they started out with propositions concerning the social nature of humankind that they then tested by applying them to various real or, in many cases, imagined worlds. Utopian literature, which appeared for the first time in 1516 with the publication of *Utopia* (from the Greek *eu-topos*, 'good place', or alternatively *ou-topos*, 'no place') by the English scholar Thomas More (1478–1535), projected imaginary environments based upon political principles or ideals (in the case of More, religious toleration, the equal education of the sexes, and the absence of money and private property). A contrary tendency later arose whereby authors fantasised about worlds in which human ideals of a perfect society were shown to be ridiculous, or at least impracticable. In *Gulliver's Travels* (1726), by the Irish writer and cleric Jonathan Swift (1667–1745), a ship's surgeon, Lemuel Gulliver, is cast away on a succession of imaginary islands, in each of which facets of human stupidity or greed are exaggerated (or, in the case of Lilliput, scaled down) so that the disparity between observed conduct and the panaceas framed by philosophers or statesmen become blatantly apparent. A book such as *Gullivers Travels* thus constituted an anti-Utopian or 'dystopian' exercise that gave the lie to particular myths of human perfectability. Voltaire knew Swift's work well and had lived in England, the relative freedom of whose institutions – relative, that is, to the absolutist monarchy of the France of his own day – attracted him. To some extent, Voltaire is writing in a Swiftean satiric vein.

There is, of course, one major difference. Swift, like his near-contemporary Daniel Defoe in *Robinson Crusoe* (1719), drew on real-life accounts left by actual travellers, but the islands he describes do not correspond to any one recognisable location. Voltaire, on the other hand, was very interested in evoking the feel of the world as it is – its hard, inescapable reality. He thus situates the environments featured in *Candide* fairly specifically on the map. However lurid his **characterisations** of cities or countries, his Westphalia is based on the real country, his Lisbon is the real capital of a real country, his Paris and his Constantinople likewise. He thus draws on the existing or surviving memoirs of travellers far more directly than do either Defoe or Swift. When writing about South America, for example, he is conscious of, and mentions, the explorations of Guiana by Sir Walter Raleigh (1554–1618) (p. 46). (Raleigh's book, *The Discovery of Guiana* (1591) was itself a major source for the idea of El Dorado, which I will discuss later.) When his narrative moves to Turkey, he is also possibly aware of the (still unpublished, though unofficially circulating) letters from Constantinople written by Lady Wortley Montagu (1689–1762), an ambassador's wife and one of the few Westerners ever to have been allowed inside a seraglio, or harem.

There was a community of insight between France and England that manifests itself in *Candide*. A contemporaneous work, published in the same month as *Candide* (that is, in January 1759), was an English text close to it in structure and theme: *The History of Rasselas Prince of Abyssinia* (or *Rasselas* for short) by the writer and lexicographer Samuel Johnson (1709–1784). Johnson dashed off this small masterpiece in order to defray his mother's burial expenses (without himself attending the funeral). In it, a pampered young aristocrat from a fairly inexactly described 'Happy Valley' (in the vicinity of Ethiopia) is cast out to make his way in the great world beyond in the company of his sister and the philosopher Imlac. He finds there nothing but misery and heartache. Though Johnson regarded Voltaire as a notorious radical, sceptic and rake, resemblances of shape and viewpoint are apparent in these two peripatetic and philosophically inclined narratives.

The genre of *Candide*?

But what genre do these works belong to? The long eighteenth century was the first great period in the evolution of the 'novel', a genre of which Behn's *Oroonoko* might be seen as an early example. In France, the form was known as the 'roman' because of its roots in medieval romance; in England, it was known as the novel because it was, well, novel. According to strict definitions of the eighteenth-century novel, *Candide* does not entirely meet the generic requirements for the novel, or indeed for the novella (novel in miniature). In shape and thrust it is far closer to a fable or parable, since its meanings lie comparatively close to the surface, and little happens within it that is not designed to make a point in the ongoing argument. Voltaire had tried his hand at this sort of thing before, for example in his eastern tale *Zadig* in 1747. The term used by the French to classify this kind of exercise was '*une conte philosophique*', which translates roughly as 'a philosophical tale'. The same description goes for Johnson's *Rasselas*. Another literary category often associated with *Candide* is that of satire, which is writing that ridicules or mocks the failings of individuals, institutions or societies. As Voltaire allows his readers to draw their own conclusions, *Candide* should probably be classified as 'indirect satire', but this in no way diminishes the intensity of the ridicule and scorn Voltaire directs at the hypocrisies and iniquities of his day. Indeed, together with his contemporaries Swift, Johnson and the poet Alexander Pope (1688–1744), Voltaire contributes in no small way to the long eighteenth century's reputation as Europe's greatest period of satire.

Activity 3

The original title page (in a variety of fonts) reads: 'Candide or Optimism / Translated from the German of Doctor Ralph / With the additions found in the doctor's pocket when he died at Minden, in the year of grace 1759'. What expectations do the words on the title page generate?

Now reread the opening paragraph of Chapter 1 of *Candide* and consider how these expectations are sustained (or disrupted).

Discussion

The words on the title page give the impression that 'Candide, or Optimism' is a translation from German of a story by one 'Doctor Ralph'. The inventions of an original German text and a Doctor Ralph lend a quasi-objectivity to the text, and distance the narrator from Voltaire himself. However, if Voltaire's readers were attuned to the literary conventions of the day, they would have recognised the idea of a German original and the existence of a 'Doctor Ralph' as inventions, as part of the fiction. English readers would of course be reading a book (purportedly) translated from German to French that had (in fact) been translated from French to English! This playful element subverts the superficially earnest account of the young man Candide's personal history in the opening paragraph. The very first words themselves – 'Once upon a time' – suggest the beginning of a fairy tale, and the combination of absurd names (Monsieur the Baron von Thunder-ten-tronckh) and the ironic tone establish immediately a distinctive narrative voice. For example, the gossip of the older servants is the source for the belief that Candide was the illegitimate son of the Baron's sister and 'a kindly and honest gentleman of the neighbourhood' (p. 3). That the narrator describes Candide's (presumed) father so indulgently – and not as an adulterer or fornicator – suggests unworldly and naive qualities, qualities we soon discover also to be characteristic of Candide himself. From the outset, the reader is thus given very clear hints not to take at face value the narrator's version of events and his judgements of individuals, peoples and places.

Like Behn before him, Voltaire therefore makes extensive use of **literary irony**: 'the use of a naive or deluded hero or unreliable narrator, whose view of the world differs widely from the true circumstances recognised by the author or readers; literary irony thus flatters its readers' intelligence at the expense of a character (or fictional narrator)' (Baldick, 1990, p. 114). The account of Candide's travels and adventures by Voltaire's unreliable fictional narrator 'Doctor Ralph' does indeed differ widely from the 'true circumstances recognised by the author or readers', and much of the humour in *Candide* is derived from the ironic distance between the narrator's words and Voltaire's satirical attack on his society.

Pangloss's journey: from theory to fact

Voltaire's philosophical views – expressed in literary works like *Candide* and in philosophical works like his *Philosophical Dictionary* – were defined in opposition to the belief in 'Optimism' which dominated the philosophy of his day. (For some extracts from Voltaire's *Philosophical Dictionary*, see Appendix 3 at the back of your edition of *Candide*, in particular the entries '*Bien* (*Tout Est*): All Is Good' (pp. 109–14) and '*Chaînes des Evénements*: Chain of Events' (pp. 114–16).) *Candide* is overtly named after his adventurous, if naive, hero but it is its subtitle, 'Optimism', that announces its theme. The character of Candide's tutor Pangloss is the inexhaustible spokesman on behalf of 'Optimism', and all of the main characters in the course of their journeys test to the very limits Pangloss's creed. The character of Pangloss was Voltaire's exaggerated comic creation, but optimism in the condition of the world, and human prospects within it, could be found pretty well everywhere in the Europe of the mid-eighteenth century. For obvious reasons, it was more common among the rich than among the poor, men than women, the healthy rather than the sick, slave owners rather than slaves. 'Optimism' had distinct intellectual sources. In his *Philosophical Dictionary*, Voltaire finds its origins in *Characteristics of Men, Manners, Opinions, Times* (1711) by Anthony Ashley Cooper, Third Earl of Shaftesbury (1671–1713), who had speculated that benevolence was an instinct deeply embedded in human nature and quite consistent with self-interest. Since we all wished for one another's well-being, all that we needed to do was to follow our own inclinations and everything, and everybody, would be fine. The highest profile attained by the creed of optimism was its articulation by one of the greatest English poets of the age, Alexander Pope.

His *Essay on Man* is the supremely confident expression of this attitude, trumpeted forth as if from the console of some great organ.

On the continent, the principal exponents of philosophical optimism resided in Germany, where their thought was more systematic and thorough since it was connected with more technical philosophical fields, such as metaphysics (the study of the first principles of things) and epistemology (the study of the acquisition of knowledge). Gottfried Wilhelm Leibniz (1646–1716), pictured in Figure 6.1, for example, had argued the case from the nature of God. Since the creator was both omniscient (all knowing) and omnipotent (all powerful) and since he wished that his creatures should be happy, it followed of necessity that the world he had made was one that secured the most contentedness he could contrive. Leibniz did not deny that nasty things happened, or that people suffered; such a position would be ridiculous. But human beings were not omniscient (they had limited knowledge) and what appeared to them to be blemishes or setbacks could very well be part of the grand universal plan. Only God, with his serene overview, saw how.

This theory was not as barmy or anachronistic as it may now seem to some. In fact, it is one of the most frequently cited answers to two dilemmas theologians call 'The Problem of Evil' and 'The Problem of Pain' (see, for example, C.S. Lewis's popular book *The Problem of Pain* (2002 [1940])). Both pain and evil seem contradictory in a world supposedly overseen by a compassionate governor. In *Candide*, Voltaire repeatedly points this out. We should not, however, fall into the trap of regarding Voltaire as necessarily right, and Leibniz and his followers as necessarily wrong. The truth is that they were tackling the same issue from opposite ends of a spectrum. Leibniz was a rationalist philosopher. His approach might be characterised as arguing forward from certain assumptions: since God is perfect by definition, it follows that he can do no wrong. Voltaire's approach might be described as empirical: he used his experience of the world around him to draw certain conclusions about it. (These two approaches are sometimes referred to as *a priori* and *a posteriori* reasoning.)

Then in 1755 something occurred that rocked the sanguine belief in optimism entirely. On 1 November, at approximately 9.40 in the morning, a fissure some five metres wide opened up under the Atlantic Ocean, off the shoreline of the Portuguese capital Lisbon, extending right across the main area of the city. Buildings tottered and fell. It was All Saints' Day, and the churches were full of people attending mass; as

Figure 6.1   Bernhard Francke, portrait of Gottfried Wilhelm Leibniz, *c.*1700, oil on canvas, 81 x 66 cm, Herzog Anton Ulrich-Museum, Braunschweig. Photo: Herzog Anton Ulrich-Museum, Braunschweig.

the walls collapsed, they were crushed in their thousands. How could a benevolent and all-seeing deity possibly have ordained this? Outside people had been cooking their breakfasts on open fires in the cool autumn air; the quake overturned the fires which raged uncontrollably across town. A few minutes later, a violent tsunami swept in from the sea, drowning many of those who had not been crushed. Estimates of the dead varied wildly: the figure suggested has been as high as 100,000 (see Braun and Radner (2005)), though in the relevant episode in

Candide Voltaire mentions a total a little less than a third of that number. Much of the infrastructure of the city was also destroyed: most of its buildings had been pulverised. If you visit Lisbon today, you will find the only medieval buildings that survive are high up in the hills where the quake did not reach.

Figure 6.2 Unknown engraver, *Lisbon*, 1755, Museu da Cidade, Lisbon. Photo: Earthquake Engineering Research Center, University of California, Berkeley.

A further impact was on the philosophical calm that had reigned in European intellectual circles for close on half a century. Voltaire himself became rapidly convinced that a tragedy on this scale spelled the death-knell of the complacent certainties put about by disciples of Leibniz. The shock of the Lisbon Earthquake was compounded by the Seven Years War, which was triggered when Frederick of Prussia (Voltaire's one-time mentor) invaded Saxony. The war subsequently spread, first across the rest of Europe and then to North America and South Asia, where France and Britain were soon at loggerheads over their colonial possessions. Among Voltaire's well-born friends at the time was the Duchess of Saxe-Gotha, who went to the front line to observe the fighting. In one of the earliest battles, her son was killed. Voltaire reported in a letter that she carried on, 'crying "Whatever Is, Is Right" in her lamentable voice' (Voltaire, 2007 [1759], p. 144).

Activity 4

1   Read the concluding stanza of the first epistle from Alexander Pope's *An Essay on Man* (1733–4), reproduced below, and then summarise his argument in your own words.

> Cease then, nor ORDER Imperfection name:
> Our proper bliss depends on what we blame.
> Know thy own point: This kind, this due degree
> Of blindness, weakness, Heav'n bestows on thee.
> Submit – In this, or any other sphere,
> Secure to be as blest as thou canst bear:
> Safe in the hand of one disposing Pow'r,
> Or in the natal, or the mortal hour.
> All Nature is but Art, unknown to thee;
> All Chance, Direction, which thou canst not see;
> All Discord, Harmony, not understood;
> All partial Evil, universal Good:
> And, spite of Pride, in erring Reason's spite,
> One truth is clear, Whatever IS, IS RIGHT.

(Pope, 1966 [1733–4], pp. 45–6)

2   Reread Chapter 5 of *Candide*, and contrast Voltaire's views on 'optimism' with those of Pope (and Leibniz – as summarised above).

Discussion

1   For the first half of the eighteenth century, this stanza from Pope was something of a mantra for paid-up, fully believing optimists, regularly rolled out in articles, tracts and public speeches. Voltaire himself quoted Pope's axiom 'Whatever IS, IS RIGHT' ironically in the subtitle of his 1756 poem, 'The Lisbon Earthquake' (see the translation of the poem, by Tobias Smollett (1721–1771), in Appendix 2 of your edition of *Candide*, pp. 100–8). Pope, in this stanza, repeats the optimistic truism of his age that all evils afflicting individuals must be understood and accepted as ultimately part of a divine plan. For the suffering individual, the appropriate response is to 'Submit – in this or in any other sphere', since he or she is 'Safe in the hand of one disposing Pow'r' (God). Four lines of **antitheses** beginning with the word 'All' then dramatise the apparent contradiction between present and immediate ills and God's beneficence, culminating in the line 'All partial Evil, universal Good'. For Pope, the 'universal Good' is the

consolation that contains and transcends the particularities of 'partial Evil'. The argument is clinched in the final line, which insists upon the 'One truth' that is 'clear', namely that whatever unfolds in life – however unpleasant – ('What IS') is part of a benevolent divine plan ('IS RIGHT').

2   Chapter 5 of *Candide* (like Voltaire's entries in his *Philosophical Dictionary*) attacks the cosmic complacency, the thin optimism, expressed in Pope's lines. The weapon used is ridicule, a technique at which Voltaire is particularly adept. Leibniz's ideas are expressed by Candide's tutor Pangloss, and are repeatedly shown up as preposterous. When the virtuous Anabaptist is drowning, Pangloss restrains Candide from rescuing him, 'arguing that Lisbon harbour was built expressly so that this Anabaptist should one day drown in it [and] offering *a priori* proofs of this' (p. 13). Pangloss berates the sailor for looting the ruins of the city with the unctuous words, 'You are flouting the laws of universal reason, and this is hardly the time or the place' (p. 14), but is roundly rebuffed by the sailor, who parades his villainy unapologetically: 'four times I've trampled on the Cross; you've picked the wrong man, with your drivel about universal reason!' (p. 14). A third example of how Voltaire exposes the limitations of Pangloss's philosophy of optimism (and by extension Pope's and Leibniz's) is during the dinner after the earthquake, when he declares, in words echoing Pope's *An Essay on Man*, 'This is all for the best ... For if there is a volcano beneath Lisbon, then it cannot be anywhere else; for it is impossible for things to be elsewhere than where they are. For all is well' (p. 14). In the context of the devastation caused by the earthquake, Pangloss's parroting of Pope's and Leibniz's creed of optimism comes across as especially platitudinous and inadequate.

Was it possible for adherents of Pope or Leibniz to square the contradiction between the dispiriting events of the Lisbon Earthquake and the Seven Years War and the view that everything in the world was perfectly conceived? They provided several stock responses to this challenge. The first was an insistence on the Leibnizian philosophical axiom that, in the ultimate scheme of things, there exists a 'sufficient reason' for each and every event, fully able to account for even its unfortunate-seeming aspects. The second was the scientific view that all happenings are part of an inexorable web of 'cause and effect' which nothing can influence or divert. The third was the religious doctrine, advanced by the agent for the Roman Catholic Inquisition, that people are responsible for much that is wrong in the world because their nature has been corrupted since the time of Adam and Eve by so-called 'Original Sin'. People can choose to act as they wish, but their will – though technically 'free' – will inevitably cause them to act badly. It is clear from the mocking portrayal of Pangloss in *Candide* that Voltaire found none of these three responses remotely convincing.

Voltaire's attack on the ideas of Leibniz and Pope is not limited to matters of content: his very style of writing is an assault upon what he saw as their self-deluding optimism. Much has been written about Voltaire's style: its alacrity, its bounce, the speed of its transitions, and these qualities so appropriate for describing travel are put to good use in *Candide*. The title of *Candide* is principally taken from the name of its protagonist, but it applies equally well to its style. This is a book that pulls no punches, makes no effort to be civil, even rejoices in its earthy rudeness. It says it how it is. Voltaire's candour is therefore integral to his message. His target is not just the illusions fed by a particular school of philosophy, but the sort of moral dishonesty, present in most ages, that flinches away from the facts and pretties them up with mealy-mouthed, sociably acceptable persiflage. In eighteenth-century English there was a term for such well-meaning linguistic avoidance. It was called 'cant', a word that had its origin in the Italian verb for 'to sing', but which had come to mean the whining of a beggar or, by extension, all manner of humbug or sanctimonious waffling. For Voltaire, it was the enemy because it led people to deceive others, and often also to deceive themselves. His view was that to write or speak simply and directly is usually to write or speak well.

Cunégonde's journey: candour not cant

The unworldly Doctor Ralph is not the only narrator in *Candide*. There are three episodes in the novel recounted by women: Chapter 8 is narrated by Candide's beloved, Cunégonde, who retells the events of the opening chapters from her perspective; Chapters 11 and 12 are narrated by the old woman, who tells Cunégonde the story of her calamitous life; and the first part of Chapter 24 is narrated by Pacquette, who disabuses Candide of his perception that she is happy by describing her decline from serving maid to prostitute. In these episodes, told from a feminine perspective, Voltaire gives us history from the point of view of its victims. Whereas Doctor Ralph describes Pangloss's philosophy of optimism uncritically, and as readers alive to literary irony, we register that Voltaire is satirising the creed of Pope and Leibniz, in these three episodes, narrated by female characters, Pangloss's sanguine apathy is exposed as an overwhelmingly masculine delusion by the blunt facts of female subservience in a male-dominated society. In the 'Introduction' to your edition of *Candide*, Michael Wood describes Pacquette's story as 'another worst-of-all-possible worlds story' (p. xxv), and, indeed, all three women tell tales of spectacular suffering and misadventure, which are nonetheless lightened (although this might be a matter of taste) by their transparent absurdities and extravagant hyperbole.

The most important of the female characters in *Candide* is Cunégonde. In terms of the **plot**, much of Candide's journeying is in search of Cunégonde, but her name warns us that she is no princess in a fairy tale rescued by a brave prince, and nor is she a sentimental heroine in a conventional eighteenth-century novel. Cunégonde's name simultaneously derives from the chaste wife of Henry II, St Kunigunde, and compounds explicit sexual references, which are exploited throughout the novel for a variety of comic effects (see 'A Note on Names' in your edition of *Candide*, pp. xxxvi–xxxvii). Aside from its comic effects, her name also discloses Voltaire's concern in *Candide* to promote the quality of candour. Voltaire's reliance on associations conjured up by her name is in keeping with her own frankness about the body. Several other implications seem to be present: that what we commonly regard as beautiful may also be quite obscene, or that what we commonly regard as obscene may in fact be quite beautiful. The third suggestion is that, during the course of her tribulations, Cunégonde has sometimes been reduced to a sexual plaything.

Activity 5

Reread Chapter 8, 'Cunégonde's Story', and think about the style, tone and the way in which the tumultuous events are narrated. How much difference does it make that the narrator of this story is a woman?

Discussion

Chapter 8 constitutes a flashback. In other words, it retells the events of Chapters 2 to 7 from a different perspective, that of Cunégonde. As such, it inserts into the tale a feminine point of view at variance with, or at least complementary to, Doctor Ralph's main narrative. Cunégonde is recounting her story in Lisbon, which gives Voltaire a chance to portray the injustices meted out in this traditionalist Catholic society on four minorities: women, Protestants, intellectuals and Jews. Like the rest of the book, however, her narrative involves journeys, beginning in Westphalia where the assault on the Baron's castle is retold from the point of view of one of its female victims. Notice how much less blushing and embarrassed Cunégonde is than Candide: after she is rescued from being raped by the Bulgar soldier, for example, she concedes that she is physically attracted to her rescuer. Cunégonde recounts all of this with supreme honesty, and in this she expresses herself very much in the same spirit as Voltaire himself, who throughout the text utilises what the translator of your edition, Theo Cuffe, calls 'a new language of plain-speaking' (p. xxxiii). Cunégonde's candour is also directed at Voltaire's philosophical targets, and in direct contrast to Doctor Ralph, Cunégonde concludes from her awful experiences that Pangloss is utterly wrong: 'Pangloss deceived me cruelly, after all, when he told me that all is for the best in this world' (p. 21).

The contrast between Doctor Ralph's and Cunégonde's narrations can be further appreciated if we pause to examine more closely the translation of Cunégonde's story from the French. Cunégonde's straightforwardness is quite beyond the naive Candide: when he hears about the blow to her thigh delivered by her assailant, he tells her with a sort of flustered self-consciousness that one day he would very much like to inspect this wound, or rather the mark of the wound (p. 19). The French original is instructive, since both 'blow' (*coup*) and 'thigh' (*flanc*) are masculine nouns, whereas mark ('*marque*') is feminine. The gendered syntax makes it clear it is something feminine and intimate that Candide confusedly wishes to see. The next example is when Cunégonde declares that the Bulgar captain 'lost all his money and his taste for me' (p. 19). Theo Cuffe's translation is a little coy, since Voltaire's own wording says bluntly that he had grown 'disgusted' with her. The fickleness and also the potential cruelty of physical desire are the point here. He then sells her to 'a Jew named Don Issacar' (p. 19), whose primary characteristic is seen as being his race. Again, Voltaire's directness wins through: anti-Semitism in the Europe of his day was a fact of life, and he does not beat about the bush in conjuring it up. In fact, he exploits it to bring out a double iniquity: when the local Grand Inquisitor finds out that a Jew is Cunégonde's keeper, he reprimands her by 'pointing out how far beneath my rank it was to be the chattel of an Israelite' (p. 20). The French word here is '*rang*', which means both someone's rank or social class, and a rung on a ladder. Voltaire is indicating an older idea: the ladder of the great chain of being which, in the Renaissance period, was thought to support all human hierarchies. The ladder reached down from God to the lowliest pebble, but women and Jews were both allotted very low rungs at the human level.

The Inquisitor is hinting to Cunégonde that if she consorts with him, she will move up a rung or two. Voltaire then mockingly endorses this view by making Cunégonde, who is temporarily at the mercy of both gentlemen, refer to the Inquisitor as 'His Eminence' (p. 20), though the French text actually gives his exact title as 'Monsignor'. Both of these accolades are reserved for the most senior clerics in the Roman Catholic Church, such as cardinals. The Inquisitor is probably entitled to neither of them. Cunégonde is now caught between the devil and the deep blue sea, but with frank realism she realises that her allure depends upon her unavailability. The Bulgar captain, who once enjoyed her favours, soon came to despise her. She is not going to make the same mistake with either the Jewish merchant or the priestly dignitary, so she keeps both of them dangling.

Activity 6

In order to appreciate the range of Voltaire's tone, read through the following passages again. Make some notes about how the tone differs in the two passages before reading the discussion.

1   The old woman's description of herself as a girl suffering terrible ordeals in Morocco, and then coming to consciousness with an Italian lying on top of her (Chapter 11, pp. 27–8).

2   Candide's encounter with the Dutch slave in Surinam (Chapter 19, pp. 51–2).

Discussion

1   In the old woman's story, the man lying on top of her had been an Italian castrato (a male singer castrated at puberty to preserve the quality of his treble voice into adulthood). In the eighteenth century, such professional singers were much prized in the opera houses of Naples: they earned considerable sums and were very popular with women. However, in this passage, Voltaire is not interested in expressing any sympathy for the castrato, or any such complexities; he is only concerned to exploit the comic potential of the scene, and to enjoy the ridiculousness of the poor man's predicament. He therefore has him complaining over and over again: 'O che sciagura d'essere senza conglione!' ('Ah, what a fate to be without balls!') (p. 25). Frankness and farce could not go much farther. Voltaire's prevailing tone here is comic, even at times consciously farcical.

2   Voltaire's tone in the second passage is rather different. The slave recounts his sufferings, from his mother selling him on the coast of Guinea, to his Dutch master in Surinam cutting off his right hand and left leg. The slave's African mother and his Dutch owner both benefit by

187

Figure 6.3   Pierre Charles Baquoy, after Jean-Michel Moreau, 'C'est à ce prix que vous mangez du sucre en Europe' ('It is the price we pay for the sugar you eat in Europe'), 1787, engraving, from Voltaire's *Candide*, in *Oeuvres Completes* (1784–9), Kehl, Germany, Beaumarchais. Photo: akg-images.

his enslavement, but the slave declares himself to be a thousand times more miserable than dogs, monkeys and parrots. The impact of the encounter with the slave upon Candide is profound, as he cries: 'Oh Pangloss! This is one abomination you could not have anticipated, and I fear it has finally done for me: I am giving up on your optimism after all' (p. 52). (It is worth recalling that Voltaire introduced this interlude at a late stage in the composition of the book specifically to make his feelings about the slave trade clear.) Voltaire's tone here is far from comic; instead his satire assumes a serious edge in order to express unequivocally how much he abominates slavery.

In order for such a counterblast to the apathy of optimism to work, it must be narrated candidly, with no avoidance of unpleasant facts. The female narrators, as well as the Dutch slave in Surinam, are not in the slightest bit delicate when it comes to telling people about the cruelties, perversities and humiliations that have been their lot. They tell their histories throughout with unflinching honesty and candour.

Cacambo's journey: the best of impossible worlds

Cacambo accompanies Candide upon most of his journeys, but the section I want to focus upon in particular is their sojourn in El Dorado, where Cacambo translates all the exchanges with El Dorado's inhabitants for Candide. The word 'El Dorado' literally means 'The Man of Gold'. By the sixteenth century, however, it had come to refer to something else: a legendary country in the far hinterland of South America where gold was as common as any other rock and where, as a consequence, it could be carried off with impunity to reward and enrich its despoilers. Of course, we now know this place to have been utterly mythical and its seekers to have been deluded. But it is not difficult to see how this opulent fairyland had welled up from the Western imagination. In the sixteenth and seventeenth centuries, many galleons laden with gold artefacts had made their way eastwards across the Atlantic towards Spain or Portugal, the main participants in this lucrative quest, leading people to suppose there was an ultimate source for all of this booty. And so men hacked their way through forests and up mountain ranges, laying waste to several complex civilisations in the process – the Inca culture in Peru, the Aztec culture in Mexico – in order to find it. And, in the eighteenth century, the myth was not quite dead.

Activity 7

Reread Chapter 18, 'What they saw in the land of Eldorado', paying particular attention to the interview with the 172-year-old citizen of El Dorado, the reception at court, and Candide and Cacambo's decision to leave the country and return to Europe.

Two related contradictions seem to be present throughout this passage. First, why in a work dedicated to the proposition that perfection is impossible should Voltaire have inserted an episode set in an environment that seemingly satisfies the most luxurious dreams of most people? Second, why, having established this haven of affluence, should he cause his footsore travellers to head back to the continent that caused most of their dissatisfaction in the first place? Jot down your thoughts in answer to these questions before reading the discussion.

Discussion

The chapter amounts to a critique of value in which the ethical and material standards of the visitors are played off against those of their hosts. Voltaire works this trick from the very beginning, contrasting the perceptions of the boggle-eyed tourists to those of the contented, if slightly blasé, natives. The old man lives in a 'modest house', the door of which is 'merely of silver and the panelling in the apartment merely of gold' (p. 46). This sounds like irony, but it is only so in the eyes of the reader and of Candide and Cacambo. To the old man, the house really is modest, the effect of its decor, to which he is quite habituated, one of 'bare simplicity' (p. 46). Those who live in this earthly Paradise are quite unaware of this fact, though they are also conscious of the unseemly and irrational effects that rumours of their land have had on the minds of outsiders. They regard these dreams with muted contempt, because in their country what is priceless to others is so common as to be without value to the inhabitants. The effect from the reader's point of view is to bring into question the whole subject of value.

With regard to the second apparent contradiction, Candide and Cacambo are subliminally aware of the unreality of the place they have stumbled upon and are soon anxious to leave it. They head for the smoke and the stress. But there is another, far more cynical, reason for their departure. The untold wealth around them is as valueless to them as it is to the indigenous people, as long as it remains where it is. If, like the Spanish before them, they can arrange to take it away, the situation would be very different. Then the value system beyond El Dorado will swing back into operation: Candide declares that if they leave El Dorado, 'we shall be richer than all the kings put together, we shall no longer have Inquisitors to fear, and we shall easily rescue Cunégonde' (p. 49).

According to the narrator, Cacambo was persuaded by Candide's argument, and so they arranged to have some sheep loaded up with gold, and are winched across the mountains to the world beyond.

Where does this leave the expectations of those raised on the philosophy of Leibniz, or his disciple Pangloss? The answer is that it again subjects such teaching to a thoroughgoing critique, with surprising results. The implication of Candide's and Cacambo's experience of El Dorado is that there are plenty of worlds that are better; they are just unrealisable. This then is Utopia; simultaneously a perfect and a non-existent place.

Candide's journey: governed by fate or free will?

Voltaire never travelled outside Europe, but *Candide* was not his first work set in an imagined East, nor was the Dervish his first attempt to portray an Eastern philosopher. In 1747, he had published *Zadig, or Destiny*. Its setting was ancient Babylon, and its protagonist was the philosopher Zadig, who, faced with an inexorable tyranny (such as ancient Babylon was always supposed to have been), ends by developing a questioning attitude to absolute authority and to fate. It is no coincidence that both Zadig and Candide have as subtitles abstract terms that also feature in Voltaire's *Philosophical Dictionary*. Dictionaries of all sorts were an important mode of information-gathering and discussion during the Enlightenment (a term used to describe an intellectual movement of the seventeenth and eighteenth centuries), one of whose facets was a strenuous questioning of received religious, social and political beliefs. In his introduction to *Candide*, Michael Wood remarks that Voltaire's *Philosophical Dictionary* is in effect a companion volume (p. 109).

Activity 8

Read Voltaire's entry on 'Destin: Fate' in his *Philosophical Dictionary* and note down its main points, commenting also on the tone. This entry is reproduced in Appendix 3 of your edition of *Candide* (pp. 116–19).

Discussion

Obedient to the dictionary convention of beginning with classical precedents, Voltaire opens his entry with a discussion of how Homer understood the meaning of fate, but his tone is far from deferential: Homer, he notes, 'is often prodigal in his poem with quite contrary ideas, as was permitted in antiquity' (p. 117). Modern philosophers, he continues, agree that 'all events are governed by immutable laws' (p. 117), and he proceeds to give several examples of how the strict application of this axiom leads to absurd conclusions (a rhetorical ploy known as *reductio ad absurdum*). With heavy irony, he then discloses his own view by quoting first unnamed 'idiots', who say that 'My doctor saved my aunt from a fatal illness, he made her live ten years longer' (pp. 117–18), and then one of the 'other idiots', the Roman satirist Juvenal, who (in Voltaire's translation) argues, 'Fortune is nothing; it is adored in vain. Prudence is the only god to whom we should pray' (p. 118, footnote 9). Voltaire does not stop at the ironic use of the abusive term 'idiots' to reveal his own beliefs; his irony extends to all the authorities he cites in his entry. If there is a pattern, it is that conventionally acclaimed authorities such as 'profound statesmen' and 'the philosopher' (p. 118) produce arguments at odds with Voltaire's ideas, whereas the conventionally disregarded opinions of 'idiots' (pp. 117–18) and 'a peasant' (p. 118) give expression to arguments in accord with Voltaire's views. Voltaire concludes the entry by insisting that it is 'our fate to be subject to prejudices and to passions' (p. 119) and applies this with a playful edge to himself and his readers: 'we are both equally foolish, equally the playthings of fate. Your nature is to do evil, mine is to love the truth and to publish in spite of you' (p. 119).

It is significant that Candide and his band of travellers conclude their journeys in Turkey, a region still dominated by the declining Ottoman Empire, widely and not entirely inaccurately supposed to be despotic. One of the most deeply rooted perceptions present in the eighteenth-century European mind was that a stubborn belief in, and quiescence before, fate or destiny was a characteristic of the peoples of the 'Orient'. In the minds of Voltaire and his contemporaries, such despotic regimes in such places were aided and abetted by the inherent fatalism of the East. The Turkish people, according to this interpretation, were oppressed largely because they believed in fate, and thus held their subjection to be inevitable. The Palestinian critic Edward Said argues in his well-known study *Orientalism* (1978) that during the centuries when the cultures of the West had predatory designs on the lands of the East, a belief in oriental passivity and fatalism served as a useful adjunct to these plans of acquisition.

Peoples who were temperamentally pessimistic were, it was inferred, easily dominated, by their own rulers or by outsiders. In the West, it was supposed, men and women were more likely to believe in freedom of choice and were therefore more inclined to resist tyranny.

Activity 9

Reread Chapter 30, 'Conclusion', paying particular attention to:

1   the characterisation of the Dervish and his philosophy

2   the characterisation of the old man and his philosophy

3   the ultimate fate of Pangloss and his arguments.

What do these final pages tell us about Voltaire's own ideas about free will and fate?

Discussion

1   Voltaire's attitude here seems to me to be one of thoroughgoing relativism. The Dervish-philosopher is 'great', but mainly in the eyes of his disciples. He is quite detached from the world and advises Candide and his band to withdraw from the world too: in reply to Pangloss's question 'So what must we do?', he says, 'Keep your mouth shut' (p. 92). The interview concludes with the Dervish-philosopher slamming the door in Pangloss's face, when the latter proposes to discuss the relative merits of freedom and destiny.

2   The old man on the farm also expresses a detached attitude towards the machinations of powerful people in the big city: 'I never enquire about what goes on in Constantinople' (p. 92), he declares. But if both these machinations and his indifference to them are predestined, who are Candide and Pangloss to object? As a matter of fact, they do not object, but retire to their own garden and do likewise.

3   Pangloss predictably considers everything that has happened to be confirmation of his creed, even though the disappointments he and his companions have endured contradict it. Pangloss's last statement is a triumphant re-assertion of his belief system to which he has remained true through all manner of vicissitudes and adversity. But notice that Candide makes no attempt to contradict him; instead, he remarks 'That is well said', before going on to express his own hard-won pragmatic nostrum, 'but we must cultivate our garden' (p. 94).

In the last chapter of *Candide*, Voltaire is therefore trying to see the idea of destiny from several points of view. These include not only different schools of philosophy, but also the perspectives on this common problem adopted by different cultures, Eastern and Western. Hence travel writing and the philosophical tale come together – the argument travels with the story. Have they then succumbed to Eastern fatalism? Have Candide and his companions found minimal fulfilment at last, or have they simply stopped trying, something that Voltaire himself never did? These are paradoxes that Voltaire, I think, quite deliberately refrains from solving for us. As Voltaire very well knows, you cannot have it both ways; you cannot believe in freedom and fate at the same time. Or can you?

In the face of all of these bewildering contradictions, Candide's recommendation that he and his friends cultivate their own private patch or garden may seem like a shrug in the face of the difficulties, as well as a gesture of complicity with the attitudes of the old man on the farm. But it is a lot more and other than this. We should not ignore the possibility that, at a practical, salutary level, Voltaire was commending gardening as a therapeutic solace. Gardens are pleasant places, and Voltaire was fond of his own. Another world very familiar to Voltaire, which is described in *Candide* with much less affection, is that of books and publishing. Recall that Candide had taken sympathy on Martin because he had been 'a poor scholar who had worked ten years for the publishing houses of Amsterdam [and] there was no occupation in the world which could more disgust a man' (p. 55). This, of course, is one of Voltaire's many in-jokes, in this case at the expense of a print trade on the services of which he had been dependent for much of his life. For Voltaire, the candid response, it seems, is to work or sit in your garden, with a book or without one.

References

Cooper, A.A., Third Earl of Shaftesbury (2001 [1711]) *Characteristics of Men, Manners, Opinions, Times* (ed. D.D. Uyl), 3 vols, New York, Liberty Fund.

Baldick, C. (1990) *Concise Dictionary of Literary Terms*, Oxford, Oxford University Press.

Braun, T.E.D. and Radner, J.B. (eds) (2005) *The Lisbon Earthquake of 1755: Representations and Reactions*, Oxford, Voltaire Foundation.

Defoe, D. (2001 [1719]) *Robinson Crusoe* (ed. J. Richetti), Harmondsworth, Penguin.

Herodotus (2004 [fifth century BCE]) *The Histories* (trans. A. de Selincourt and revised by J. Marincola), Harmondsworth, Penguin Classics.

Johnson, S. (2009 [1759]) *The History of Rasselas, Prince of Abissinia* (ed. T. Keymer), Oxford World's Classics, Oxford, Oxford University Press.

Leibniz, G. (1951) *Selections* (ed. P.P. Wiener), New York, Scribners Modern Student's Library.

Lewis, C.S. (2002 [1940]) *The Problem of Pain*, London, Harper Collins.

Montagu, M.W. (1986) *Selected Letters* (ed. I. Grundy), Harmondsworth, Penguin.

More, T. (2004 [1516]) *Utopia* (trans. and ed. P. Turner), Harmondsworth, Penguin Classics.

Naipaul, V.S. (1969) *The Loss of El Dorado: A History*, Harmondsworth, Penguin.

Pausanias (1971 [second century CE]) *Description of Greece* (trans. P. Levi), Harmondsworth, Penguin.

Pope, A. (1966 [1733–4]) *An Essay on Man* in *An Essay on Man; Epistle to Dr. Arbuthnot* (ed. A. Trott and M. Axford), London, Macmillan.

Said, E. (1979) *Orientalism*, New York, Vintage.

Swift, J. (2003 [1726]) *Gulliver's Travels* (ed. R. DeMaria), Harmondsworth, Penguin.

Voltaire (2005 [1759]) *Candide, or Optimism* (trans. and ed. T. Cuffe, with an introduction by M. Wood), Harmondsworth, Penguin.

Voltaire (2006 [1747]) *Zadig or L'Ingenu* (ed. J. Butt), Harmondsworth, Penguin.

Voltaire (2007 [1759]) *Candide ou l'Optimisme* (ed. Y. Bomati), Paris, Petits Classiques Larousse.

Yeazell, R.B. (2000) *Harems of the Mind: Passages of Western Art and Literature*, New Haven and London, Yale University Press.

Further reading

Naipaul, V.S. (1969) *The Loss of El Dorado: A History*, Harmondsworth, Penguin.

Syms, L.C. (2009) *Selected Letters of Voltaire*, London, Bibliobazaar.

Voltaire (2003 [1733]) *Letters on England*, Harmonsdworth, Penguin.

Voltaire (2004) *Philosophical Dictionary* (trans. T. Besterman), Harmondsworth, Penguin.

Yeazell, R.B. (2000) *Harems of the Mind: Passages of Western Art and Literature*, New Haven and London, Yale University Press.

Chapter 7
The narrative of James Albert Ukawsaw Gronniosaw

David Johnson

Aims

This chapter will:

- analyse the physical and spiritual journeys described in Ukawsaw Gronniosaw's autobiography

- locate Gronniosaw's text in the contexts of Christian theology, pre-colonial West Africa and Atlantic slavery

- contrast Gronniosaw's descriptions of the 'middle passage' with those of Hannah More, Olaudah Equiano and James Stanfield.

Introduction

Unlike the fictional travels of Oroonoko and Candide, *A Narrative of the Most Remarkable Particulars in the Life of James Albert Ukawsaw Gronniosaw, An African Prince, Written by Himself* (which I will refer to in this chapter as *A Narrative*) describes the journeys of an actual historical figure: the one-time African slave Gronniosaw. Recounted via an amanuensis (an 1809 edition suggests this was the abolitionist Hannah More (1745–1833)), Gronniosaw in this short book looks back over a peripatetic and eventful life. *A Narrative* was first published in Bath in about 1770 and went through nineteen more editions before Britain's emancipation of the slaves in 1834. In this chapter, we will analyse the first edition of Gronniosaw's *A Narrative* and focus in particular on the narrator's many journeys, not only his physical travels (from Africa to the Americas to Europe), but also his spiritual journey from 'heathen African' to 'redeemed Christian'.

The chapter begins by considering the text of Gronniosaw's travels, analysing the details of his physical and spiritual journeys, and drawing preliminary conclusions about how he represents himself and his world in his writings. The balance of the chapter then proceeds to consider the contexts framing Gronniosaw's writings, namely:

- The cultural context – specifically, the religious context. Gronniosaw's text belongs to the genre of the Christian conversion narrative. In order to understand the genre and its **ideology**, I discuss the influence of the writings of Hannah More, John Bunyan (1628–1688) and Richard Baxter (1615–1691).

- The historical context. The transporting of slaves from Africa to the Americas was the basis of Britain's economy in the eighteenth century. Accordingly, we examine Gronniosaw's text in relation to two connected contexts:

  1   The African society of Gronniosaw's childhood.

  2   Gronniosaw's journey across the Atlantic to the Americas, a journey known as 'the middle passage'. We expand upon Gronniosaw's description of the middle passage by discussing other factual descriptions of this journey, by the slave Olaudah Equiano (*c.*1745–1797) and by the Irish sailor James Field Stanfield (*c.*1750–1824), as well as the

fictitious version contained in Hannah More's poem 'The Sorrows of Yamba; or, The Negro Woman's Lamentation' (1795).

All of the required reading associated with this chapter can be found at the back of this part of the book in 'Readings for Part 2'.

The text

To familiarise ourselves with Gronniosaw's *A Narrative*, we need to begin by establishing the chronology and itinerary of Gronniosaw's travels.

Activity 1

Read Gronniosaw's *A Narrative*, which you will find reprinted as Reading 7.1 at the back of this part of the book. Read it quite quickly and in its entirety. As you read, list 'the Most Remarkable Particulars', that is, the key dates and destinations of his journeys. Refer to the footnotes to the reading to supplement your summary. You could also look back to Figure 1 in the 'Introduction to Part 2', which includes the route of Gronniosaw's journey.

Discussion

The dates and destinations of Gronniosaw's many journeys that I noted are:

1   Gronniosaw was born in the kingdom of Bornu (also spelled Borno) in about 1710. The 'Preface', written by W. Shirley, tells us that Gronniosaw was sixty in 1770, when *A Narrative* was published, which gives us his approximate date of birth.

2   When he was about fifteen (around 1725), Gronniosaw was duped by a travelling merchant into joining up with him and undertaking the long journey to the Gold Coast. When they arrived at the coast (probably Fort Elmina), Gronniosaw was sold as a slave to a Dutch sea captain.

3   Gronniosaw's next journey was to cross the Atlantic Ocean for Barbados.

4   In Barbados, Gronniosaw was soon sold again, this time for fifty dollars to a young gentleman called Vanhorn, who transported him to New York to work as a domestic slave.

5   Gronniosaw was then sold for fifty pounds to the Dutch minister 'Mr Freelandhouse' (Frelinghuysen). He remained with him and his

family in the Raritan Valley of New England for about thirty years (from about 1726 to 1754, that is, from the age of sixteen to forty-four).

6   Gronniosaw is vague as to how he earned his livelihood in the years immediately after he left the Frelinghuysen family but, when he fell into debt, he joined up as a privateer on British ships plundering French craft in the Caribbean in the early years of the Seven Years War (the late 1750s).

7   Returning to New York, he worked as a servant for a merchant called Dunscum and then, when he was in his late forties or early fifties, he joined the Royal Navy and fought in the concluding battles of the Seven Years War.

8   After his demobilisation, Gronniosaw undertook his next major journey: from the Americas to Europe, travelling first to Spain and then on to England. Gronniosaw arrived in Portsmouth in 1762 or 1763, when he was in his fifties.

9   From Portsmouth, Gronniosaw travelled to London, where he met his future wife, Betty, who was a weaver. Instead of remaining in London, however, Gronniosaw travelled to Amsterdam, where he worked for a year as a butler before returning to London.

10 Unsettled by the lack of employment and by the 1765 weavers' riots in London, Gronniosaw and Betty moved first to Colchester and then to Norwich in search of work.

11 The final journey in *A Narrative* is from Norwich to Kidderminster, where Gronniosaw was living when, at the age of sixty, he recounted his life story.

By any standards, Gronniosaw's travels were extensive, but the many gaps and silences in *A Narrative* regarding the geographical and chronological details of his journeys suggest that he was at least as concerned to communicate to his readers the details of his spiritual journey.

Having established the bare facts and dates of Gronniosaw's *A Narrative*, we turn now to analyse what kind of narrator he is. You will recall how in Chapter 5 on *Oroonoko* you focused on Behn's narrative technique, and in particular on the qualities of the novel's narrator. In non-fictional texts like Gronniosaw's autobiography, it is just as important to register how the narrator is constructed.

Activity 2

Reread the first five paragraphs of *A Narrative* under the heading 'An account of James Albert, &c.' (pp. 264–8). Take it more slowly this time. Circle every use of first-person pronouns ('I'/'me'/'we'/'us') and sum up how Gronniosaw-the-narrator represents himself in the text.

Discussion

You will have circled many more instances of the first-person singular form ('I'/'me') than of the first-person plural form ('we'/'us'), which conveys the strong sense that *A Narrative* is the autobiography of an individual rather than the memoir of a community. Looking back on his life from the age of sixty, Gronniosaw describes his younger self as curious, naive and well-intentioned, but also solitary, melancholy and prone to depression. He claims from an early age to have yearned inchoately for a monotheistic spiritual universe:

> I had, from my infancy, a curious turn of mind; was more grave and reserved, in my disposition, than either of my brothers and sisters … I was, at times, very unhappy in myself: It being strongly impressed on my mind that there was some GREAT MAN of power which resided above the sun, moon and stars, the objects of our worship … I often raised my hand to heaven, and asked [my mother] who lived there? Was much dissatisfied when she told me the sun, moon and stars, being persuaded, in my own mind, that there must be some SUPERIOR POWER.
>
> (p. 265)

Gronniosaw also makes much of his royal birth, and of the fact that in Africa he enjoyed a life of material privilege, but this does not diminish the urgency of his quest for spiritual truths inaccessible in Africa. Intrinsic to Gronniosaw's Christian impulses and virtues is his life-long sense of isolation within a sinful world. He describes the painful experience of being singled out for abuse by his peers: as a consequence of his great curiosity, his brothers and sisters disliked him, 'as they supposed that I was either foolish or insane' (p. 265), and when he contemplates leaving Bornu for the Gold Coast with the merchant, he repeats that his 'brothers and sisters despised me … even my servants slighted me, and disregarded all I said to them' (p. 267). His only ally was his albino sister, Logwy.

The critic Henry Louis Gates Jr argues that, from the outset of
A Narrative, Gronniosaw 'represents himself as an ebony admixture of
Oroonoko and the Lord's questing Pilgrim' (Gates, 1988, p. 133). The
unworldly and trusting qualities Gronniosaw-the-narrator establishes in
the opening paragraphs remain to the fore in the balance of *A
Narrative*. There are many examples. When he repeats to his young
white mistress the old slave Ned's warning that swearing leads directly
to the Devil, he notes that she 'was not angry with me, but rather
diverted at my simplicity' (p. 271). A second example is the theft of his
nineteen pounds by the Portsmouth landlady, which he regrets not so
much for the loss of the money as for his failure to find any worthy
Christians in England: 'Still I did not mind my loss in the least; all that
grieved me was, that I had been disappointed in finding some Christian
friends' (p. 281). Through the telling of short anecdotes from his life
story, Gronniosaw indirectly declares his virtues. His compassion is
evident in the story from his privateer days of the 'very amiable'
(p. 278) young gentleman who was captured, mistreated and later killed:
'he was so thankful and pretty in his manner that my heart bled for
him' (p. 278). His charitableness (even to his own detriment) is evident
in his description of his visits with Betty to listen to the minister Dr
Gifford: 'I had always a propensity to relieve every object in distress as
far as I was able' (p. 282). Gronniosaw also repeatedly emphasises his
capacities as a good and loyal servant. A succession of benevolent white
men rescue him from destitution – the Dutch slave captain, Vanhorn,
Frelinghuysen, Dunscum, Handbarrar, Daniel, Gurdney, Watson – and
he repays their kindnesses with unwavering loyalty. By contrast, he is
ambiguous, to say the least, about his relationships with his fellow
slaves, sailors or even simply other poor people. When he was a slave,
he prefaces the story of the jealous maid hiding a fork in order to get
him into trouble by observing: 'The servants were all jealous, and
envied me the regard, and favour shewn me by my master and mistress'
(p. 273). When he was a sailor, he did not form any collective bond
with his fellow crew; on the contrary, he records, 'I met with many
enemies, and much persecution, among the sailors' (p. 278). When he
was among England's poorer classes, he again found himself alone and
surrounded by enemies: in Portsmouth, he concluded that 'I was got
among bad people, who defrauded me of my money and watch'
(p. 280), and, in Norwich, his initial success in making money from
chopping chaff was soon reversed when '[m]any of the inferior people
were envious and ill-natur'd … and worked under price on purpose to
get my business from me' (pp. 288–9). In his own terms, Gronniosaw

therefore stands over and again as the righteous individual beset by hordes of the ignorant, the desperate and the ungodly. One final quality Gronniosaw demonstrates in abundance is his remarkable resourcefulness. He himself makes no great claims to this quality, preferring to give God's guiding hand the credit for his survival, but nonetheless his own agency in overcoming extraordinary difficulties is certainly apparent.

Although Gronniosaw-the-narrator is constant in that he retains these virtuous qualities throughout his life, he does undergo important spiritual changes in the course of *A Narrative*, and these changes are described in the metaphor of a journey.

Activity 3

Reread 'The Preface to the Reader', by W. Shirley (the Reverend Walter Shirley) at the beginning of *A Narrative*. Consider the language used to describe Gronniosaw's life.

Discussion

The dominant metaphor running through Shirley's 'Preface' is of a journey from darkness to light. In Gronniosaw's pre-Christian African phase, Shirley asserts that he was 'born under every outward disadvantage, and in the regions of the grossest darkness and ignorance' (p. 263). Shirley argues that God 'brings [Africans] to the means of spiritual information, gradually opens to their view the light of his truth' (p. 263); the young Gronniosaw's inarticulate sense of a Being superior to the sun, moon and stars confirms God's mysterious workings. In Gronniosaw's journey from his home to the coast, and then on to the Americas, he is guided by the hand of God: 'the Lord undertook to bring him by a way he knew not, out of darkness into his marvellous light, that he might lead him to a saving heart-acquaintance and union with the triune God in Christ' (p. 264). His remarkable journeys having culminated in conversion to Christianity, Gronniosaw then had his faith severely tested by 'the most distressing and pitiable trials and calamities' (p. 264). Even 'his wife and children perishing for want before his eyes' (p. 264) did not diminish his faith in God. Shirley concludes with a stirring tribute to Gronniosaw's Christian fortitude: 'though born in an exalted station of life, and now under the Pressure of various afflicting Providences ... [Gronniosaw] would rather embrace the dunghill having Christ in his heart, than give up his spiritual possessions and enjoyments, to fill the throne of Princes' (p. 264). Shirley thus imposes a Christian teleology upon the complex events of Gronniosaw's life, scripting his narrative as an ultimately happy journey, which begins (in the first phase) in 'darkness and ignorance' in Africa, progresses (in the second phase) by God's hand to conversion and redemption, and is sustained (in the third phase) as Gronniosaw remains true to his new-found faith, despite being severely tested.

Gronniosaw's *A Narrative* then proceeds to repeat in greater detail Shirley's three-stage sequence. The descriptions of his state of mind during the first phase (his African childhood) dwell upon his unhappiness, ignorance and state of confusion. In the second paragraph, he declares ''Twas certain that I was, at times, very unhappy in myself' (p. 265); following the great storm, he repeats, 'But I grew very unhappy in myself'; and, facing execution for being a spy on the Gold Coast, he 'suffered misery that cannot be described' (p. 269). His sense of being excluded from the Word of God on account of his race is painfully conveyed in his description of himself trying to emulate the Dutch slave captain reading from the 'talking book':

> As soon as my master had done reading I follow'd him to the place where he put the book, being mightily delighted with it, and when nobody saw me, I open'd it and put my ear down close upon it, in great hope that it would say something to me; but was very sorry and greatly disappointed when I found it would not speak, this thought immediately presented itself to me, that every body and every thing despised me because I was black.

> (p. 270)

The second phase of Gronniosaw's spiritual journey (his conversion to Christianity) took place in North America. From our reconstruction of Gronniosaw's physical travels, we know he spent well over twenty years in North America, but it is difficult to establish quite when during his time there he converted to Christianity. What is clear, however, is that his religious struggles were painful and protracted. In the Vanhorn household, he learned from the old slave Ned to fear the devil, and from Frelinghuysen he was 'somewhat enlightened' to learn that God is 'a good Spirit, [who] created every body, and every thing' (p. 272) and that God 'would judge the whole world; *Ethiopia*, *Asia*, and *Africa*, and every where' (p. 273). Despite these encouraging messages, Gronniosaw was driven to the brink of suicide by the thought that 'there was no way for me to be saved unless I came to *Christ*, and I could not come to Him: I thought that it was impossible He should receive such a sinner as me' (p. 274). In this desperate state, the words from the Bible '*Behold the Lamb of God*' came to him at night, and he was 'comforted at this, and began to grow easier' (p. 275). The next morning, he went to his schoolmaster, Mr Vanosdore, who encouraged him to pray to God for further guidance. Gronniosaw then describes how he spent many solitary hours praying and seeking comfort from God at an oak tree in a nearby wood, and how eventually he was saved:

> I was one day in a most delightful frame of mind; my heart so overflowed with love and gratitude to the author of all my comforts: – I was so drawn out of myself, and so fill'd and awed by the presence of God, that I saw (or thought I saw) light inexpressible dart down from heaven upon me, and shone around me for the space of a minute. – I continued on my knees, and joy unspeakable took possession of my soul. – The peace and serenity which filled my mind after this was wonderful, and cannot be told. – I would not have changed situations, or been any one but myself for the whole world. I blest God for my poverty, that I had no worldly riches or grandeur to draw my heart from him.

(pp. 275–6)

The third phase of Gronniosaw's spiritual journey is dominated by a succession of hardships and disappointments, all of which he construes as sent by God to test and ultimately strengthen his faith. The first test of Gronniosaw's new-found faith followed the death of Mr Frelinghuysen, as it precipitated once again grave doubts about whether he was worthy enough to be a Christian: 'the great enemy of my soul … would present my own misery to me in such striking light, and distress me with doubts, fears, and such a deep sense of my own unworthiness, that … I was often tempted to believe I should be a cast-away' (p. 276). Gronniosaw faced difficulties of a different order as a privateer, but saw the hand of God in his survival. Not only did God protect him in bloody sea battles ('I was near death several times, but the LORD preserv'd me' (p. 278)), but he also punished the enemies of Gronniosaw, as in the cases of the sailor who threw his favourite book in the sea, and of the ship's captain who cheated him of his rightful payment. Gronniosaw describes many testing experiences in England, notably having his money stolen in Portsmouth, struggling in London to overcome obstacles in order to marry Betty, and failing to find work during the weavers' riots – but even greater tests of his faith followed in Colchester and Norwich. In Norwich, a short period of profitable work was succeeded by desperate poverty and the death from fever of one of their daughters. Gronniosaw recounts his unsuccessful efforts to persuade Baptist and Quaker ministers to give her a Christian burial, describing the ordeal as 'one of the greatest trials I ever met with' (p. 289). When the parson of the local parish eventually agreed to bury her, but without the burial service, Gronniosaw's conclusion for once does not cast this painful event as a trial sent by God to test his faith; rather, he concludes, 'I told him I did not mind whether he would or not, as the child could not hear it' (p. 289). The final journey is to Kidderminster, which is described as a kind of 'promised land', where Gronniosaw and his family join a community of good Christians true to the teachings of Richard Baxter. Living off charity and his wife's meagre earnings from weaving, Gronniosaw's concluding words look forward to his journey onward to heaven.

We can draw certain provisional conclusions about Gronniosaw's distinctive qualities as a narrator: he has a curious and restless temperament; a naive and unworldly trust in people; a charitableness and generosity of spirit; an unwavering respect for authority; and a great resourcefulness in overcoming obstacles. Gronniosaw represents his spiritual journey as synchronous with his physical travels, as each of the three phases of his religious development corresponds with a major stage of his travels: in Africa, he is lost in the darkness, unhappy, and searching for a spiritual truth he cannot articulate; in the Americas, he undergoes a protracted experience of conversion; and in England, his faith is subjected to a series of tests. By the end of his narrative, his spiritual and physical journeys culminate in the promised land of Kidderminster.

Contexts

The religious context: Evangelical Christianity

A Narrative is punctuated by sixteen direct quotations from the Bible, and many more allusions, with an especially high concentration of biblical references in the paragraphs on Gronniosaw's conversion. These quotations from the Bible, however, are brief and elliptical, and should be read in the context of the particular variety of Christian belief Gronniosaw encountered. To this end, we need to attend to the ideas of three religious thinkers invoked in *A Narrative*, namely Gronniosaw's amanuensis Hannah More, and two of the writers he refers to in the text, John Bunyan and Richard Baxter.

Hannah More grew up in Bristol, one of Britain's major slave ports, but only took an interest in opposing slavery when she was in her forties. In the 1770s, she enjoyed the patronage of the great actor and theatre impresario, David Garrick (1717–1779), and produced a number of successful plays and ballads. After Garrick's death, she withdrew from the London theatre world, and turned her energies to producing didactic tracts teaching Tory politics and Evangelical morals to Britain's poor. After meeting the famous abolitionist William Wilberforce (1759–1833) in 1787, More start writing pamphlets and poems opposing the slave trade. Her abolitionism, however, never interrupted her conservative politics, and in the 1790s she published more than fifty 'Cheap Repository Tracts', most of which attacked English radicals like Thomas Paine (1737–1809) and tried to dissuade Britain's working classes from following the example of France's revolutionary poor. More set out how African slaves transported to the Americas should be saved in several publications, but perhaps the most accessible expression of her views is the poem 'The Sorrows of Yamba', which appeared in one of her Cheap Repository Tracts in 1795 (see Figure 7.1).

Activity 4

Read Hannah More's poem, 'The Sorrows of Yamba', which you can find reprinted as Reading 7.2. Summarise the story in the poem and the argument it presents. How does this poem compare with Gronniosaw's *A Narrative*?

Discussion

The poem uses the **persona** and the **idiom** of the African woman slave, Yamba, in order to tell a representative story of abduction in Africa, the middle-passage crossing of the Atlantic, slave labour in the Caribbean and conversion to Christianity. The concluding stanzas of the poem switch from narrative to polemic, as a direct appeal is made to British readers to abolish the slave trade. In attempting to address the widest possible audience, a simple and accessible ballad form is adopted: there are forty-seven stanzas, each of four lines (with seven syllables in each), organised in an *abab* rhyme scheme, accompanied by the recommendation that they are sung to the tune of 'Hosier's Ghost'. These devices derived from popular poetry are thus utilised in order to make the case for Evangelical abolitionism. The elements of protest in the poem are directed at the greed of the slave traders (Yamba condemns their love of 'filthy Gold' (ll. 29, 60)) and the needless cruelty of the plantation owners ('I was sold to Massa hard, / Some have Massas kind and good; / And again my back was scarr'd, / Bad and stinted was my food' (ll. 61–4)). In much the same way that More argued in other tracts for the amelioration of the sufferings of Britain's poor while preserving aristocratic privilege, 'The Sorrows of Yamba' argues that the

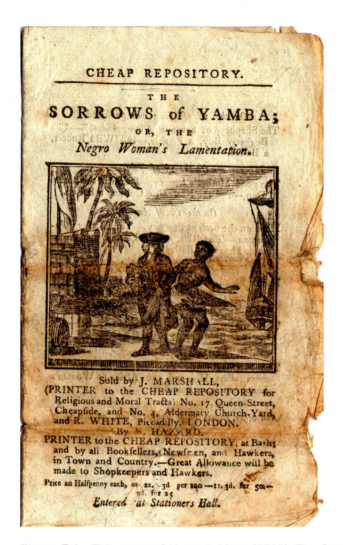

Figure 7.1   Title page of Hannah More (1795) *The Sorrows of Yamba*, engraving. Photo: National Education Network.

plight of the slaves should be improved without violence or retribution towards the masters: 'O ye slaves whom Massas beat, / Ye are stain'd with guilt within; / As ye hope for mercy sweet, / So forgive your Massa's sin' (ll. 113–6). Essential in reconciling Yamba to benevolent British paternalism is the acquisition of the Christian faith: 'Think how all her pain and woe / Brought the Captive home to God' (ll. 119–20), and 'Now I'll bless my cruel capture, / (Hence I've known a Saviour's name)' (ll. 130–1). The contrast is drawn between the singular Yamba seeking salvation through Christ, and the many unconverted slaves rebelling against their oppressors: 'Here an injured Slave forgives, / There a Host for vengeance cry; / Here a single Yamba lives, / There a thousand droop and die' (ll. 138–41). The message is clear: Africans transported into slavery in the Americas might suffer hardships, but the painful journey does enable them to encounter the teachings of Christ, and if they as individuals embrace the Word of God, they will be saved. In the final stanzas, Yamba yearns for Britain to abolish the slave trade, and in its stead to send missionaries to save African souls: 'Where ye gave to war its birth, / Where your traders fix'd their den, / There go publish 'Peace on Earth,' / Go proclaim 'good-will to men.' (ll. 174–7).

'The Sorrows of Yamba' differs in many ways from Gronniosaw's A Narrative. Most obviously, it combines narrative and polemic in the poetic genre of the popular ballad, whereas A Narrative frames Gronniosaw's life story in the prose genre of the spiritual autobiography. 'The Sorrows of Yamba' accordingly tells a compressed and linear tale, whereas A Narrative provides a more attenuated and conflicted story. It is nonetheless striking that the poem about the fictional slave woman and the autobiography of the historical figure of the freed slave share the same fundamental narrative structure. Godless ignorance in Africa is followed by the middle passage, and in both More's poem and Gronniosaw's autobiography, conversion to Christianity in the Americas transforms the experience of slavery into a redemptive journey from darkness and despair to light and salvation.

Gronniosaw mentions John Bunyan in describing the initial phases of his conversion. Troubled by Frelinghuysen's sermon proclaiming the ubiquity of God's judgement, Gronniosaw was given Bunyan to read. But Bunyan's writings failed to have the intended impact: '[S]he gave me John Bunyan on the holy war, to read; I found his experience similar to my own, which gave me reason to suppose he must be a bad man; as I was convinced of my own corrupt nature, and the misery of my own heart' (p. 274). Why would reading Bunyan so trouble Gronniosaw? We can speculate by looking briefly at Bunyan's writings. In *The Holy War* (1682), Bunyan tells the story of the town of Mansoul, and the fluctuating struggles for control of the town between the righteous ruler, El Shaddai, and the wicked Diabolus. According to the historian Christopher Hill, *The Holy War* combines at least four allegories: the first is the history of the universe from the fall of Diabolus/Satan and the rebel angels, and their protracted rebellion against El Shaddai/God; the second is about the process of conversion within the individual soul, brought about by a combination of external and internal factors; the third is 'the history of the English Revolution, from the anti-Christian tyranny of Charles I and his bishops, through the all-too-brief rule of the saints, to the return of Diabolus in 1660, and his ultimate overthrow' (Hill, 1988, p. 240); and finally, the fourth **allegory** refers to the history of Bunyan's home town of Bedford, and its fortunes during and after the English Civil War. Of these four allegorical layers, Gronniosaw is most likely to have been directly troubled by the second (the difficulties of conversion), a theme more obviously to the fore in Bunyan's better-known work, *The Pilgrim's Progress* (1678), and in his spiritual biography, *Grace Abounding* (1666). (Indeed, from Gronniosaw's description of what he was reading in Bunyan, it is tempting to conclude that he was mistaken in citing *The Holy War*, and that he had in fact read one of these other works.)

It is not difficult to imagine Gronniosaw being dismayed by Bunyan's descriptions of the process of conversion because they dramatise vividly the uncompromising rules of predestination prescribed by Calvinist theology. According to this view, the majority of mankind is assigned to damnation (reprobation) and only the chosen few achieve salvation (election). The process of conversion therefore involves finding signs that one is a member of the elect rather than a reprobate. This is a long and arduous process and involves many stages. The elect would progress from 'Effectual Calling' to 'Justification' and 'Sanctification' before, finally, 'Glorification', whereas the reprobate would regress from 'No calling at all' to 'Yielding to God's calling', 'Relapse', 'Fullness of Sin' and, finally, 'Damnation' (see Stachniewski with Pacheco, 1998, p. xii). Whatever work of Bunyan's he was reading, Gronniosaw would have encountered this terrifying dichotomy, and in identifying as he does with Bunyan's character of the 'wicked man as bad as myself' (p. 274), he understandably shrinks from the fearful prospect of damnation. One further reason Gronniosaw might have been upset by reading *The Holy War* is contained in the figure of Diabolus, who is introduced as: 'This *Gyant* was King of the *Blacks* or *Negroes*, and a most raving Prince he was' (Bunyan, 1980 [1682], p. 9). *The Holy War* from the outset thus constructs a racial binary, with Christian virtue on the side of the fair El Shaddai, and the wickedness of the devil on the side of Diabolus and his '*Blacks* or *Negroes*'. As an African reader, Gronniosaw might well have been alienated by this identification of the devil, damnation and blackness.

The writer Gronniosaw refers to most frequently in *A Narrative* is the seventeenth-century Puritan, Richard Baxter, whose book *A Call to the Unconverted* (1658) at first 'occasioned as much distress in me as [Bunyan] had before done' (p. 274). After his conversion, however, Gronniosaw records, 'I now began to relish the book my master gave

Figure 7.2   Edward Whymper, John Bunyan preaching in front of the Mote – or Moot – Hall, Bedford, engraving, in Brown, J. (1885) *John Bunyan, His Life, Times and Work*, London, W. Isbister Ltd.

me, Baxter's *call to the unconverted*, and took great delight in it' (p. 275), and he later cites Baxter's *Saint's Everlasting Rest* (1650) as another of his favourite books. Baxter's theology is summarised by his biographer N.H. Keeble as a 'combination of commitment with catholicity, of zeal with reasonableness, qualities which commended him to Church of England clergy quite as strongly as to nonconformists' (Keeble, 2009). It is therefore hardly surprising that Gronniosaw found Baxter more appealing than the much more austere and uncompromising Bunyan. In being so moved by Baxter's writings, Gronniosaw was far from being alone. *A Call to the Unconverted* was immensely popular in its day. Baxter himself records that 20,000 copies were printed by his own consent, and many thousands more 'by stolen Impressions, which poor Men stole for Lucre sake: Through God's Mercy I have had information of almost whole Households converted by this small Book' (quoted in Keeble, 1982, p. 8). Its reach extended well beyond England, as it was translated into Welsh (1659), French (1666), German (1667), Romansch (1669), Swedish (1683) and Dutch (1684). Gronniosaw would have read Baxter in the Dutch translation, and would have encountered exactly the same conversion paradigm prescribed by Bunyan and, later, by Shirley and More. After a lengthy preface, Baxter begins his tract with the familiar opposition between the elect and the damned: 'It hath been the astonishing Wonder of many a Man, as well as to me, to read in the Holy Scripture, how *few* will be saved, and that the greatest part, even of those that are called, will be everlastingly shut out of the Kingdom of Heaven' (Baxter, 1717, p. 1). With great rhetorical energy, Baxter sets out seven key doctrines which lay down the route to salvation. The first three are:

> Doctrine 1. It is the unchangeable Law of God, that wicked men must turn, or die.
>
> Doctrine 2. It is the Promise of God, that the Wicked shall live, if they will but Turn.
>
> Doctrine 3. God takes pleasure in Men's Conversion and Salvation, but not in their Death or Damnation: He had rather they would return and live, than go on and die.
>
> (Baxter, 1717, p. 4)

Baxter thus provides both a stern warning and a clear programme to the unconverted for escaping damnation and joining the elect. Gronniosaw follows Baxter's doctrines, as he progresses from his initial terror at the prospect of being 'everlastingly shut out of the Kingdom of Heaven', to finding consolation in Baxter's generous doctrine that God takes more pleasure in 'Men's Conversion and Salvation' than in their 'Death or Damnation'.

It is worth pausing to reflect upon how this account of the religious context of Gronniosaw's *A Narrative* influences our understanding of the text. Our initial textual analysis disclosed a resourceful but somewhat unworldly individual buffeted by slavery, exploitation and unemployment, who was ultimately saved by his conversion to Christianity. By registering the sheer weight of Christian teaching encountered by Gronniosaw (through More and Shirley directly, and through Bunyan and Baxter in their writings), a slightly different reading of his text emerges. Removed from the Africa of his childhood, transported across the Atlantic, and having suffered extreme and protracted poverty in the Americas, the Christian doctrines Gronniosaw encountered offered him both an explanation of and an escape from his difficult material circumstances. The cultural critic Raymond Williams has defined the verb 'determine' as 'the setting of limits [and] the exertion of pressures' (Williams, 1977, p. 87), and, on this definition, we might argue that Gronniosaw's text was determined to a substantial degree by its religious context. In other words, Gronniosaw's experiences of slavery and poverty, and his exposure to Christian teachings, set certain limits and exerted certain pressures on how he was able to recount his experiences in *A Narrative*. We might even formulate this more bluntly: Gronniosaw's vulnerable personal circumstances meant that in order first to be heard and then to be published by his benefactors, he was obliged to tell them what they wanted to hear, namely a Christian conversion narrative. That he told them the story they wanted to hear with such conviction was, of course, much the better for all parties to the transaction. But the vast power differences between Gronniosaw and his interlocutors should alert us to read his words cautiously. In order to explore further the degree to which Gronniosaw might have tailored his narrative to please his amanuensis and her fellow Christians in England, I turn now to Gronniosaw's African context.

The historical context (1): Gronniosaw's African childhood

In order to satisfy the generic rules of the Christian conversion narrative favoured by More and Shirley, Gronniosaw was obliged to produce a retrospective account of the Africa of his childhood as a place of ignorance, darkness and unhappiness. He meets this requirement handsomely, as he dwells upon the negatives in the opening pages of *A Narrative*. Despite references to being loved by his mother, his sister Logwy and his grandfather, Gronniosaw emphasises his sense of spiritual desolation and of being ostracised by his siblings and servants. But let us now try to place Gronniosaw's testimony in the context of an alternative history of Bornu in the early eighteenth century.

Activity 5

Read the following extract from a recent history of Bornu in the eighteenth century, and make a list of the key features of this society. When you've done that, ask yourself: how does this version of Bornu's history affect your understanding of Gronniosaw's *A Narrative*?

> The term Kanuri probably came into use in the early seventeenth century. It refers to the dominant ethnic group of Borno upon whom the power of the Sēfuwa kings was based. It was produced by the inter-marriage of the peoples and

cultures of the immigrant Magumi from Kānem and the Chadic speakers of Borno. ... Within the Kanuri group itself there were many sub-ethnic distinctions. ... It was the Kanuri culture that formed the base of the Bornoan culture which spread beyond the metropolitan province as the Kanuri travelled out or as other groups adopted the Kanuri culture through political or economic domination or association through Islamization. ... Kanuri society was highly stratified. It was broadly divided into two classes, the *Kontuowa* (ruling class or nobility) and the *tala'a* (commoners) and both these had several divisions. Differences of speech, dress, household furniture, architecture and residence distinguished the classes and their sub-divisions. Status was based on ethnic membership, occupation, birth, age and residence. ... Islam was one of the bases of Kanuri culture. Islam was deeply rooted in everyday life and even penetrated the fabric of Kanuri folklore. Much of the technical vocabulary of Islam had been so 'Kanurised' that its original meaning had been modified. ... Borno at this time was a centre of learning which attracted large numbers of students and visiting scholars for the *Bilād al Sūdān*, North Africa and the Middle East. Borno specialised in *tafsīr* (commentary on the Kur'ān) in the Kānembu language and the art of writing the Borno language in Arabic letters must have been developed in the seventeenth century.

(Barkindo, 1992, pp. 504–8)

Discussion

There are several points about Bornu in the period of Gronniosaw's childhood to note:

1 The inhabitants of the region of Bornu are designated Kanuri. They are a composite nation, which evolved and emerged from the intermarriage of several migrating nations. The Kanuri themselves constituted something of a regional super-power, as once they had consolidated a power base, they expanded and incorporated various smaller nations.

2 Kanuri society was stratified into two main classes (a ruling elite (*Kontuowa*) and a class of 'commoners' (*tala'a*)), but there were further sub-divisions within these two classes.

3 Islam was the dominant religion, and was thoroughly assimilated into Kanuri folklore and religious vocabularies.

4   Bornu was a centre of learning and scholarship and, even by the seventeenth century, was a highly literate culture.

Having read only the text of Gronniosaw's *A Narrative*, some of this information will come as a great surprise. Gronniosaw does indeed claim to be from a substantial African kingdom, and he does claim to be a prince, but he is silent about the fact that he was brought up in the Muslim faith and that he came from a highly literate culture.

Let us revisit a couple of the early passages from *A Narrative* in the light of these contextual details. First, Gronniosaw's claims to be searching for 'some GREAT MAN', 'some SUPERIOR POWER' anterior to the sun, moon and stars, must now surely be rejected, since Islam is a monotheistic religion, and Gronniosaw would indubitably have been raised as a Muslim. By concealing from his amanuensis the fact that he was brought up in the Islamic faith, and by feigning dissatisfaction with African pagan religions, Gronniosaw effectively manipulates the prejudices of his audience in order to ingratiate himself. Further, the critic Jennifer Harris points out that, in Bornu, Gronniosaw would have had access to a second creation myth aside from the Islamic one: 'Obassi Osaw' is an indigenous northern Nigerian god, who 'lives in the sky and creates the world and populates it' (2005, p. 47). 'Osaw' is, of course, incorporated in Gronniosaw's name, and Harris argues that 'one can admire [Gronniosaw's] cheek in opening his narrative with an incident which covertly puns upon his own name' (2005, p. 47).

The second incident in *A Narrative* we must rethink is Gronniosaw's description of his awestruck reaction to watching the Dutch sea captain reading from a book during their Atlantic crossing. Given his status in Bornu, Gronniosaw would certainly have been familiar with books, and he would in all likelihood have been literate. The critic Sylviane Anna Diouf reinforces the point that '[a] large proportion of the Muslims [in West Africa] could read and write in Arabic and in *ajami*, the generic name given to their own language transcribed in the Arabic alphabet'; indeed, she argues that 'the literacy rate among Muslim slaves was in all probability higher than it was among slaveholders' (1998, pp. 8, 108). To understand why Gronniosaw dissembles in *A Narrative* about his religious and educational background, we need once again to appreciate the unequal power relationship between the poverty-stricken ex-slave and his much wealthier, white, English patrons. Harris explains the exchange thus: 'Gronniosaw is engaging in the economics of race, giving the charitable customer what he or she wanted ideologically from the

Christianized African in exchange for the economic support he was unable to secure as a market-based laborer' (2005, p. 47).

How does this affect our assessment of Gronniosaw? Clearly, our judgement of him as naive and unworldly – based exclusively on our reading of the text of *A Narrative* – must be revised. By remaining silent about his Islamic and literate childhood in Africa, Gronniosaw displays a strategic intelligence, which enables him to disarm his benefactors and acquire some temporary economic relief. The anti-colonial theorist Frantz Fanon has argued that colonialism (with slavery at its root) 'turns to the past of the oppressed people, and distorts, disfigures and destroys it' (1967, p. 169). The impact on the colonised, he argues, is devastating, as in desperation 'the native intellectual has thrown himself greedily upon Western culture. … [He] will try to make European culture his own' (Fanon, 1967, p. 176). Fanon describes this as the first phase of colonialism, the phase when the 'native intellectual gives proof that he has assimilated the culture of the occupying power' (1967, p. 178). Fanon's argument can be applied to Gronniosaw: Shirley's description, in the preface, of Africa as a region of 'grossest darkness and ignorance' qualifies as a distortion or disfigurement of African history, and Gronniosaw's *A Narrative* could certainly be read as evidence of an African intellectual giving 'proof that he has assimilated the culture of the occupying power'. However, by paying attention to specific colonial contexts – in this case, the kingdom of Bornu in the first half of the eighteenth century – a more complex picture emerges. Gronniosaw might well mimic, very plausibly and with great conviction, the required Christian conversion narrative, but having registered the sophistication of his pre-abduction African world, we can now also recognise the ingenuity and agency he displays in securing his material survival.

The historical context (2): the middle passage

The term 'middle passage' was first coined by the abolitionist Thomas Clarkson (1760–1846) in 1788 to designate the bottom line of the slave-trading triangle between the 'outward passage', from Europe to Africa, and the 'homeward passage', from the Americas to Europe. It is worth registering that the journey from Africa to the Americas was only a 'middle' passage from a European perspective; from the perspective of captured African slaves, it was a single 'outward' passage terminating in an American plantation. Gronniosaw describes his experience of the journey across the Atlantic in one sentence: 'I was exceedingly sea-sick at first; but when I became more accustom'd to the sea, it wore off' (p. 270). This brevity in describing the most momentous leg of his travels can be attributed to Gronniosaw attuning his life story to the requirements of his audience. Gronniosaw assumed that More and other English Christian readers wanted to hear less about his sufferings as a slave, and more about his deprived childhood and miraculous conversion. With such concerns paramount, descriptions of the middle passage were incidental. Other writers, however, particularly in the 1780s and 1790s, provided much more detailed descriptions, and the final section of this chapter considers three such versions: Hannah More's poetic description, and the eye-witness accounts of the ex-slave Olaudah Equiano and the slave-ship sailor James Field Stanfield.

Before proceeding to these accounts, however, the scale of the Atlantic slave trade in the eighteenth century should be noted. Historians have disagreed about the statistics of the slave trade, and it is indeed impossible to provide precise numbers. The current scholarly consensus is summarised by Marcus Rediker in his recent study, *The Slave Ship: A Human History* (2007), which argues that during the 400 years of the Atlantic slave trade 14 million Africans were transported from Africa to the Americas. Breaking down the journey from the point of being captured in Africa to the point of slaving on the plantations in the Americas, Rediker summarises the death rate: 1.8 million Africans died between point of enslavement and boarding the ship; on the middle passage itself, another 1.8 million slaves died; and, during the first year on the plantations, another 1.5 million would expire. Rediker offers this perspective: 'an estimated 14 million people were enslaved to produce a "yield" of 9 million longer-surviving enslaved Atlantic workers' (2007, p. 5). Between 1700 and 1808, two-thirds of the total numbers of slaves were transported, and 3 million were shipped in British and American slave ships. Rediker concedes that, during this period, the mortality rate dropped slightly, but notes that still nearly a million slaves died in transit to the Americas, half of them on British and American ships.

There were relatively few descriptions of conditions on slave ships in the eighteenth century, but as the campaign for the abolition of the slave trade gathered momentum in the 1780s, publications describing its horrors started appearing more frequently. The two eye-witness accounts selected for analysis here are by the ex-slave Olaudah Equiano and by a ship's doctor, James Field Stanfield. Equiano was born in about 1745 in what is now south-eastern Nigeria. He was kidnapped at the age of ten and transported first to the West Indies, and then sold to

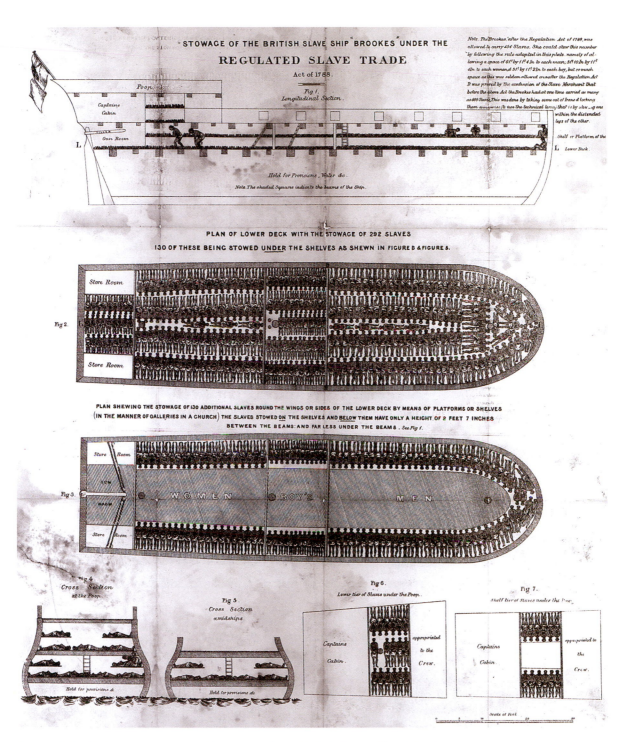

Figure 7.3   Unknown engraver, 'Stowage of the British Slave Ship "Brookes" under the Regulated Slave Trade Act of 1788', *c.*1790. Photo: Private Collection/The Bridgeman Art Gallery.

a Virginia planter. He was resold to an English officer, travelled with his owner to London, and then (like Gronniosaw) fought in the Seven Years War. After the war, he was sold again into West Indian slavery, but purchased his freedom in 1766 and survived by trading and working on ships. In the late 1770s, he settled in England and threw himself into the abolitionist movement, publishing *The Interesting Narrative* in 1789 to further the cause. The authenticity of Equiano's narrative has recently been questioned by one leading historian of slavery, who has argued that he was in fact born in South Carolina and never experienced the middle passage himself (see Carretta, 2005). However, this argument has been vigorously disputed (see Byrd, 2006, and Lovejoy, 2006), and the balance of scholarly opinion remains on the side of treating Equiano's *The Interesting Narrative* as based on his direct experience of the middle passage. Stanfield, meanwhile, was born in Ireland in about 1750 and, while being educated as a priest, underwent 'a secular awakening' (Rediker, 2007, p. 134), leaving the seminary to go to sea. He was already an experienced (and unusually well-educated) seaman when he undertook several slave voyages from 1774–7. Thereafter, he became a successful actor, but at the same time published his critical impressions of the slave trade in 1788 with the help of the leading abolitionist Thomas Clarkson.

Activity 6

Read the following extracts, which contain descriptions of the middle passage. They can be found in the 'Readings' section at the end of this part of the book.

- Reading 7.2: lines 9–60 of More's 'The Sorrows of Yamba'
- Reading 7.3: an extract from Equiano's *The Interesting Narrative*
- Reading 7.4: an extract from Stanfield's *Observations*.

Now answer the following questions:

How does each extract describe the slave's journey across the Atlantic? What literary techniques does each of them use in their description?

Discussion

Reading 7.2: More

We have already looked at 'The Sorrows of Yamba', but there are a few further points to note with regard to the poem's representation of the middle passage. Written in the 1790s, at the height of the campaign for the abolition of the slave trade, these opening stanzas on the middle passage are the most shocking in the poem, as they describe the increasingly well-known horrors of the trade: the violence of the original abduction; the over-crowding, whippings and terrible food; the infant mortalities; and the yearning for death to escape such suffering. Written in the voice of Yamba, the poem addresses English readers directly in an attempt to register a common humanity: 'Born on Afric's Golden Coast, / Once I was as blest as you' (ll. 13–14). Two **similes** emphasise how the cruelty of the slave traders strips away the humanity of the slaves: 'Now like Brutes they make us prance' (l. 38) and 'Driven like Cattle to a fair' (l. 57). The realism of these opening stanzas contrasts with the didactic evangelising conclusion of the poem, a contrast the critic Alan Richardson attributes to the fact that More in fact adopted and extended a shorter poem by the obscure poet Eaglesfield Smith (c.1770–1838). According to Richardson, exactly who wrote which stanzas of 'The Sorrows of Yamba' is somewhat unclear – but it is most likely that More appropriated Smith's original and 'added the stanzas on Yamba's conversion and some concluding material, while thickening the dialect' (Richardson, 1999, p. 224).

Reading 7.3: Equiano

Aside from the obvious generic difference between 'The Sorrows of Yamba' and *The Interesting Narrative*, Equiano's narrative also contrasts with 'The Sorrows of Yamba' (and indeed with Gronniosaw's narrative) in that he writes of his experiences as a collective trauma. This is most obvious in his frequent use of the first-person plural pronouns 'we' and 'us', as opposed to the 'I' and 'me' used in 'The Sorrows of Yamba' and Gronniosaw's narrative. In both 'The Sorrows of Yamba' and Gronniosaw's narrative, the key relationship is between the individual slave and the white Christian minister or master who brings salvation, whereas for Equiano the companionship of his fellow slaves is much more central. In addition to his frequent use of the first-person plural, Equiano refers to the slaves as a community of fellow-sufferers, describing them with a dehumanising simile like those used in 'The Sorrows of Yamba': 'we were all pent up together like so many sheep in a fold' (p. 298). Equiano's description of the middle passage discloses a more precisely detailed catalogue of the sufferings of the slaves and the callousness of the slavers than 'The Sorrows of Yamba'. He describes the terrible stench, the rampant disease, the floggings, the suicides, and the want of fresh air in the hold, and he also notes the arbitrary cruelty of the slavers, as in when they refused to give leftover fish to the starving slaves. In an acute **aside**, Equiano makes an economic argument against such gross maltreatment of the slaves, when he suggests that the dying slaves are falling victim to 'the improvident avarice … of their purchasers' (p. 296). Prudent avarice would guide the slavers to deliver their captives healthy and intact to their purchasers in the Americas. The descriptions of relentless suffering are relieved by the brief moments when Equiano recounts his pleasure in seeing the flying fish and the sailors demonstrating the quadrant to him. However, these two moments in no way diminish the horrors of the journey, and on two occasions, Equiano suggests that the suffering he witnessed is beyond understanding, beyond expression: 'The shrieks of the women, and the groans of the dying, rendered the whole a scene of horror almost inconceivable' (p. 296); and 'we continued to undergo more hardships than I can now relate' (p. 297).

Reading 7.4: Stanfield

With serving the abolitionist cause paramount, Stanfield framed his *Observations* as a series of letters to Clarkson and focused upon the terrible conditions for British seamen involved in the slave trade. There are significant similarities with Equiano's account. Like Equiano, Stanfield declares the suffering he witnessed on the middle passage to be inexpressible. In the final sentence of the Fifth Letter, the sight of the man eaten while still alive by the hogs is 'too shocking to relate' (p. 301). In the Sixth Letter, Stanfield observes that 'no pen, no abilities, can give more than a very faint resemblance of the horrid situation' and that one minute on a slave ship would do more for the cause of humanity than 'the pen of a *Robertson*, or the whole collective eloquence of the British senate' (p. 301). Stanfield refers here to the Scottish Enlightenment historian and abolitionist sympathiser William Robertson (1721–1793), suggesting that his arguments are less persuasive than the experience of observing slave ships. The third point at which Stanfield is at a loss for words is in referring to the captain's rape of an eight- or nine-year-old slave girl, an act 'too atrocious and bloody to be passed over in silence, yet … I cannot express it in any words' (p. 302). Like Equiano, Stanfield also notes that the cruelty directed at the slaves is against the slavers' best economic interests: 'even AVARICE, the author of the destructive business, when struggling with CRUELTY, loses its force, and finds its powers of dominion foiled by the very monster that it begat' (p. 301). **Personifying** the vices of avarice and cruelty, Stanfield argues that the parent 'AVARICE' is ultimately foiled by its child 'CRUELTY'. Writing sympathetically of both the sailors and the slaves, he describes how the many deaths of the crew forced them to free the slaves so that '*they* pulled and hawled as they were directed by the inefficient sailors' – adding, 'We were fortunate in having favourable weather' (p. 300). It is not clear whether Stanfield's 'we' in this sentence refers only to the sailors, or includes sailors and slaves alike, but Stanfield continues to emphasise their shared suffering: 'I never could see any difference in the cruelty of their treatment' (p. 301). Stanfield thus rejects the pro-slavery denial of common humanity to the slaves, noting ironically that '[the grieving slaves] are the people whom the good traders represent, as wanting every kind of sensibility' (p. 302). Finally, unlike Gronniosaw, More and Equiano, Stanfield's letters do not attempt to frame the cruelties inflicted upon the slaves and seamen within a Christian narrative of suffering and redemption.

Conclusion

Studying the different contexts of Gronniosaw's *A Narrative* influences how we read his work: the religious context reveals the normative power of the Christian conversion narrative he was encouraged to produce; the context of Gronniosaw's African childhood discloses the amount of personal information he suppressed in order to 'fit' his complicated life into the sequence of the conversion narrative; and the context of the middle passage reveals just how much Gronniosaw's single-sentence description conceals. There are, of course, further contexts of Gronniosaw's text we might explore, like the slave economies of the Americas in the decades from 1720 to 1760, and the England of the early Industrial Revolution in the 1760s, but one final context we should consider is that of the present.

The eighteenth-century slave journeys of the middle passage have been consigned to the past, but recently historians have expanded the meaning of the term to define all cases of forced transportation and exploitation: 'the middle passage is not merely a maritime phrase to describe one part of an oceanic voyage; it can, rather, be utilized as a concept – the structuring link between expropriation in one geographic location and exploitation in another' (Christopher, Pybus and Rediker, 2007, p. 2). In other words, Gronniosaw's capture, coerced journey and forced labour was not a uniquely eighteenth-century experience: comparable versions of his experience have been repeated in many different contexts, including the present. Campaigns in 2007 commemorating the two hundredth anniversary of the end of the slave trade emphasised that new forms of slavery and trafficking flourish today. An International Labour Organisation (ILO) survey in 2005 estimated that there are 12.3 million victims of 'the new slavery' and that 2.4 million of them will have been trafficked (see ILO, 2005). The critical methods we have developed in studying the texts and contexts of these eighteenth-century journeys might as readily be applied to non-fictional and fictional accounts of these contemporary journeys.

References

Barkindo, B.M. (1992) 'Kānem-Borno: its relation with the Mediterranean Sea, Bagirmi and other states in the Chad basin' in Ogot, B.A. (ed.) *General History of Africa. Volume 5. Africa from the Sixteenth to the Eighteenth Century*, Paris, UNESCO/Oxford, Heinemann, pp. 492–514.

Baxter, R. (1717 [1658]) *A Call to the Unconverted to Turn and Live*, 31st edn, Boston, John Allen.

Bunyan, J. (1980 [1682]) *The Holy War* (ed. R. Sharrock and J. F. Forrest), Oxford, Clarendon Press.

Byrd, A.X. (2006) 'Eboe, country, nation, and Gustavus Vassa's *Interesting Narrative*', *William and Mary Quarterly*, vol. 63, pp. 123–48.

Carretta, V. (2005) *Equiano the African: Biography of a Self-Made Man*, Athens and London, University of Georgia Press.

Christopher, E., Pybus, C. and Rediker, M. (2007) *Many Middle Passages: Forced Migration and the Making of the Modern World*, Berkeley, University of California Press.

Diouf, S.A. (1998) *Servants of Allah: African Muslims Enslaved in the Americas*, New York, New York University Press.

Fanon, F. (1967) *The Wretched of the Earth* (trans. C. Farrington), Harmondsworth, Penguin.

Gates, H.L. Jr (1988) *The Signifying Monkey: A Theory of African-American Literary Criticism*, New York, Oxford University Press.

Gronniosaw, J.A.U. (1774) *A Narrative of the Most Remarkable Particulars in the Life of James Albert Ukawsaw Gronniosaw, An African Prince, Written by Himself*, Bath, W. Gye and T. Mills.

Harris, J. (2005) 'Seeing the light: re-reading James Albert Ukawsaw Gronniosaw', *English Language Notes*, vol. 42, no. 4, pp. 43–57.

Hill, C. (1988) *A Turbulent, Seditious, and Factious People: John Bunyan and his Church 1628–1688*, Oxford, Clarendon Press.

ILO (2005) 'A global alliance against forced labour', http://www.ilo.org/public/english/region/asro/manila/mtgevents/flglobal.htm (Accessed 10 December 2009).

Keeble, N.H. (1982) *Richard Baxter: Puritan Man of Letters*, Oxford, Clarendon Press.

Keeble, N.H. (2009) 'Baxter, Richard (1615–1691)' in Goldman, L. (ed.) *Oxford Dictionary of National Biography*, Oxford, Oxford University Press; available online at http://www.oxforddnb.com/view/article/1734 (Accessed 20 April 2010).

Lovejoy, P. (2006) 'Autobiography and memory: Gustavus Vassa, alias Olaudah Equiano the African', *Slavery and Abolition*, vol. 27, pp. 317–47.

Rediker, M. (2007) *The Slave Ship: A Human History*, London, John Murray.

Richardson, A. (ed.) (1999) *Slavery, Abolition and Emancipation: Writings in the British Romantic Period. Vol. 4. Verse*, London, Pickering and Chatto.

Stachniewski, J. with Pacheco, A. (eds) (1998) *John Bunyan: 'Grace Abounding' with Other Spiritual Autobiographies*, Oxford, Oxford University Press.

Williams, R. (1977) *Marxism and Literature*, Oxford, Oxford University Press.

Further reading

Linebaugh, L. and Rediker, M. (2000) *The Many-Headed Hydra: Sailors, Slaves, Commoners, and the Hidden History of the Revolutionary Atlantic*, London, Verso.

Potkay, A. and Burr, S. (eds) (1995) *Black Atlantic Writers of the Eighteenth Century*, Basingstoke, Macmillan.

Thomas, H. (2000) *Romanticism and Slave Narratives: Transatlantic Testimonies*, Cambridge, Cambridge University Press.

Chapter 8
The mutiny on the *Bounty*

David Johnson

Aims

This chapter will:

- analyse the competing non-fictional and fictional accounts of journeys during the mutiny on the *Bounty*
- locate these competing accounts in the historical context of Britain's presence in the Pacific Ocean
- discuss the reception history of the mutiny on the *Bounty* by considering a selection of subsequent literary and cinematic versions.

Introduction

In the final chapter of Part 2, we will focus principally upon a second non-fiction travel narrative: the narrative of the voyage of William Bligh (1754–1817) and eighteen sailors from Tonga to Timor. Bligh's journey of 3,618 nautical miles in 49 days on an open launch was precipitated by a mutiny led by Fletcher Christian (1764–1793) against Bligh on HMS *Bounty* on 28 April 1789. Many competing versions of the mutiny have been produced in the last two centuries in histories, novels and films. We analyse in the first instance those of the main antagonists: Bligh and Christian. Bligh wrote up and published his version of the mutiny and the voyage to Timor soon after he returned to Portsmouth in *A Narrative of the Mutiny on Board His Majesty's Ship 'Bounty'* (1790) (which I will refer to as *A Narrative* in this chapter). To appreciate the distinctiveness of Bligh's account, we contrast his version of the voyage briefly with the competing factual account, *The Journal of John Fryer* (written in the 1790s, published 1934), and the fictional account contained in Charles Nordhoff and James Norman Hall's bestseller *Men Against the Sea* (1934). Bligh's version of events held sway in the short term, but was challenged when the lawyer Stephen Barney and Fletcher Christian's brother Edward published a partial transcript of the trial of the *Bounty* mutineers, along with 'an Appendix, Containing a Full Account of the Real Causes and Circumstances of the Unhappy Transaction, the most material of which have hitherto been withheld from the Public' (1794).

Our first concern is to establish the contexts of these texts: the histories of British exploration in the South Pacific; the typical conditions on board British sailing ships in the eighteenth century; the family histories of the principal protagonists in the conflict; and the political climate of 1790s Britain. Having established these contexts, we examine the texts of Bligh, Fryer, Nordhoff and Hall, and Christian, attending to the literary techniques used to narrate journeys and the rhetorical strategies employed in order to manipulate readers' sympathies. Thirdly, we look at the **reception history** of the mutiny on the *Bounty* and discuss two exemplary film versions of the story, *The Mutiny on the Bounty* (1935) and *The Bounty* (1984).

All of the required reading associated with this chapter can be found at the end of this part of the book in 'Readings for Part 2'.

Contexts

Francis Drake circumnavigated the globe in 1577–80, but British ships only began appearing in the Pacific Ocean in significant numbers in the period 1680–1760. Their presence nonetheless remained 'essentially parasitic' (Williams, 1997, p. xiii), as British privateers like William Dampier (1652–1715) and Lionel Wafer (1660–1705) plundered the ships of other European nations with the long-distance support of sponsors in England. A second phase can be dated from the 1760s, and was characterised by voyages of scientific discovery, with the acquisition and recording of cartographical, astronomical and botanical knowledge their explicit goal. The defining achievements of this phase were the three voyages of Captain James Cook (1728–1779) in 1768–71, 1772–5 and 1776–80, which enjoyed the support of Sir Joseph Banks (1743–1820), President of the Royal Society for forty-one years. The voyage of the *Bounty* represented the beginnings of a third phase, in which British ships to the Pacific sought to turn the scientific discoveries to commercial advantage. Breadfruit had been identified on one of Cook's voyages as a nutritious and easy-to-grow source of protein, and Banks's plan was for the *Bounty* to transplant breadfruit plants from Tahiti to Britain's Caribbean colonies as cheap sustenance for the slaves. Forging such trans-oceanic connections enabled Britain's economy to assume global dimensions: cheap labour from Africa plus cheap food from the Pacific would converge in the Caribbean to produce cheaper sugar for consumers in Britain (and ultimately larger profits for British plantation owners).

Life on British sailing ships in the eighteenth century was ordered by a strict hierarchy, with the captain enjoying absolute power. Captains had a range of coercive means at their disposal to enforce their authority, with recourse to flogging the most frequent. The historian Greg Dening has summarised the record of floggings on British ships in the period of the *Bounty*. From 1765 to 1793, 15 British naval vessels carrying a total of 1,556 sailors entered the Pacific Ocean: 21.5 per cent of the crew on these vessels were flogged, with Cook flogging 20 per cent, 26 per cent, and 37 per cent of his crew on each of his three voyages, and Bligh flogging 19 per cent on the *Bounty* voyage and 8 per cent on his subsequent journey on the *Providence*. Dening concludes that 'Bligh was milder in displaying physical violence than most British captains who came into the Pacific in the eighteenth century' (1992, p. 63). Floggings did not always terrify seamen into obedience, as the large number of mutinies in the eighteenth century attest. The mutiny on the *Bounty* is unarguably the most famous, but from 1700–50 there were sixty recorded mutinies on British ships (Rediker, 1987, p. 309), and the mutinies at Spithead near Portsmouth and Nore in the Thames estuary in 1797 involved far more mutinous sailors and far more hangings. Mutinies had many causes: cruelty inflicted by captains and officers; inadequate provisions; too much work for too few hands; poor medical care; breaches of wage agreements; delays in being paid; and sustained low-level abuse. The historian Marcus Rediker argues that most mutinies had several overlapping causes, and tended to develop over an extended period of time. Navigational knowledge was essential for a gang of mutineers, and a mutiny 'could be put into effect with the support of only 20–30 percent of the crew so long as the majority of the seamen could be counted upon to remain neutral or join up once the seizure of power was underway' (Rediker, 1987, p. 229).

The personal histories of Bligh and Christian, the two chief protagonists in the mutiny on the *Bounty*, have been much pored over in the search for clues as to why their relationship ended in such bitter conflict. Bligh was born near Plymouth into a family of sailors, and he began his life at sea at the age of seven as a captain's servant. Like Cook, his initial route into maritime service was through a tradition of apprenticeship as a boy midshipman, with promotion dependent upon merit and achievement rather than patronage. By 1770, he had graduated to serving as an able seaman, and at the age of twenty-two, he was appointed sailing-master on Cook's third voyage to the Pacific. Bligh witnessed his hero Cook being killed on Hawaii in 1779, and on his return to England assisted in the publication of Cook's journals. Bligh owed his appointment as master of the *Bounty* to Cook's great patron, Sir Joseph Banks, who continued to support Bligh's career after the failure of the *Bounty* expedition. Christian was born into the landed gentry in Cockermouth, in England's Lake District, where he attended the same school as William Wordsworth (1770–1850). When his family went bankrupt, Christian moved with his mother to live on the Isle of Man. Despite his family's decline in fortune, their connections enabled Christian to begin his career at sea as a midshipman in 1783. He served with distinction under Bligh in the merchant service in the late 1780s, and Bligh enrolled him as acting lieutenant on the *Bounty*. We might therefore identify a class difference between the upwardly mobile yeoman Bligh from Devon-Cornwall, and the impoverished but genteel Christian from Manx-Cumberland, but the significance of their differences relates less to their respective origins, and more to the social networks each could access. Whereas Bligh relied upon the support of the naval hierarchy and the scientific establishment, Christian's support was based upon extended family influence and connections to the land-owning elites.

The very same day that Christian confronted Bligh on the *Bounty* in the South Pacific, Parisian workers sacked the factories of Reveillon and Henriot (Lefebvre, 1971, p. 122), and by 1790, when Bligh published his account of the mutiny, Britain's rulers were anxious that the French Revolution might spread across the Channel. These anxieties are vividly captured in another publication of 1790, *Reflections on the Revolution in France* by Edmund Burke (1729–1797). Burke argued that in the Revolution of the year before, '[t]hey have seen the French rebel against a mild and lawful monarch with more fury, outrage and insult, than ever any people has been known to rise against the most illegal usurper. … This was unnatural' (1986 [1790], p. 126). In direct contrast to France, Burke argues that England's national character is built on respect for order: 'We fear God; we look up with awe to kings; with affection to parliaments; with duty to magistrates; with reverence to priests; and with respect to nobility' (1986 [1790], p. 182). As we will see, Bligh's version of the mutiny parallels Burke's diagnosis of the dichotomy between the French monarchy and the revolutionaries: Bligh represents the embodiment of lawfulness, order, duty, reverence and respect, whereas Christian and the mutineers epitomise fury, outrage, insult, illegality and unnaturalness.

If Bligh's sufferings during and after the mutiny won the sympathy of much of the British establishment, the mutineers too had their supporters. For example, in the early 1790s, the Romantic poet Robert Southey (1774–1843) expressed sympathy both for the French Revolution and for the mutineers on the *Bounty* (Rennie, 1995, p. 163). By 1794, when Edward Christian published the partial transcript of their trial and 'Appendix' defending his brother's actions, there was widespread enthusiasm for individual liberties across Britain. In 1791 and 1792, Thomas Paine had published *The Rights of Man,*

Part I and *Part II*, in which he argued *contra* Burke that 'in the instance of France, we see a revolution generated in the rational contemplation of the rights of man' (Paine, 1989 [1791–2], p. 62). For Paine, these rights are natural, and include 'all those rights of acting as an individual for his own comfort and happiness, which are not injurious to the rights of others' (Paine, 1989 [1791–2], p. 78). Pre-eminent among Paine's natural rights is the right of individuals to rebel against tyrants – as the French people had done in the Revolution, and as the mutineers had done on the *Bounty*. Christian's version of the mutiny therefore parallels Paine's sympathy for the French rising up to challenge the tyrannical authority of the monarchy: Christian and the mutineers represent individuals claiming their natural right to resist tyranny, whereas Bligh stands for despotic, autocratic and unjust power. The critic Rod Edmond summarises the political resonances of the mutiny in 1790s Britain: 'ships are a microcosm of the political order, and however spontaneous the mutiny might have been it was received in Britain as an act against constituted authority, welcomed by some, but anathema to the ruling classes' (1997, p. 72).

Activity 1

Read the 'Extended chronology of the mutiny on the *Bounty*' (Reading 8.1 in 'Readings for Part 2'). Then read the section entitled 'Advertisement' in Bligh's *A Narrative* (in Reading 8.2), and the first three paragraphs of Christian's 'Appendix' (in Reading 8.5). With the extended chronology in mind, comment on Bligh's and Christian's selection of material for inclusion in their respective texts.

Discussion

From the extended chronology, it is clear that there were several dramatic events in the months before the mutiny, notably the desperate failure to round Cape Horn in April 1788, and the desertion and capture of the three sailors on Tahiti in January 1789. The *Bounty* on its long voyage also visited a number of unfamiliar and exotic locales that would have been of great interest to readers of Bligh's account in Britain. However, Bligh makes it clear in his advertisement for *A Narrative* that from the many experiences on his journeys, stretching from December 1787 to March 1790, he has selected only the most exciting ones. He has chosen to focus upon the events from the moment of the mutiny (28 April 1789) to the moment of the arrival of the launch in Coupang (14 June 1789). (See Figure 8.1 for a map of the route followed by Bligh's launch.) Although *A Narrative* advertises itself as an objective recounting of facts, by beginning with the

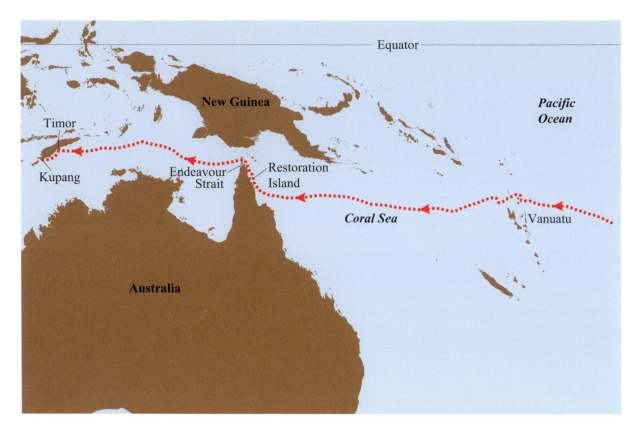

Figure 8.1   Bligh's voyage after the mutiny.

departure from Tahiti with breadfruit on 4 April 1789, Bligh leaves out many prior facts which might explain the causes of the mutiny. By describing the mutiny in isolation, and by detailing the forty-nine-day voyage on the launch, Bligh edits his account in such a way that he appears as the brave and resourceful hero, who prevails over villainous mutineers, treacherous indigenes and the cruel sea. By contrast, Christian's 'Appendix', in its first two paragraphs, concedes the wickedness of the mutineers and the heroism of Bligh in sailing the launch to Timor. But in the third paragraph, it introduces a crucial contextual counter-argument; namely that 'what passed at the time of the mutiny was so immediately connected with what had happened previously in the ship' (p. 351). In other words, Bligh's and Christian's respective cases rest upon casting the mutiny in quite different contexts: for Bligh, there is nothing of any great significance in the events preceding the mutiny, whereas for Christian it is precisely the context of Bligh's cruel regime on the *Bounty* before the mutiny that must be registered.

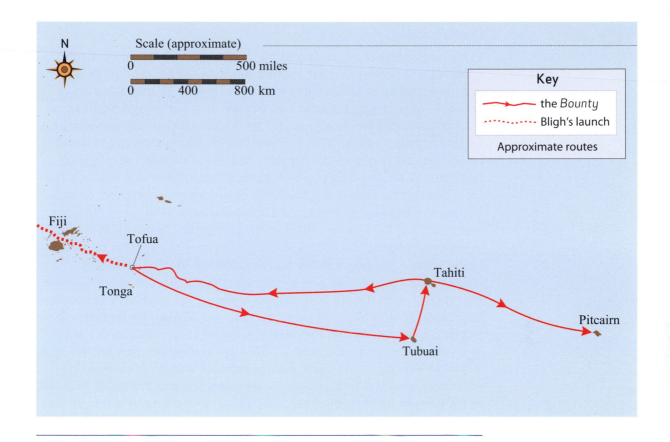

Keeping the contexts we have examined in mind, we turn now to consider in close detail how Bligh's and Christian's texts disclose such contradictory versions of events.

The case for William Bligh

It is difficult to forget Bligh's image as one of history's great bullies and tyrants, as two centuries of historical, fictional and cinematic versions of Bligh have created this mythic figure. Before we discuss Bligh-the-myth, however, let us study Bligh in his own terms by analysing his text.

Activity 2

Read the whole of Reading 8.2, which contains extracts from Bligh's *A Narrative*. In the same way that you did when reading Gronniosaw's text in Chapter 7, circle the first-person pronouns (I/we, me/us) in order to draw preliminary conclusions about how Bligh-as-narrator represents himself.

Discussion

In his description of the mutiny at the beginning of *A Narrative*, Bligh uses the first-person singular in order to represent his own credentials in the most positive possible light, and the mutineers as negatively as possible. Accordingly, he describes himself as a competent professional (he had gathered the breadfruit and the return journey was perfectly set); as courageous in adversity (he is unafraid of the mutineers, and when he '[dared] the ungrateful wretches to fire, they uncocked [their guns]' (p. 309)); as an able leader with a trusting relationship with his crew (he mentions that he always slept with his cabin door open in order to allow access to himself at all times); and as utterly conscientious in pursuing and protecting the mission. Bligh switches from the first-person singular in his description of the mutiny to the first-person plural in his description of the voyage. He refers to the survivors on the launch on several occasions as 'my people' and emphasises their collective sufferings and moments of relief. On 15 May, his log records: 'We were very little better than starving, with plenty in view' (p. 324). On 26 May, he reports catching a booby, 'so that Providence seemed to be relieving our wants in a very extraordinary manner' (p. 325). Bligh does not shift entirely from 'I'/'me' to 'we'/'us'; he remains the commander, and on occasions, he enforces his authority over his crew with violence and threats of violence. In his entry of 31 May, Bligh reports that some of the crew's 'fatigue and weakness so far got the better of their sense of duty, that some of them began to mutter' (p. 331), and when one of the crew looked at him 'with a mutinous look [and said] he was as good a man as myself' (p. 331), Bligh's response was decisive: 'seizing a cutlass, I ordered him to take hold of another and defend himself; on which he called out I was going to kill him, and began to make concessions' (p. 331). By contrast, towards the end of the voyage, there are two entries in which Bligh represents himself as the selfless servant and saviour of his crew. In his entry of 4 June, he claims to have borne the burden of worrying about their survival so that the crew's morale might be lifted: 'Miserable as our situation was in every respect, I was secretly surprised to see that it did not appear to affect any one so strongly as myself' (p. 333). And in his entry of 11 June, he reports the boatswain telling him 'that he really thought I looked worse than any one in the boat' (p. 334).

To understand why Bligh represented himself in this fashion, we need to register who he was writing for. In other words, who is the **implied reader** of *A Narrative*? Bligh identifies his sponsors as the audience he is most anxious to reassure, as he consoles himself in the immediate aftermath of the mutiny with the hope that 'I should one day be able to account to my King and country for the misfortune' (p. 313). Conscious that he would face a court martial, a second closely related audience Bligh addresses is an imagined judge and jury. Every word of *A Narrative* is dedicated to persuading these two audiences that his version of the mutiny is the truthful one. There is, however, a third reader implied in the text, and that is the book-buying public. Not only does Bligh want to convince Banks and his royal sponsors to keep him on their payroll and to fund further expeditions, and to persuade a court of law that his case against the mutineers is unanswerable; he also seeks to tell a compelling story that will sell as many books as possible. Persuading these three readerships is especially important in Bligh's description of the mutiny.

Activity 3

Reread Bligh's description of events on 28 April 1789 (pp. 308–14), including his explanation as to why the mutiny occurred. What words does Bligh repeat for emphasis? What is his explanation for the mutiny?

Discussion

Given its remarkable afterlife, you might be surprised at how short Bligh's description of the mutiny is. In the original 1790 edition of *A Narrative*, the mutiny occupies eleven pages out of the total eighty-eight, with the balance taken up with describing the journey to Timor. Bligh's *A Narrative* commences with a confident declaration of how successful his mission has been, and the next two paragraphs describe the beginnings of the voyage home, with the dates, co-ordinates and daily routine set down. The neutral **register** changes suddenly in the fourth paragraph, as the mutineers enter Bligh's cabin and manhandle him. The sentence, 'I demanded the reason of such violence, but received no other answer than threats of instant death' (p. 308), establishes Bligh's opposition between his own reasonable/professional/ordered/efficient/dutiful/peaceful regime and the irrational/criminal/chaotic/violent alternative asserted by Christian and the mutineers. Bligh repeats the key word 'reason' a few pages later when he asks, 'what could be the reason for such a revolt?' (p. 313). For Bligh, reason underwrites the scientific and commercial aims of the *Bounty*'s mission, and to sabotage the mission simply goes against reason. A second key word aligned to 'reason' is 'duty', which Bligh appeals to twice in the opening pages: at an early stage of the mutiny, he tries to 'persuade some one to a sense of duty; but it was to no effect' (p. 308); and once in the boat, he again attempts 'to bring back the offenders to a sense of their duty; but it was to no effect' (p. 308). A third word repeated by Bligh is 'endeavour' – he uses the word six times in the space of ten paragraphs – in order to emphasise how desperately hard he tried to oppose the mutiny. Not surprisingly, Christian and the mutineers are described as Bligh's polar opposites: 'villains' (p. 309), 'ungrateful wretches' (p. 309), 'the mutinous crew' (p. 310), 'a tribe of armed ruffians' (p. 310) and 'unfeeling wretches' (p. 311).

Assessing the reasons for the mutiny, Bligh concludes that the mutineers were convinced they would have a better life in Tahiti than in England. The main advantage of Tahiti over England, Bligh suggests, is the women of the island: they are 'handsome, mild and chearful in their manners and conversation, possessed of great sensibility, and have sufficient delicacy to make them admired and beloved' (p. 313). Bligh draws a further contrast: on Tahiti, the mutineers have 'some female connections [which] have most probably been the principal cause of the whole transaction' (p. 313), whereas in England, the majority of them are 'void of connections' (p. 313). Bligh's euphemistic language could be paraphrased more bluntly: the sailors have formed happier sexual relationships with the Tahitian women than they could ever hope for in England. In addition to these female 'connections', Bligh lists further attractions: the Tahitian chiefs encouraged the mutineers to stay, and promised they would be able to settle 'in the midst of plenty, on the finest island in the world' (p. 313); they would not be obliged to labour; and the 'allurements of dissipation [were] beyond any thing that can be conceived' (p. 313). Furthermore, Bligh expresses absolute certainty that his crew had no grounds to complain about his leadership: 'Had their mutiny been occasioned by any grievances, either real or imaginary, I must have discovered symptoms of their discontent' (p. 314). In placing full responsibility for the mutiny on the women of Tahiti and the weak character of his crew, Bligh thus refuses even to consider that his own actions might in any way have caused the mutiny.

What lent authority to Bligh's condemnation of the Tahitian women was the fact that feminised and eroticised images of the South Pacific islanders had accumulated in eighteenth-century British travelogues. Most influential in this respect was the official account of Cook's first voyage by John Hawkesworth (1715–1773), which both titillated and scandalised English readers with extensive descriptions of the islanders' relaxed sexual mores: 'there is a scale in dissolute sensuality, which these people have ascended, wholly unknown to every other nation whose manners have been recorded from the beginning of the world to the present hour, and which no imagination could possibly conceive' (Hawkesworth, 1773, p. 206). Bligh's accusation that the mutineers had formed 'some female connections' on Tahiti therefore coincided with existing stereotypes of the Pacific, and for British readers constituted a most plausible reason for mutiny.

Figure 8.2   John Webber, *Poedooa, the Daughter of Oree*, 1777, oil on canvas, 145 x 96 cm, National Maritime Museum, Greenwich, London. Photo: National Maritime Museum, Greenwich, London.

Aside from the mutiny, arguably the most dramatic event on the journey of the *Bounty*'s launch to Timor was the killing of John Norton on Tofua. I have already noted the feminised **imagery** used to describe the South Pacific in British travel writing, but such images alternated with a second **discourse**, which described the South Pacific islanders as violent savages, even as cannibals. In such descriptions, there was a tendency to occlude or downplay the violence perpetrated by the British against the South Pacific islanders. To address this imbalance, the historian Dening tallies all the deaths arising during the *Bounty*'s time in the Pacific between 1789 and 1794. With Christian and his crew inflicting heavy fatalities upon the natives of Tubuai after the mutiny, and the many subsequent murders on Pitcairn Island, Dening's final total adds up to 139 islanders as against seven Britons killed violently (Dening, 1992, p. 321). If Bligh's descriptions of sexual exchanges between the mutineers and Tahitian women reinforced one stereotype of the South Pacific, his account of the fatal encounter on Tofua therefore lent weight to the second dominant stereotype of the islanders as dangerous savages.

Figure 8.3   Johann Zoffany, *The Death of Captain James Cook, 14 February 1779*, *c*.1795, oil on canvas, 137 x 183 cm, National Maritime Museum, Greenwich, London. Photo: National Maritime Museum, Greenwich, London.

In order to appreciate the distinctiveness of Bligh's account, we turn now to compare his version of the clash with the indigenes of Tofua and of Norton's death with two other versions: the first-hand factual account of the Master John Fryer, and the fictional account narrated by the surgeon Thomas Ledward in Charles Nordhoff and James Norman Hall's *Men Against the Sea*. Fryer's version was lost in an archive until its publication in 1934, and Nordhoff and Hall's novel of the same year was the second volume in a best-selling trilogy.

Activity 4

Reread Bligh's account of the escape from Tofua (pp. 319–21 of Reading 8.2) and then read Fryer's version (Reading 8.3) and the extract from Nordhoff and Hall's novel (Reading 8.4). Summarise each narrator's version of events, identifying their similarities and differences. As well as focusing upon the events, consider their respective uses of language.

Discussion

1 **Bligh's version:** Bligh and his men had landed on Tofua with only four cutlasses, and the islanders soon registered their vulnerability. After a couple of days of limited bartering, on 3 May tensions between the islanders and Bligh's crew escalated. Bligh observed that their superficially friendly demeanour belied 'treacherous behaviour' (p. 320). The islanders attacked as the crew were escaping in the launch, and John Norton was killed. Bligh describes Norton as a 'worthy character' (p. 321) whose loss he much lamented. Bligh secured their ultimate escape by 'throwing overboard some cloaths' (p. 321), which the pursuing islanders stopped to gather rather than keep up the chase. He regrets his inability on this occasion to assert military superiority over the islanders – 'Here unhappily I was without arms, and the Indians knew it' (p. 321) – and generalises from this bitter experience: 'I considered their good behaviour hitherto to proceed from a dread of our fire-arms, which, now knowing us destitute of, would cease' (p. 321). Taking stock in the launch after their narrow escape, Bligh concludes on the basis of their unhappy experiences on Tofua that attempting to gather supplies at other inhabited islands would be a mistake, and he convinces the crew that sailing to Timor was their best option. Bligh emphasises both his own role in making this decision – 'I was solicited by all hands to take them towards home' (p. 321) – and the importance of his unique navigational expertise: we had 'nothing but my own recollection and general knowledge of the situation of places' (pp. 321–2). Bligh writes in the rational and scientific discourse of an educated professional, narrating the most alarming events with understated detachment.

2 **Fryer's version:** Much less polished in style than Bligh's account, Fryer describes the events leading up to the death of Norton and their flight from Tofua with much more emphasis on his own role and that of the other sailors (notably Purcel) in securing their escape. His insistence on keeping the launch in deeper water (against Bligh's orders) saved it from filling with water, and Purcel's heroics in helping Bligh onto the boat ensured that Norton was the only sailor left to a violent death. Fryer's version of how decisions were reached regarding the proposed route of the launch differs fundamentally from Bligh's. According to Fryer, notwithstanding their narrow escape on Tofua, Bligh still wanted to stop at other inhabited islands to trade, but he was overruled by the crew, with Fryer himself and Cole speaking for the majority: 'Mr Cole said that he would soon[er] trust to providence and live on an ounce of Bread than go to Tongataboo [Tonga], if we could get there as he was sure that the Natives would take every thing from us if not cut us all to pieces – then the rest said they thought that would be the case' (p. 344). Fryer also challenges Bligh's claim to have been the only one on the launch with the requisite navigational skills to complete the journey to Timor. In a key phrase, he insists that 'where Captain Bligh have wrote single he should have wrote plurel' (p. 345), not only because decisions on the launch were collectively made, but specifically because both he himself and Peckover had also had Timor in mind as a destination. Bligh in his version of the voyage 'has not mentioned any body['s] services but his own'; in truth (according to Fryer), 'there was others in the Boat that would have found their way to Timor as well as Captain Bligh and made every one with them more pleasant' (p. 345).

3 **The version in *Men Against the Sea*:** Surgeon Thomas Ledward was a historical figure, one of the survivors on the launch, but Nordhoff and Hall have appropriated him and used him as their narrator. In Ledward's version of events, the crew are 'a well-knit band' (p. 346), led by the resourceful and courageous Bligh: 'Bligh's actions at this time were beyond praise. To see him rise to a desperate occasion was an experience to be treasured in the memory. He was cool and clear-headed' (pp. 347–8). His rallying cry to the crew appealed to their national pride: 'Let these bastards see how Englishmen behave in a tight place' (p. 348). Bligh and the crew's virtues contrast with the wickedness of the Pacific islanders, who are described as 'masters at the art of dissembling' (p. 346), as 'treacherous villains' (p. 349) and as 'savages' (p. 349). The rising tension in the scene is carefully paced, with the polarised descriptions of the two contending parties alternating with terse dialogue. For the most part, the facts as recorded in Bligh's *A Narrative* are followed in

the novel (for example, Bligh's successful distraction of throwing clothes overboard), but there are details added for dramatic effect, like one of the pursuing islanders being 'struck squarely in the face by a stone cast by the boatswain' (p. 349).

If the violent confrontation with the inhabitants of Tofua coloured Bligh's previously sympathetic perception of the South Pacific islanders, his struggle to survive on the launch also affected his perception of the landscapes and seascapes of the Pacific. The geographer Dennis Cosgrove has argued that the capacity to view and appreciate landscapes is conventionally the privilege of those he defines as 'outsiders'. By contrast, those he defines as 'insiders' are denied this capacity: 'The insider does not enjoy the privilege of being able to walk away from a scene as we can walk away from a framed picture or from a tourist viewpoint' (Cosgrove, 1998, p. 19). Typically for Cosgrove, 'outsiders' are the wealthy and powerful, who own land and can survey it from a distance (and often from an elevated vantage point), whereas 'insiders' are those who work the land. In the contexts of European colonialism, 'outsiders' are generally European travellers observing the lands and oceans they traverse, whereas 'insiders' are the original inhabitants of those lands and

Figure 8.4   William Hodges, *Oaitepeha Bay, Tahiti*, 1776, oil on canvas, 93 x 138 cm, National Maritime Museum, Greenwich, London. Photo: National Maritime Museum, Greenwich, London.

oceans, and are the objects of European observation or surveillance. The painting, by William Hodges, of *Oaitepeha Bay, Tahiti* (1776) is a good example of an 'outsider' view of the Pacific islands (see Figure 8.4).

Activity 5

Bearing in mind Cosgrove's distinction, how does Bligh describe the landscapes and seascapes of the Pacific? Specifically, what qualities or attributes does Bligh most value in his descriptions of islands and headlands?

Discussion

All of Bligh's descriptions of the island landscapes he and his crew encountered are governed by pragmatic concerns: do they provide food and water? On Tofua, their difficulties in finding sustenance prompt Bligh's conclusion that 'the country … has a most dreary appearance', leading him to comment how 'we considered ourselves on as miserable spot of land as could well be imagined' (p. 316). The same criterion is applied explicitly in Bligh's description of the northernmost reaches of Australia: 'we had now a miserable low sandy coast in view, with very little verdure, or any thing to indicate that it was at all habitable to a human being' (p. 330). As the journey nears its conclusion, the landscape improves markedly, and again it is its capacity for providing food that draws Bligh's praise: 'The day gave us a most agreeable prospect of the land [Timor], which was interspersed with woods and lawns … We were greatly delighted with the general look of the country, which exhibited many cultivated spots and beautiful situations' (p. 335). Only once he knew they were safe, on the penultimate day of the journey, does Bligh allow considerations other than the practical to colour his descriptions: 'We had a view of a beautiful-looking country, as if formed by art lawns and parks' (p. 336). Given their desperate plight, it is hardly surprising that Bligh was blind to the aesthetics of the land- and seascapes he traversed, and that he only allowed himself to enjoy the view once their safety was assured. In Cosgrove's terms, Bligh might initially have been an 'outsider' enjoying the beauty of the Pacific land- and seascapes but, stripped of his military and material resources on the launch, he becomes an 'insider' and sees the Pacific vistas exclusively in terms of how they might help him to survive. Bligh remains an 'insider' until he feels safe again, and only then can he look at islands 'as if formed by art'.

One of the aims of this chapter is to appreciate the relationship between non-fictional and fictional forms of travel narrative, and, in concluding this section on Bligh's *A Narrative*, it is therefore useful to summarise how Bligh's text makes use of these two related modes of writing.

Activity 6

First, in what ways does Bligh's *A Narrative* seem to you like a non-fiction travelogue? Second, in what ways does the text seem to borrow from prose fiction?

Discussion

The most obvious feature of *A Narrative* is the captain's daily log. Bligh has an entry for every day of the journey in which he records the location of the launch, wind directions and weather conditions, and how much food and water they consume. His regular summaries of these factual details establish a sense of authenticity, not only because they communicate Bligh's professional competence as a navigator and seaman, but also because they have the status of objective historical record. To the general reader, much of this information might well be quite boring and repetitive, but its rhetorical effect is to constitute Bligh as the authoritative witness. This effect is reinforced by Bligh's frequent references to Captain Cook, who had explored the coastline on the launch's route about twenty years earlier. If Bligh can be trusted with regard to his record of the launch's progress on its perilous voyage (and his very survival suggests that readers can rely on his word), the assumption might well be that his statements about the mutineers, the survivors on the launch, and the islanders, are also a truthful record.

Bligh's text differs from most eighteenth-century non-fiction travel narratives in at least two respects. In the first place, the completion of the journey is significant because it ensures that the mutineers will be brought to justice. More than just an account of an arduous journey, *A Narrative* therefore has the greater purpose of exposing the mutineers, with Bligh a kind of prosecutor assembling evidence against the accused to put before a court of public opinion. In the second place, *A Narrative* shares many of the characteristics of eighteenth-century adventure novels like *Robinson Crusoe* (and, indeed, twentieth-century ones like *Men Against the Sea*): Bligh is the brave hero who undertakes a difficult journey; he overcomes obstacles both natural (the sea and adverse weather) and human (treacherous mutineers, seductive island women and violent island men); and he returns to the safety of home, having done his duty and ultimately prevailing against all the odds. By employing this popular literary form so skilfully, Bligh produces what one recent critic praises as a 'good unified piece of story-telling [which] belongs to the literary genre of sea voyages and discoveries of the eighteenth century' (Dunphy, 1982, p. 287). Bligh does not perpetrate obvious fictions in his narrative, but he does structure his factual account in accordance with this particular subgenre of the novel in order both to win his argument and to thrill his readers.

Closing arguments for Bligh

Bligh's actions on the *Bounty* and on the launch were guided by his unswerving commitment to Banks and the Royal Society, and to the example of Cook and the Royal Navy. Essential to serving these commitments was the need to maintain order, as is illustrated in his entry on 29 May, when he names 'Restoration Island':

> This being the day of the restoration of king Charles the Second, and the name not being inapplicable to our present situation (for we were restored to fresh life and strength), I named this Restoration Island; for I thought it probable that captain Cook might not have taken notice of it.

(p. 329)

Bligh's explanation for thus naming the island is limited to the fact that it provided oysters and berries for them to eat, and fresh water for them to drink. However, the (unconscious?) associations of Bligh's choice of name are more interesting. A number of beleaguered British sea captains, including Bartholomew Sharp, William Dampier and George Shevlocke, had likened their difficulties with mutinous crews to the Stuart monarchy struggling (and failing) to impose order on the Puritan revolutionaries of the seventeenth century (Lamb, 2001, p. 57). The breakdown of social order on the ship echoed the destruction in the 1640s of the social order headed by King Charles I. By invoking King Charles II in the naming of Restoration Island, Bligh thus identifies his successful voyage of survival on the launch with the re-establishment of monarchical order during the Restoration. The mutineers, like the Puritan revolutionaries, had enjoyed a brief period of ascendancy, but once Bligh had been rejuvenated on Restoration Island, their fate was sealed. Bligh (like King Charles I) had had his authority challenged by traitors to Britain, but in performing his duty and completing his heroic voyage, he was destined (like King Charles II) to return to restore the monarchy, exact justice, and re-impose order.

The case for Fletcher Christian

In 1794, Stephen Barney, the lawyer who had successfully defended some of the mutineers in 1792, published a partial transcript of the trial, together with 'an Appendix, Containing a Full Account of the Real Causes and Circumstances of the Unhappy Transaction, the most material of which have hitherto been withheld from the Public' by Edward Christian, Cambridge law professor and brother of Fletcher Christian. The partial transcript includes extracts from the minutes of the cross-examination of seven of the ten accused and very brief passages from the evidence of Captain Edwards of the *Pandora* and two of his lieutenants. Christian's legal discourse – based upon judicial procedure and witness statements made under oath – frames Bligh's individual account of the mutiny and the voyage as but one piece of highly contested evidence in a complicated and multi-faceted conflict. By citing as evidence statements by many other witnesses, and by synthesising such evidence into a single coherent version of events quite contrary to Bligh's *A Narrative*, Christian presents a powerful counter-account of the mutiny.

I noted in the discussion to Activity 1 how Christian's opening paragraphs strategically concede the wickedness of the mutiny and heroism of Bligh in sailing to Timor, but then insist that the context for assessing the mutiny must be extended to include all events on the outward voyage of the *Bounty* and during the months on Tahiti. Where Bligh used the captain's log as a rhetorical device to enhance the authority of his version of events, Christian relies on the language and procedures of the law. He builds a legal case by introducing the evidence of twelve witnesses: six survivors who were on the launch with Bligh; three mutineers who were acquitted; and another three mutineers who were convicted but subsequently pardoned. To validate the evidence, Christian lists the eleven respectable gentlemen who accompanied him when he gathered the witness statements and who functioned as his independent court of inquiry. One recent critic has noted that Christian's eleven-man jury was entirely made up of 'members of the Manx-Cumberland network of Church, Navy, the Bench, and the literary world of Cambridge' (Dunphy, 1982, p. 292) – close connections of the Christian family. Christian insists that 'there is no contradiction or variance' (p. 352) in the witness statements gathered by his unimpeachable authorities and that they all tell the same story: on the *Bounty*, Bligh was a tyrant deposed by men who had been bullied beyond reason.

Activity 7

Read the appendix to Stephen Barney's transcript of the 1792 trial by Edward Christian (Reading 8.5). How does Christian discredit Bligh, and how does he rescue the reputation of his brother Fletcher Christian? Pay attention to Christian's use of language.

Discussion

The character of Bligh comes under sustained attack, as his acts of cruelty towards the crew, and Christian in particular, are described in detail. Crucial facts left out of Bligh's *A Narrative* are added (for example, the bitter conflicts between Bligh and the islanders of Tofua before the mutiny, the islanders' theft of a cooper's adze on 26 April, and Bligh's anger at Christian for taking a coconut on 27 April) and certain key details are challenged (for example, whereas Bligh considered the mutiny a carefully plotted conspiracy, Christian argued that it was a spontaneous act of defiance). These matters of fact all contribute to Christian's principal strategy, which is to damage Bligh's reputation before the public.

The attack on Bligh is complemented by an even more exhaustive accumulation of evidence vouching for Fletcher Christian's excellent character. The most striking quality emphasised is Christian's acute sensitivity to Bligh's harsh treatment: the day before the mutiny, he was seen to be upset by Bligh's abuse, with 'tears … running fast from his eyes in big drops' (p. 353); immediately after the mutiny, Christian told the crew that when Bligh mentioned his wife and children, 'my heart melted, and I would then have jumped overboard' (p. 357); even at an early stage of the voyage, it was clear that 'the poignancy of [Christian's] distress had begun to prey upon his mind' (p. 358); and when Bligh humiliated Christian before the Tahitians, he was 'much mortified at being thus degraded in the opinion of his friend' (p. 359). In the aftermath of the mutiny, Christian's abjection is stressed: he is quoted by one witness as having rejected a return to Tahiti (and inevitable capture) by declaring, '*I will never live where I may be carried home to be a disgrace to my family*' (p. 361); and another witness recorded that 'Christian was always sorrowful and dejected [and] had become such an altered man in his looks and appearance, as to render it probable that he would not long survive this dreadful catastrophe' (p. 362). Having established how utterly remorseful Christian was for leading the mutiny, Edward Christian then stoutly rejects Bligh's explanation of the mutiny as caused by the Tahitian women. The 'Appendix' quotes an allegation that Christian had been inspired to mutiny by 'a *favourite female*' (p. 362) on the island, but insists that both those who remained in Tahiti and the officers with Christian at the time of the mutiny 'declare, that he never had a female favourite at Otaheite, nor any attachment or particular connexion among the women' (p. 363). The final pages of the 'Appendix' provide a long paragraph of very favourable quotations praising Christian's many excellent qualities, followed by a sympathetic summary of his career prior to the mutiny. Bligh's own generous role in promoting Christian's career before the *Bounty*, in particular, is highlighted. Edward Christian concludes his case with elevated rhetoric, suggesting that the mutiny on the *Bounty* should stand as a warning to the Navy to reform its ways by controlling tyrants like Bligh. He contrasts the judgements of 'public justice and the public safety' (which must condemn the mutiny), and those of 'reason and humanity' (p. 365) (which must recognise the injustice of Fletcher Christian's suffering under Bligh).

Closing arguments for Christian

Edward Christian rejects Bligh's explanation of the mutiny as the result of weak-willed seamen choosing an indolent life with Tahitian women, and casts it instead as the story of a sensitive young man leading a righteous rebellion against a tyrant. More precisely, Fletcher Christian's case is presented as the exposé of a tyrannical commander, who destroyed the career of a talented individual from a respectable family. The closing lines are especially resonant, as they rewrite the mutiny on the *Bounty* in the literary genre of tragedy. Fletcher Christian assumes the status of a tragic hero. He is one of 'the best formed and principled mind[s]' (p. 365), a potentially great young man undone by a combination of his own fatal flaw of giving in to an 'unpremeditated act of desperation and phrenzy' (p. 365) and his desperate misfortune in being under Bligh on the *Bounty*. After the catastrophe of the mutiny, his fate is to be 'condemned to perpetual infamy' (p. 365).

The judgement?

A superficial interpretation of the mutiny on the *Bounty* might read the fundamental opposition as one between the tyrant Bligh and the oppressed seamen led by Christian, with Bligh's case a version of Burke on the French Revolution, and Christian's a version of Paine. However, a more careful reading of the respective cases of Bligh and Christian suggests a more complicated opposition. Bligh's case is presented as the reasoned account of a highly trained professional dedicated to single-mindedly doing his duty for king and country. The mutiny is a consequence of the desires of weak and lazy men for Tahitian women. His case is framed in the literary genre of the sea-adventure/travel narrative, and support for Bligh included Banks and the scientific establishment, and the reformist and modernising factions of the Navy inspired by the example of Cook. Christian's case is presented as an appeal to feelings of justice and compassion for a respectable and gifted young man destroyed by a bullying commander. The mutiny is the result of a sensitive individual being sorely provoked into leading an uprising against a vicious tyrant. Christian's case is framed in the literary genre of tragedy, and support for Christian was made up of an elite of land-owning families from the north-west of England and the Isle of Man, members of the traditional Cambridge intelligentsia, conservative elements of the Navy and the Law, and senior figures in the Church of England. The opposition between Bligh and Christian might therefore be seen more accurately as a conflict between two competing factions within Britain's ruling elite: Bligh represents an upwardly mobile professional class trained in the sciences and driven by commercial ambition, whereas Christian represents a defensive land-owning class dependent upon family connections and strategic compromises with the emergent market economy.

Finally, before we conclude this section, it is important to register that we have not discussed several other fascinating, if less well-known, texts on the mutiny. Indeed, some of these more obscure accounts dramatise complex questions skirted in both Bligh's and Christian's texts, questions of class exclusion, colonial violence and gender oppression. For example, boatswain's mate and mutineer James Morrison's articulate record of events was only published for the first time in 1935 (and republished in 2010), and it presents a very different image of the mutineers and their lives on Tahiti (Morrison, 2010 [1935]). In direct contrast to Bligh's account, Morrison describes the mutineers on Tahiti as unhappy exiles forced to survive in a hostile environment by desperate circumstances (Neill, 2002, p. 176). Second, the oral account of the Tahitian woman known as Jenny, who was the partner of the mutineer Isaac Martin on Pitcairn, was transcribed in the 1820s, and first published in 1829 in the *United Service Journal and Naval and Military Magazine* (see Madison, 2001, pp. 228–34). Her descriptions of the difficult and murderous life led by the mutineers and the islander women on Pitcairn call into question the effusive descriptions of Fletcher Christian in his brother's Appendix, although they are consistent with what we now know of the slaughter and kidnapping perpetrated at Tubuai by Christian and the mutineers immediately after the mutiny.

The reception history

Since 1789, there have been many rewritings of the mutiny on the *Bounty*, with the court of public opinion in the vast majority of cases finding in favour of Christian. Arguably, the most influential version of the mutiny has been the 1935 Hollywood film, *Mutiny on the Bounty*, starring Charles Laughton as Bligh and Clark Gable as Christian (see Figure 8.5). Within six weeks of its release, 600,000 people had seen the movie (Dening, 1998, p. 33). Based loosely upon the first volume of Nordhoff and Hill's best-selling novel trilogy, *Mutiny on the Bounty*, Laughton's Bligh is a monster, and the allurements of the Tahitian women are secondary to Bligh's cruelty as the reason for the mutiny. Louis B. Meyer, the Hollywood studio magnate backing the movie, had been unenthusiastic about making a movie of the mutiny, as he 'disliked the idea of good order being overturned by "seductive" natives' (Sturma, 2002, p. 46), but two framing devices placated his concerns. The first was the fade-in foreword, which explains the mutiny as a necessary and ultimately helpful warning to the Royal Navy to address isolated instances of poor captaincy:

> In December, 1787, HMS *Bounty* lay in Portsmouth Harbour on the eve of departure for Tahiti in the unchartered waters of the Great South Sea. The *Bounty*'s mission was to procure breadfruit trees for transplanting to the West Indies as cheap food for slaves. Neither ship nor bread reached the West Indies. Mutiny prevented it – mutiny against the abuse of harsh eighteenth-century sea law. But this mutiny, famous in history and legend, helped bring about a new discipline, based upon mutual respect between officers and men, by which Britain's sea power is maintained and security for all who pass upon the seas.
>
> (*Mutiny on the Bounty*, film, 1935)

In other words, the ultimate effect of the mutiny was to secure Britain's maritime supremacy by encouraging 'a new discipline, based upon mutual respect between officers and men'. Order, undermined in the moment of the mutiny on the *Bounty*, is maintained in the long term by the institution of the Royal Navy. The second device was the final image of Christian on Pitcairn with his 'wife', holding their child, an image in line with Meyer's commitment to American family values, and consistent with all other MGM films of the 1930s.

Figure 8.5   Charles Laughton in the role of William Bligh, with Clark Gable as Fletcher Christian, *Mutiny on the Bounty*, dir. Frank Lloyd (Metro-Goldwyn-Mayer, 1935). Photo: Rex Features.

The 1984 film version of the mutiny, *The Bounty*, was scripted by Robert Bolt, and starred Anthony Hopkins as Bligh and Mel Gibson as Christian (see Figure 8.6). Based upon Richard Hough's 1972 novel, *Captain Bligh and Mr Christian*, this version is framed by Bligh's account to the Admiralty. A series of long takes opens the film, with Bligh arriving to give an account of the mutiny at his court martial. Camera angles contribute to conveying his relative vulnerability in relation to the panel of judges from the Admiralty, and sympathy for Bligh is further created by shots of him with wife and children. The sequences in Tahiti dwell at greater length on the attractions of the island women, and the difficulties of the voyage to Timor on the launch – including a vivid depiction of Norton's death – also demonstrate a greater fidelity to Bligh's version of events as set out in *A Narrative*. Despite its greater efforts to reflect the historical record of the mutiny, *The Bounty*, like all the other Hollywood versions of the mutiny, still fails to represent the scale of violence between the mutineers and the indigenous populations of the islands. Neither the mutineers' murderous interlude at Tubuai, immediately after the mutiny, nor the subsequent killings on Pitcairn are shown on screen.

Figure 8.6   Anthony Hopkins in the role of William Bligh, with Liam Neeson as Charles Churchill, Philip Davis as Edward Young, Mel Gibson as Fletcher Christian and Dexter Fletcher as Thomas Ellison, *The Bounty*, dir. Roger Donaldson (Dino De Laurentiis Company/Bounty Productions Ltd, 1984). Photo: Everett Collection/Rex Features.

The fascination with the mutiny on the *Bounty* has yet to abate, with recent popular novels rewriting the mutiny from either Bligh's or Christian's perspective. For example, Val McDermid's thriller, *The Grave Tattoo* (2006), weaves a contemporary murder plot together with a sympathetic portrayal of Fletcher Christian returning to England and being sheltered by William Wordsworth. By contrast, John Boyne's slight historical novel, *Mutiny on the Bounty* (2008), retells the story of the mutiny and voyage to Timor through the eyes of the fictional pickpocket/captain's servant John Jacob Turnstile, and provides a sympathetic portrait of Bligh. How do we explain this continuing fascination of the mutiny? At least part of the answer lies in the resilience of the powerful but irreconcilable readings of the mutiny laid down in the 1790s: first, Christian as irrational revolutionary defying the legitimate authority of Bligh (paralleling Burke's reading of the French Revolution), or, second, Christian as reluctant rebel standing up to the bully Bligh (following Paine). Starting with these strongly polarised readings, Bligh and Christian have over the last two centuries become universal archetypes of the individual versus authority. We have done our best here to restore their competing texts to their historical context(s), but the arguments over their respective and collective meanings are unlikely to be settled.

References

Burke, E. (1986 [1790]) *Reflections on the Revolution in France* (ed. C.C. O'Brien), Harmondsworth, Penguin.

Cosgrove, D. (1998) *Social Formation and Symbolic Landscape*, Madison, University of Wisconsin Press.

Dening, G. (1992) *Mr Bligh's Bad Language*, Cambridge, Cambridge University Press.

Dening, G. (1998) '"Captain Bligh" as mythic cliché: the films' in Barta, T. (ed.) *Screening the Past: Film and the Representation of History*, Westport, CT, Praeger, pp. 19–44.

Dunphy, J. (1982) 'Insurrection and repression: Bligh's 1790 *Narrative of the mutiny on board H.M. Ship Bounty*' in Barker, F. et al (eds) *1789: Reading Writing Revolution*, Colchester, University of Essex, pp. 281–301.

Edmond, R. (1997) *Representing the South Pacific: Colonial Discourse from Cook to Gauguin*, Cambridge, Cambridge University Press.

Hawkesworth, J. (1773) *An Account of the Voyages Undertaken by the Order of His Present Majesty for Making Discoveries in the Southern Hemisphere: Volume II*, London, W. Strahan and T. Cadell.

Lamb, J. (2001) *Preserving the Self in the South Seas, 1680–1840*, Chicago and London, University of Chicago Press.

Lefebvre, G. (1971) *The French Revolution from its Origins to 1793* (trans. E.M. Evanson), London, Routledge and Kegan Paul.

Madison, R.D. (ed.) (2001) *The Bounty Mutiny: William Bligh and Edward Christian*, London, Penguin.

Morrison, J. (2010 [1935]) *After the Bounty: A Sailor's Account of the Mutiny and Life in the South Seas* (ed. D.A. Maxton), Dulles, VA, Potomac Books.

Mutiny on the Bounty, film, directed by D. Lloyd, USA, Metro-Goldwyn Mayer, 1935.

Neill, A. (2002) *British Discovery Literature and the Rise of Global Commerce*, Basingstoke, Palgrave.

Paine, T. (1989 [1791–92]) *The Rights of Man* in *Political Writings* (ed. B. Kuklick), Cambridge, Cambridge University Press.

Rediker, M. (1987) *Between the Devil and the Deep Blue Sea*, Cambridge, Cambridge University Press.

Rennie, N. (1995) *Far-Fetched Facts: The Literature of Travel and the Idea of the South Seas*, Oxford, Clarendon Press.

Sturma, M. (2002) *South Sea Maidens: Western Fantasy and Sexual Politics in the South Pacific*, Westport, CT, Greenwood Press.

Williams, G. (1997) *The Great South Sea: English Voyages and Encounters 1570–1750*, New Haven and London, Yale University Press.

Further reading

Dening, G. (1992) *Mr Bligh's Bad Language*, Cambridge, Cambridge University Press.

Lamb, J., Smith, V. and Thomas, N. (eds) (2000) *Exploration and Exchange: A South Seas Anthology, 1680–1900*, Chicago, University of Chicago Press.

Madison, R.D. (ed.) (2001) *The Bounty Mutiny: William Bligh and Edward Christian*, London, Penguin.

Conclusion to Part 2

David Johnson

The second part of this book has demonstrated the centrality of journeys in the long eighteenth century. Specifically, the four chapters have explored a variety of fictional and non-fictional writings about journeys. In your study of Aphra Behn's novel *Oroonoko*, you analysed the overlapping narratives of the female narrator and of Oroonoko describing their different journeys between West Africa, England and Surinam; in Voltaire's philosophical tale *Candide*, you examined the travel tales of the eponymous hero, his beloved Cunégonde, and his servant Cacambo, as well as the philosophical journey Candide undertakes in wrestling with his tutor Pangloss's creed of optimism; in Ukawsaw Gronniosaw's spiritual autobiography, you studied how he narrates both his physical journey (from West Africa to the Caribbean, to the eastern seaboard of the United States and, finally, to England) and his spiritual journey from heathen to Christian; and, in William Bligh's first-person account of his journey on the launch after the mutiny on the *Bounty*, you appreciated Bligh's rhetorical skill in combining fictional and non-fictional narrative devices in order to diminish his own culpability for the mutiny.

In all four chapters, close textual analysis was the necessary first step in coming to grips with how journeys were narrated in the long eighteenth century. You have noted in *Oroonoko* the contradictions in the attempts of the female narrator to reconcile her sympathy for the heroic African prince and her fear of slave rebellion, and in *Candide* the irony in the narrator Doctor Ralph's efforts to cast the Lisbon earthquake as confirmation of the axiom that 'whatever is, is right'. You have also seen Gronniosaw's attempt to narrate his difficult life story in accordance with the generic imperatives of the Christian conversion narrative, as well as Bligh's manipulation of novelistic techniques in order to cast his heroism on the launch in the most positive possible light. This close analysis of the set texts was accompanied by extended attention to their many contexts, the argument being that our understanding of the texts is in all cases enhanced by reading them in juxtaposition with their contexts. In each of the four chapters, we therefore foregrounded significant elements of their respective contexts: for *Oroonoko*, European colonisation, African slavery, and Britain's Glorious Revolution; for *Candide*, the philosophical and literary ideas of eighteenth-century Europe; for Gronniosaw, Islamic West Africa, the

Atlantic slave triangle and Protestant Christianity; and for the narratives of the mutiny on the *Bounty*, eighteenth-century British maritime exploration and the English class system, as well as Hollywood cinema in the twentieth century. In all cases, how we have understood the diverse journeys narrated in these texts has been enriched by an expanded knowledge of their multiple contexts.

Readings for Part 2

Contents

Reading 7.1 *A Narrative of the Life of James Albert Ukawsaw Gronniosaw Written by Himself*

Source: James Albert Ukawsaw Gronniosaw (1774) *A Narrative of the Most Remarkable Particulars in the Life of James Albert Ukawsaw Gronniosaw, An African Prince, Written by Himself*, Bath, W. Gye and T. Mills, pp. 27–53. Footnotes are by David Johnson. The text has been revised slightly from the original (some old English spellings have been modernised).

The preface to the reader

This account of the life and spiritual experience of James Albert, *was taken from his own mouth, and committed to paper by the elegant pen of a young* Lady *of the town of* Leominster[1], *for her own private satisfaction, and without any intention, at first, that it should be made public. But she has now been prevailed on to commit it to the press, both with a view to serve* Albert *and his distressed family, who have the sole profits arising from the sale of it; and likewise, as it is apprehended, this little history contains matter well worthy the notice and attention of every Christian reader.*

Perhaps we have here, in some degree, a solution of that question that has perplex'd the minds of so many serious persons, viz. In what manner will God deal with those benighted parts of the world where the gospel of Jesus Christ hath never reached? Now, it appears, from the experience of this remarkable person, that God does not save without the knowledge of the truth; but, with respect to those whom he hath foreknown, though born under every outward disadvantage, and in the regions of the grossest darkness and ignorance, he most amazingly acts upon, and influences, their minds, and in the course of wisely and most wonderfully appointed providence, he brings them to the means of spiritual information, gradually opens to their view the light of his truth, and gives them full possession and enjoyment of the inestimable blessings of his gospel. Who can doubt but that the suggestion so forcibly press'd upon the mind of Albert *(when a boy) that there was a Being superior to the sun, moon, and stars (the objects of African idolatry) came from the Father of lights, and was, with respect to him, the first fruit of the display of gospel glory? His long and perilous journey to the coast of* Guinea,[2] *where he was sold for a slave, and so brought into a Christian land; shall we consider this as the alone*

---

[1]   The 1809 edition of *A Narrative* names Hannah More (1745–1833) as the '*young* Lady *of the town of* Leominster'.

[2]   In the eighteenth century, 'Guinea' referred to the entire stretch of African coast from Senegal to Angola.

effect of a curious and inquisitive disposition? Shall we, in accounting for it refer to nothing higher than mere chance & accidental circumstances? Whatever Infidels & Deists may think, I trust the Christian reader will easily discern an all wise and omnipotent appointment and direction in these movements. He belonged to the Redeemer of lost sinners; he was the purchase of his cross; and therefore the Lord undertook to bring him by a way he knew not, out of darkness into his marvellous light, that he might lead him to a saving heart-acquaintance and union with the triune God in Christ, reconciling the world unto himself; and not imputing their trespasses. As his call was very extraordinary, so there are certain particulars exceedingly remarkable in his experience. God has put singular honor upon him in the exercise of his faith and patience, which, in the most distressing and pitiable trials and calamities, have been found to the praise and glory of God. How deeply must it affect a tender heart, not only to be reduc'd to the last extremity himself, but to have his wife and children perishing for want before his eyes! Yet his faith did not fail him; he put his trust in the Lord, and he was delivered. And, at this instant, though born in an exalted station of life, and now under the Pressure of various afflicting Providences, I am persuaded (for I know the man) he would rather embrace the dunghill, having Christ in his heart, than give up his spiritual possessions and enjoyment, to fill the throne of Princes. It perhaps may not be amiss to observe, that James Albert *left his native country (as near as I can guess from certain circumstances) when he was about* 15 *years old. He now appears to be turn'd of* 60*; has a good natural understanding; is well acquainted with the scriptures, and the things of God; has an amiable and tender disposition; and his character can be well attested not only at* Kidderminster, *the place of his residence, but likewise by many creditable persons in* London *and other places. Reader, recommending this* Narrative *to your perusal, and him who is the subject of it, to your charitable regard,*

I am your faithful and obedient servant,
For Christ's sake,
W. SHIRLEY.[3]

An account of James Albert, &c.

I was born in the city of *Baurnou*,[4] my mother was the eldest daughter of the reigning King there. I was the youngest of six children, and particularly loved by my mother, and my grand-father almost doated on me.

---

[3]   'W. Shirley' is the Reverend Walter Shirley (1726–1786), the first cousin of Selina, the Countess of Huntingdon, to whom Gronniosaw dedicated the first edition of his narrative. Shirley was a successful preacher, who met Gronniosaw in the 1760s in Kidderminster.

[4]   '*Baurnou*' is the region today known as Bornu (also sometimes spelt 'Borno') in north-eastern Nigeria which borders Lake Chad.

I had, from my infancy, a curious turn of mind; was more grave and reserved, in my disposition, than either of my brothers and sisters, I often teazed them with questions they could not answer; for which reason they disliked me, as they supposed that I was either foolish or insane. 'Twas certain that I was, at times, very unhappy in myself: It being strongly impressed on my mind that there was some GREAT MAN of power which resided above the sun, moon and stars, the objects of our worship. – My dear, indulgent mother would bear more with me than any of my friends beside. – I often raised my hand to heaven, and asked her who lived there? Was much dissatisfied when she told me the sun, moon and stars, being persuaded, in my own mind, that there must be some SUPERIOR POWER. – I was frequently lost in wonder at the works of the creation: Was afraid, and uneasy, and restless, but could not tell for what. I wanted to be informed of things that no person could tell me; and was always dissatisfied. – These wonderful impressions began in my childhood, and followed me continually till I left my parents, which affords me matter of admiration and thankfulness.

To this moment I grew more and more uneasy every day, insomuch that one Saturday (which is the day on which we kept our sabbath) I laboured under anxieties and fears that cannot be expressed; and, what is more extraordinary, I could not give a reason for it.– – I rose, as our custom is, about three o'clock (as we are obliged to be at our place of worship an hour before the sun rise) we say nothing in our worship, but continue on our knees with our hands held up, observing a strict silence till the sun is at a certain height, which I suppose to be about 10 or 11 o'clock in *England*: When, at a certain sign made by the Priest, we get up (our duty being over) and disperse to our different houses. – Our place of meeting is under a large palm tree; we divide ourselves into many congregations; as it is impossible for the same tree to cover the inhabitants of the whole city, though they are extremely large, high and majestic; the beauty and usefulness of them are not to be described; they supply the inhabitants of the country with meat, drink and clothes; the body of the palm tree is very large; at a certain season of the year they tap it, and bring vessels to receive the wine, of which they draw great quantities, the quality of which is very delicious: The leaves of this tree are of a silky nature; they are large and soft; when they are dried and pulled to pieces, it has much the same appearance as the English flax, and the inhabitants of BOURNOU manufacture it for clothing, &c. This tree likewise produces a plant, or substance, which has the appearance of a cabbage, and very like it, in taste almost the same: It grows between the branches. Also the palm tree produces a nut, something like a cocoa, which contains a kernel, in which is a large quantity of milk, very pleasant to the taste: The shell is of a hard substance, and of a very beautiful appearance, and serves for basons, bowls, &c.

I hope this digression will be forgiven. – I was going to observe, that after the duty of our sabbath was over (on the day in which I was more distressed and afflicted than ever) we were all on our way home as usual, when a remarkable black cloud arose and covered the sun; then followed very heavy rain and thunder, more dreadful than ever I had heard: The heavens roared, and the earth trembled at it: I was highly affected and cast down; insomuch that I wept sadly, and could not follow my relations & friends home. – I was obliged to stop, and felt as if my legs were tied, they seemed to shake under me: So I stood still, being in great fear of the MAN of POWER, that I was persuaded, in myself, lived above. One of my young companions (who entertained a particular friendship for me, and I for him) came back to see for me: He asked me why I stood still in such very hard rain? I only said to him that my legs were weak, and I could not come faster: He was much affected to see me cry, and took me by the hand, and said he would lead me home, which he did. My mother was greatly alarmed at my tarrying out in such terrible weather; she asked me many questions, such as what I did so for? And if I was well? My dear mother, says I, pray tell me who is the GREAT MAN of POWER that makes the thunder? She said, there was no power but the sun, moon and stars; that they made all our country.– – I then inquired how all our people came? She answered me, from one another; and so carried me to many generations back. – Then says I, who made the *first man*? And who made the first cow, and the first lion, and where does the fly come from, as no one can make him? My mother seemed in great trouble; she was apprehensive that my senses were impaired, or that I was foolish. My father came in, and seeing her in grief asked the cause, but when she related our conversation to him he was exceedingly angry with me, and told me he would punish me severely if ever I was so troublesome again; so that I resolved never to say any thing more to him. But I grew very unhappy in myself; my relations and acquaintance endeavoured, by all the means they could think on, to divert me, by taking me to ride upon goats (which is much the custom of our country) and to shoot with a bow and arrow; but I experienced no satisfaction at all in any of these things; nor could I be easy by any means whatever: My parents were very unhappy to see me so dejected and melancholy.

About this time there came a merchant from the *Gold Coast*[5] (the third city in GUINEA) he traded with the inhabitants of our country in ivory, &c. he took great notice of my unhappy situation, and inquired into the cause; he expressed vast concern for me, and said, if my parents would part with me for a little while, and let him take me home with him, it would be of more service to me than any thing they could do for me. – He told me that if I would go with him I should see houses with wings to them walk upon the water, and should also see the white folks; and that he had many sons of my age, which should be my companions; and he added to all this that he would bring me safe back again soon. – I was highly pleased with the account of this strange place, and was very desirous of going. – I seemed sensible of a secret impulse upon my mind, which I could not resist, that seemed to tell me I must go. When my dear mother saw that I was willing to leave them, she spoke to my father and grandfather and the rest of my relations, who all agreed that I should accompany the merchant to the Gold Coast. I was the more willing as my brothers and sisters despised me, and looked on me with contempt on the account of my unhappy disposition; and even my servants slighted me, and disregarded all I said to them. I had one sister who was always exceeding fond of me, and I loved her entirely; her name was LOGWY, she was quite white, and fair, with fine light hair, though my father and mother were black.[6] – I was truly concerned to leave my beloved sister, and she cry'd most sadly to part with me, wringing her hands, and discovered every sign of grief that can be imagined. Indeed if I could have known when I left my friends and country that I should never return to them again my misery on that occasion would have been inexpressible. All my relations were sorry to part with me; my dear mother came with me upon a camel more than three hundred miles, the first of our journey lay chiefly through woods: At night we secured ourselves from the wild beasts by making fires all around us; we and our camels kept within the circle, or we must have been torn to pieces by the lions, and other wild creatures, that roared terribly as soon as night came on, and continued to do so till morning. – There can be little said in favour of the country through which we passed; only a valley of marble that we came through which is unspeakably beautiful. – On each side of this valley are exceedingly high

---

[5] The Gold Coast refers to the area between the Benyori and Volta Rivers, the location of modern-day Ghana.

[6] It is most probable that Logwy was an albino.

and almost inaccessible mountains – Some of these pieces of marble are of prodigious length and breadth but of different sizes and colour, and shaped in a variety of forms, in a wonderful manner. – It is most of it veined with gold mixed with striking and beautiful colours; so that when the sun darts upon it, it is as pleasing a sight as can be imagined. – – The merchant that brought me from BOURNOU was in partnership with another gentleman who accompanied us; he was very unwilling that he should take me from home, as, he said, he foresaw many difficulties that would attend my going with them. – He endeavoured to prevail on the merchant to throw me into a very deep pit that was in the valley, but he refused to listen to him, and said, he was resolved to take care of me: But the other was greatly dissatisfied; and when we came to a river, which we were obliged to pass through, he purposed throwing me in and drowning me; but the merchant would not consent to it, so that I was preserved.

We travel'd till about four o'clock every day, and then began to make preparations for night, by cutting down large quantities of wood, to make fires to preserve us from the wild beasts. – I had a very unhappy and discontented journey, being in continual fear that the people I was with would murder me. I often reflected with extreme regret on the kind friends I had left, and the idea of my dear mother frequently drew tears from my eyes. I cannot recollect how long we were in going from *Bournou* to the *Gold Coast*; but as there is no shipping nearer to *Bournou* than that city, it was tedious in travelling so far by land, being upwards of a thousand miles. – I was heartily rejoiced when we arrived at the end of our journey:[7] I now vainly imagined that all my troubles and inquietudes would terminate here; but could I have looked into futurity, I should have perceived that I had much more to suffer than I had before experienced, and that they had as yet but barely commenced.

I was now more than a thousand miles from home, without a friend or any means to procure one. Soon after I came to the merchant's house I heard the drums beat remarkably loud, and the trumpets blow – the persons accustom'd to this employ, are oblig'd to go upon a very high structure appointed for that purpose, that the sound might be heard at a great distance: They are higher than the steeples are in *England*. I was mightily pleased with sounds so entirely new to me, and was very inquisitive to know the cause of this rejoicing, and asked many

---

[7] Gronniosaw's likeliest destination would have been Fort Elmina, the major Dutch slave-trading port on the Gold Coast in the eighteenth century.

questions concerning it; I was answered that it was meant as a compliment to me, because I was grandson to the King of *Bournou*.

This account gave me a secret pleasure; but I was not suffered long to enjoy this satisfaction, for, in the evening of the same day, two of the merchant's sons (boys about my own age) came running to me, and told me, that the next day I was to die, for the King intended to behead me. – I reply'd, that I was sure it could not be true, for that I came there to play with them, and to see houses walk upon the water, with wings to them, and the white folks; but I was soon informed that their King imagined I was sent by my father as a spy, and would make such discoveries, at my return home, that would enable them to make war with the greater advantage to ourselves; and for these reasons he had resolved I should never return to my native country. – When I heard this, I suffered misery that cannot be described. – I wished, a thousand times, that I had never left my friends and country. – But still the Almighty was pleased to work miracles for me.

The morning I was to die, I was washed and all my gold ornaments made bright and shining, and then carried to the palace, where the King was to behead me himself (as is the custom of the place). – He was seated upon a throne at the top of an exceeding large yard, or court, which you must go through to enter the palace, it is as wide and spacious as a large field in *England*. – I had a lane of life-guards to go through. – I guessed it to be about three hundred paces.

I was conducted by my friend, the merchant, about half way up; then he durst proceed no further: I went up to the King alone – I went with an undaunted courage, and it pleased God to melt the heart of the King, who sat with his scymitar in his hand ready to behead me; yet, being himself so affected, he dropped it out of his hand, and took me upon his knee and wept over me. I put my right hand round his neck, and prest him to my heart. – He set me down and blest me; and added that he would not kill me, and that I should not go home, but be sold for a slave, so then I was conducted back again to the merchant's house.

The next day he took me on board a French brig; the Captain did not chuse to buy me: He said I was too small; so the merchant took me home with him again.

The partner, whom I have spoken of as my enemy, was very angry to see me return, and again purposed putting an end to my life; for he represented to the other, that I should bring them into troubles and difficulties, and that I was so little that no person would buy me.

The merchant's resolution began to waver, and I was indeed afraid that I should be put to death: But however he said he would try me once more.

A few days after a *Dutch* ship came into the harbour, and they carried me on board, in hopes that the Captain would purchase me. – As they went, I heard them agree, that, if they could not sell me *then*, they would throw me overboard. – I was in extreme agonies when I heard this; and as soon as ever I saw the *Dutch* Captain, I ran to him, and put my arms round him, and said, 'Father save me.' (for I knew that if he did not buy me I should be treated very ill, or, possibly murdered) And though he did not understand my language, yet it pleased the Almighty to influence him in my behalf, and he bought me *for two yards of check*, which is of more value *there*, than in *England*.

When I left my dear mother I had a large quantity of gold about me, as is the custom in our country, it was made into rings, and they were linked into one another, and formed into a kind of chain, and so put round my neck, and arms and legs, and a large piece hanging at one ear almost in the shape of a pear. I found all this troublesome, and was glad when my new master took it from me. – I was now washed, & clothed in the *Dutch* or *English* manner. – My master grew very fond of me, and I loved him exceedingly. I watched every look, was always ready when he wanted me, and endeavoured to convince him, by every action, that my only pleasure was to serve him well. – I have since thought that he must have been a serious man. His actions corresponded very well with such a character. – He used to read prayers in public to the ship's crew every sabbath day; and when first I saw him read, I was never so surprised in my whole life as when I saw the book talk to my master; for I thought it did, as I observed him to look upon it, and move his lips. – I wished it would do so to me. – As soon as my master had done reading I follow'd him to the place where he put the book, being mightily delighted with it, and when nobody saw me, I open'd it and put my ear down close upon it, in great hope that it would say something to me; but was very sorry and greatly disappointed when I found it would not speak, this thought immediately presented itself to me, that every body and every thing despised me because I was black.

I was exceedingly sea-sick at first; but when I became more accustom'd to the sea, it wore off. – My master's ship was bound for *Barbados*. When we came there, he thought fit to speak of me to several gentlemen of his acquaintance, and one of them exprest a particular desire to see me. – He had a great mind to buy me; but the Captain could not immediately be prevail'd on to part with me; but however, as the gentleman seemed very solicitous, he at length let me go, and I was sold for fifty dollars (*four and six penny pieces in English*.) My new master's name was *Vanhorn*, a young gentleman; his home was in *New-England*, in the city of *New-York*; to which place he took me with him. He dress'd me in his livery, & was very good to me. My chief business was to wait at table, and tea, & clean knives, & I had a very easy place; but the servants used to curse & swear surprizingly; which I learnt faster than any thing, 'twas almost the first English I could speak. If any of them affronted me, I was sure to call upon God to damn them immediately; but I was broke of it all at once, occasioned by the correction of an old black servant that lived in the family. – One day I had just clean'd the knives for dinner, when one of the maids took one to cut bread and butter with; I was very angry with her, and called upon God to damn her; when this old black man told me I must not say so: I ask'd him why? He replied there was a wicked man, call'd the Devil, that liv'd in hell, and would take all that said these words and put them in the fire and burn them. – This terrified me greatly, and I was entirely broke of swearing. Soon after this, as I was placing the china for tea, my mistress came into the room just as the maid had been cleaning it; the girl had unfortunately sprinkled the wainscot with the mop; at which my mistress was angry; the girl very foolishly answered her again, which made her worse, and she called upon God to damn her. – I was vastly concern'd to hear this, as she was a fine young lady, and very good to me, insomuch that I could not help speaking to her: Madam, says I, you must not say so: Why, says she? Because there is a black man, call'd the Devil, that lives in hell, and he will put you in the fire and burn you, and I shall be very sorry for that. Who told you this, replied my lady? Old Ned, says I. Very well was all her answer; but she told my master of it, who ordered that old Ned should be tied up and whipp'd, and was never suffered to come into the kitchen, with the rest of the servants, afterwards. – My mistress was not angry with me, but rather diverted at my simplicity, and, by way of talk, she repeated what I had said to many of her acquaintance that visited her; among the rest, *Freelandhouse*,[8] a very gracious, good minister, heard it, and he took a great deal of notice of me, and desired my master to part with me to him. He would not hear of it at first, but, being greatly persuaded, he let me go; and Mr. *Freelandhouse* gave £.50 for me. – He took me home

---

[8]   '*Freelandhouse*' was the Reverend Theodorus Jacobus Frelinghuysen (1691–1747/8), an Evangelical Dutch Reformed minister in the Raritan Valley of New Jersey from the 1720s to the 1740s.

with him, and made me kneel down, and put my two hands together, and prayed for me, and every night and morning he did the same. – I could not make out what it was for, nor the meaning of it, nor what they spoke to when they talked – I thought it comical, but I liked it very well. – After I had been a little while with my new master I grew more familiar, and asked him the meaning of prayer: (I could hardly speak *English* to be understood) he took great pains with me, and made me understand that he pray'd to God, who liv'd in Heaven; that he was my father and *best* friend. – I told him that this must be a mistake; that *my* father lived at *Bournou*, and I wanted very much to see him, and likewise my dear mother, and sister, and I wished he would be so good as to send me home to them; and I added, all I could think of to induce him to convey me back, I appeared in great trouble, and my good master was so much affected that the tears run down his face. He told me that God was a great and good Spirit, that he created all the world, and every person and thing in it, *Ethiopia*, *Africa* and *America*, and every where. I was delighted when I heard this: There, says I, I always thought so when I lived at home! Now, if I had wings like an eagle, I would fly to tell my dear mother that God is greater than the sun, moon and stars; and that they were made by him.

I was exceedingly pleas'd with this information of my master's, because it corresponded so well with my own opinion; I thought now if I could but get home, I should be wiser than all my country-folks, my grandfather, or father, or mother, or any of them. – But though I was somewhat enlightened, by this information of my master's, yet I had no other knowledge of God than that he was a good Spirit, and created every body, and every thing. – I never was sensible, in myself, nor had any one ever told me, that he would punish the wicked, and love the just. I was only glad that I had been told there was a God, because I had always thought so.

My dear kind master grew very fond of me, as was his lady; she put me to school, but I was uneasy at that, and did not like to go; but my master and mistress requested me to learn in the gentlest terms, and persuaded me to attend my school without any anger at all; that, at last, I came to like it better, and learnt to read pretty well. My schoolmaster was a good man, his name was *Vanosdore*,[9] and very indulgent to me. – I was in this state when, one Sunday, I heard my master preach from these words out of the *Revelations*, chap. i. v. 7. '*Behold, He cometh in the clouds and every eye shall see him and they that pierc'd Him.*' These words

---

[9] '*Vanosdore*' was most probably Peter van Arsdalen, one of Frelinghuysen's close associates.

affected me excessively; I was in great agonies because I thought my master directed them to me only; and, I fancied, that he observed me with unusual earnestness – I was farther confirm'd in this belief as I looked round the church, and could see no one person beside myself in such grief and distress as I was; I began to think that my master hated me, and was very desirous to go home, to my own country; for I thought that if God did come (as he said) He would be sure to be most angry with me, as I did not know what He was, nor had ever heard of him before.

I went home in great trouble, but said nothing to any body. – I was somewhat afraid of my master; I thought he disliked me. – The next text I heard him preach from was, *Heb.* xii. 14. *'Follow peace with all men, and holiness, without which no man shall see the LORD.'* He preached the law so severely, that it made me tremble. – He said, that GOD would judge the whole world; *Ethiopia*, *Asia*, and *Africa*, and every where. – I was now excessively perplexed, and undetermined what to do; as I had now reason to believe that my situation would be equally bad to go as to stay. – I kept these thoughts to myself, and said nothing to any person whatever.

I should have complained to my good mistress of this great trouble of mind, but she had been a little strange to me for several days before this happened, occasioned by a story told of me by one of the maids. The servants were all jealous, and envied me the regard, and favour shewn me by my master and mistress; and the Devil being always ready, and diligent in wickedness, had influenced this girl to make a lie on me. – This happened about hay harvest, and one day, when I was unloading the wagon to put the hay into the barn, she watched an opportunity, in my absence, to take the fork out of the stick, and hide it: When I came again to my work, and could not find it, I was a good deal vexed, but I concluded it was dropt somewhere among the hay; so I went and bought another with my own money: When the girl saw that I had another, she was so malicious that she told my mistress I was very unfaithful, and not the person she took me for; and that she knew, I had, without my master's permission, ordered many things in his name, that he must pay for; and as a proof of my carelessness produced the fork she had taken out of the stick, and said, she had found it out of doors – My Lady, not knowing the truth of these things, was a little shy to me, till she mentioned it, and then I soon cleared myself, and convinced her that these accusations were false.

I continued in a most unhappy state for many days. My good mistress insisted on knowing what was the matter. When I made known my situation, she gave me John Bunyan[10] on the holy war, to read; I found his experience similar to my own, which gave me reason to suppose he must be a bad man; as I was convinced of my own corrupt nature, and the misery of my own heart: And as he acknowledged that he was likewise in the same condition, I experienced no relief at all in reading his work, but rather the reverse. – I took the book to my lady, and informed her I did not like it at all, it was concerning a wicked man as bad as myself; and I did not chuse to read it, and I desired her to give me another, wrote by a better man, that was holy, and without sin. – She assured me that John Bunyan was a good man, but she could not convince me; I thought him to be too much like myself to be upright, as his experience seemed to answer with my own.

I am very sensible that nothing but the great power and unspeakable mercies of the Lord could relieve my soul from the heavy burden it laboured under at that time. – A few days after my master gave me Baxter's *call to the unconverted*.[11] This was no relief to me neither; on the contrary it occasioned as much distress in me as the other had before done, *as it* invited all to come to *Christ*; and I found myself so wicked and miserable that I could not come –. This consideration threw me into agonies that cannot be described; insomuch that I even attempted to put an end to my life – I took one of the large case-knives, and went into the stable with an intent to destroy myself; and as I endeavoured with all my strength to force the knife into my side, it bent double. I was instantly struck with horror at the thought of my own rashness, and my conscience told me that had I succeeded in this attempt I should probably have gone to hell.

I could find no relief, nor the least shadow of comfort; the extreme distress of my mind so affected my health that I continued very ill for three days, and nights; and would admit of no means to be taken for my recovery, though my lady was very kind, and sent many things to me; but I rejected every means of relief and wished to die – I would not go into my own bed, but lay in the stable upon straw – I felt all the horrors of a troubled conscience, so hard to be born, and saw all the vengeance of God ready to overtake me – I was sensible that there was no way for me to be saved unless I came to *Christ*, and I could not come to Him: I thought that it was impossible He should receive such a sinner as me.

[10] John Bunyan (1628–1688) was a devout English Baptist preacher and writer, best known for *A Pilgrim's Progress* (1678) and his spiritual autobiography *Grace Abounding* (1666), but also the author of *The Holy War* (1682).

[11] Richard Baxter (1615–1691) was another English Protestant thinker, more moderate than Bunyan, and the author of *A Call to the Unconverted* (1658).

The last night that I continued in this place, in the midst of my distress these words were brought home upon my mind, '*Behold the Lamb of God,*' I was something comforted at this, and began to grow easier and wished for day that I might find these words in my bible – I rose very early the following morning, and went to my school-master, Mr. Vanosdore, and communicated the situation of my mind to him; he was greatly rejoiced to find me inquiring the way to Zion, and blessed the Lord who had worked so wonderfully for me a poor heathen. – I was more familiar with this good gentleman than with my master, or any other person; and found my self more at liberty to talk to him: He encouraged me greatly, and prayed with me frequently, and I was always benefited by his discourse.

About a quarter of a mile from my master's house stood a large, remarkably fine oak-tree, in the midst of a wood; I often used to be employed there in cutting down trees, (a work I was very fond of) I seldom failed going to this place every day; sometimes twice a day if I could be spared. It was the highest pleasure I ever experienced to sit under this oak; for there I used to pour out all my complaints to the LORD: And when I had any particular grievance I used to go there, and talk to the tree, and tell my sorrows, as if it had been to a friend.

Here I often lamented my own wicked heart, and undone state; and found more comfort and consolation than I ever was sensible of before. – Whenever I was treated with ridicule or contempt, I used to come here and find peace. I now began to relish the book my master gave me, Baxter's *call to the unconverted*, and took great delight in it. I was always glad to be employed in cutting wood, 'twas a great part of my business, and I followed it with delight, as I was than quite alone and my heart lifted up to GOD, and I was enabled to pray continually; and blessed for ever be his holy name, he faithfully answered my prayers. I can never be thankful enough to Almighty GOD for the many comfortable opportunities I experienced there.

It is possible the circumstance I am going to relate will not gain credit with many; but this I know, that the joy and comfort it conveyed to me, cannot be expressed, and only conceived by those who have experienced the like.

I was one day in a most delightful frame of mind; my heart so over-flowed with love and gratitude to the author of all my comforts: – I was so drawn out of myself, and so fill'd and awed by the presence of God, that I saw (or thought I saw) light inexpressible dart down from heaven upon me, and shone around me for the space of a minute. – I continued on my knees, and joy unspeakable took possession of my soul. – The peace and serenity which filled my mind after this was wonderful, and cannot be told. – I would not have changed situations, or been any one but myself for the whole world. I blest God for my poverty, that I had no worldly riches or grandeur to draw my heart from him. I wished at that time, if it had been possible for me, to have continued on that spot forever. I felt an unwillingness in myself to have any thing more to do with the world, or to mix with society again. I seemed to possess a full assurance that my sins were forgiven me. I went home all my way rejoicing, and this text of scripture came full upon my mind. *'And I will make an everlasting covenant with them, that I will not turn away from them, to do them good; but I will put my fear in their hearts that they shall not depart from me.'* The first opportunity that presented itself, I went to my old school-master, and made known to him the happy state of my soul who joined with me in praise to God for his mercy to me the vilest of sinners. – I was now perfectly easy and had hardly a wish to make beyond what I possessed, when my temporal comforts were all blasted by the death of my dear and worthy master Mr. *Freelandhouse*, who was taken from this world rather suddenly: He had but a short illness, and died of a fever. I held his hand in mine when he departed; he told me he had given me my freedom. I was at liberty to go where I would. – He added that he had always prayed for me and hoped I should be kept unto the end. My master left me by his will ten pounds, and my freedom.

I found that if he had lived twas his intention to take me with him to Holland, as he had often mentioned me to some friends of his there that were desirous to see me; but I chose to continue with my mistress who was as good to me as if she had been my mother.

The loss of Mr. *Freelandhouse* distressed me greatly, but I was rendered still more unhappy by the clouded and perplexed situation of my mind; the great enemy of my soul being ready to torment me, would present my own misery to me in such striking light, and distress me with doubts, fears, and such a deep sense of my own unworthiness, that after all the comfort and encouragement I had received, I was often tempted to believe I should be a cast-away at last. – The more I saw of the beauty and glory of God, the more I was humbled under a sense of my own vileness. I often repaired to my old place of prayer; I seldom came away without consolation. One day this scripture was wonderfully apply'd to my mind, *And ye are complete in him which is the head of all principalities and power* – The Lord was pleased to comfort me by the application of many gracious promises at times when I was ready to sink under my troubles. *Wherefore he is able also to save them to the uttermost that come unto God by him, seeing he ever liveth to make intercession for them,* Heb. x. xiv. *For by one offering he hath perfected forever them that are sanctified.*

My kind, indulgent mistress liv'd but two years after my master. Her death was a great affliction to me. She left five sons, all gracious young men, and ministers of the gospel. – I continued with them all, one after another, till they died; they lived but four years after their parents. When it pleased God to take them to himself. I was left quite destitute, without a friend in the world. But I, who had so often experienced the goodness of God, trusted in him to do what he pleased with me. – In this helpless condition I went in the wood to prayer as usual; and though the snow was a considerable height, I was not sensible of cold, or any other inconveniency. – At times, indeed, when I saw the world frowning round me, I was tempted to think that the LORD had forsaken me. I found great relief from the contemplation of these words in Isai. xlix. 16. *Behold I have graven thee on the palms of my hands; thy walls are continually before me.* And very many comfortable promises were sweetly applied to me. The 89th Psal. and 34th ver. *My covenant will I not break, nor alter the thing that is gone out of my lips.* Heb. xvi. 17, 18. Phil. i. 6. and several more.

As I had now lost all my dear and valued friends, every place in the world was alike to me. I had for a great while entertained a desire to come to *England.* – I imagined that all the inhabitants of this island were *holy;* because all those that had visited my master from thence were good (Mr. Whitefield[12] was his particular friend) and the authors of the books that had been given me were all English. – But, above all places in the world, I wish'd to see Kidderminster, for I could not but think that on the spot where Mr. Baxter had lived, and preach'd, the people must be all *righteous.*

The situation of my affairs required that I should tarry a little longer in *New York,* as I was something in debt, and was embarrassed how to pay it. About this time a young gentleman that was a particular acquaintance of my young master's, pretended to be a friend to me, and promis'd to pay my debts, which was three pounds; and he assured me he would never expect the money again. – But, in less than a month, he came and demanded it; and when I assured him I had nothing to pay, he threatened to sell me. – Though I knew he had no right to do that,

---

[12]   George Whitefield (1714–1770) was an energetic and influential Evangelical preacher in both England and the North American colonies. In his lifetime, he delivered over 18,000 sermons at an average of 500 per year, and (it is calculated) preached to at least 10 million people.

yet, as I had no friend in the world to go to, it alarm'd me greatly. – At length he purpos'd my going a privateering,[13] that I might, by these means, be enabled to pay him, to which I agreed. – Our Captain's name was – – –. I went in character of cook to him. – Near St. *Domingo* we came up to five French ships, merchantmen. – We had a very smart engagement, that continued from eight in the morning till three in the afternoon; when victory declared on our side. – Soon after this we were met by three English ships which join'd us, and that encouraged us to attack a fleet of 36 ships. – We boarded the three first, and then followed the others, and had the same success with twelve; but the rest escaped us. – There was a great deal of blood shed, and I was near death several times, but the LORD preserv'd me.

I met with many enemies, and much persecution, among the sailors; one of them was particularly unkind to me, and studied ways to vex and teaze me. I can't help mentioning one circumstance that hurt me more than all the rest, which was, that he snatched a book out of my hand, that I was very fond of, and used frequently to amuse myself with, & threw it into the sea. – But, what is remarkable, he was the first that was killed in our engagement. – I don't pretend to say that this happened because he was not my friend; but I thought 'twas a very awful providence, to see how the enemies of the LORD are cut off.

Our Captain was a cruel, hard-hearted man. I was excessively sorry for the prisoners we took in general: But the pitiable case of one young gentleman grieved me to the heart. – He appeared very amiable; was strikingly handsome. – Our Captain took four thousand pounds from him; but that did not satisfy him, as he imagined he was possessed of more, and had somewhere concealed it, so that the Captain threatened him with death, at which he appeared in the deepest distress, and took the buckles out of his shoes, and untied his hair, which was very fine, and long; and in which several very valuable rings were fastened. He came into the cabin to me, and in the most obliging terms imaginable asked for something to eat and drink; which when I gave him he was so thankful and pretty in his manner that my heart bled for him; and I heartily wished that I could have spoken in any language in which the ship's crew would not have understood me; that I might have let him know his danger; for I heard the Captain say he was resolved upon his

---

[13] 'Privateering' was the term used to describe the practice in time of war of seizing enemy ships in the name of the nation, and subsequently dividing the booty between the privateers and the government. In this case, Gronniosaw would have sailed and fought as privateer on Britain's behalf in the early years of the Seven Years War against France.

death; and he put his barbarous design into execution, for he took him on shore with one of the sailors, and there they shot him.

This circumstance affected me exceedingly. I could not put him out of my mind a long while. – When we returned to *New York* the Captain divided the prize-money among us, that we had taken. When I was called upon to receive my part, I waited upon Mr. – – –, (the gentleman that paid my debt and was the occasion of my going abroad) to know if he chose to go with me to receive my money, or if I should bring him what I owed. – He chose to go with me; and when the Captain laid my money on the table ('twas an hundred and thirty-five pounds) I desired Mr. – – – to take what I was indebted to him; and he swept it all into his handkerchief, and would never be prevailed on to give a farthing of money, nor any thing at all beside. – And he likewise secured a hogshead of sugar which was my due from the same ship. The Captain was very angry with him for this piece of cruelty to me, as was every other person that heard it. – But I have reason to believe (as he was one of the principal merchants in the city) that he transacted business for him and on that account did not chuse to quarrel with him.

At this time a very worthy gentleman, a wine merchant, his name *Dunscum*, took me under his protection, and would have recovered my money for me if I had chose it; but I told him to let it alone; that I would rather be quiet. – I believed that it would not prosper with him, and so it happened, for by a series of losses and misfortunes he became poor, and was soon after drowned, as he was on a party of pleasure. – The vessel was driven out to sea, and struck against a rock by which means every soul perished.

I was very much distressed when I heard it, and felt greatly for his family who were reduced to very low circumstances. – I never knew how to set a proper value on money, if I had but a little meat and drink to supply the present necessaries of life, I never wished for more; and when I had any I always gave it if ever I saw an object in distress. If it was not for my dear wife and children I should pay as little regard to money now as I did at any time. – I continued some time with Mr. *Dunscum* as his servant; he was very kind to me. – But I had a vast inclination to visit *England*, and wished continually that it would please providence to make a clear way for me to see this island. I entertained a notion that if I could get to *England* I should never more experience either cruelty or ingratitude, so that I was very desirous to get among Christians. I knew Mr. *Whitefield* very well. – I had heard him preach often at *New-York*. In this disposition I listed in the twenty-eight regiment of foot, who were designed for *Martinico* in the late war. – We went in Admiral Pocock's fleet from *New York* to *Barbados*; from thence to *Martinico.* – When that was taken we proceeded to the *Havanna*, and took that place likewise.[14] – There I got discharged.

I was then worth about thirty pounds, but I never regarded money in the least, nor would I tarry to receive my prize-money lest I should lose my chance of going to *England.* – I went with the *Spanish* prisoners to *Spain*; and came to *Old England* with the English prisoners. – I cannot describe my joy when we were within sight of *Portsmouth*. But I was astonished when we landed to hear the inhabitants of that place curse and swear, and otherwise profane. I expected to find nothing but goodness, gentleness and meekness in this Christian land, I then suffered great perplexities of mind.

I inquired if any serious Christian people resided there, the woman I made this inquiry of, answered me in the affirmative; and added that she was one of them. – I was heartily glad to hear her say so. I thought I could give her my whole heart: She kept a public house. I deposited with her all the money that I had not an immediate occasion for; as I thought it would be safer with her. – It was 25 guineas, but 6 of them I desired her to lay out to the best advantage, to buy me some shirts, hat, and some other necessaries. I made her a present of a very handsome large looking-glass, that I brought with me from Martinico, in order to recompence her for the trouble I had given her. I must do this woman the justice to acknowledge that she did lay out some little for my use, but the 19 guineas, and part of the 6, with my watch, she would not return, and denied that I ever gave it her.

I soon perceived that I was got among bad people, who defrauded me of my money and watch; and that all my promis'd happiness was blasted, I had no friend but GOD, and I prayed to him earnestly. I could scarcely believe it possible that the place where so many eminent Christians had lived and preached could abound with so much wickedness and deceit. I thought it worse than *Sodom* (considering the great advantages they have) I cry'd like a child, and that almost continually: At length GOD heard my prayers and raised me a friend indeed.

This publican had a brother who lived on *Portsmouth* common, his wife was a serious good woman. When she heard of the treatment I had met with, she came and inquired into my real situation, and was

---

[14] As an enlisted soldier, Gronniosaw fought for Britain in the concluding battles of the Seven Years War: against the French in Martinique (February 1762), and against the Spanish in Havana, Cuba (August 1762).

greatly troubled at the ill usage I had received, and took me home to her own house. – I began now to rejoice, and my prayer was turned into praise. She made use of all the arguments in her power to prevail on her who had wronged me, to return my watch and money, but it was to no purpose, as she had given me no receipt, and I had nothing to show for it, I could not demand it. – My good friend was excessively angry with her, and obliged her to give me back four guineas, which she said she gave me out of charity: Though in fact it was my own, and much more. She would have employed some rougher means to oblige her to give up my money, but I would not suffer her, let it go, says I, 'My GOD is in heaven.' Still I did not mind my loss in the least; all that grieved me was, that I had been disappointed in finding some Christian friends, with whom I hoped to enjoy a little sweet and comfortable society.

I thought the best method that I could take now, was to go to *London*, and find out Mr. *Whitefield*, who was the only living soul I knew in *England*, and get him to direct me to some way or other to procure a living without being troublesome to any person. – I took leave of my Christian friend at *Portsmouth*, and went in the stage to *London*. – A creditable tradesman in the city, who went up with me in the stage, offered to show me the way to Mr. *Whitefield's* tabernacle. Knowing that I was a perfect stranger, I thought it very kind, and accepted his offer; but he obliged me to give him half-a-crown for going with me, and likewise insisted on my giving him five shillings more for conducting me to Dr. *Gifford's*[15] meeting.

I began now to entertain a very different idea of the inhabitants of *England* than what I had figured to myself before I came among them. – Mr. *Whitefield* received me very friendly, was heartily glad to see me, and directed me to a proper place to board and lodge in Petticoat-lane, till he could think of some way to settle me in, and paid for my lodging, and all my expences. The morning after I came to my new lodging, as I was at breakfast with the gentlewoman of the house, I heard the noise of some looms over our heads: I inquired what it was; she told me a person was weaving silk. – I expressed a great desire to see it, and asked if I might: She told me she would go up with me: She was sure I should be very welcome. She was as good as her word, and as soon as we entered the room, the person that was weaving looked about, and smiled upon us, and I loved her from that moment. She asked me many questions, and I in turn talked a great deal to her.

---

[15] Dr Andrew Gifford (1700–1784) was a Baptist minister, who preached for over fifty years in London.

I found she was a member of Mr *Allen's*[16] meeting, and I began to entertain a good opinion of her, though I was almost afraid to indulge this inclination, least she should prove like all the rest I had met with at *Portsmouth* &c. and which had almost given me a dislike to all white women. – But after a short acquaintance I had the happiness to find she was very different, and quite sincere, and I was not without hope that she entertained some esteem for me. We often went together to hear Dr. *Gifford*, and as I had always a propensity to relieve every object in distress as far as I was able, I used to give to all that complained to me; sometimes half a guinea at a time, as I did not understand the real value of it. – This gracious, good woman took great pains to correct and advise me in that and many other respects.

After I had been in *London* about six weeks I was recommended to the notice of some of my late master Mr. *Freelandhouse's* acquaintance, who had heard him speak frequently of me. I was much persuaded by them to go to *Holland*. My master lived there before he bought me, and used to speak of me so respectfully among his friends there, that it raised in them a curiosity to see me; particularly the gentlemen engaged in the ministry, who expressed a desire to hear my experience and examine me. I found that it was my good old master's design that I should have gone if he had lived; for which reason I resolved upon going to *Holland*, and informed my dear friend Mr. *Whitefield* of my intention; he was much averse to my going at first, but after I gave him my reasons appeared very well satisfied. I likewise informed my *Betty* (the good woman that I have mentioned above) of my determination to go to *Holland*, and I told her that I believed she was to be my wife: That if it was the LORD's will I desired it, but not else. – She made me very little answer, but has since told me, she did not think it at that time.

I embarked at tower-wharf at four o'clock in the morning, and arrived at *Amsterdam* the next day by three o'clock in the afternoon. I had several letters of recommendation to my old master's friends, who received me very graciously. Indeed, one of the chief ministers was particularly good to me, he kept me at his house a long while, and took great pleasure in asking questions, which I answered with delight, being always ready to say, '*Come unto me all ye that fear GOD, and I will tell what he hath done for my soul.*' I cannot but admire the footsteps of *Providence*; astonished that I should be so wonderfully preserved! Though the

[16] John Allen (1741–*c*.1780) was a controversial Evangelical minister in London, who moved to the North American colonies in the 1770s after incurring debts and being charged with forgery.

grandson of a King, I have wanted bread, and should have been glad of the hardest crust I saw. I who, at home, was surrounded and guarded by slaves, so that no indifferent person might approach me, and clothed with gold, have been inhumanly threatened with death; and frequently wanted clothing to defend me from the inclemency of the weather; yet I never murmured, nor was I discontented. – I am willing, and even desirous, to be counted as nothing, a stranger in the world, and a pilgrim here; for '*I know that my* REDEEMER *liveth*,' and I'm thankful for every trial and trouble that I've met with, as I am not without hope that they have been all sanctified to me.

The Calvinist ministers desired to hear my experience from myself, which proposal I was very well pleased with: So I stood before 48 ministers every Thursday for seven weeks together, and they were all very well satisfied, and persuaded I was what I pretended to be. – They wrote down my experience as I spoke it; and the Lord almighty was with me at that time in a remarkable manner, and gave me words, and enabled me to answer them; so great was his mercy to take me in hand a poor blind Heathen.

At this time a very rich merchant at *Amsterdam* offered to take me into his family, in the capacity of his butler, and I very willingly accepted it. – He was a gracious, worthy gentleman, and very good to me. – He treated me more like a friend than a servant. – I tarried there a twelve-month, but was not thoroughly contented, I wanted to see my wife (that is now) and for that reason I wished to return to *England*. I wrote to her once in my absence, but she did not answer my letter; and I must acknowledge if she had, it would have given me a less opinion of her. – My master and mistress persuaded me not to leave them, and likewise their two sons, who entertained a good opinion of me; and if I had found my Betty married, on my arrival in *England*, I should have returned to them again immediately.

My lady proposed my marrying her maid; she was an agreeable young woman, had saved a good deal of money, but I could not fancy her, though she was willing to accept of me, but I told her my inclinations were engaged in *England*, and I could think of no other person. – On my return home I found my Betty disengaged. – She had refused several offers in my absence, and told her sister that she thought if ever she married I was to be her husband.

Soon after I came home I waited on Dr. Gifford, who took me into his family, and was exceedingly good to me. The character of this pious, worthy gentleman is well known; my praise can be of no use or signification at all. – I hope I shall ever gratefully remember the many favours I have received from him. Soon after I came to Dr. Gifford, I expressed a desire to be admitted into their church, and set down with them; they told me I must first be baptized; so I gave in my experience before the church, with which they were very well satisfied, and I was baptized by Dr. Gifford, with some others. I then made known my intentions of being married; but I found there were many objections against it, because the person I had fixed on was poor. She was a widow, her husband had left her in debt, and with a child, so that they persuaded me against it out of real regard to me. But I had promised, and was resolved to have her; as I knew her to be a gracious woman, her poverty was no objection to me, as they had nothing else to say against her. When my friends found that they could not alter my opinion, respecting her, they wrote Mr. Allen, the minister she attended, to persuade her to leave me; but he replied that he would not interfere at all, that we might do as we would. I was resolved that all my wife's little debts should be paid before we were married; so that I sold almost every thing I had, and with all the money I could raise, cleared all that she owed; and I never did any thing with a better will in all my life, because I firmly believed that we should be very happy together, and so it proved, for she was given me from the Lord. And I have found her a blessed partner, and we have never repented, though we have gone through many great troubles and difficulties.

My wife got a very good living by weaving, and could do extremely well; but just at that time there was great disturbance among the weavers, so that I was afraid to let my wife work, least they should insist on my joining the rioters, which I could not think of, and, possibly, if I had refused to do so they would have knock'd me on the head.[17] So that by these means my wife could get no employ, neither had I work enough to maintain my family. We had not yet been married a year before all these misfortunes overtook us.

Just at this time a gentleman, that seemed much concerned for us, advised me to go into *Essex* with him, and promised to get me employed. I accepted his kind proposal, and he spoke to a friend of his, a Quaker, a gentleman of large fortune, who resided a little way out of the town of *Colchester*, his name was *Handbarrar*, he ordered his steward to set me to work.

There were several employed in the same way with myself. I was very thankful and contented though my wages were but small. I was

---

[17]   After the end of the Seven Years War, there was widespread unemployment in England, with weavers in London especially severely affected. The weavers' riots culminated in May 1765 with the weavers besieging the Duke of Bedford's house in Bloomsbury.

allowed but eight pence a day, and found myself; but after I had been in this situation for a fortnight, my master, being told that a Black was at work for him, had an inclination to see me. He was pleased to talk to me for some time, and at last inquired what wages I had; when I told him, he declared it was too little, and immediately ordered his steward to let me have eighteen pence a day, which he constantly gave me after; and I then did extremely well.

I did not bring my wife with me: I came first alone, and it was my design, if things answered according to our wishes, to send for her. I was now thinking to desire her to come to me, when I received a letter to inform me she was just brought to bed, and in want of many necessaries. This news was a great trial to me, and a fresh affliction: But my God, *faithful and abundant in mercy*, forsook me not in this trouble. As I could not read English, I was obliged to apply to some one to read the letter I received, relative to my wife. I was directed by the good providence of God to a worthy young gentleman, a Quaker, and friend of my master. – I desired he would take the trouble to read my letter for me, which he readily complied with, and was greatly moved and affected at the contents; insomuch that he said he would undertake to make a gathering for me, which he did and was the first to contribute to it himself. The money was sent that evening to London, by a person who happened to be going there; nor was this all the goodness that I experienced from these kind friends, for as soon as my wife came about and was fit to travel, they sent for her to me, and were at the whole expence of her coming; so evidently has the love and mercy of God appeared through every trouble that ever I experienced.

We went on very cordially all the summer. We lived in a little cottage near Mr. *Handbarrar*'s house; but when the winter came on I was discharged, as he had no further occasion for me. And now the prospect began to darken upon us again. We tho't it most adviseable to move our habitation a little nearer to the town, as the house we lived in was very cold and wet, and ready to tumble down.

The boundless goodness of God to me has been so very great, that, with the most humble gratitude, I desire to prostrate myself before him; for I have been wonderfully supported in every affliction. – My God never left me. I perceived light *still*, thro' the thickest darkness.

My dear wife and I were now both unemployed, we could get nothing to do. The winter proved remarkably severe, and we were reduced to the greatest distress imaginable. – I was always very shy of asking for any thing; I could never beg; neither did I chuse to make known our wants to any person, for fear of offending, as we were entire strangers; but our last bit of bread was gone, and I was obliged to think of something to do for our support. I did not mind for myself at all; but to see my dear wife and children in want, pierc'd me to the heart. – I now blam'd myself for bringing her from London, as doubtless had we continued there we might have found friends to keep us from starving. The snow was remarkably deep; so that we could see no prospect of being relieved. In this melancholy situation, not knowing what step to pursue, I resolved to make my case known to a gentleman's gardener that lived near us, and entreat him to employ me; but when I came to him my courage fail'd me, and I was ashamed to make known our real situation. – I endeavoured all I could to prevail on him to set me to work, but to no purpose; he assured me it was not in his power: But just as I was about to leave him, he asked me if I would accept of some carrots? I took them with great thankfulness, and carried them home; he gave me four, they were very large and fine. – We had nothing to make fire with, so consequently could not boil them; but was glad to have them to eat raw. Our youngest child was quite an infant; so that my wife was obliged to chew it, and fed her in that manner for several days. We allowed ourselves but one every day, lest they should not last till we could get some other supply. I was unwilling to eat at all myself; nor would I take any the last day that we continued in this situation, as I could not bear the thought that my dear wife and children would be in want of every means of support. We lived in this manner till our carrots were all gone: Then my wife began to lament because of our poor babes; but I comforted her all I could; still hoping, and believing, that my God would not let us die; but that it would please him to relieve us, which he did by almost a miracle.

We went to bed, as usual, before it was quite dark (as we had neither fire nor candle) but had not been there long before some person knocked at the door, and inquired if *James Albert* lived there? I answer'd in the affirmative, and rose immediately; as soon as I opened the door I found it was the servant of an eminent attorney who resided at *Colchester*. He asked me how it was with me? If I was not almost starved? I burst out a crying, and told him I was indeed. He said his master suppos'd so, and that he wanted to speak with me, and I must return with him. This gentleman's name was *Daniel*, he was a sincere, good Christian. He used to stand and talk with me frequently, when I work'd in the road for Mr. *Handbarrar*, and would have employed me himself if I had wanted work. – When I came to his house he told me that he had thought a good deal about me of late, and was apprehensive that I must be in want, and could not be satisfied till he sent to inquire after me. I made known my distress to him, at which he was greatly affected; and generously gave me a guinea; and promised to be kind to me in future. I could not help exclaiming, *O the boundless mercies of my God!* I prayed unto him, and he has heard me; I trusted in him, and he has preserv'd me: Where shall I begin to praise him? Or how shall I love him enough?

I went immediately and bought some bread and cheese and coal and carried then home. My dear wife was rejoiced to see me return with something to eat. She instantly got up and dressed our babies, while I made a fire; and the first nobility in the land never made a more comfortable meal. We did not forget to thank the Lord for all his goodness to us. Soon after this, as the spring came on, Mr. *Peter Daniel* employed me in pulling down a house, and rebuilding it. I had then very good work, and full employ: He sent for my wife and children to *Colchester*, and provided us a house, where we lived very comfortably. I hope I shall always gratefully acknowledge his kindness to myself and family. I worked at this house for more than a year, till it was finished; and after that I was employed by several successively, and was never so happy as when I had something to do; but perceiving the winter coming on, and work rather slack, I was apprehensive that we should again be in want, or become troublesome to our friends.

I had at this time an offer made me of going to *Norwich*, and having constant employ. My wife seemed pleased with this proposal, as she supposed she might get work there in the weaving manufactory, being the business which she was brought up to, & more likely to succeed there than any other place; and we thought as we had an opportunity of moving to a town where we could both be employed, it was most adviseable to do so; and that probably we might settle there for our lives. When this step was resolved on, I went first alone to see how it would answer; which I very much repented after, for it was not in my power immediately to send my wife any supply, as I fell into the hands of a master that was neither kind nor considerate; and she was reduced to great distress, so that she was obliged to sell the few goods that we had, and when I sent for her was under the disagreeable necessity of parting with our bed.

When she came to *Norwich* I hired a room ready furnished. – I experienced a great deal of difference in the carriage of my master from what I had been accustomed to from some of my other masters. He was very irregular in his payments to me. – My wife hired a loom and wove all the leisure time she had and we began to do very well, till we were overtaken by fresh misfortunes. Our three poor children fell ill of the small pox; this was a great trial to us; but still I was persuaded in myself we should not be forsaken. – And I did all in my power to keep my dear partner's spirits from sinking. Her whole attention now was taken up with the children, as she could mind nothing else, and all I could get was but little to support a family in such a situation, beside paying for the hire of our room, which I was obliged to omit doing for several weeks: But the woman to whom we were indebted would not excuse us, though I promised she should have the very first money we could get after my children came about, but she would not be satisfied, and had the cruelty to threaten us that if we did not pay her immediately, she would turn us all into the street.

The apprehension of this plunged me in the deepest distress, considering the situation of my poor babies: If they had been in health I should have been less sensible of this misfortune. But my God, *still faithful to his promise*, raised me a friend. Mr. *Henry Gurdney*,[18] a Quaker, a gracious gentleman heard of our distress, he sent a servant of his own to the woman we hired the room of, paid our rent, and bought all the goods, with my wife's loom, and gave it us all.

Some other gentlemen, hearing of his design, were pleased to assist him in these generous acts, for which we never can be thankful enough; after this my children soon came about; we began to do pretty well again; my dear wife worked hard and constant when she could get work, but it was upon a disagreeable footing, as her employ was so uncertain, sometimes she could get nothing to do, and at other times when the weavers of *Norwich* had orders from *London*, they were so excessively hurried, that the people they employed were often obliged to work on the Sabbath-day: But this my wife would never do, and it was matter of uneasiness to us that we could not get our living in a regular manner, though we were both diligent, industrious, and willing to work. I was far from being happy in my master, he did not use me well. I could scarcely ever get my money from him; but I continued patient till it pleased GOD to alter my situation.

My worthy friend Mr. *Gurdney* advised me to follow the employ of chopping chaff, and bought me an instrument for that purpose. There were but few people in the town that made this their business beside myself; so that I did very well indeed and we became easy and happy. – But we did not continue long in this comfortable state. Many of the inferior people were envious and ill-natur'd, and set up the same employ, and worked under price on purpose to get my business from

---

[18] Henry Gurney was a wealthy Quaker wool merchant who in 1770 together with his brother John founded Gurney's Bank, a direct ancestor of Barclays Bank.

me, and they succeeded so well that I could hardly get any thing to do, and became again unfortunate: Nor did this misfortune come alone, for just at this time we lost one of our little girls, who died of a fever; this circumstance occasioned us new troubles, for the Baptist minister refused to bury her because we were not their members. The parson of the parish denied us because she had never been baptized. I applied to the Quakers, but met with no success; this was one of the greatest trials I ever met with, as we did not know what to do with our poor baby – At length I resolved to dig a grave in the garden behind the house, and bury her there; when the parson of the parish sent for me to tell me he would bury the child, but did not chuse to read the burial service over her. I told him I did not mind whether he would or not, as the child could not hear it.

We met with a great deal of ill treatment after this, and found it very difficult to live. – We could scarcely get work to do, and were obliged to pawn our clothes. We were ready to sink under our troubles. – When I proposed to my wife to go to *Kidderminster*, and try if we could do there. I had always an inclination for that place, and now more than ever, as I had heard Mr. *Fawcet*[19] mentioned in the most respectful manner, as a pious worthy gentleman, and I had seen his name in a favourite book of mine, Baxter's *Saints everlasting rest*; and as the manufactory of *Kidderminster* seemed to promise my wife some employment, she readily came into my way of thinking.

I left her once more, and set out for *Kidderminster* in order to judge if the situation would suit us. – As soon as I came there I waited immediately on Mr. *Fawcet*, who was pleased to receive me very kindly and recommended me to Mr. *Watson*, who employed me in twisting silk and worsted together. I continued here about a fortnight, and when I thought it would answer our expectation, I returned to *Norwich* to fetch my wife; she was then near her time, and too much indisposed. So we were obliged to tarry until she was brought to bed, and as soon as she could conveniently travel we came to *Kidderminster*, but we brought nothing with us, as we were obliged to sell all we had to pay our debts, and the expences of my wife's illness, &c.

Such is our situation at present. – My wife, by hard labor at the loom, does every thing that can be expected from her towards the maintenance of our family; and God is pleased to incline the hearts of his people at times to yield us their charitable assistance; being myself

---

[19] Benjamin Fawcett (1715–1780) was a popular Evangelical minister in Kidderminster, who worked closely with Walter Shirley, and published edited versions of Richard Baxter's sermons.

through age and infirmity able to contribute but little to their support. As pilgrims, and very poor pilgrims we are traveling through many difficulties towards our heavenly home, and waiting patiently for his glorious call, when the Lord shall deliver us out of the evils of this present world, and bring us to the everlasting glories of the world to come. – To HIM be praise for ever and ever. AMEN.

Reading 7.2 Hannah More, 'The Sorrows of Yamba'

Source: Hannah More (1795) *The Sorrows of Yamba; or, The Negro Woman's Lamentation*, London, J. Marshall and R. White, pp. 3–12.

The Sorrows of Yamba, &c.
To the Tune of Hosier's Ghost.

In St. Lucie's distant isle,
Still with Afric's love I burn;
Parted many a thousand mile,
Never, never to return.

Come kind death! and give me rest,   5
Yamba has no friend but thee;
Thou can'st ease my throbbing breast,
Thou can'st set the Prisoner free.

Down my cheeks the tears are dripping,
Broken is my heart with grief;   10
Mangled my poor flesh with whipping,
Come kind death! and bring relief.

Born on Afric's Golden Coast,
Once I was as blest as you;
Parents tender I could boast,   15
Husband dear, and children too.

Whity man he came from far,
Sailing o'er the briny flood,
Who, with help of British Tar,
Buys up human flesh and blood.   20

With the Baby at my breast
(Other two were sleeping by)
In my Hut I sat at rest,
With no thought of danger nigh.

From the Bush at even tide   25
Rush'd the fierce man-stealing Crew;
Seiz'd the Children by my side,
Seiz'd the wretched Yamba too.

Then for love of filthy Gold
Strait they bore me to the Sea;   30
Cramm'd me down a Slave Ship's hold,
Where were Hundreds stow'd like me.

Naked on the Platform lying,
Now we cross the tumbling wave;
Shrieking, sickening, fainting, dying,   35
Deed of shame for Britons brave.

At the savage Captain's beck
Now like Brutes they make us prance:
Smack the Cat about the Deck,
And in scorn they bid us dance.   40

Nauseous horse beans they bring nigh.
Sick and sad we cannot eat;
Cat must cure the Sulks they cry,
Down their throats we'll force the meat.

I in groaning passed the night,   45
And did roll my aching head;
At the break of morning light,
My poor Child was cold and dead.

Happy, happy, there she lies,
Thou shalt feel the lash no more,   50
Thus full many a Negro dies
Ere we reach the destin'd shore.

Thee, sweet infant, none shall sell,
Thou hast gained a wat'ry Grave;
Clean escap'd the Tyrants fell,   55
While thy mother lives a Slave.

Driven like Cattle to a fair,
See they sell us young and old;
Child from Mother too they tear,
All for love of filthy Gold.   60

I was sold to Massa hard,
Some have Massas kind and good;
And again my back was scarr'd,
Bad and stinted was my food.

Poor and wounded, faint and sick,   65
All expos'd to burning sky;
Massa bids me grass to pick,
And I now am near to die.

What and if to death he send me,
Savage murder tho' it be,   70
British Law shall ne'er befriend me,
They protect not Slaves like me.

Mourning thus my wretched state,
(Ne'er may I forget the day)
Once in dusk of evening late   75
Far from home I dar'd to stray;

Dar'd, alas! with impious haste
Tow'rds the roaring Sea to fly;
Death itself I long'd to taste,
Long'd to cast me in and Die.   80

There I met upon the Strand
English Missionary Good,
He had Bible book in hand,
Which poor me no understood.

Led by pity from afar   85
He had left his native ground;
Thus if some inflict a scar,
Others fly to cure the wound.

Strait he pull'd me from the shore,
Bid me no self-murder do;   90
Talk'd of state when life is o'er,
All from Bible good and true.

Then he led me to his Cot,
Sooth'd and pity'd all my woe;
Told me 'twas the Christian's lot   95
Much to suffer here below.

Told me then of God's dear Son,
(Strange and wond'rous is the story;)
What sad wrong to him was done,
Tho' he was the Lord of Glory.   100

Told me too, like one who knew him,
(Can such love as this be true?)
How he died for them that slew him,
Died for wretched Yamba too.

Freely he his mercy proffer'd,   105
And to Sinners he was sent;
E'en to Massa pardon's offer'd;
O if Massa would repent!

Wicked deed full many a time
Sinful Yamba too hath done   110
But she wails to God her crime,
But she trusts his only Son.

O ye slaves whom Massas beat,
Ye are stain'd with guilt within;
As ye hope for mercy sweet,   115
So forgive your Massa's sin.

And with grief when sinking low,
Mark the Road that Yamba trod;
Think how all her pain and woe
Brought the Captive home to God.   120

Now let Yamba too adore
Gracious Heaven's mysterious Plan;
Now I'll count my mercies o'er,
Flowing thro' the guilt of man.

Now I'll bless my cruel capture,   130
(Hence I've known a Saviour's name)
Till my Grief is turn'd to Rapture,
And I half forget the blame.

But tho' here a Convert rare
Thanks her God for Grace divine,   135
Let not man the glory share,
Sinner, still the guilt is thine.

Here an injured Slave forgives,
There a Host for vengeance cry;
Here a single Yamba lives,   140
There a thousand droop and die.

Duly now baptiz'd am I
By good Missionary Man;
Lord my nature purify
As no outward water can!   145

All my former thoughts abhorr'd,
Teach me now to pray and praise;
Joy and Glory in my Lord,
Trust and serve him all my days.

Worn indeed with Grief and Pain,   150
Death I now will welcome in:
O the Heavenly Prize to gain!
O to 'scape the power of Sin!

True of heart, and meek and lowly,
Pure and blameless let me grow!   155
Holy may I be, for Holy,
Is the place to which I go.

But tho' death this hour may find me,
Still with Afric's love I burn,
(There I've left a spouse behind me)   160
Still to native land I turn.

And when Yamba sinks in Death,
This my latest prayer shall be,
While I yield my parting breath,
O that Afric might be free.   165

Cease, ye British Sons of murder!
Cease from forging Afric's chain;
Mock your Saviour's name no further,
Cease your savage lust of gain.

Ye that boast '*Ye rule the waves*,'   170
Bid no Slave Ship soil the sea,
Ye that '*never will be slaves*,'
Bid poor Afric's land be free.

Where ye gave to war its birth,
Where your traders fix'd their den,   175
There go publish '*Peace on Earth*,'
Go proclaim '*good-will to men.*'

Where ye once have carried slaughter,
Vice, and Slavery, and Sin;
Seiz'd on Husband, Wife, and Daughter,   180
Let the Gospel enter in.

Thus where Yamba's native home,
Humble Hut of Rushes stood,
Oh if there should chance to roam
Some dear Missionary good;   185

Thou in Afric's distant land,
Still shalt see the man I love;
Join him to the Christian band,
Guide his Soul to Realms above.

There no Fiend again shall sever   190
Those whom God hath join'd and blest
There they dwell with Him for ever,
There '*the weary are at rest.*'

Reading 7.3 *The Interesting Narrative of the Life of Olaudah Equiano*

Source: Olaudah Equiano (1789) *The Interesting Narrative of the Life of Olaudah Equiano, or Gustavus Vassa, The African*, **vol. 1, London, T. Wilkins, pp. 78–85.**

At last, when the ship we were in had got in all her cargo, they made ready with many fearful noises, and we were all put under deck, so that we could not see how they managed the vessel. But this disappointment was the least of my sorrow. The stench of the hold while we were on the coast was so intolerably loathsome, that it was dangerous to remain there for any time, and some of us had been permitted to stay on the deck for the fresh air; but now that the whole ship's cargo were confined together, it became absolutely pestilential. The closeness of the place, and the heat of the climate, added to the number in the ship, which was so crowded that each had scarcely room to turn himself, almost suffocated us. This produced copious perspirations, so that the air soon became unfit for respiration, from a variety of loathsome smells, and brought on a sickness among the slaves, of which many died, thus falling victims to the improvident avarice, as I may call it, of their purchasers. This wretched situation was again aggravated by the galling of the chains, now become insupportable; and the filth of the necessary tubs, into which the children often fell, and were almost suffocated. The shrieks of the women, and the groans of the dying, rendered the whole a scene of horror almost inconceivable. Happily perhaps for myself I was soon reduced so low here that it was thought necessary to keep me almost always on deck; and from my extreme youth I was not put in fetters. In this situation I expected every hour to share the fate of my companions, some of whom were almost daily brought upon deck at the point of death, which I began to hope would soon put an end to my miseries. Often did I think many of the inhabitants of the deep much more happy than myself. I envied them the freedom they enjoyed, and as often wished I could change my condition for theirs. Every circumstance I met with served only to render my state more painful, and heighten my apprehensions, and my opinion of the cruelty of the whites. One day they had taken a number of fishes; and when they had killed and satisfied themselves with as many as they thought fit, to our astonishment who were on the deck, rather than give any of them to us to eat as we expected, they tossed the remaining fish into the sea again, although we begged and prayed for some as well as we could, but in vain; and some of my countrymen being pressed by hunger, took an opportunity, when they thought no one saw them, of trying to get a little privately; but they were discovered, and the attempt procured them some very severe floggings. One day, when we had a smooth sea and moderate wind, two of my wearied countrymen who were chained together (I was near them at the time), preferring death to such a life of misery, somehow made through the nettings and jumped into the sea: immediately another quite dejected fellow, who, on account of his illness, was suffered to be out of irons, also followed their example; and I believe many more would very soon have done the same if they had not been prevented by the ship's crew, who were instantly alarmed. Those of us that were the most active were in a moment put down under the deck, and there was such a noise and confusion amongst the people of the ship as I never heard before, to stop her, and get the boat out to go after the slaves. However two of the wretches were drowned, but they got the other, and afterwards flogged him unmercifully for thus attempting to prefer death to slavery. In this manner we continued to undergo more hardships than I can now relate, hardships which are inseparable from this accursed trade. Many a time we were near suffocation from the want of fresh air, which we were often without for whole days together. This, and the stench of the necessary tubs, carried off many. During our passage I first saw flying fishes, which surprised me very much: they used frequently to fly across the ship, and many of them fell on the deck. I also now first saw the use of the quadrant; I had often with astonishment seen the mariners make observations with it, and I could not think what it meant. They at last took notice of my surprise; and one of them, willing to increase it, as well as to gratify my curiosity, made me one day look through it. The clouds appeared to me to be land, which disappeared as they passed along. This heightened my wonder; and I was now more persuaded than ever that I was in another world, and that every thing about me was magic. At last we came in sight of the island of Barbadoes, at which the whites on board gave a great shout, and made many signs of joy to us. We did not know what to think of this; but as the vessel drew nearer we plainly saw the harbour, and other ships of different kinds and sizes; and we soon anchored amongst them off Bridge Town. Many merchants and planters now came on board, though it was in the evening. They put us in separate parcels, and examined us attentively. They also made us jump, and pointed to the land, signifying we were to go there. We thought by this we should be eaten by these ugly men, as they appeared to us; and, when soon after we were all put down under the deck again, there was much dread and trembling among us, and nothing but bitter cries to be heard all the night from these apprehensions, insomuch that at last the white people got some old slaves from the land to pacify us. They told us we were not to be eaten, but to work, and were soon to go on land, where we should see many of our country people. This report eased us much; and sure enough, soon after we were landed, there came to us Africans of all languages. We were conducted immediately to the merchant's yard, where we were all pent up together like so many sheep in a fold, without regard to sex or age.

Reading 7.4 James Field Stanfield, *Observations on a Guinea Voyage*

Source: James Field Stanfield (1788) *Observations on a Guinea Voyage in a Series of Letters Addressed to the Rev. Thomas Clarkson,* **London, James Phillips, pp. 26–34. Footnote is by James Field Stanfield.**

Letter the fifth

In this fresh ship, and with this fresh crew we left the coast, and entered on what is called the *Middle Passage*.

This horrid portion of the voyage was but one continued scene of barbarity, unremitting labour, mortality, and disease. Flogging, as in the outward passage, was a principal amusement in this.

The captain was so feeble that he could not move, but was obliged to be carried up and down: yet his illness, so far from abating his tyranny, seemed rather to increase it. When in this situation, he has often asked the persons who carried him, whether they could judge of the torment he was in; and being answered, No – he has laid hold of their faces, and darting his nails into their checks with all his strength, on the person's crying out with the pain, he would than add, with the malignity of a demon, 'There, – that is to give you a taste of what I feel.' He had always a parcel of trade knives within his reach, which he would also dart at them with ferocity on the most trifling occasions.

The bed of this wretch, which he kept for weeks together, was in one corner of the cabin, and raised to a good height from the deck. To the posts of this bed he would order those to be tied that were to be flogged, so that their faces almost met his, and there he lay, enjoying their agonizing screams, while their flesh was lacerated without mercy: this was a frequent and a favourite mode of punishment.

The chief mate whom we brought off the coast, died soon; the second mate soon after: their united duties devolved on me. While the latter was in his illness, he got up one night, made a noise, tumbled some things about the half-deck, untied a hammock, and played some other delirious but innocent tricks. The captain, being a little recovered at that time, came out, and knocked him down. I do not at this time remember the weapon, but I know his head was sadly cut, and bleeding – in short, he was beat in a most dreadful manner; and, before the morning, he *was dead*. This man had not been many weeks on the coast, and left it in remarkably good health.

The cook, one day, burned some meat in the roasting: he was called to the cabin on that account, and beaten most violently with the spit. He begged and cried for mercy, but without effect, until the strength of his persecutor was exhausted. He crawled some where – but *never did duty afterwards*. He died in a day or two!

The poor creatures, as our numbers were thinned, were obliged to work when on the very verge of death. The *certainty*, that they could not live a day longer, did not procure them a grain of mercy. The boatswain, who had left the coast, a healthy, hearty man, had been seized with the flux: he was in the last stage of it, but no remission from work was allowed him. He grew at last so bad, that the mucus, blood, and whole strings of his intestines came from him without intermission. Yet, even in this situation – when he could not stand – he was forced to the wheel, to steer a large vessel; an arduous duty, that in all likelihood would have required two men, had we had people enough for the purpose. He was placed upon one of the mess-tubs, as not being able to stand, and that he might not dirty the deck. He remained at this painful duty as long as he could move his hands – he died on the same night! The body was, as usual, thrown overboard, without any covering but the shirt. It grew calm in the night, and continued to be so for a good part of the next day – in the morning his corps was discovered floating alongside, and kept close to us for some hours – it was a horrid spectacle, and seemed to give us an idea of the body of a victim, calling out to heaven for vengeance on our barbarity!

As the crew fell off, an accumulated weight of labour pressed upon the few survivors – and, towards the end of the middle passage, all idea of keeping the slaves in chains was given up; for there was not strength enough left among all the white men, to pull a single rope with effect. The slaves (at least a great number of them) were therefore freed from their irons, and *they* pulled and hawled as they were directed by the inefficient sailors. We were fortunate in having favourable weather: a smart gale of wind, such as with an able crew would not have created us more trouble than reefing our sails a little, must have inevitably sent us to destruction, and added us to a numerous list of people, that have perished in the same circumstances; but which list has been kept from the publick eye by the most studied circumspection.

In this state of weakness, it may be readily supposed, that but little attention can be paid to those, whose approach to the last stage of their misery renders them helpless, and in want of aid: I remember that a man, who was ill, had one night crawled out of his hammock: he was so weak that he could not get back, but laid himself down on the gratings. There was no person to assist him – In the morning, when I came upon the main deck – (I shudder at the bare recollection) he was still alive, but covered with blood – the hogs had picked his toes to the bones, and his body was otherwise mangled by them in a manner too shocking to relate.

Letter the sixth

Though the unabating cruelty, exercised upon *seamen* in the Slave-Trade, first prompted me to give in my mite of information to the cause, yet it may not be thought foreign to the subject to make a few remarks on the treatment of the *slaves*. Mr. *Falconbridge*'s account, which carries truth and conviction on the face of it, gives a most just description of their package, diet, and treatment. But no pen, no abilities, can give more than a very faint resemblance of the horrid situation. One *real* view – one MINUTE, absolutely spent in the slave rooms on the middle passage, would do more for the cause of humanity, than the pen of a *Robertson*, or the whole collective eloquence of the British senate.

That interest must operate on the captain to treat the slaves with kindness, has been advanced by those who have cogent reasons for wishing the continuance of this trade: but, like most of the arguments they advance, it has more of speciousness than of truth. The infernal passions, that seem to be nourished in the very vitals of this employ, bid defiance to every power of controul. Humanity, justice, religion, have long lost their influence there. But even AVARICE, the author of the destructive business, when struggling with CRUELTY, loses its force, and finds its powers of dominion foiled by the very monster that it begat.

The slaves, with regard to attention to their health and diet, claim, from the purpose of the voyage, a consideration superior to the seamen: but when the capricious and irascible passions of their general tyrant were once set afloat, I never could see any difference in the cruelty of their treatment.

Flogging, that favourite exercise, was in continual use with the poor Negroes as well as the seamen. So incessant was the practice, that it is impossible to discriminate the particular occasions or circumstances. One or two, however, I may mention.

Just before we left the coast, and when the rooms were so crowded, that the slaves were packed together to a degree of pain, there came a boat-load of slaves along-side in the night, after all those on board had been put below. The new comers were also put down, to shift for themselves, and of course much noise ensued. In the women's room, this was sadly increased by one of the strangers being so unfortunate as to throw down a certain tub. In the morning she was tied up to the captain's bed, with her face close to his, and a person was ordered to flog her. The idea of the sex operating on the unwilling executioner, she did not receive her punishment with all the severity that was expected. The executioner was himself immediately tied up, and, for the lenity he had shewn, received a violent lashing. The woman was then flogged till her back was full of holes. I remember, that in healing them, they were so thick, that I was forced to cut two or three of them into one, to apply the dressings.

That the chief tortures are applied to the unhappy sufferers, on refusing the diet that is offered them, has been fully mentioned by others. We had our share of them; and the lash was often inflicted, untill the poor victims fainted away with the pain. Two women, by many degrees the two finest slaves in the ship, felt a severity of this kind with such poignancy, that folding themselves in each others arms, they plunged over the poop of the vessel into the sea, and were drowned. We were obliged to put all the women immediately below, as they cried out in a most affecting manner, and many of them were preparing to follow their companions. These are the people whom the good traders represent, as wanting every kind of sensibility.

Were I to transcribe a regular journal of the usage of the slaves on the middle passage, it would be but a repetition of acts similar to the above, and varied perhaps only by the circumstances that attended it. One instance more of brutality I would, however, willingly relate, as practised by the captain on an unfortunate female slave, of the age of eight or nine, but that I am *obliged* to withhold it; for though my heart bleeds at the recollection, though the act is too atrocious and bloody to be passed over in silence, yet as I cannot express it in any words, that would not severely wound the feelings of the *delicate* reader, I must be content with suffering it to escape among those numerous hidden and unrevealed enormities, the offspring of barbarity and despotism, that are committed daily in the prosecution of this execrable trade.

Before I quit this subject of the slaves, I must mention a circumstance, that, I dare say very often occurs, though perhaps seldom with so advantageous a succedaneum.[1] The doctor and his mate being both dead, the medicine chest was given into my charge and disposal: a knowledge of Latin, and a little medical reading, were all my qualifications. What a situation would it have been for an ignorant, an

---

[1] Substitute.

unfeeling, or an indolent man! Medicines or poisons to be dealt out promiscuously to such a number of persons, all afflicted with disease, during a passage through the tedious latitudes across the Atlantic. The only directions I had to go by, were a few remarks on the last stage of the flux, written in a minute or two, by a surgeon at St. Thomas's, on a bit of cartridge-paper.

Reading 8.1 Extended chronology of the mutiny on the *Bounty*

Source: Written by David Johnson.

February 1787: Sir Joseph Banks successfully petitions the British government on behalf of West Indies plantation owners to finance an expedition to Tahiti to transplant breadfruit plants to the West Indies.

August 1787: Banks acquires HMS *Bethia* for the voyage, renames it HMS *Bounty*, oversees refitting the ship for the transport of breadfruit, and appoints William Bligh as commander.

December 1787: The *Bounty* sets sail from Spithead, England, on a westward course around Cape Horn for Tahiti.

April 1788: Bligh tries for thirty days to round Cape Horn, but is driven back by strong winds and bad weather, and is forced to sail east for the Cape of Good Hope.

May 1788: The *Bounty* stops for one month at the Cape of Good Hope, before continuing the journey eastward.

August 1788: The *Bounty* stops at Van Dieman's Land[1], and then continues on the final leg of the journey.

26 October 1788: The *Bounty* arrives at Matavai Bay, Tahiti, and commences with the collecting of breadfruit plants.

5 January 1789: Three sailors steal a boat and desert, but are captured three weeks later, and sentenced by Bligh to flogging.

4 April 1789: The *Bounty* – with 1,015 breadfruit plants – sets sail for the return journey.

28 April 1789: The mutiny on the *Bounty* takes place off the island of Tofua,[2] resulting in Bligh and eighteen loyal seamen joining him on the launch, and the balance of twenty-five remaining with Fletcher Christian on board the *Bounty*.

3 May 1789: Having landed on Tofua to negotiate for provisions, Bligh and his crew on the launch are forced to flee, with one of the seamen killed during their escape.

---

[1] Now Tasmania.
[2] Spelled 'Tofoa' by Bligh. An island in Tonga.

25 May 1789: The *Bounty* under Christian stops at the island of Tubuai, where conflict with the local inhabitants escalates, and the next day the mutineers kill twelve of them.

28 May 1789: Bligh navigates the launch through the Great Barrier Reef off New Holland,[3] and lands a day later to search for food.

14 June 1789: The launch arrives at the Dutch settlement of Coupang on West Timor,[4] with no further fatalities.

September 1789: The unsuccessful attempt of the *Bounty* mutineers to settle on Tubuai culminates in a second violent confrontation, and over fifty Tubuaians are killed. The *Bounty* leaves Tubuai on 15 September and arrives at Tahiti five days later. Sixteen of the mutineers elect to remain on Tahiti; the remaining nine leave with Christian on the *Bounty* together with several Tahitians and Tubuians – twelve women, one girl and six men – to search for an alternative island refuge beyond the British Navy.

January 1790: After a protracted search, the *Bounty* lands and settles at Pitcairn Island, and on 23 January the *Bounty* is burned to avoid subsequent detection. The land and women are divided between the nine *Bounty* mutineers, and the six Tahitian and Tubuaian men work as servants and share three women.

March 1790: Bligh arrives back in Portsmouth, England, and within months is exonerated by the Admiralty of any responsibility for the mutiny on the *Bounty*.

August 1790: Captain Edward Edwards is given command of the frigate *Pandora*, and leaves for Tahiti to arrest the mutineers.

March 1791: Edwards reaches Tahiti, discovers fourteen of the mutineers there, and arrests them.

May 1791: The *Pandora* leaves Tahiti to continue searching (unsuccessfully) for the *Bounty* survivors, but in August 1791 is wrecked on the Great Barrier Reef, with four of the mutineer–prisoners drowned.

August 1791: Bligh is given command of the *Providence* to complete (successfully, on this second attempt) the transplanting of breadfruit from Tahiti to the West Indies.

---

[3] Now Australia.
[4] Now Kupang in Indonesia.

March 1792: The ten surviving mutineers reach England.

12 August 1792: The surviving mutineers are court-martialled in Portsmouth. Three are found guilty and hanged on 29 October 1789, but the remaining seven are either pardoned, or have their verdicts set aside.

7 August 1793: Bligh returns to England on the *Providence*, having successfully delivered the second breadfruit consignment to the West Indies.

September 1793: On Pitcairn Island, a mutiny by the Tahitian and Tubuaian men results in the killing of five of the *Bounty* mutineers, including Christian. In retaliatory attacks, all the Tahitian and Tubuaian men are killed, leaving four of the mutineers, ten women and several children.

November 1794: A mutiny by the Tahitian women on Pitcairn against the four surviving mutineers is thwarted.

September 1808: Captain Mayhew Folger of the US ship *Topaz* reaches Pitcairn Island, and finds one surviving mutineer and a community of about thirty-five.

Reading 8.2 William Bligh, *A Narrative of the Mutiny on Board His Majesty's Ship 'Bounty'*

Source: William Bligh (1790) *A Narrative of the Mutiny on Board His Majesty's Ship 'Bounty'*, **London, George Nicol.**

Advertisement

The following *Narrative* is only a part of a voyage undertaken for the purpose of conveying the Bread-fruit Tree from the South Sea Islands to the West Indies. The manner in which this expedition miscarried, with the subsequent transactions and events, are here related. This part of the voyage is not first in the order of time, yet the circumstances are so distinct from that by which it was preceded, that it appears unnecessary to delay giving as much early information as possible concerning so extraordinary an event. The rest will be laid before the Public as soon as it can be got ready; and it is intended to publish it in such a manner, as, with the present *Narrative*, will make the account of the voyage compleat.

At present, for the better understanding the following pages, it is sufficient to inform the reader, that in August, 1787, I was appointed to command the *Bounty*, a ship of 215 tons burthen, carrying 4 fix-pounders, 4 swivels, and 46 men, including myself and every person on board. We sailed from England in December, 1787, and arrived at Otaheite[1] the 26th of October, 1788. On the 4th of April, 1789, we left Otaheite, with every favourable appearance of completing the object of the voyage, in a manner equal to my most sanguine expectations. At this period the ensuing *Narrative* commences.

Narrative of the mutiny on board His Majesty's ship 'Bounty'

I sailed from Otaheite on the 4th of April 1789, having on board 1015 fine bread-fruit plants, besides many other valuable fruits of that country, which, with unremitting attention, we had been colleting for three and twenty weeks, and which were now in the highest state of perfection.

---

[1] Now Tahiti.

On the 11th of April, I discovered an island in latitude 18° 52' S. and longitude 200° 19' E. by the natives called Whytootackee. On the 24th we anchored at Annamooka, one of the Friendly Islands;[2] from which, after completing our wood and water, I sailed on the 27th, having every reason to expect, from the fine condition of the plants, that they would continue healthy.

On the evening of the 28th, owing to light winds, we were not clear of the islands, and at night I directed my course towards Tofoa. The master had the first watch; the gunner the middle watch; and Mr. Christian, one of the mates, the morning watch. This was the turn of duty for the night.

Just before sun-rising, Mr. Christian, with the master at arms, gunner's mate, and Thomas Burket, seaman, came into my cabin while I was asleep, and seizing me, tied my hands with a cord behind my back, and threatened me with instant death, if I spoke or made the least noise: I, however, called so loud as to alarm every one; but they had already secured the officers who were not of their party, by placing centinels at their doors. There were three men at my cabin door, besides the four within; Christian had only a cutlass in his hand, the others had muskets and bayonets. I was hauled out of bed, and forced on deck in my shirt, suffering great pain from the tightness with which they had tied my hands. I demanded the reason of such violence, but received no other answer than threats of instant death, if I did not hold my tongue. Mr. Elphinston, the master's mate, was kept in his birth; Mr. Nelson, botanist, Mr. Peckover, gunner, Mr. Ledward, surgeon, and the master, were confined to their cabins; and also the clerk, Mr. Samuel, but he soon obtained leave to come on deck. The fore hatchway was guarded by centinels; the boatswain and carpenter were, however, allowed to come on deck, where they saw me standing abast the mizen-mast, with my hands tied behind my back, under a guard, with Christian at their head.

The boatswain was now ordered to hoist the launch out, with a threat, if he did not do it instantly, to take care of himself.

The boat being out, Mr. Hayward and Mr. Hallet, mid-shipmen, and Mr. Samuel, were ordered into it; upon which I demanded the cause of such an order, and endeavoured to persuade some one to a sense of duty; but it was to no effect: 'Hold your tongue, Sir, or you are dead this instant,' was constantly repeated to me.

---

[2] Now Tonga.

The master, by this time, had sent to be allowed to come on deck, which was permitted; but he was soon ordered back again to his cabin.

I continued my endeavours to turn the tide of affairs, when Christian changed the cutlass he had in his hand for a bayonet, that was brought to him, and, holding me with a strong gripe by the cord that tied my hands, he with many oaths threatened to kill me immediately if I would not be quiet: the villains round me had their pieces cocked and bayonets fixed. Particular people were now called on to go into the boat, and were hurried over the side: whence I concluded that with these people I was to be set adrift.

I therefore made another effort to bring about a change, but with no other effect than to be threatened with having my brains blown out.

The boatswain and seamen, who were to go in the boat, were allowed to collect twine, canvas, lines, sails, cordage, an eight and twenty gallon cask of water, and the carpenter to take his tool chest. Mr. Samuel got 150 lbs of bread, with a small quantity of rum and wine. He also got a quadrant and compass into the boat; but was forbidden, on pain of death, to touch either map, ephemeris, book of astronomical observations, sextant, time-keeper, or any of my surveys or drawings.

The mutineers now hurried those they meant to get rid of into the boat. When most of them were in, Christian directed a dram to be served to each of his own crew. I now unhappily saw that nothing could be done to effect the recovery of the ship: there was no one to assist me, and every endeavour on my part was answered with threats of death.

The officers were called, and forced over the side into the boat, while I was kept apart from every one, abast the mizen-mast; Christian, armed with a bayonet, holding me by the bandage that secured my hands. The guard round me had their pieces cocked, but, on my daring the ungrateful wretches to fire, they uncocked them.

Isaac Martin, one of the guard over me, I saw, had an inclination to assist me, and, as he fed me with shaddock, (my lips being quite parched with my endeavours to bring about a change) we explained our wishes to each other by our looks; but this being observed, Martin was instantly removed from me; his inclination then was to leave the ship, for which purpose he got into the boat; but with many threats they obliged him to return.

The armourer, Joseph Coleman, and the two carpenters, McIntosh and Norman, were also kept contrary to their inclination; and they begged of me, after I was astern in the boat, to remember that they declared they had no hand in the transaction. Michael Byrne, I am told, likewise wanted to leave the ship.

It is of no moment for me to recount my endeavours to bring back the offenders to a sense of their duty: all I could do was by speaking to them in general; but my endeavours were of no avail, for I was kept securely bound, and no one but the guard suffered to come near me.

To Mr. Samuel I am indebted for securing my journals and commission, with some material ship papers. Without these I had nothing to certify what I had done, and my honour and character might have been suspected, without my possessing a proper document to have defended them. All this he did with great resolution, though guarded and strictly watched. He attempted to save the time-keeper, and a box with all my surveys, drawings, and remarks for fifteen years past, which were numerous; when he was hurried away, with 'Damn your eyes, you are well off to get what you have.'

It appeared to me, that Christian was some time in doubt whether he should keep the carpenter, or his mates; at length he determined on the latter, and the carpenter was ordered into the boat. He was permitted, but not without some opposition, to take his tool chest.

Much altercation took place among the mutinous crew during the whole business: some swore 'I'll be damned if he does not find his way home, if he gets any thing with him,' (meaning me); others, when the carpenter's chest was carrying away, 'Damn my eyes, he will have a vessel built in a month.' While others laughed at the helpless situation of the boat, being very deep, and so little room for those who were in her. As for Christian, he seemed meditating instant destruction on himself and every one.

I asked for arms, but they laughed at me, and said I was well acquainted with the people where I was going, and therefore did not want them; four cutlasses, however, were thrown into the boat, after we were veered astern.

When the officers and men, with whom I was suffered to have no communication, were put into the boat, they only waited for me, and the master at arms informed Christian of it; who then said – 'Come, captain Bligh, your officers and men are now in the boat, and you must go with them; if you attempt to make the least resistance you will instantly be put to death:' and, without any farther ceremony, holding me by the cord that tied my hands, with a tribe of armed ruffians about me, I was forced over the side, where they untied my hands. Being in the boat we were veered astern by a rope. A few pieces of pork were then thrown to us, and some cloaths, also the cutlasses I have already mentioned; and it was now that the armourer and carpenters called out to me to remember that they had no hand in the transaction. After having undergone a great deal of ridicule, and been kept some time to make sport for these unfeeling wretches, we were at length cast adrift in the open ocean.

I had with me in the boat the following persons:

Names	Stations
John Fryer	Master.
Thomas Ledward	Acting Surgeon.
David Nelson	Botanist.
William Peckover	Gunner.
William Cole	Boatswain.
William Purcell	Carpenter.
William Elphinston	Master's Mate.
Thomas Hayward	Midshipman.
John Hallet	Midshipman.
John Norton	Quarter Master.
Peter Linkletter	Quarter Master.
Lawrence Lebogue	Sailmaker.
John Smith	Cook.
Thomas Hall	Cook.
George Simpson	Quarter Master's Mate.
Robert Tinkler	A boy.
Robert Lamb	Butcher.
Mr. Samuel	Clerk.

There remained on board the *Bounty*, as pirates,

Fletcher Christian	Master's Mate.
Peter Haywood	Midshipman.
Edward Young	Midshipman.
George Stewart	Midshipman.

Names	Stations
Charles Churchill	Master at Arms.
John Mills	Gunner's Mate.
James Morrison	Boatswain's Mate.
Thomas Burkitt	Able Seaman.
Matthew Quintal	Ditto.
John Sumner	Ditto.
John Millward	Ditto.
William McKoy	Ditto.
Henry Hillbrant	Ditto.
Michael Byrne	Ditto.

William Musprat	Ditto.
Alexander Smith	Ditto.
John Williams	Ditto.
Thomas Ellison	Ditto.
Isaac Martin	Ditto.
Richard Skinner	Ditto.
Matthew Thompson	Ditto.
William Brown	Gardiner.
Joseph Coleman	Armourer.
Charles Norman	Carpenter's Mate.
Thomas McIntosh	Carpenter's Crew.

In all 25 hands, and the most able men of the ship's company.

Having little or no wind, we rowed pretty fast towards Tofoa, which bore N E about 10 leagues from us. While the ship was in sight she steered to the W N W, but I considered this only as a feint; for when we were sent away – 'Huzza for Otaheite,' was frequently heard among the mutineers.

Christian, the captain of the gang, is of a respectable family in the north of England. This was the third voyage he had made with me; and, as I found it necessary to keep my ship's company at three watches, I gave him an order to take charge of the third, his abilities being thoroughly equal to the task; and by this means my master and gunner were not at watch and watch.

Haywood is also of a respectable family in the north of England, and a young man of abilities, as well as Christian. These two were objects of my particular regard and attention, and I took great pains to instruct them, for they really promised, as professional men, to be a credit to their country.

Young was well recommended, and appeared to me an able stout seaman; therefore I was glad to take him: he, however, fell short of what his appearance promised.

Stewart was a young man of creditable parents, in the Orkneys; at which place, on the return of the Resolution from the South Seas, in 1780, we received so many civilities, that, on that account only, I should gladly have taken him with me: but, independent of this recommendation, he was a seaman, and had always borne a good character.

Notwithstanding the roughness with which I was treated, the remembrance of past kindnesses produced some signs of remorse in Christian. When they were forcing me out of the ship, I asked him, if this treatment was a proper return for the many instances he had received of my friendship? he appeared disturbed at my question, and answered, with much emotion, 'That, – captain Bligh, – that is the thing; – I am in hell – I am in hell.'

As soon as I had time to reflect, I felt an inward satisfaction, which prevented any depression of my spirits: conscious of my integrity, and anxious solicitude for the good of the service in which I was engaged, I found my mind wonderfully supported, and I began to conceive hopes, notwithstanding so heavy a calamity, that I should one day be able to account to my King and country for the misfortune. – A few hours before, my situation had been peculiarly flattering. I had a ship in the most perfect order, and well stored with every necessary both for service and health: by early attention to those particulars I had, as much as lay in my power, provided against any accident, in case I could not get through Endeavour Straits, as well as against what might befal me in them; add to this, the plants had been successfully preserved in the most flourishing state: so that, upon the whole, the voyage was two thirds completed, and the remaining part in a very promising way; every person on board being in perfect health, to establish which was ever amongst the principal objects of my attention.

It will very naturally be asked, what could be the reason for such a revolt? in answer to which, I can only conjecture that the mutineers had assured themselves of a more happy life among the Otaheiteans, than they could possibly have in England; which, joined to some female connections, have most probably been the principal cause of the whole transaction.

The women at Otaheite are handsome, mild and chearful in their manners and conversation, possessed of great sensibility, and have sufficient delicacy to make them admired and beloved. The chiefs were so much attached to our people, that they rather encouraged their stay among them than otherwise, and even made them promises of large possessions. Under these, and many other attendant circumstances, equally desirable, it is now perhaps not so much to be wondered at, though scarcely possible to have been foreseen, that a set of sailors, most of them void of connections, should be led away; especially when, in addition to such powerful inducements, they imagined it in their power to fix themselves in the midst of plenty, on the finest island in the world, where they need not labour, and where the allurements of dissipation are beyond any thing that can be conceived. The utmost, however, that any commander could have supported to have happened is, that some of the people would have been tempted to desert. But if it should be asserted, that a commander is to guard against an act of mutiny and piracy in his own ship, more than by the common rules of service, it is as much as to say that he must sleep locked up, and when awake, be girded with pistols.

Desertions have happened, more or less, from many of the ships that have been at the Society Islands; but it ever has been in the commanders power to make the chiefs return their people: the knowledge, therefore, that it was unsafe to desert, perhaps, first led mine to consider with what ease so small a ship might be surprized, and that so favourable an opportunity would never offer to them again.

The secrecy of this mutiny is beyond all conception. Thirteen of the party, who were with me, had always lived forward among the people; yet neither they, nor the messmates of Christian, Stewart, Haywood, and Young, had ever observed any circumstance to give them suspicion of what was going on. With such close-planned acts of villainy, and my mind free from any suspicion, it is not wonderful that I have been got the better of. Perhaps, if I had had marines, a centinel at my cabin-door might have prevented it; for I slept with the door always open, that the officer of the watch might have access to me on all occasions. The possibility of such a conspiracy was ever the farthest from my thoughts. Had their mutiny been occasioned by any grievances, either real or imaginary, I must have discovered symptoms of their discontent, which would have put me on my guard: but the case was far otherwise. Christian, in particular, I was on the most friendly terms with; that very day he was engaged to have dined with me; and the preceding night he excused himself from supping with me, on pretence of being unwell; for which I felt concerned, having no suspicions of his integrity and honour.

It now remained with me to consider what was best to be done. My first determination was to seek a supply of bread-fruit and water at Tofoa, and afterwards to sail for Tongataboo, and there risk a solicitation to Poulaho, the king, to equip my boat, and grant a supply of water and provisions, so as to enable us to reach the East Indies.

The quantity of provisions I found in the boat was 150 lb. of bread, 16 pieces of pork, each piece weighing 2 lb. 6 quarts of rum, 6 bottles of wine, with 28 gallons of water, and four empty barrecoes.

Wednesday, April 29th. Happily the afternoon kept calm, until about 4 o'clock, when we were so far to windward, that, with a moderate easterly breeze which sprung up, we were able to sail. It was nevertheless dark when we got to Tofoa, where I expected to land; but the shore proved to be so steep and rocky, that I was obliged to give up all thoughts of it, and keep the boat under the lee of the island with two oars; for there was no anchorage. Having fixed on this mode of proceeding for the night, I served to every person half a pint of grog, and each took to his rest as well as our unhappy situation would allow.

In the morning, at dawn of day, we set off along shore in search of landing, and about ten o'clock we discovered a stony cove at the N W part of the island, where I dropt the grapnel within 20 yards of the rocks. A great deal of surf ran on the shore; but, as I was unwilling to diminish our stock of provisions, I landed Mr. Samuel, and some others, who climbed the cliffs, and got into the country to search for supplies. The rest of us remained at the cove, not discovering any way to get into the country, but that by which Mr. Samuel had proceeded. It was great consolation to me to find, that the spirits of my people did not sink, notwithstanding our miserable and almost hopeless situation. Towards noon Mr. Samuel returned, with a few quarts of water, which he had found in holes; but he had met with no spring, or any prospect of a sufficient supply in that particular, and had only seen signs of inhabitants. As it was impossible to know how much we might be in want, I only issued a morsel of bread, and a glass of wine, to each person for dinner.

I observed the latitude of this cove to be 19° 41' S.

This is the N W part of Tofoa, the north-westernmost of the Friendly Islands.

Thursday, April 30th. Fair weather, but the wind blew so violently from the E S E that I could not venture to sea. Our detention therefore made it absolutely necessary to see what we could do more for our support; for I determined, if possible, to keep my first stock entire: I therefore weighed, and rowed along shore, to see if any thing could be got; and at last discovered some cocoa-nut trees, but they were on the top of high precipices, and the surf made it dangerous landing; both one and the other we, however, got the better of. Some, with much difficulty, climbed the cliffs, and got about 20 cocoa-nuts, and others slung them to ropes, by which we hauled them through the surf into the boat. This was all that could be done here; and, as I found no place so eligible as the one we had left to spend the night at, I returned to the cove, and, having served a cocoa-nut to each person, we went to rest again in the boat.

At dawn of day I attempted to get to sea; but the wind and weather proved so bad, that I was glad to return to my former station; where, after issuing a morsel of bread and a spoonful of rum to each person, we landed, and I went off with Mr. Nelson, Mr. Samuel, and some others, into the country, having hauled ourselves up the precipice by long vines, which were fixed there by the natives for that purpose; this being the only way into the country.

We found a few deserted huts, and a small plantain walk, but little taken care of; from which we could only collect three small bunches of plantains. After passing this place, we came to a deep gully that led towards a mountain, near a volcano; and, as I conceived that in the rainy season very great torrents of water must pass through it, we hoped to find sufficient for our use remaining in some holes of the rocks; but, after all our search, the whole that we found was only nine gallons, in the course of the day. We advanced within two miles of the foot of the highest mountain in the island, on which is the volcano that is almost constantly burning. The country near it is all covered with lava, and has a most dreary appearance. As we had not been fortunate in our discoveries, and saw but little to alleviate our distresses, we filled our cocoa-nut shells with the water we found, and returned exceedingly fatigued and faint. When I came to the precipice whence we were to descend into the cove, I was seized with such a dizziness in my head, that I thought it scarce possible to effect it: however, by the assistance of Mr. Nelson and others, they at last got me down, in a weak condition. Every person being returned by noon, I gave about an ounce of pork and two plantains to each, with half a glass of wine. I again observed the latitude of this place 19° 41' south. The people who remained by the boat I had directed to look for fish, or what they could pick up about the rocks; but nothing eatable could be found: so that, upon the whole, we considered ourselves on as miserable a spot of land as could well be imagined.

I could not say positively, from the former knowledge I had of this island, whether it was inhabited or not; but I knew it was considered inferior to the other islands, and I was not certain but that the Indians only resorted to it at particular times. I was very anxious to ascertain this point; for, in case there had only been a few people here, and those could have furnished us with but very moderate supplies, the remaining in this spot to have made preparations for our voyage, would have been preferable to the risk of going amongst multitudes, where perhaps we might lose every thing. A party, therefore, sufficiently strong, I determined should go another route, as soon as the sun became lower; and they cheerfully undertook it.

Friday, May the 1st: stormy weather, wind E S E and S E. About two o'clock in the afternoon the party set out; but, after suffering much fatigue, they returned in the evening, without any kind of success.

At the head of the cove, about 150 yards from the water-side, was a cave; across the stony beach was about 100 yards, and the only way from the country into the cove was that which I have already described. The situation secured us from the danger of being surprised, and I determined to remain on shore for the night, with a part of my people, that the others might have more room to rest in the boat, with the master; whom I directed to lie at a grapnel, and be watchful, in case we should be attacked. I ordered one plantain for each person to be boiled; and, having supped on this scanty allowance, with a quarter of a pint of grog, and fixed the watches for the night, those whose turn it was, laid down to sleep in the cave; before which we kept a good fire, yet notwithstanding we were much troubled with flies and musquitoes.

At dawn of day the party set out again in a different route, to see what they could find; in the course of which they suffered greatly for want of water: they, however, met with two men, a woman, and a child; the men came with them to the cove, and brought two cocoa-nut shells of water. I immediately made friends with these people, and sent them away for bread-fruit, plantains, and water. Soon after other natives came to us; and by noon I had 30 of them about me, trading with the articles we were in want of: but I could only afford one ounce of pork, and a quarter of a bread-fruit, to each man for dinner, with half a pint of water; for I was fixed in not using any of the bread or water in the boat.

No particular chief was yet among the natives: they were, notwithstanding, tractable, and behaved honestly, giving the provisions they brought for a few buttons and beads. The party who had been out, informed me of having discovered several neat plantations; so that it became no longer a doubt of there being settled inhabitants on the island; and for that reason I determined to get what I could, and sail the first moment the wind and weather would allow me to put to sea.

Saturday, May the 2d: stormy weather, wind E S E It had hitherto been a weighty consideration with me, how I was to account to the natives for the loss of my ship: I knew they had too much sense to be amused with a story that the ship was to join me, when she was not in sight from the hills. I was at first doubtful whether I should tell the real fact, or say that the ship had overset and sunk, and that only we were saved: the latter appeared to me to be the most proper and advantageous to us, and I accordingly instructed my people, that we might all agree in one story. As I expected, enquiries were made after the ship, and they seemed readily satisfied with our account; but there did not appear the least symptom of joy or sorrow in their faces, although I fancied I discovered some marks of surprise. Some of the natives were coming and going the whole afternoon, and we got enough of bread-fruit, plantains, and cocoa-nuts for another day; but water they only brought us about five pints. A canoe also came in with four men, and brought a few cocoa-nuts and bread-fruit, which I bought as I had done the rest. Nails were much enquired after, but I would not suffer one to be shewn, as I wanted them for the use of the boat.

Towards evening I had the satisfaction to find our stock of provisions somewhat increased: but the natives did not appear to have much to spare. What they brought was in such small quantities, that I had no reason to hope we should be able to procure from them sufficient to stock us for our voyage. At sunset all the natives left us in quiet possession of the cove. I thought this a good sign, and made no doubt that they would come again the next day with a larger proportion of food and water, with which I hoped to sail without farther delay: for if, in attempting to get to Tongataboo, we should be blown away from the islands altogether, there would be a larger quantity of provisions to support us against such a misfortune.

At night I served a quarter of a bread-fruit and a cocoa-nut to each person for supper; and, a good fire being made, all but the watch went to sleep.

At day-break I was happy to find every one's spirits a little revived, and that they no longer regarded me with those anxious looks, which had constantly been directed towards me since we lost sight of the ship: every countenance appeared to have a degree of cheerfulness, and they all seemed determined to do their best.

As I doubted of water being brought by the natives, I sent a party among the gullies in the mountains, with empty shells, to see what they could get. In their absence the natives came about us, as I expected, but more numerous; also two canoes came in from round the north side of the island. In one of them was an elderly chief, called Maccaackavow. Soon after some of our foraging party returned, and with them came a good-looking chief, called Eegijeefow, or perhaps more properly Eefow, Egij or Eghee, signifying a chief. To both these men I made a present of an old shirt and a knife, and I soon found they either had seen me, or had heard of my being at Annamooka. They knew I had been with captain Cook, who they enquired after, and also captain Clerk. They were very inquisitive to know in what manner I had lost my ship. During this conversation a young man appeared, whom I remembered to have seen at Annamooka, called Nageete: he expressed much pleasure at seeing me. I now enquired after Poulaho and Feenow, who, they said, were at Tongataboo; and Eefow agreed to accompany me thither, if I would wait till the weather moderated. The readiness and affability of this man gave me much satisfaction.

This, however, was but of short duration, for the natives began to increase in number, and I observed some symptoms of a design against us; soon after they attempted to haul the boat on shore, when I threatened Eefow with a cutlass, to induce him to make them desist; which they did, and every thing became quiet again. My people, who had been in the mountains, now returned with about three gallons of water. I kept buying up the little bread-fruit that was brought to us, and likewise some spears to arm my men with, having only four cutlasses, two of which were in the boat. As we had no means of improving our situation, I told our people I would wait until sun-set, by which time, perhaps, something might happen in our favour: that if we attempted to go at present, we must fight our way through, which we could do more advantageously at night; and that in the mean time we would endeavour to get off to the boat what we had bought. The beach was now lined with the natives, and we heard nothing but the knocking of stones together, which they had in each hand. I knew very well this was the sign of an attack. It being now noon, I served a cocoa-nut and a bread-fruit to each person for dinner, and gave some to the chiefs, with whom I continued to appear intimate and friendly. They frequently importuned me to sit down, but I as constantly refused; for it occured both to Mr. Nelson and myself, that they intended to seize hold of me, if I gave them such an opportunity. Keeping, therefore, constantly on our guard, we were suffered to eat our uncomfortable meal in some quietness.

Sunday, 3d May, fresh gales at S E and E S E, varying to the N E in the latter part, with a storm of wind.

After dinner we began by little and little to get our things into the boat, which was a troublesome business, on account of the surf. I carefully watched the motions of the natives, who still increased in number, and found that, instead of their intention being to leave us, fires were made, and places fixed on for their stay during the night. Consultations were also held among them, and every thing assured me we should be attacked. I sent orders to the master, that when he saw us coming down, he should keep the boat close to the shore, that we might the more readily embark.

I had my journal on shore with me, writing the occurrences in the cave, and in sending it down to the boat it was nearly snatched away, but for the timely assistance of the gunner.

The sun was near setting when I gave the word, on which every person, who was on shore with me, boldly took up his proportion of things, and carried them to the boat. The chiefs asked me if I would not stay with them all night, I said, 'No, I never sleep out of my boat; but in the morning we will again trade with you, and I shall remain until the weather is moderate, that we may go, as we have agreed, to see Poulaho, at Tongataboo.' Maccaackavow then got up, and said, 'You will not sleep on shore? then Mattie,' (which directly signifies we will kill you) and he left me. The onset was now preparing; every one, as I have described before, kept knocking stones together, and Eefow quitted me. We had now all but two or three things in the boat, when I took Nageete by the hand, and we walked down the beach, every one in a silent kind of horror.

When I came to the boat, and was seeing the people embark, Nageete wanted me to stay to speak to Eefow; but I found he was encouraging them to the attack, and I determined, had it then begun, to have killed him for his treacherous behaviour. I ordered the carpenter not to quit me until the other people were in the boat. Nageete, finding I would not stay, loosed himself from my hold and went off, and we all got into the boat except one man, who, while I was getting on board, quitted it, and ran up the beach to cast the stern fast off, notwithstanding the master and others called to him to return, while they were hauling me out of the water.

I was no sooner in the boat than the attack began by about 200 men; the unfortunate poor man who had run up the beach was knocked down, and the stones flew like a shower of shot. Many Indians got hold of the stern rope, and were near hauling us on shore, and would certainly have done it if I had not had a knife in my pocket, with which I cut the rope. We then hauled off to the grapnel, every one being more or less hurt. At this time I saw five of the natives about the poor man they had killed, and two of them were beating him about the head with stones in their hands.

We had no time to reflect, before, to my surprise, they filled their canoes with stones, and twelve men came off after us to renew the attack, which they did so effectually as nearly to disable all of us. Our grapnel was foul, but Providence here assisted us; the fluke broke, and we got to our oars, and pulled to sea. They, however, could paddle round us, so that we were obliged to sustain the attack without being able to return it, except with such stones as lodged in the boat, and in this I found we were very inferior to them. We could not close, because our boat was lumbered and heavy, and that they knew very well: I therefore adopted the expedient of throwing overboard some cloaths, which they lost time in picking up; and, as it was now almost dark, they gave over the attack, and returned towards the shore, leaving us to reflect on our unhappy situation.

The poor man I lost was John Norton: this was his second voyage with me as a quarter-master, and his worthy character made me lament his loss very much. He has left an aged parent, I am told, whom he supported.

I once before sustained an attack of a similar nature, with a smaller number of Europeans, against a multitude of Indians; it was after the death of captain Cook, on the Morai at Owhyhee, where I was left by lieutenant King: yet, notwithstanding, I did not conceive that the power of a man's arm could throw stones, from two to eight pounds weight, with such force and exactness as these people did. Here unhappily I was without arms, and the Indians knew it; but it was a fortunate circumstance that they did not begin to attack us in the cave: in that case our destruction must have been inevitable, and we should have had nothing left for it but to die as bravely as we could, fighting close together; in which I found every one cheerfully disposed to join me. This appearance of resolution deterred them, supposing they could effect their purpose without risk after we were in the boat.

Taking this as a sample of the dispositions of the Indians, there was little reason to expect much benefit if I persevered in my intention of visiting Poulaho; for I considered their good behaviour hitherto to proceed from a dread of our fire-arms, which, now knowing us destitute of, would cease; and, even supposing our lives not in danger, the boat and every thing we had would most probably be taken from us, and thereby all hopes precluded of ever being able to return to our native country.

We were now sailing along the west side of the island Tofoa, and my mind was employed in considering what was best to be done, when I was solicited by all hands to take them towards home: and, when I told them no hopes of relief for us remained, but what I might find at New Holland, until I came to Timor, a distance of full 1200 leagues, where was a Dutch settlement, but in what part of the island I knew not, they all agreed to live on one ounce of bread, and a quarter of a pint of water, per day. Therefore, after examining our stock of provisions, and recommending this as a sacred promise for ever to their memory, we bore away across a sea, where the navigation is but little known, in a small boat, twenty-three feet long from stern to stern, deep laden with eighteen men; without a chart, and nothing but my own recollection and general knowledge of the situation of places, assisted by a book of latitudes and longitudes, to guide us. I was happy, however, to see every one better satisfied with our situation in this particular than myself.

Our stock of provisions consisted of about one hundred and fifty pounds of bread, twenty-eight gallons of water, twenty pounds of pork, three bottles of wine, and five quarts of rum. The difference between this and the quantity we had on leaving the ship, was principally owing to loss in the bustle and confusion of the attack. A few cocoa-nuts were in the boat, and some bread-fruit, but the latter was trampled to pieces.

It was about eight o'clock at night when I bore away under a reefed lug fore-sail: and, having divided the people into watches, and got the boat in a little order, we returned God thanks for our miraculous preservation, and, fully confident of his gracious support, I found my mind more at ease than for some time past.

At day-break the gale increased; the sun rose very fiery and red, a sure indication of a severe gale of wind. At eight it blew a violent storm, and the sea ran very high, so that between the seas the sail was becalmed, and when on the top of the sea it was too much to have set: but I was obliged to carry to it, for we were now in very imminent danger and distress, the sea curling over the stern of the boat, which obliged us to bale with all our might. A situation more distressing has, perhaps, seldom been experienced.

Our bread was in bags, and in danger of being spoiled by the wet: to be starved to death was inevitable, if this could not be prevented: I therefore began to examine what cloaths there were in the boat, and what other things could be spared; and, having determined that only two suits should be kept for each person, the rest was thrown overboard, with some rope and spare sails, which lightened the boat considerably, and we had more room to bale the water out. Fortunately the carpenter had a good chest in the boat, into which I put the bread the first favourable moment. His tool chest also was cleared, and the tools stowed in the bottom of the boat, so that this became a second convenience.

I now served a tea-spoonful of rum to each person, (for we were very wet and cold) with a quarter of a bread-fruit, which was scarce eatable, for dinner; but our engagement was now strictly to be carried into execution, and I was fully determined to make what provisions I had last eight weeks, let the daily proportion be ever so small.

At noon I considered my course and distance from Tofoa to be W N W 3/4 W. 86 miles, my latitude 19° 27' S. I directed my course to the W N W, that I might get a sight of the islands called Feejee,[3] if they laid in the direction the natives had pointed out to me.

Monday, 4th May. This day the weather was very severe, it blew a storm from N E to E S E. The sea ran higher than yesterday, and the fatigue of baling, to keep the boat from filling, was exceedingly great. We could do nothing more than keep before the sea; in the course of which the boat performed so wonderfully well, that I no longer dreaded any danger in that respect. But among the hardships we were to undergo, that of being constantly wet was not the least: the nights were very cold, and at day light our limbs were so benumbed, that we could scarce find the use of them. At this time I served a tea-spoonful of rum to each person, which we all found great benefit from.

As I have mentioned before, I determined to keep to the W N W, until I got more to the northward, for I not only expected to have better weather, but to see the Feejee Islands, as I have often understood, from the natives of Annamooka, that they lie in that direction; Captain Cook likewise considers them to be N W by W from Tongataboo. Just before noon we discovered a small flat island of a moderate height, bearing W S W, 4 or 5 leagues. I observed in latitude 18° 58' S; our longitude, by account, 3° 4' W from the island Tofoa, having made a N 72° W course, distance 95 miles, since yesterday noon. I divided five small cocoa-nuts for our dinner, and every one was satisfied.

…

Friday, May the 15th. Fresh gales at S E, and gloomy weather with rain, and a very high sea; two people constantly employed baling.

At four in the afternoon I passed the westernmost island. At one in the morning I discovered another, bearing W N W, five leagues distance, and at eight o'clock I saw it for the last time, bearing N E seven leagues. A number of gannets, boobies, and men of war birds were seen.

These islands lie between the latitude of 13° 16' S and 14° 10' S: their longitude, according to my reckoning, 15° 51' to 17° 6' W from the island Tofoa. The largest island may be twenty leagues in circuit, the others five or six. The easternmost is the smallest island, and most remarkable, having a high sugar-loaf hill.

---

[3] Now Fiji.

The sight of these islands served but to increase the misery of our situation. We were very little better than starving, with plenty in view; yet to attempt procuring any relief was attended with so much danger, that pro-longing of life, even in the midst of misery, was thought preferable, while there remained hopes of being able to surmount our hardships. For my own part, I consider the general run of cloudy and wet weather to be a blessing of Providence. Hot weather would have caused us to have died with thirst; and perhaps being so constantly covered with rain or sea protected us from that dreadful calamity.

As I had nothing to assist my memory, I could not determine whether these islands were a part of the New Hebrides[4] or not: I believed them perfectly a new discovery, which I have since found to be the case; but, though they were not seen either by Monsieur Bougainville or Captain Cook, they are so nearly in the neighbourhood of the New Hebrides, that they must be considered as part of the same group. They are fertile, and inhabited, as I saw smoke in several places.

…

Monday, May the 25th. Fresh gales and fair weather. Wind S S E.

This afternoon we had many birds about us, which are never seen far from land, such as boobies and noddies.

About three o'clock the sea began to run fair, and we shipped but little water, I therefore determined to know the exact quantity of bread I had left; and on examining found, according to my present issues, sufficient for 29 days allowance. In the course of this time I hoped to be at Timor; but, as that was very uncertain, and perhaps after all we might be obliged to go to Java, I determined to proportion my issues to six weeks. I was apprehensive that this would be ill received, and that it would require my utmost resolution to enforce it; for, small as the quantity was which I intended to take away, for our future good, yet it might appear to my people like robbing them of life, and some, who were less patient than their companions, I expected would very ill brook it. I however represented it so essentially necessary to guard against delays in our voyage by contrary winds, or other causes, promising to enlarge upon the allowance as we got on, that it was readily agreed to. I therefore fixed, that every person should receive one 25th of a pound of bread for breakfast, and one 25th of a pound for dinner; so that by omitting the proportion for supper, I had 43 days allowance.

[4] Now Vanuatu.

At noon some noddies came so near to us, that one of them was caught by hand. This bird is about the size of a small pigeon. I divided it, with its entrails, into 18 portions, and by the method of, Who shall have this? it was distributed with the allowance of bread and water for dinner, and eat up bones and all, with salt water for sauce. I observed the latitude 13° 32' S; longitude made 35° 19' W; and course N 89° W; distance 108 miles.

Tuesday, May the 26th. Fresh gales at S S E, and fine weather.

In the evening we saw several boobies flying near to us, that we caught one of them by hand. This bird is as large as a good duck; like the noddy, it has received its name from seamen, for suffering itself to be caught on the masts and yards of ships. They are the most presumptive proofs of being in the neighbourhood of land of any seafowl we are acquainted with. I directed the bird to be killed for supper, and the blood to be given to three of the people who were the most distressed for want of food. The body, with the entrails, peak, and feet, I divided into 18 shares, and with an allowance of bread, which I made a merit of granting, we made a good supper, compared with our usual fare.

In the morning we caught another booby, so that Providence seemed to be relieving our wants in a very extraordinary manner. Towards noon we passed a great many pieces of the branches of trees, some of which appeared to have been no long time in the water. I had a good observation for the latitude, and found my situation to be in 13° 41' S; my longitude, by account, from Tofoa, 37° 13' W; course S 85° W, 112 miles. Every person was now overjoyed at the addition to their dinner, which I distributed as I had done in the evening; giving the blood to those who were the most in want of food.

To make our bread a little savoury we frequently dipped it in salt water; but for my own part I generally broke mine into small pieces, and eat it in my allowance of water, out of a cocoa-nut shell, with a spoon, economically avoiding to take too large a piece at a time, so that I was as long at dinner as if it had been a much more plentiful meal.

...

Friday, May the 29th. Moderate breezes and fine weather, wind E S E.

As we advanced within the reefs, the coast began to shew itself very distinctly, with a variety of high and low land; some parts of which were covered with wood. In our way towards the shore we fell in with a point of a reef, which is connected with that towards the sea, and here I came to a grapnel, and tried to catch fish, but had no success. The island Direction now bore S three or four leagues. Two islands lay about four miles to the W by N, and appeared eligible for a resting-place, if nothing more; but on my approach to the first I found it only a heap of stones, and its size too inconsiderable to shelter the boat. I therefore proceeded to the next, which was close to it and towards the main, where, on the N W side, I found a bay and a fine sandy point to land at. Our distance was about a quarter of a mile from a projecting part of the main, bearing from SW by S, to N N W ¾ W. I now landed to examine if there were any signs of the natives being near us; but though I discovered some old fire-places, I saw nothing to alarm me for our situation during the night. Every one was anxious to find something to eat, and I soon heard that there were oysters on the rocks, for the tide was out; but it was nearly dark, and only a few could be gathered. I determined therefore to wait till the morning, to know how to proceed, and I consented that one half of us should sleep on shore, and the other in the boat. We would gladly have made a fire, but, as we could not accomplish it, we took our rest for the night, which happily was calm and undisturbed.

The dawn of day brought greater strength and spirits to us than I expected; for, notwithstanding every one was very weak, there appeared strength sufficient remaining to make me conceive the most favourable hopes of being able to surmount the difficulties we might yet have to encounter.

As soon as I saw that there were not any natives immediately near us, I sent out parties in search of supplies, while others were putting the boat in order, that I might be ready to go to sea in case any unforeseen cause might make it necessary. The first object of this work, that demanded our attention, was the rudder: one of the gudgeons had come out, in the course of the night, and was lost. This, if it had happened at sea, would probably have been the cause of our perishing, as the management of the boat could not have been so nicely preserved as these very heavy seas required. I had often expressed my fears of this accident, and, that we might be prepared for it, had taken the precaution to have grummets fixed on each quarter of the boat for oars; but even our utmost readiness in using them, I fear, would not have saved us. It appears, therefore, a providential circumstance, that it happened at this place, and was in our power to remedy the defect; for by great good luck we found a large staple in the boat that answered the purpose.

The parties were now returned, highly rejoiced at having found plenty of oysters and fresh water. I also had made a fire, by help of a small magnifying glass, that I always carried about me, to read off the divisions of my sextants; and, what was still more fortunate, among the few things which had been thrown into the boat and saved, was a piece of brimstone and a tinder-box, so that I secured fire for the future.

One of my people had been so provident as to bring away with him a copper pot: it was by being in possession of this article that I was enabled to make a proper use of the supply we found, for, with a mixture of bread and a little pork, I made a stew that might have been relished by people of more delicate appetites, of which each person received a full pint.

The general complaints of disease among us, were a dizziness in the head, great weakness of the joints, and violent tenesmus, most of us having had no evacuation by stool since we left the ship. I had constantly a severe pain at my stomach; but none of our complaints were alarming; on the contrary, every one retained marks of strength, that, with a mind possessed of any fortitude, could bear more fatigue than I hoped we had to undergo in our voyage to Timor.

As I would not allow the people to expose themselves to the heat of the sun, it being near noon, every one took his allotment of earth, shaded by the bushes, for a short sleep.

The oysters we found grew so fast to the rocks that it was with difficulty they could be broke off, and at last we discovered it to be the most expeditious way to open them where they were found. They were very sizeable, and well tasted, and gave us great relief. To add to this happy circumstance, in the hollow of the land there grew some wire grass, which indicated a moist situation. On forcing a stick, about three feet long, into the ground, we found water, and with little trouble dug a well, which produced as much as we were in need of. It was very good, but I could not determine if it was a spring or not. Our wants made it not necessary to make the well deep, for it flowed as fast as we emptied it; which, as the soil was apparently too loose to retain water from the rains, renders it probable to be a spring. It lies about 200 yards to the S E of a point in the S W part of the island.

I found evident signs of the natives resorting to the island; for, besides fire-places, I saw two miserable wig-wams, having only one side loosely covered. We found a pointed stick, about three feet long, with a slit in the end of it, to sling stones with, the same as the natives of Van Diemen's land use.

The track of some animal was very discernible, and Mr. Nelson agreed with me that it was the Kanguroo; but how these animals can get from the main I know not, unless brought over by the natives to breed, that they may take them with more ease, and render a supply of food certain to them; as on the continent the catching of them may be precarious, or attended with great trouble, in so large an extent of country.

The island may be about two miles in circuit; it is a high lump of rocks and stones covered with wood; but the trees are small, the soil, which is very indifferent and sandy, being barely sufficient to produce them. The trees that came within our knowledge were the manchineal and a species of purow: also some palm-tress, the tops of which we cut down, and the soft interior part or heart of them was so palatable that it made a good addition to our mess. Mr. Nelson discovered some fern-roots, which I thought might be good roasted, as a substitute for bread, but it proved a very poor one: it however was very good in its natural state to allay thirst, and on that account I directed a quantity to be collected to take into the boat. Many pieces of cocoa-nut shells and husk were found about the shore, but we could find no cocoa-nut trees, neither did I see any like them on the main.

I had cautioned every one not to touch any kind of berry or fruit that they might find; yet they were no sooner out of my sight than they began to make free with three different kinds, that grew all over the island, eating without any reserve. The symptoms of having eaten too much, began at last to frighten some of them; but on questioning others, who had taken a more moderate allowance, their minds were a little quieted. The others, however, became equally alarmed in their turn, dreading that such symptoms would come on, and that they were all poisoned, so that they regarded each other with the strongest marks of apprehension, uncertain what would be the issue of their imprudence. Happily the fruit proved wholesome and good. One sort grew on a small delicate kind of vine; they were the size of a large gooseberry, and very like in substance, but had only a sweet taste; the skin was a pale red, streaked with yellow the long way of the fruit: it was pleasant and agreeable. Another kind grew on bushes, like that which is called the sea-side grape in the West Indies; but the fruit was very different, and more like elder-berries, growing in clusters in the same manner. The third sort was a black berry, not in such plenty as the others, and resembled a bullace, or large kind of sloe, both in size and taste. Seeing these fruits eaten by the birds made me consider them fit for use, and those who had already tried the experiment, not finding any bad effect, made it a certainty that we might eat of them without danger.

Wild pigeons, parrots, and other birds, were about the summit of the island, but, as I had no fire-arms, relief of that kind was not to be expected, unless I met with someone unfrequented spot where we might take them with our hands.

On the south side of the island, and about half a mile from the well, a small run of water was found; but, as its source was not traced, I know nothing more of it.

The shore of this island is very rocky, except the part we landed at, and here I picked up many pieces of pumice-stone. On the part of the main next to us were several sandy bays, but at low-water they became an extensive rocky flat. The country had rather a barren appearance, except in a few places where it was covered with wood. A remarkable range of rocks lay a few miles to the S W, or a high peaked hill terminated the coast towards the sea, with other high lands and islands to the southward. A high fair cape showed the direction of the coast to the N W, about seven leagues, and two small isles lay three or four leagues to the northward.

I saw a few bees or wasps, several lizards, and the black-berry bushes were full of ants nests, webbed as a spider's, but so close and compact as not to admit the rain.

A trunk of a tree, about 50 feet long, lay on the beach; from whence I conclude a heavy sea runs in here with the northerly winds.

This being the day of the restoration of king Charles the Second, and the name not being inapplicable to our present situation (for we were restored to fresh life and strength), I named this Restoration Island; for I thought it probable that captain Cook might not have taken notice of it. The other names I have presumed to give the different parts of the coast, will be only to show my route a little more distinctly.

At noon I found the latitude of the island to be 12° 39' S; our course having been N 66° W; distance 18 miles from yesterday noon.

...

Sunday, May the 31st. Early in the afternoon, the people returned with the few oysters they had time to pick up, and every thing was put into the boat. I then examined the quantity of bread remaining and found 38 days allowance, according to the last mode of issuing a 25th of a pound at breakfast and at dinner.

Fair weather, and moderate breezes at E S E and S E.

Being all ready for sea, I directed every person to attend prayers, and by four o'clock we were preparing to embark; when twenty natives appeared, running and holloaing to us, on the opposite shore. They were armed with a spear or lance, and a short weapon which they carried in their left hand: they made signs for us to come to them. On the top of the hills we saw the heads of many more; whether these were their wives and children, or others who waited for our landing, until which they meant not to show themselves, lest we might be intimidated, I cannot say; but, as I found we were discovered to be on the coast, I thought it prudent to make the best of my way, for fear of canoes; though, from the accounts of captain Cook, the chance was that there were very few or none of any consequence. I passed these people as near as I could, which was within a quarter of a mile; they were naked, and apparently black, and their hair or wool bushy and short.

I directed my course within two small islands that lie to the north of Restoration Island, passing between them and the main land, towards Fair Cape, with a strong tide in my favour; so that I was abreast of it by eight o'clock. The coast I had passed was high and woody. As I could see no land without Fair Cape, I concluded that the coast inclined to the N W and W N W, which was agreeable to my recollection of captain Cook's survey. I therefore steered more towards the W; but by eleven o'clock at night I found myself mistaken: for we met with low land, which inclined to the N E; so that at three o'clock in the morning I found we were embayed, which obliged us to stand back to the southward.

At day-break I was exceedingly surprised to find the appearance of the country all changed, as if in the course of the night I had been transported to another part of the world; for we had now a miserable low sandy coast in view, with very little verdure, or any thing to indicate that it was at all habitable to a human being, if I except some patches of small trees or brush-wood.

I had many small islands in view to the N E, about six miles distant. The E part of the main bore N four miles, and Fair Cape S S E five or six leagues. I took the channel between the nearest island and the main land, about one mile apart, leaving all the islands on the starboard side. Some of these were very pretty spots, covered with wood, and well situated for fishing: large shoals of fish were about us, but we could not catch any. As I was passing this strait we saw another party of Indians, seven in number, running towards us, shouting and making signs for us to land. Some of them waved green branches of the bushes which were near them, as a sign of friendship; but there were some of their other motions less friendly. A larger party we saw a little farther off, and coming towards us. I therefore determined not to land, though I wished much to have had some intercourse with these people; for which purpose I beckoned to them to come near to me, and laid the boat close to the rocks; but not one would come within 200 yards of us. They were armed in the same manner as those I had seen from Restoration Island, were stark naked, and appeared to be jet black, with short bushy hair or wool, and in every respect the same people. An island of good height now bore N 1/2 W, four miles from us, at which I resolved to see what could be got, and from thence to take a look at the coast. At this isle I landed about eight o'clock in the morning. The shore was rocky, with some sandy beaches within the rocks: the water, however, was smooth, and I landed without difficulty. I sent two parties out, one to the northward, and the other to the southward, to seek for supplies, and others I ordered to stay by the boat. On this occasion their fatigue and weakness so far got the better of their sense of duty, that some of them began to mutter who had done most, and declared they would rather be without their dinner than go in search of it. One person, in particular, went so far as to tell me, with a mutinous look, he was as good a man as myself. It was not possible for me to judge where this might have an end, if not stopped in time; I therefore determined to strike a final blow at it, and either to preserve my command, or die in the attempt: and, seizing a cutlass, I ordered him to take hold of another and defend himself; on which he called out I was going to kill him, and began to make concessions. I did not allow this to interfere further with the harmony of the boat's crew, and every thing soon became quiet.

The parties continued collecting what could be found, which consisted of some fine oysters and clams, and a few small dog-fish that were caught in the holes of the rocks. We also found about two tons of rain-water in the hollow of the rocks, on the north part of the island, so that of this essential article we were again so happy as not to be in want.

After regulating the mode of proceeding, I set off for the highest part of the island, to see and consider of my route for the night. To my surprise I could see no more of the main than I did from below, it extending only from S 1/2 E, four miles, to W by N, about three leagues, full of sand-hills. Besides the isles to the E S E and south, that I had seen before, I could only discover a small key N W by N. As this was considerably farther from the main than where I was at present, I resolved to get there by night, it being a more secure resting-place; for I was here open to an attack, if the Indians had canoes, as they undoubtedly observed my landing. My mind being made up on this point, I returned, taking a particular look at the spot I was on, which I found only to produce a few bushes and coarse grass, and the extent of the whole not two miles in circuit. On the north side, in a sandy bay, I saw an old canoe, about 33 feet long, lying bottom upwards, and half buried in the beach. It was made of three pieces, the bottom entire, to which the sides were sewed in the common way. It had a sharp projecting prow rudely carved, in resemblance of the head of a fish; the extreme breadth was about three feet, and I imagine it was capable of carrying 20 men.

At noon the parties were all returned, but had found difficulty in gathering the oysters, from their close adherence to the rocks, and the clams were scarce: I therefore saw, that it would be of little use to remain longer in this place, as we should not be able to collect more than we could eat; nor could any tolerable sea-store be expected, unless we fell in with a greater plenty. I named this Sunday Island: it lies N by W 3/4 W from Restoration Island; the latitude, by a good observation, 11° 58' S.

...

Thursday, June the 4th. A fresh gale at S E, and fair weather.

At two o'clock, as we were steering to the S W, towards the westernmost part of the land in sight, we fell in with some large sand-banks that run off from the coast. We were therefore obliged to steer to the northward again, and, having got round them, I directed my course to the W.

At four o'clock, the westernmost of the islands to the northward bore N four leagues; Wednesday island E by N five leagues; and Shoal Cape S E by E two leagues. A small island was now seen bearing W, at which I arrived before dark, and found that it was only a rock, where boobies resort, for which reason I called it Booby Island. A small key also lies close to the W part of the coast, which I have called Shoal Cape. Here terminated the rocks and shoals of the N part of New Holland, for, except Booby Island, we could see no land to the westward of S, after three o'clock this afternoon.

I find that Booby Island was seen by Captain Cook, and, by a remarkable coincidence of ideas, received from him the same name; but I cannot with certainty reconcile the situation of many parts of the coast that I have seen, to his survey. I ascribe this to the very different form in which land appears, when seen from the unequal heights of a ship and a boat. The chart I have given, is by no means meant to supersede that made by Captain Cook, who had better opportunities than I had, and was in every respect properly provided for surveying. The intention of mine is chiefly to render the narrative more intelligible, and to shew in what manner the coast appeared to me from an open boat. I have little doubt that the opening, which I named the Bay of Islands, is Endeavour Straits; and that our track was to the northward of Prince of Wales's Isles. Perhaps, by those who shall hereafter navigate these seas, more advantage may be derived from the possession of both our charts, than from either singly.

At eight o'clock in the evening, we once more launched into the open ocean. Miserable as our situation was in every respect, I was secretly surprised to see that it did not appear to affect any one so strongly as myself; on the contrary, it seemed as if they had embarked on a voyage to Timor, in a vessel sufficiently calculated for safety and convenience. So much confidence gave me great pleasure, and I may assert that to this cause their preservation is chiefly to be attributed; for if any one of them had despaired, he would most probably have died before we reached New Holland.

I now gave every one hopes that eight or ten days might bring us to a land of safety; and, after praying to God for a continuance of his most gracious protection, I served an allowance of water for supper, and kept my course to the W S W, to counteract the southerly winds, in case they should blow strong.

We had been just six days on the coast of New Holland, in the course of which we found oysters, a few clams, some birds, and water. But perhaps a benefit nearly equal to this we received from not having fatigue in the boat, and enjoying good rest at night. These advantages certainly preserved our lives; for, small as the supply was, I am very sensible how much it relieved our distresses. About this time nature would have sunk under the extremes of hunger and fatigue. Some would have ceased to struggle for a life that only promised wretchedness and misery; while others, though possessed of more bodily strength, must soon have followed their unfortunate companions. Even in our present situation, we were most wretched spectacles; yet our fortitude and spirit remained; every one being encouraged by the hopes of a speedy termination to his misery.

For my own part, wonderful as it may appear, I felt neither extreme hunger nor thirst. My allowance contented me, knowing I could have no more.

I served one 25th of a pound of bread, and an allowance of water, for breakfast, and the same for dinner, with an addition of six oysters to each person. At noon, latitude observed 10° 48' S; course since yesterday noon S 81 W; distance 111 miles; longitude, by account, from Shoal Cape 1° 45' W.

...

Thursday, June the 11th. Fresh gales and fair weather. Wind S E and S S E.

Birds and rock-weed showed that we were not far from land; but I expected such signs must be here, as there are many islands between the east part of Timor and New Guinea. I however hoped to fall in with Timor every hour, for I had great apprehensions that some of my people could not hold out. An extreme weakness, swelled legs, hollow and ghastly countenances, great propensity to sleep, with an apparent debility of understanding, seemed to me melancholy presages of their approaching dissolution. The surgeon and Lebogue, in particular, were most miserable objects. I occasionally gave them a few tea-spoonfuls of wine, out of the little I had saved for this dreadful stage, which no doubt greatly helped to support them.

For my own part, a great share of spirits, with the hopes of being able to accomplish the voyage, seemed to be my principal support; but the boatswain very innocently told me, that he really thought I looked worse than any one in the boat. The simplicity with which he uttered such an opinion diverted me, and I had good humour enough to return him a better compliment.

Every one received his 25th of a pound of bread, and quarter of a pint of water, at evening, morning, and noon, and an extra allowance of water was given to those who desired it.

At noon I observed in latitude 9° 41' S; course S 77° W; distance 109 miles; longitude made 13° 49' W. I had little doubt of having now passed the meridian of the eastern part of Timor, which is laid down in 128° E. This diffused universal joy and satisfaction.

Friday, June the 12th. Fresh breezes and fine weather, but very hazy. Wind from E to S E.

All the afternoon we had several gannets, and many other birds, about us, that indicated we were near land, and at sun-set we kept a very anxious look-out. In the evening we caught a booby, which I reserved for our dinner the next day.

At three in the morning, with an excess of joy, we discovered Timor bearing from W S W to W N W, and I hauled on a wind to the N N E till day-light, when the land bore from S W by S about two leagues to N E by N seven leagues.

It is not possible for me to describe the pleasure which the blessing of the fight of land diffused among us. It appeared scarce credible, that in an open boat, and so poorly provided, we should have been able to reach the coast of Timor in forty-one days after leaving Tofoa, having in that time run, by our log, a distance of 3618 miles, and that, notwithstanding our extreme distress, no one should have perished in the voyage.

I have already mentioned, that I knew not where the Dutch settlement was situated; but I had a faint idea that it was at the S W part of the island. I therefore, after day-light, bore away along shore to the S S W, and the more readily as the wind would not suffer us to go towards the N E without great loss of time.

The day gave us a most agreeable prospect of the land, which was interspersed with woods and lawns; the interior part mountainous, but the shore low. Towards noon the coast became higher, with some remarkable head-lands. We were greatly delighted with the general look of the country, which exhibited many cultivated spots and beautiful situations; but we could only see a few small huts, whence I concluded no European resided in this part of the island. Much sea ran on the shore, so that landing with a boat was impracticable. At noon I was abreast of a very high head-land; the extremes of the land bore S W 1/ 2 W, and N N E 1/2 E; our distance off shore being three miles; latitude, by observation, 9° 59' S; and my longitude, by dead reckoning, from the north part of New Holland, 15° 6' W.

With the usual allowance of bread and water for dinner, I divided the bird we had caught the night before, and to the surgeon and Lebogue I gave a little wine.

Saturday, June the 13th. Fresh gales at E, and E S E, with very hazy weather.

During the afternoon, we continued our course along a low woody shore, with innumerable palm-trees, called the Fan Palm from the leaf spreading like a fan; but we had now lost all signs of cultivation, and the country had not so fine an appearance as it had to the eastward. This, however, was only a small tract, for by sun-set it improved again, and I saw several great smokes where the inhabitants were clearing and cultivating their grounds. We had now ran 25 miles to the W S W since noon, and were W five miles from a low point, which in the afternoon I imagined had been the southernmost land, and here the coast formed a deep bend, with low land in the bight that appeared like islands. The west shore was high; but from this part of the coast to the high cape which we were abreast of yesterday noon, the shore is low, and I believe shoal. I particularly remark this situation, because here the very high ridge of mountains, that run from the east end of the island, terminate, and the appearance of the country suddenly changes for the worse, as if it was not the same island in any respect.

That we might not run past any settlement in the night, I determined to preserve my station till the morning, and therefore hove to under a close-reefed fore-sail, with which the boat lay very quiet. We were here in shoal water, our distance from the shore being half a league, the westernmost land in sight bearing W S W 1/2 W. Served bread and water for supper, and the boat lying too very well, all but the officer of the watch endeavoured to get a little sleep.

At two in the morning, we wore, and stood in shore till day-light, when I found we had drifted, during the night, about three leagues to the W S W, the southernmost land in sight bearing W. On examining the coast, and not seeing any sign of a settlement, we bore away to the westward, having a strong gale, against a weather current, which occasioned much sea. The shore was high and covered with wood, but we did run far before low land again formed the coast, the points of which opening at west, I once more fancied we were on the south part of the island; but at ten o'clock we found the coast again inclining towards the south, part of it bearing W S W 1/2 W. At the same time high land appeared from S W to S W by W 1/2 W; but the weather was so hazy, that it was doubtful whether the two lands were separated, the opening only extending one point of the compass. I, for this reason, stood towards the outer land, and found it to be the island Roti.

I returned to the shore I had left, and in a sandy bay I brought to a grapnel, that I might more conveniently calculate my situation. In this place we saw several smokes, where the natives were clearing their grounds. During the little time we remained here, the master and carpenter very much importuned me to let them go in search of supplies; to which, at length, I assented; but, finding no one willing to be of their party, they did not choose to quit the boat. I stopped here no longer than for the purpose just mentioned, and we continued steering along shore. We had a view of a beautiful-looking country, as if formed by art lawns and parks. The coast is low, and covered with woods, in which are innumerable fan palm-trees, that look like cocoa-nut walks. The interior part is high land but very different from the more eastern parts of the island, where it is exceedingly mountainous, and to appearance the soil better.

At noon, the island Roti bore S W by W seven leagues. I had no observation for the latitude, but, by account, we were in 10° 12' S; our course since yesterday noon being S 77 W, 54 miles. The usual allowance of bread and water was served for breakfast and dinner, and to the surgeon and Lebogue, I gave a little wine.

Sunday, June the 14th. A strong gale at E S E, with hazy weather, all the afternoon; after which the wind became moderate.

At two o'clock this afternoon, having run through a very dangerous breaking sea, the cause of which I atributed to a strong tide setting to windward, and shoal water, we discovered a spacious bay or sound, with a fair entrance about two or three miles wide. I now conceived hopes that our voyage was nearly at an end, as no place could appear more eligible for shipping, or more likely to be chosen for an European settlement: I therefore came to a grapnel near the east side of the entrance, in a small sandy bay, where we saw a hut, a dog, and some cattle; and I immediately sent the boatswain and gunner away to the hut, to discover the inhabitants.

The S W point of the entrance bore W 1/2 S three miles; the S E point S by W three quarters of a mile; and the island Roti from S by W 3/4 W to S W 3/4 W, about five leagues.

While we lay here I found the ebb came from the northward, and before our departure the falling of the tide discovered to us a reef of rocks, about two cables length from the shore; the whole being covered at high-water, renders it dangerous. On the opposite shore also appeared very high breakers; but there is nevertheless plenty of room, and certainly a safe channel for a first-rate man of war.

The bay or sound within, seemed to be of a considerable extent; the northern part, which I had now in view, being about five leagues distant. Here the land made in moderate risings joined by lower grounds. But the island Roti, which lies to the southward, is the best mark to know this place.

I had just time to make these remarks, when I saw the boatswain and gunner returning with some of the natives: I therefore no longer doubted of our success, and that our most sanguine expectations would be fully gratified. They brought five Indians, and informed me that they had found two families, where the women treated them with European politeness. From these people I learned, that the governor resided at a place called Coupang, which was some distance to the N E. I made signs for one of them to go in the boat, and show me Coupang, intimating that I would pay him for his trouble; the man readily complied, and came into the boat.

These people were of a dark tawny colour, and had long black hair; they chewed a great deal of beetle, and wore a square piece of cloth round their hips, in the folds of which was stuck a large knife. They had a handkerchief wrapped round their heads, and at their shoulders hung another tied by the four corners, which served as a bag for their beetle equipage.

They brought us a few pieces of dried turtle, and some ears of Indian corn. This last was most welcome to us; for the turtle was so hard, that it could not be eaten without being first soaked in hot water. Had I staid they would have brought us something more; but, as the pilot was willing, I was determined to push on. It was about half an hour past four when we sailed.

By direction of the pilot we kept close to the east shore under all our sail; but as night came on, the wind died away, and we were obliged to try at the oars, which I was surprised to see we could use with some effect. However, at ten o'clock, as I found we got but little ahead, I came to a grapnel, and for the first time I issued double allowance of bread and a little wine to each person.

At one o'clock in the morning, after the most happy and sweet sleep that ever men had, we weighed, and continued to keep the east shore on board, in very smooth water; when at last I found we were again open to the sea, the whole of the land to the westward, that we had passed, being an island, which the pilot called Pulo Samow. The northern entrance of this channel is about a mile and a half or two miles wide, and I had no ground at ten fathoms.

Hearing the report of two cannon that were fired, gave new life to every one; and soon after we discovered two square-rigged vessels and a cutter at anchor to the eastward. I endeavoured to work to windward, but we were obliged to take to our oars again, having lost ground on each tack. We kept close to the shore, and continued rowing till four o'clock, when I brought to a grapnel, and gave another allowance of bread and wine to all hands. As soon as we had rested a little, we weighed again, and rowed till near day-light, when I came to a grapnel, off a small fort and town, which the pilot told me was Coupang.

Among the things which the boatswain had thrown into the boat before we left the ship, was a bundle of signal flags that had been made for the boats to show the depth of water in sounding; with these I had, in the course of the passage, made a small jack, which I now hoisted in the main shrouds, as a signal of distress; for I did not choose to land without leave.

Soon after day-break a soldier hailed me to land, which I instantly did, among a croud of Indians, and was agreeably surprised to meet with an English sailor, who belonged to one of the vessels in the road. His captain, he told me, was the second person in the town; I therefore desired to be conducted to him, as I was informed the governor was ill, and could not then be spoken with.

Captain Spikerman received me with great humanity. I informed him of our miserable situation; and requested that care might be taken of those who were with me, without delay. On which he gave directions for their immediate reception at his own house, and went himself to the governor, to know at what time I could be permitted to see him; which was fixed to be at eleven o'clock.

I now desired every one to come on shore, which was as much as some of them could do, being scarce able to walk: they, however, got at last to the house, and found tea with bread and butter provided for their breakfast.

The abilities of a painter, perhaps, could never have been displayed to more advantage than in the delineation of the two groups of figures, which at this time presented themselves. An indifferent spectator would have been at a loss which most to admire; the eyes of famine sparkling at immediate relief, or the horror of their preservers at the sight of so many spectres, whose ghastly countenances, if the cause had been unknown, would rather have excited terror than pity. Our bodies were nothing but skin and bones, our limbs were full of sores, and we were cloathed in rags; in this condition, with the tears of joy and gratitude flowing down our cheeks, the people of Timor beheld us with a mixture of horror, surprise, and pity.

The governor, Mr. William Adrian Van Este, notwithstanding his extreme ill-health, became so anxious about us, that I saw him before the appointed time. He received me with great affection, and gave me the fullest proofs that he was possessed of every feeling of a humane and good man. Sorry as he was, he said, that such a calamity could ever have happened to us, yet he considered it as the greatest blessing of his life that we had fallen under his protection; and, though his infirmity was so great that he could not do the office of a friend himself, he would give such orders as I might be certain would procure me every supply I wanted. In the mean time a house was hired for me, and, till matters could be properly regulated, victuals for every one were ordered to be dressed at his own house. With respect to my people, he said I might have room for them either at the hospital or on board of captain Spikerman's ship, which lay in the road; and he expressed much uneasiness that Coupang could not afford them better accommodations, the house assigned to me being the only one uninhabited, and the situation of the few families such, that they could not accommodate any one. After this conversation an elegant repast was set before me, more according to the custom of the country, than with design to alleviate my hunger: so that in this instance he happily blended, with common politeness, the greatest favour I could receive.

On returning to my people, I found every kind relief had been given to them. The surgeon had dressed their sores, and the cleaning of their persons had not been less attended to, besides several friendly gifts of apparel.

I now desired to be shewn to the house that was intended for me, and I found it ready, with servants to attend, and a particular one, which the governor had directed to be always about my person. The house consisted of a hall, with a room at each end, and a loft over-head; and was surrounded by a piazza, with an outer apartment in one corner, and a communication from the back part of the house to the street. I therefore determined, instead of separating from my people, to lodge them all with me; and I divided the house as follows: One room I took to myself, the other I allotted to the master, surgeon, Mr. Nelson, and the gunner; the loft to the other officers; and the outer apartment to the men. The hall was common to the officers, and the men had the back piazza. Of this I informed the governor, and he sent down chairs, tables, and benches, with bedding and other necessaries for the use of every one.

The governor, when I took my leave, had desired me to acquaint him with every thing of which I stood in need; but I was now informed it was only at particular times that he had a few moments of ease, or could attend to any thing; being in a dying state, with an incurable disease. On this account, whatever business I had to transact would be with Mr. Timotheus Wanjon, the second of this place, and the governor's son-in-law; who now also was contributing every thing in his power to make our situation comfortable. I had been, therefore, misinformed by the sea-man, who told me that captain Spikerman was the next person to the governor.

At noon a very handsome dinner was brought to the house, which was sufficient to make persons, more accustomed to plenty, eat too much. Cautions, therefore, might be supposed to have had little effect;

but I believe few people in such a situation would have observed more moderation. My greatest apprehension was, that they would eat too much fruit.

Having seen every one enjoy this meal of plenty, I dined with Mr. Wanjon; but I found no extraordinary inclination to eat or drink. Rest and quiet, I considered, as more necessary to my doing well, and therefore retired to my room, which I found furnished with every convenience. But, instead of rest, my mind was disposed to reflect on our late sufferings, and on the failure of the expedition; but, above all, on the thanks due to Almighty God, who had given us power to support and bear such heavy calamities, and had enabled me at last to be the means of saving eighteen lives.

In times of difficulty there will generally arise circumstances that bear more particularly hard on a commander. In our late situation, it was not the least of my distresses, to be constantly assailed with the melancholy demands of my people for an increase of allowance, which it grieved me to refuse. The necessity of observing the most rigid economy in the distribution of our provisions was so evident, that I resisted their solicitations, and never deviated from the agreement we made at setting out. The consequence of this care was, that at our arrival we had still remaining sufficient for eleven days, at our scanty allowance: and if we had been so unfortunate as to have missed the Dutch settlement at Timor, we could have proceeded to Java, where I was certain every supply we wanted could be procured.

Another disagreeable circumstance, to which my situation exposed me, was the caprice of ignorant people. Had I been incapable of acting, they would have carried the boat on shore as soon as we made the island of Timor, without considering that landing among the natives, at a distance from the European settlement, might have been as dangerous as among any other Indians.

The quantity of provisions with which we left the ship, was not more than we should have consumed in five days, had there been no necessity for husbanding our stock. The mutineers must naturally have concluded that we could have no other place of refuge than the Friendly Islands; for it was not likely they should imagine, that, so poorly equipped as we were in every respect, there could have been a possibility of our attempting to return homewards: much less will they suspect that the account of their villainy has already reached their native country.

When I reflect how providentially our lives were saved at Tofoa, by the Indians delaying their attack, and that, with scarce any thing to support life, we crossed a sea of more than 1200 leagues, without shelter from the inclemency of the weather; when I reflect that in an open boat, with so much stormy weather, we escaped foundering, that not any of us were taken off by disease, that we had the great good fortune to pass the unfriendly natives of other countries without accident, and at last happily to meet with the most friendly and best of people to relieve our distresses; I say, when I reflect on all these wonderful escapes, the remembrance of such great mercies enables me to bear, with resignation and chearfulness, the failure of an expedition, the success of which I had so much at heart, and which was frustrated at a time when I was congratulating myself on the fairest prospect of being able to complete it in a manner that would fully have answered the intention of his Majesty, and the honourable promoters of so benevolent a plan.

With respect to the preservation of our health, during a course of 16 days of heavy and almost continual rain, I would recommend to every one in a similar situation the method we practised, which is to dip their cloaths in the salt-water, and wring them out, as often as they become filled with rain; it was the only resource we had, and I believe was of the greatest service to us, for it felt more like a change of dry cloaths than could well be imagined. We had occasion to do this so often, that at length all our cloaths were wrung to pieces: for, except the few days we passed on the coast of New Holland, we were continually wet either with rain or sea.

Thus, through the assistance of Divine Providence, we surmounted the difficulties and distresses of a most perilous voyage, and arrived safe in an hospitable port, where every necessary and comfort were administered to us with a most liberal hand.

Reading 8.3 John Fryer, 'The Journal of John Fryer'

Source: Owen Rutter (ed.) (1934) *The Voyage of the Bounty's Launch as Related William Bligh's despatch to the Admiralty and the Journal of John Fryer,* **London, Golden Cockerel Press. Editorial changes (in square brackets) are by the editor of this edition.**

May 3d Sunday. Fresh Gales the first part, latter part a hard Gale wind from E.S.E to N.E – first part employ'd getting our things into the Boat. The Natives began to make fires on the beach, and put stones into their canoes. One man swam off and alongside the Boat and played some time alongside, at last went astern and [we] thought that he had been gone onshore but he swam and toke hold of the Boat stern – and took a blanket out – but [on] my calling out he let it go – under his feet – in the water where he kept it some time untill I took hold of an oar – when he emmedially swam for the shore – soon after Captain Bligh sent word that [when] I saw him coming down to hauld the boat close to the shore – just at sun set I saw Captain Bligh coming down when I emmedeatly veer'd on the Grapnel Rope and hauld in on the beach Rope – untill the Boats stern struck the Ground – the natives, got hold of the Rope in order to hauld the boat on shore – when they hauld I slack the Rope by which means several of [them] fell down – Captain Bligh kept calling Mr Fryer let the boat come onshore. I call'd to him, Sir she is onshore and if she beat she will fill with [water.] You must come into the water and I will haul you [in] – At this time John Norton a very good man was going up to cast the beach Rope off. I call'd him to come into the Boat, but poor fellow he could not hear me. I then call to Mr Bligh to come into the Boat or she would knock her bottom out at the same time kept playing with the Rope that was fast on shore – when the natives hauld I slack and then hauld in – Mr Purcel stood by Captain Bligh longer than one man in twenty would have done in that situation, if Mr Bligh had thought of that he would not have tryed him by a court martial. At last Mr Bligh came to the Boat, when the stones began to fly pretty thick Mr Purcel lifted and I hauld him into the Boat. Purcel was hauld off his legs but hung at the Boat's stern – I then call'd out to cut the Rope as it had caught foul in the Bottom of the boat – at the same time the People were hauling on the grapnel Rope – the small Rope was cut by whom I do not know. Mr Bligh say it was him – luckly for us the grapnel broke it had caugh [t] hold of a Rock; had this not been the case we should most certainly been all cut to pieces – After the Grapnel broke we got our oars out but not without a little confusion as every body will suppose at a time when people are alarmed – we pulled out before the wind. I steerd the Boat myself with an oar. By this time the canoes was off close too us pelting us with stones. Mr Peckover the Gunner was the first wounded by a stone which struck him on the ball of the Cheek and swelld his head very much – however he still kept his oar – we hove several stones at them which fell into the Boat – several stones was caugh[t] by Mr Bligh and myself that would have struck the People that were rowing. Captain Bligh and Mr Nelson hove several things overboard – among which was the provisions that we had bought from them, which jump'd overboard from their canoes and pickd it up – in doing this they lost time and we got a good Distance from the Land and the sea began to run pretty high – they told us to come onshore for the man that we left – and we in return made signs for them to lay us along, but that the[y] would not do – our fear was that other canoes would come off from other parts of the Island – so that we kept off from the Land and night coming on they left us – we then got the Fore mast up and I hung the Rudder after which we set the sail and stood to the Southward. Captain Bligh was desirous of going to Tongataboo where he said that we should get any thing. Mr Cole the Boatswain told him that we should be treated the same at Tongataboo as we had been at Tofoa – O no Captain said, they are a different kind of People – All this conversation I was silent too for some [time], at last I said to Captain Bligh pray sir had you any words with the Natives of Tongataboo when you was there with Captain Cook, he said yes they had several of them in confinement for theft – then I said if that is the case Sir they will play us some trick – well then Mr Fryer what is best to be done? I said Sir providence may heave us on some friendly shore, by making a fair wind of it sooner than working to windward – Mr Cole said that he would soon[er] trust to providence and live on an ounce of Bread than go to Tongataboo, if we could get there as he was sure that the Natives would take every thing from us if not cut us all to pieces – then the rest said they thought that would be the case – that we had better make a fair wind of it – we then estimated the Quantity of Bread that we had in the boat would last six weeks at two ounces each per Day and the water to last half that time at a Gill each per Day – after we had done this Captain Bligh said well Mr Fryer what shall we do – I said Sir make a fair wind of it and trust to providence. He then spoke to every one saying well my lads are you all agreeable to live on two ounces of Bread and a Gill of water per day – Every one made answer yes Sir – with a great deal of cheerfullness – I then said to Captain Bligh as I was steering the Boat shall I put the helm up Sir? He said yes in God's name – it was done and [we] steerd before the wind and sea this was between seven and eight oclock at Night – as we run off from the Land the wind increased and the sea running very high obliged us to reef the foresail which was the small cutter sail that the Boatswain hove into the Boat – had those people that came into the Boat thought as much about there Books as Captain Bligh and his Clerk did, the Boat would have turn adrift without oar or sail, and [I] do farther say probably in a Boat with her bottom almost out which most certainly wou'd have been the case had it not been for the intercession of those whom the mutineers had more regard for than they had for there Captain. However we were all happy that we had made such a narrow escape – put the boat a little in order and set the watch half and half – there was no sleeping as the sea was constantly breaking into the Boat. I steer the boat myself [from] the time we bore away untill eight aclock in the morning – when I was releeved by Mr Cole the Boatswain.

I will now refer the reader to Captain Bligh *Narrative* which is true and just except some few omittinces, where Captain Bligh have wrote single he should have wrote plurel – Mr Bligh say that there was no one in the boat that know any thing about Timor but himself – Now Mr Peckover the Gunner was the first that mentioned Timor as he had seen the Island when he came through the Straits of New Holland with Captain Cook – and from this circumstance we lookd into Hammilton Moors Book and likewise the Requisite Tables – which were in the boat belonging to Mr Hallet Midshipman, and found that Timor laid very little to the Northward of Endeavour Straits – therefore I knew where Timor lay as well as Captain Bligh – but as Captain Bligh has not mentioned any body['s] services but his own I must till my Friends that there was others in the Boat that would have found their way to Timor as well as Captain Bligh and made every one with them more pleasant.

Reading 8.4 Charles Nordhoff and James Normal Hall, *Men Against the Sea*

Source: Charles Nordhoff and James Normal Hall (1934) *Men Against the Sea*, **London, Chapman and Hall, pp. 47–54.**

We had not long to wait for evidence of their intentions. Savages, although they invariably recognise and respect the authority of their chiefs, lack discipline, and when a course of action is decided upon, are impatient to put it into effect. So it was here. Shortly after this we heard from a distance, an ominous sound: the knocking of stones together, which we rightly supposed was a signal amongst them previous to an attack. At first only a few of them did this, but gradually the sound spread, increasing in volume, to all parts of the cove; at moments it became all but deafening and then would die away only to be resumed with even greater insistence, as though the commoners were growing increasingly impatient with their chiefs for withholding the signal for slaughter. The effect upon our little band may be imagined; we believed that our last hour had come; we stood together, a well-knit band, every man resolved to sell his life as dearly as possible.

It was late afternoon when Cole and his party returned with about two quarts of water which they had collected amongst the rocks. Mr. Bligh had kept a record of everything we had been able to secure in the way of provision, and the water we had either bought or found for ourselves had been just sufficient for our needs. We had added nothing to our twenty-eight gallons in the launch, but neither had we taken anything from that supply. Now that the shore party was again united, we waited only for a suitable opportunity before making an attempt to embark. Meanwhile, the clapping of stones went on, now here, now there, and yet it was necessary for us to keep up the pretence that we suspected nothing.

Nageete, who had been with us during this time, was becoming increasingly restless, and was only seeking some pretext for getting away, but Bligh kept him engaged in conversation. We were all gathered before the entrance of the cavern in such a way that the Indians could not pass behind us. For the most part they were gathered in groups of twenty or thirty, at some distance, and we saw the two chiefs passing from group to group. Presently they returned to where we stood and I must do them the credit to say that they were masters at the art of dissembling. We asked them the meaning of the stone-clapping, and they gave us to understand that it was merely a game in which their followers indulged to while away the time. They then attempted to persuade Captain Bligh and Nelson to accompany them away from the rest of us, as though they wished to confer with him in private, but Bligh pretended not to understand. We were all on our feet, in instant readiness to defend ourselves; nevertheless, I believe that we did succeed by our actions – for a time at least – in convincing the chiefs that we were ignorant of their intentions. Immediately they returned to us the clapping of stones had ceased, and the ensuing silence seemed the more profound.

Eefow then asked: 'You will sleep on shore to-night?'

Captain Bligh replied: 'No, I never sleep away from my boat, but it may be that I shall leave a part of my men in the cavern.'

Our hope was, of course, that we could persuade the Indians of an intention to remain in the cove until the following day. I think there must have been a difference of opinion between the two chiefs as to when the attack upon us should be made, and that the elder one was for immediate action and Eefow for a night attack. They again conversed together, in their figurative speech, of which we understood nothing. Bligh said to us, very quietly: 'Be ready, lads. If they make a hostile move we will kill them both and fight our way to the launch.'

We were, of course, in the unfortunate position of not being able to begin the attack, and yet we were almost at the point where action, however desperate, would have seemed preferable to further delay.

Eefow now turned again to Nelson. 'Tell your captain,' he said, 'that we shall spend the night here. … To-morrow I will go with you in your boat to Tongataboo.'

Nelson interpreted this message, and Bligh replied, 'That is good.' The chiefs then left us, but when they had gone a distance of fifteen or twenty paces, Macca-ackavow turned with an expression on his face that I shall not soon forget.

'You will not spend the night ashore?' he again asked.

'What does he say, Nelson?' asked Bligh. Nelson interpreted.

'God damn him, tell him no!' said Bligh.

Nelson conveyed this message at some length, and in a more diplomatic manner than Bligh had used. The chief stood facing us, glancing swiftly from side to side amongst his followers. Then he again spoke, very briefly, and having done so, strode swiftly away.

'What is it, Nelson?' asked Bligh.

Nelson smiled, grimly. '*Te mo maté gimotoloo*,' he replied. 'Their intentions are clear enough now. It means: "then you shall die!"'

Bligh's actions at this time were beyond praise. To see him rise to a desperate occasion was an experience to be treasured in the memory.

He was cool and clear-headed, and he talked quietly, even cheerfully to us. 'It is now or never, lads,' he said. 'Hall, serve out quickly the water Mr. Cole has brought in.' The calabash was passed rapidly from hand to hand, for we knew it would be impossible to get the water to the launch, each man had a generous sup, and it was needed, for we had been on short rations for three days. All this while Bligh had kept a firm grip with his left hand on Nageete's arm, holding his cutlass in his right. He was determined that, if we were to die, Nageete should die with us. The man's face was a study. I have not been able to determine, in my own mind, to this day, whether he was playing a part, or was genuinely friendly towards us. I imagine, however, that he had a heart as treacherous as those of his countrymen.

Bligh had already instructed us in what order we should proceed to the beach. Cole, also armed with a cutlass, took his station with the captain on the other side of Nageete, and the rest of us fell in behind, with Purcell and Norton bringing up the rear.

'Forward, lads!' said Bligh. 'Let these bastards see how Englishmen behave in a tight place!'

We then proceeded towards the beach, everyone in a kind of silent horror.

I believe it was the promptness, the unexpectedness of our action alone that saved us. Had we shown the least hesitation we must have all been slain; but Bligh led us straight on, directly toward one large group of Indians who were between us and the launch. They parted to let us through, and I well remember my feeling of incredulous wonder at finding myself still alive when we had passed beyond them. Not a word was spoken nor was a hand lifted against us until we reached the beach.

Fryer had, of course, seen us coming and had slacked away until the launch was within half a dozen paces of the beach, in about four feet of water. 'In with you, lads! Look alive!' Bligh shouted. 'Purcell, stand by with me, you and Norton!' Within half a minute we were all in the boat, save Bligh and the two men with him. Nageete now wrenched himself free from Bligh's grasp and ran up the beach. The captain and Purcell made for the boat, wisely not attempting to bring in the grapnel on shore; but Norton, whom Bligh thought was immediately behind him, ran back to fetch it. We shouted to him to let it go, but either he did not or would not hear. The Indians by this time had been roused to action, and they were upon Norton in an instant, beating out his brains with stones. Meanwhile we had hauled Bligh and Purcell into the boat and gotten out the oars. The natives seized the line which held us to the shore, but Bligh severed it with a stroke of his cutlass, and the men forward quickly hauled us out to the other grapnel and attempted to pull it up. To our dismay one of the flukes had caught and two or three precious minutes were lost before it was gotten clear. It was fortunate for us that the savages were unarmed; had they been possessed of spears, or bows and arrows, the chance of any man's escaping would have been small indeed. The only spears amongst them were those carried by the two chiefs. Macca-ackavow hurled his, which passed within a few inches of Peckover's head and fell into the water a dozen yards beyond us.

But whilst they had no man-made weapons, the beach offered them an inexhaustible supply of stones, and we received such a shower of these that, had we not been a good thirty yards distant, a number of us might have met Norton's fate. As it was, Purcell was knocked senseless by a blow on the head, and various others were badly hurt. The speed and accuracy with which they cast the stones was amazing. We protected ourselves as well as we could with bundles of clothing which we held before us. Meanwhile the men forward were hauling desperately on the grapnel, which at last gave way and came up with one fluke broken. Bligh at the tiller was in the most exposed position of any; that he escaped serious injury was due to the efforts of Elphinstone and Cole, who shielded him with floorboards from the stern-sheets.

We now began to pull away from them, but the treacherous villains were not done with us yet. They got one of their canoes into the water, which they loaded with stones, whereupon a dozen of them leaped into her to pursue us. Our six men at the oars pulled with all their strength, but we were so heavily laden that the savages gained swiftly upon us. Nevertheless we had gotten out of the cove and beyond view of the throng on the beach before we were overtaken. They now had us at their mercy and began throwing stones with such deadly accuracy that it seemed a miracle some of us were not killed. A few of the stones fell into the boat and were hurled back at them; we had the satisfaction of seeing one of their paddlers struck squarely in the face by a stone cast by the boatswain; however, that was a chance shot; we would have been no match for them at this kind of warfare, even had we possessed a supply of ammunition. In the hope of distracting their attention from us, Mr. Bligh threw some articles of clothing into the water, and to our joy they stopped to take them in. It was now getting dark, and, as they could have had but a few stones left in the canoe, they gave up the attack and a moment later disappeared past the headland at the entrance to the cove. We were by no means sure that others would not attempt to come after us, so we pulled straight out to sea until we caught the breeze. With our sails set we were soon past all danger of pursuit.

Reading 8.5 Edward Christian's defence of Fletcher Christian's role in the mutiny on the *Bounty*

Source: Edward Christian (1794) Appendix to *Minutes of the Proceedings of the Court-Martial held at Portsmouth, August 12, 1792. On Ten Persons charged with Mutiny on Board His Majesty's Ship the 'Bounty'. With an Appendix, Containing a Full Account of the Real Causes and Circumstances of the Unhappy Transaction, the most material of which have hitherto been withheld from the Public*, London, J. Deighton.

The circumstances communicated in this Appendix have been collected by a person nearly related to Christian: and it is far from his intention or wish to insinuate a vindication of the crime which has been committed. Justice, as well as policy, requires that mutiny, from whatever causes produced, or with whatever circumstances accompanied, should be punished with inexorable rigour. The publication of the trial, and of these extraordinary facts, it is presumed, will in no degree impede the pursuit of justice, yet it will administer some consolation to the broken hearts, which this melancholy transaction has occasioned. And whilst the innocent families and relations of twenty-one unhappy men are deeply interested in reducing to its just measure the infamy which this dreadful act has brought upon them; every friend to truth and strict justice must feel his attention awakened to the true causes and circumstances, which have hitherto been concealed or misrepresented, of one of the most remarkable events in the annals of the navy. It is the aim of the writer of this Appendix to state facts as they are, and to refrain, as far as possible, from invective and reproach.

It will naturally be asked from whom, and how have these facts been collected? and why have they been so long suppressed? It may be answered, That the writer of this Appendix, with the other relations of the mutineers, entertained no distrust of the narratives published to the world, or the accounts which they received in private; and as they came from those whose sufferings had unquestionably been extreme, and preservation almost miraculous; and thus carrying with them the stamp of even greater authenticity than the solemn declarations of a death-bed, they precluded all suspicion and enquiries among those who were most concerned in the horrid representation. Their lips were closed, they mourned in silence, and shuddering at the most distant allusion to this melancholy subject, they were of all persons the least likely to discover the real truth of the transaction.

All the circumstances stated here could not be produced at the trial, as the Court confined the witnesses, as much as possible, to the question, Who were actually engaged in the mutiny? for that being a crime which will admit of no legal justification, the relation of previous circumstances could not be material or legal evidence; yet what passed at the time of the mutiny was so immediately connected with what had happened previously in the ship, that in the testimony of most of the witnesses there will be found an allusion to, or confirmation of, what is here advanced.

Some time after the trial of the mutineers, the writer of this Appendix received such information as surprized him greatly, and in consequence of which, he resolved to make every possible enquiry into this unhappy affair. The following circumstances have been collected from many interviews and conversations, in the presence and hearing of several respectable gentlemen, with Mr. Fryer, master of the *Bounty*; Mr. Hayward, midshipman; Mr. Peckover, gunner; Mr. Purcell, carpenter; John Smith, cook; Lawrence Lebogue, sail maker; all these returned in the boat with Captain Bligh: and with Joseph Coleman, armourer; Thomas McIntosh, carpenter's mate; Michael Byrne, seaman; these are three of the four, who were tried and honourably acquitted, even with Captain Bligh's testimony in their favour; and with Mr. Heywood, midshipman, who has received his Majesty's pardon; and William Musprat, discharged by the opinion of the judges in his favour, upon a point of evidence: the writer of this has received letters also upon the subject from James Morrison, the boatswain's mate; who was pardoned. Mr. Heywood is now serving again as midshipman, under Lord Howe, in the Queen Charlotte, and is much respected by all who know him; and Morrison and Musprat are also employed again in the king's service; yet the writer of this Appendix thinks it necessary to assure the reader that no material fact here stated stands in need of their testimony or confirmation. The gentlemen who were present at different conversations with the persons just mentioned, are; John Farhill, Esq. No. 38, Mortimer street; Samuel Romilly, Esq. Lincoln's Inn; Mr. Gilpin, No. 432, Strand; the Rev. Dr. Fisher, Canon of Windsor; the Rev. Mr. Cookson, Canon of Windsor; Captain Wordsworth, of the Abergavenny East Indiaman; Rev. Mr. Antrobus, Chaplain to the Bishop of London; John France, Esq. Temple; James Losh, Esq. Temple; Rev. Dr. Frewen, Colchester; and John Atkinson, Esq. Somerset Herald.

Each of these gentlemen has heard the declarations of one at the least of the persons before mentioned; some have had an interview with five or six of them at different times, together with the writer of this Appendix, who is confident that every one of these gentlemen will bear testimony that what he has heard is not here exaggerated or misrepresented. There is no contradiction or variance whatever, in the account given by the gentlemen and people of the *Bounty*, though they could not upon every occasion, be all present together, and therefore cannot all relate exactly the same circumstances.

They declare that Captain Bligh used to call his officers 'scoundrels, damned rascals, hounds, hell-hounds, beasts, and infamous wretches'; that he frequently threatened them, that when the ship arrived at Endeavour Straits, 'he would kill one half of the people, make the officers jump overboard, and would make them eat grass like cows'; and that Christian, and Stewart, another midshipman were as much afraid of Endeavour Straits, as any child is of a rod.

Captain Bligh was accustomed to abuse Christian much more frequently and roughly than the rest of the officers, or as one of the persons expressed it, 'whatever fault was found, Mr. Christian was sure to bear the brunt of the Captain's anger.' In speaking to him in this violent manner, Captain Bligh frequently 'shook his fist in Christian's face.' But the immediate cause of the melancholy event is attributed to what happened on the 26th and 27th of April, the mutiny broke out on the morning of the 28th of April 1789. The *Bounty* had stopped at Annamooko, one of the Friendly Islands; on the 26th Christian was sent upon a watering party, with express orders from the Captain, by no means to fire upon the natives; upon their return, the Captain was informed that the natives had stolen the cooper's adze; at this, Captain Bligh was in a great rage, and abused Christian much; saying to him, 'G–damn your blood, why did not you fire, – you an officer!' At this island the Captain and ship's company had bought quantities of cocoa nuts, at the rate of 20 for a nail; the Captain's heap lay upon deck, and on the morning of the 27th, Captain Bligh fancied that the number was diminished, but the master, Mr. Fryer, told him he supposed they were pressed closer from being run over by the men in the night. The Captain then ordered the officer of the morning watch, Mr. Christian, to be called; when he came, the Captain accosted him thus, 'Damn your blood, you have stolen my cocoa nuts'; Christian answered, 'I was dry, I thought it of no consequence, I took one only, and I am sure no one touched another.' Captain Bligh then replied, 'You lie, you scoundrel, you have stolen one half.' Christian appeared much hurt and agitated, and said, 'Why do you treat me thus, Captain Bligh?' Captain Bligh then shook his hand in his face and said, 'No reply'; and called him 'a thief,' and other abusive names. He then ordered the quarter masters to go down and bring all the cocoa nuts both from man and officer, and put them upon the quarter deck. They were brought. The Captain then called all hands upon deck, and desired 'the people to look after the officers, and the officers to look after the people, for there never were such a set of damned thieving rascals under any man's command in the world before.' And he told the men, 'You are allowed a pound and a half of yams to-day, but to-morrow I shall reduce you to three quarters of a pound.' All declare that the ship's company were before greatly discontented at their short allowance of provisions, and their discontent was increased from the consideration that they had plenty of provisions on board, and that the Captain was his own purser. About four o'clock on the same day, Captain Bligh abused Christian again. Christian came forward from Captain Bligh, crying, 'tears were running fast from his eyes in big drops.' Purcell, the Carpenter, said to him, 'What is the matter Mr. Christian?' He said, 'Can you ask me, and hear the treatment I receive?' Purcell replied, 'Do not I receive as bad as you do?' Christian said, 'You have something to protect you, and can speak again; but if I should speak to him as you do, he would probably break me, turn me before the mast, and perhaps flog me; and if he did, it would be the death of us both, for I am sure I should take him in my arms, and jump overboard with him.' Purcell said, 'Never mind it, it is but for a short time longer.' Christian said, 'In going through Endeavour Straits, I am sure the ship will be a hell.' He was heard by another person to say, when he was crying, 'I would rather die ten thousand deaths, than bear this treatment; I always do my duty as an officer and as a man ought to do, yet I receive this scandalous usage.' Another person heard him say, 'That flesh and blood cannot bear this treatment.' This was the only time he ever was seen in tears on board the ship; and one of the seamen being asked, if he had ever observed Christian in tears before, answered, 'No, he was no milksop.' It is now certainly known, that Christian after this had prepared to leave the ship that night upon a raft; those who came with Captain Bligh, can only know it by circumstances, which they afterwards recollected, and which were the subject of conversation in the boat. He gave away that afternoon all his Otaheite curiosities; he was seen tearing his letters and papers, and throwing them overboard; he applied to the carpenter for nails, who told him to take as many as he pleased out of the locker; and the ship intending to stop at no other island, these could have been of no use to him, but in case of his escape to land. Mr. Tinkler, a young boy, one of Christian's messmates, was hungry in the evening, and went below to get some pig which was left at dinner; this he missed, and after some search, found it packed up with a bread fruit, in a dirty cloaths bag in Christian's cot; when the launch was hoisted out, the two masts were lashed to a plank, which they were obliged to untie. This was the raft or stage upon which he intended to leave the ship. These circumstances are remembered by those who came in the boat, but his design of going off upon the raft was frequently the subject of conversation afterwards in the ship. Norman, one of the four who were honourably acquitted, said to him after the mutiny, 'This is a hard case upon me, Mr. Christian, who have a wife and family in England.' Christian replied, 'It is a hard case, Norman, but it never would have happened, if I could have left the ship alone.' Christian told them afterwards in the ship, 'that he did not expect to reach the shore upon the raft, but he was in hopes of being seen and taken up by some of the natives in their canoes.' The reason of his disappointment is said to have been owing to the people being upon deck in greater numbers than usual, looking at a volcano in the island of Tofoa.

All agree that there was no plot or intention to mutiny before Christian went upon his watch, at four in the morning. The mutiny broke out at five o'clock, and all the mutineers were in bed when it began, except those who were in Christian's watch; how soon after four o'clock the conspiracy was entered into, before it was put in execution, does not appear. That there had been some agreement previous to the breaking out of the mutiny is manifest from the evidence of Mr. Fryer, who was told by two of them, 'Sir, there is no one means to hurt you; no, that was our agreement, not to commit murder.' This statement cannot be reconciled with the testimony of Mr. Hayward and Mr. Hallet, who were both in Christian's watch; if the reader were not apprized of a circumstance which was not mentioned before the court-martial; viz. that these gentlemen who were very young at that time, viz. about fifteen, had both fallen asleep. The circumstance of the rest of the mutineers being in bed when the mutiny began, proves that it had not been preconcerted with them; and it is remarkable that Mr. Young was the only person among Christian's messmates, who was concerned in it, and he was in bed when it broke out. On the 26th, before the ship left Annamooko, Christian and some other officers threw away their beads and trifles among the natives, as articles for which they would have no further occasion.

It appears from the testimony of every witness, that the original intent was to put the Captain on shore, with three other persons only, and if the smallest boat, which was hoisted out for that purpose, had not been leakey, it is probable that this design would have been carried into execution; but by the time that the second cutter or boat was got into the water, a great number desired to leave the ship, and requested the launch. It is agreed by all, that every person who went into the launch, went voluntarily, or might have continued on board if he had wished to stay, except the four who were first ordered into the small boat; and afterwards Mr. Fryer, who was commanded to go in consequence of his design to retake the ship being overheard. It is indeed expressly proved by Mr. Hallet, that 'the boatswain and carpenters told Christian, they would prefer going in the boat, to staying in the ship; and he said he did not wish them, or any other, to stay against their inclination, or to go; and that the most part went voluntarily.' And Mr. Hayward in his evidence has also deposed, 'I heard no one ordered to go into the boat, but Mr. Hallet, Mr. Samuel, and myself.' Although Mr. Fryer himself wished to stay, from a very laudable motive, viz. that of retaking the ship; yet being obliged to go, he earnestly requested that his brother-in-law, Tinkler, then a young boy, might be permitted to follow him. In such a dilemma, the alternative was dreadful, yet those who went voluntarily into the launch, were sure of getting to shore, where they expected to live, until an European ship arrived, or until they could raise their boat or build a greater, as one of the mutineers said of the carpenter, 'you might as well give him the ship as his tool chest.' It is proved by Mr. Hallet, that they were veered astern, in order to be towed towards the land, which was so near, that it is said they might see them reach the shore from the mast head of the ship.

After the mutiny commenced, it was between three and four hours before the launch left the ship, and one reason, besides the number of persons, why she was so deeply laden, was, that almost all Captain Bligh's property in boxes and trunks was put on board. A short time after it had quitted the ship, Christian declared, that 'he would readily sacrifice his own life, if the persons in the launch were all safe in the ship again.'

At Annamooko, besides the cooper's adze being stolen, the natives, by diving, had cut and carried off a grapnel by which a boat was fastened. Captain Bligh, in order to compel the natives to restore it, had made them believe he would sail away with their chiefs whom he had on board; this was unattended with success, as they assured him the grapnel had been carried away in a canoe belonging to another island; but the people of the island, who crowded round the ship to entreat the deliverance of their chiefs, and the chiefs themselves, were greatly frightened and distressed, before they were set at liberty. For Captain Bligh carried them out some distance to sea, and they were followed and taken back in canoes. This unfortunate circumstance is supposed to have been the cause of the rough reception which the people in the launch met with at Tofoa. For Nageete, one of the chiefs, who had been thus frightened, had come upon a visit from Annamooko, though ten leagues distant, and was one of the first persons they saw at Tofoa. He appeared at the first friendly, yet it is thought that he was glad of having this opportunity of resenting the treatment he had received in the ship at Annamooko.

Those who came in the boat, though they gave vent to no open complaints, yet sometimes made allusions in the hearing of the Captain, to what had passed previous to the mutiny. Captain Bligh was one day observing, that it was surprising that this should have happened after he had been so kind to the people, by making them fine messes of wheat; upon which Mr. Hallet replied, 'If it had not been for your fine messes, and fine doings, we should have had the ship for our resource instead of the boat.'

In a misunderstanding about some oysters, between the Captain and the carpenter, Captain Bligh told him, 'If I had not taken so much pains with you, you would never have been here'; the carpenter replied, 'Yes, if you had not taken so much pains with us, we should never have been here.'

In the evidence of Mr. Peckover and Mr. Fryer, it is proved that Mr. Nelson the botanist said, upon hearing the commencement of the mutiny, 'We know whose fault this is, or who is to blame; and oh! Mr. Fryer, what have we brought upon ourselves?' In addition to this, it ought to be known that Mr. Nelson, in conversation afterwards with an officer at Timor, who was speaking of returning with Captain Bligh if he got another ship, observed, 'I am surprized that you should think of going a second time with one, (using a term of abuse,) who has been the occasion of all our losses.'

In Captain Bligh's *Narrative* no mention is made of the two little boats or cutters, the least boat would not hold more than six, and the larger more than nine persons. But after Captain Bligh relates that he was brought upon deck, he proceeds thus in the two next paragraphs:

'The boatswain was now ordered to hoist out the *launch*, with a threat if he did not do it instantly, to take care of himself.

'The *boat* being out, Mr. Heywood and Mr. Hallet, midshipmen, and Mr. Samuel, were ordered into it.

Every reader must have supposed that the boat mentioned in the latter paragraph, was the same as the launch in the former, and that these four were the first of the nineteen who were ordered into it.

If the small boats had been distinctly mentioned in Captain Bligh's *Narrative*, it would have been manifest to all the world that the mutiny could not have been the result of a conspiracy of twenty-five of the people, to turn the other nineteen into one or both of them.

Indeed, many readers had the penetration to think that it was incredible, and almost beyond any calculation of probability, that twenty-five persons could have been seduced to have concurred in such a horrid plot, without a single one having the virtue to resist the temptation, and to disclose the design to the Captain.

In the *Narrative*, there is this memorable paragraph:

> Notwithstanding the roughness with which I was treated, the remembrance of past kindnesses produced some signs of remorse in Christian. When they were forcing me out of the ship, I asked him, If this treatment was a proper return for the many instances he had received of my friendship? He appeared disturbed at my question, and answered with much emotion, 'That, Captain Bligh, – that is the thing; I am in hell – I am in hell.'

In Mr. Purcell's evidence before the Court, this conversation is sworn to thus: 'Captain Bligh attempted to speak to Christian, who said, "Hold your tongue, and I'll not hurt you; it is too late to consider now, I have been in hell for weeks past with you."' But all, who were upon deck and overheard the whole of this conversation, state it thus: 'Captain Bligh, addressing himself to Christian, said, "Consider Mr. Christian, I have a wife and four children in England, and you have danced my children upon your knee."' Christian replied, 'You should have thought of them sooner yourself, Captain Bligh, it is too late to consider now, I have been in hell for weeks past with you.' Christian afterwards told the people in the ship, that when Bligh spoke of his wife and children, 'my heart melted, and I would then have jumped overboard, if I could have saved you, but as it was too late to do that, I was obliged to proceed.' One person, who heard what passed, immediately after Captain Bligh was brought upon deck, says, that Captain Bligh asked Christian, 'What is the meaning of all this?' And Christian answered, 'Can you ask, Captain Bligh, when you know you have treated us officers, and all these poor fellows, like Turks?'

Captain Bligh in his *Narrative* asserts, 'When we were sent away, Huzza for Otaheite, was frequently heard among the mutineers.' But every one of those who came in the boat, as well as all who staid in the ship, declare, that they neither heard nor observed any huzzaing whatever in the ship.

In Captain Bligh's *Narrative*, there is the following paragraph:

> Had their mutiny been occasioned by any grievances, either real or imaginary, I must have discovered symptoms of their discontent, which would have put me upon my guard, but the case was far otherwise. Christian in particular I was on the most friendly terms with; that very day he was engaged to have dined with me; and the preceding night he excused himself from supping with me, on pretence of being unwell, for which I felt concerned, having no suspicions of his integrity and honour.

It is said that the Captain had his officers to dine with him in rotation, and Christian's turn might have fallen on the day of the mutiny; but in consequence of the charge of stealing the cocoa nuts, the gentlemen (or most of them) had resolved not to dine again at the Captain's table. Mr. Fryer had not dined there for a long time before. It is true that Captain Bligh had asked Christian to supper; but it now appears, he excused himself, not to meditate the destruction of his benefactor, but his own flight.

It was proved on the trial, that Christian, during the mutiny, told Mr. Fryer, 'You know, Mr. Fryer, I have been in hell on board this ship for weeks past'; and that he said to the Captain, 'I have been in hell for weeks past with you': but what particular period Christian referred to, or when the poignancy of his distress had begun to prey upon his mind, does not appear. But instances are mentioned of Christian's being hurt by Captain Bligh's treatment, even at the Cape of Good Hope, in their outward bound voyage. Christian had the command of the tent on shore at Otaheite, where Captain Bligh sometimes entertained the Chiefs of the island, and before all the company used to abuse Christian for some pretended fault or other, and the Chiefs would afterwards take an opportunity of observing to Christian, 'Titriano, Brie worrite beha': i.e. 'Christian, Bligh is perhaps angry with you.' Christian would turn it off by saying, No, no. But he afterwards complained to the officers, of the Captain's cruelty in abusing him before the people of the country, observing, that he would not regard it, if he would only find fault with him in private. There is no country in the world, where the notions of aristocracy and family pride are carried higher than at Otaheite; and it is a remarkable circumstance, that the Chiefs are naturally distinguished by taller persons, and more open and intelligent countenances, than the people of inferior condition; hence these are the principal qualities by which the natives estimate the gentility of strangers; and Christian was so great a favourite with them, that according to the words of one person, 'They adored the very ground he trod upon.' He was Tyo, or friend, to a Chief of the first rank in the island, whose name, according to the custom of the country, he took in exchange for his own; and whose property he participated. This Chief dined one day with Captain Bligh, and was told by him, That his Tyo Christian, was only his Towtow, or servant. The Chief upbraided Christian with this, who was much mortified at being thus degraded in the opinion of his friend, and endeavoured to recommend himself again to the Chief, by assuring him, that he, Captain Bligh, and all the officers, were Towtows of the King of Bretane.

These circumstances, although comparatively trifling, are such as to be distinctly remembered; but they prove that there could be little harmony, where such painful sensations were so frequently and unnecessarily excited.

A regard to truth obliges the writer of this Appendix to add, That Captain Bligh has told some of Christian's relations, that after they sailed from Otaheite, Christian, when he was upon duty, had put the ship in great danger; from which Captain Bligh supposed that it had been his intention to cripple the ship, that they might be obliged to return to Otaheite to repair. But no such circumstance is remembered by any person besides the Captain. Captain Bligh has also declared that the persons in the launch 'were turned out to certain destruction, because the mutineers had not the courage to embrue their hands in blood.' It has already been observed, that it is proved before the court-martial, that most of the persons went into the launch voluntarily. And it is certainly true, that, although the sufferings of the persons in the boat were distressful to the last degree, they were not the occasion of the death of Mr. Nelson at Timor, or of those who died at Batavia; for all recovered from the extremity to which they had been reduced by this unhappy voyage.

It is agreed that Christian was the first to propose the mutiny, and the project of turning the Captain on shore at Tofoa, to the people in his watch; but he declared afterwards in the ship, he never should have thought of it, if it had not been suggested to his mind by an expression of Mr. Stewart, who knowing of his intention of leaving the ship upon the raft, told him, 'When you go, Christian, we are ripe for any thing.'

The mutiny is ascribed by all who remained in the ship, to this unfortunate expression, which probably proceeded rather from a regard for Christian, than from a mutinous disposition; for all declare that Stewart was an excellent officer, and a severe disciplinarian; severe to such a degree as to be disliked by the seamen, though much respected for his abilities. Mr. Stewart was in bed when the mutiny broke out, and afterwards was neither in arms, nor active on the side of the mutineers; yet it ought not to be concealed, that during the mutiny he was dancing and clapping his hands in the Otaheite manner, and saying, 'It was the happiest day of his life.' He was drowned in the wreck of the Pandora. This gentleman is spoken of by all in terms of great praise and respect. He is said to have been the best practical navigator on board, even superior in that character to Captain Bligh and Christian. Soon after the launch had left the ship, Christian told the people that he had no right to the command, and that he would act in any station they would assign him. But they all declared that he should be their Captain, and after some persuasion from Christian, they permitted Mr. Stewart to be the second in command, though they were desirous, from Stewart's former severity, of preferring Mr. Heywood; but being told by Christian, that as the ship must be at watch and watch, he thought Mr. Heywood, who was then only sixteen, too young and inexperienced for such a charge, with some reluctance they acceded to his recommendation of Mr. Stewart. The other arrangements being settled, instead of insisting upon going back to Otaheite, they told Christian he might carry them wherever he thought proper. Christian advised them to go to an island called Tobooy, which was laid down in the charts by Captain Cook, though no European ship had ever landed there. This lies about seven degrees south of Otaheite, and it was chosen because it was out of the track of European ships. When they arrived there, and with difficulty had made a landing, although it was full of inhabitants, they found no quadrupeds but a species of small rats, with which the island was completely overrun. They staid there a few days, and then resolved to sail to Otaheite for a ship load of hogs, goats, dogs, cats, and fowls, to stock the island of Tobooy, which they had fixed upon for their settlement.

When they had reached Otaheite, in order to acquire what they wanted more expeditiously, Christian told the Chiefs and people, that Captain Bligh had returned to Captain Cook, who had sent Christian back to purchase for him the different articles which they wished to obtain.

This story was the more plausible, as the people of Otaheite had been told by Captain Bligh, that Captain Cook was still living, and that he had sent him for the bread-fruit. Such is still their love and veneration for the memory of Captain Cook, that the natives even contended for the honour of sending their best hogs and animals to Toote. The ship by this artifice being soon filled, they returned with some Otaheite men and women to Tobooy. It was thought that the Otaheite men would be useful in introducing them to the friendship and good offices of the natives. At Tobooy they built a fort, and having staid there three months, and finding the inhabitants always inhospitable and treacherous, the people of the ship grew discontented; all hands were called up, and it being put to the vote what should be done, sixteen out of the twenty-five voted that they should go back to Otaheite. Christian, thinking that this was the general wish, said, *'Gentlemen, I will carry you, and land you wherever you please; I desire no one to stay with me, but I have one favour to request, that you will grant me the ship, tie the foresail, and give me a few gallons of water, and leave me to run before the wind, and I shall land upon the first island the ship drives to. I have done such an act that I cannot stay at Otaheite. I will never live where I may be carried home to be a disgrace to my family.'*

Upon this, Mr. Young, the midshipman, and seven others declared, *'We shall never leave you, Mr. Christian, go where you will.'* It was then agreed, that the other sixteen should be landed at Otaheite, and have their share of the arms and other necessary articles; and he proposed to the rest, that they should go and seek an island, not before discovered, where they were not likely to be found, and having run the ship aground, and taken out every thing of value, and scuttled and broke up the ship, they should endeavour to make a settlement. They reached Otaheite on the 27th of September 1789, and came to an anchor in Matavai Bay about eleven o'clock in the forenoon, and the sixteen were disembarked with their portions of the arms and other necessaries. Christian took leave of Mr. Stewart and Mr. Heywood, and told them he should sail that evening; and desired them, if they ever got to England, to inform his friends and country what had been the cause of his committing so desperate an act; but to guard against any obstruction, he concealed the time of his sailing from the rest.

The natives came on board in crowds as usual, and about twelve o'clock at night he cut his cable, and sailed from the Bay. The people on board consisted of nine Englishmen, about twenty-five men, women, boys, and girls, of different ages, from Otaheite, and two men from Tobooy. It does not appear that any selection was made of the

Otaheiteans, who are always eager to be carried away in an English ship. The ship was seen standing off the island the next morning, but from that day, for the nineteen months the others lived at Otaheite, they never saw nor heard any thing more of Christian; and upon the arrival of Captain Edwards in the Pandora, they could give him no further account of the *Bounty* than what is here stated.

During his short stay at Otaheite, Christian was much pressed to go on shore to visit the King, but he declined it, saying, '*How can I look him in the face, after the lie I told him when I was here last?*' These circumstances concerning the *Bounty*, subsequent to the mutiny, must necessarily be collected from the seven persons who were left in the ship, and who are now, or were lately, in England. These say, that Christian was always sorrowful and dejected after the mutiny; and before he left them, had become such an altered man in his looks and appearance, as to render it probable that he would not long survive this dreadful catastrophe. Indeed, it is impossible that he should have appeared otherwise, if he deserved the character which all unite in giving him.

In the *Royal Jamaica Gazette*, dated February 9, 1793, which announced the arrival of Captain Bligh in the Providence, the following was one of the paragraphs, and it has been copied into all the English newspapers:

> Captain Bligh could gain no intelligence of the mutineer Christian and his accomplices, who were on board the *Bounty*. When they returned to Otaheite, after executing their infernal project, the natives, suspecting some mischief from the non-appearance of the Commander and the gentlemen with him, laid a plan to seize the vessel and crew; but a *favourite female* of Christian's betrayed the design of her countrymen. He put to sea in the night, and the next morning the ship was nearly out of sight.

It is immaterial to inquire who was the author of this paragraph, yet it cannot but be remarked, that it is totally different from the account which has been given by those who staid at Otaheite, and who can have no possible interest in concealing this circumstance, if in fact it had existed; nor can it be reconciled with probability, or the treatment and protection which the Englishmen experienced from the natives when the ship had left them.

As this paragraph contains an assertion, that Christian had a *favourite female* at Otaheite, it is proper that it should be known, that although Christian was upon shore, and had the command of the tent all the time that Captain Bligh was at Otaheite with the *Bounty*, yet the officers who were with Christian upon the same duty declare, that he never had a female favourite at Otaheite, nor any attachment or particular connexion among the women. It is true that some had what they call *their girls*, or women with whom they constantly lived all the time they were upon the island, but this was not the case with Christian.

Until this melancholy event, no young officer was ever more affectionately beloved for his amiable qualities, or more highly respected for his abilities and brave and officer-like conduct. The world has been led to suppose, that the associates in his guilt were attached to him only by his seducing and diabolical villainy. But all those who came in the boat, whose sufferings and losses on his account have been so severe, not only speak of him without resentment and with forgiveness, but with a degree of rapture and enthusiasm. The following are, word for word, some of the unpremeditated expressions, used by the gentlemen and people of the *Bounty*, in speaking of this unfortunate mutineer: '*His Majesty might have his equal, but he had not a superior officer in his service.*' This probably had a reference to his age, which was about twenty-three. '*He was a gentleman, and a brave man; and every officer and seaman on board the ship would have gone through fire and water to have served him.*' – '*He was a good and worthy gentleman, and was dear to all who ever knew him; and before the fatal day, his conduct was in every respect such as became an officer, a gentleman, and a man of honour.*' – '*He was adorned with every virtue, and beloved by all.*' – '*He was a gentleman every inch of him, and I would still wade up to the arm-pits in blood to serve him.*' – '*As much as I have lost and suffered by him, if he could be restored to his country, I should be the first to go without wages in search of him.*' – '*He was as good and as generous a man as ever lived.*' – '*Mr. Christian was always good-natured, I never heard him say Damn you, to any man on board the ship.*' – '*Every body under his command did their duty at a look from Mr. Christian, and I would still go through fire and water for him.*' These are respectively the expressions of nine different persons, and it is the language of one and all. Mr. Hayward in his evidence, no doubt with a proper sentiment of the crime of mutiny, has used the words, '*Christian, and his gang*': yet that gentleman has declared, that, until the desperate act, Christian deserved the character described by the strongest of the above expressions.

Christian, having staid at school longer than young men generally do who enter into the navy, and being allowed by all who knew him to possess extraordinary abilities, is an excellent scholar, and every one acquainted with him from a boy, till he went on board the *Bounty*, can testify, that no young man was ever more ambitious of all that is esteemed right and honourable among men, or more anxious to acquire distinction and advancement by his good conduct in his profession. He had been an acting Midshipman but a short time in the service, when Captain Courtenay, the late brave Commander of the Boston frigate, entrusted him with the charge of a watch in the Eurydice all the way home from the East Indies. This, no doubt, was extremely flattering to him, and he declared to a relation who met him at Woolwich, 'he had been extremely happy under Captain Courtenay's command'; and at the same time observed, that *it was very easy to make one's self beloved and respected on board a ship; one had only to be always ready to obey one's superior officers, and to be kind to the common men, unless there was occasion for severity, and if you are severe when there is a just occasion, they will not like you the worse for it.* This was after the conclusion of the peace, and within a few days the ship was paid off; and being out of employ, he wished to be appointed a Mate of a West-Indiaman, a situation for which he thought himself qualified. Whilst he was in treaty with a merchant in the city to go in that capacity in his ship, Captain Taubman, a relation of Christian's, came to London from the Isle of Man, and suggested to Christian, that it would be very desirable for him to serve under so experienced a navigator as Captain Bligh, who had been Sailing-master to Captain Cook, and who was then in the merchants' service; and as Captain Taubman was acquainted with Captain Bligh, he offered to make an application to him in Christian's favour. The application was made, and Captain Bligh returned a polite answer, that he was sorry he could not take Christian, having then his complement of officers. Upon this, Christian of his own accord observed, that 'wages were no object, he only wished to learn his profession, and if Captain Bligh would permit him to mess with the gentlemen, he would readily enter his ship as a Foremast-man, until there was a vacancy among the officers': and at the same time added, *we Midshipmen are gentlemen, we never pull at a rope; I should even be glad to go one voyage in that situation, for there may be occasions, when officers may be called upon to do the duties of a common man.*

To this proposal Captain Bligh had no objection, and in that character he sailed one voyage, and upon his return spoke of Captain Bligh with great respect: he said, that although he had his share of labour with the common men, the Captain had been kind to him in shewing him the use of his charts and instruments; but at the same time he observed, that Captain Bligh was very passionate; yet he seemed to pride himself in knowing how to humour him. In the next voyage, Captain Bligh took him out as his Second Mate, and before his return the Captain was chosen to command the *Bounty.* Christian wishing to go upon a voyage where so much service would be seen, in which he would complete his time as a Midshipman, and if it had been successful, he would, no doubt, with little difficulty upon his return have been raised to the rank of Lieutenant, was recommended to the Admiralty by Captain Bligh himself, as one of his officers; and as it was understood that great interest had been made to get Midshipmen sent out in this ship, Christian's friends thought this recommendation, as they do still, a very great obligation. Captain Bligh had no Lieutenants on board, and the ship at the first was divided into two watches, the charge of which was entrusted to the Master and the Gunner: but after they had sailed about a month, the Captain divided the ship into three watches, and gave the charge of one to Christian, on whom Captain Bligh has always declared he had the greatest reliance. Such was his introduction to, and connexion with, Captain Bligh; and every one must sincerely lament, that what in its commencement had been so honourable to both, should in its event and consequences have proved to both so disastrous and fatal.

The writer of this Appendix would think himself an accomplice in the crime which has been committed, if he designedly should give the slightest shade to any word or fact different from its true and just representation; and lest he should be supposed to be actuated by a vindictive spirit, he has studiously forborn to make more comments than were absolutely necessary upon any statement which he has been obliged to bring forward. He has felt it a duty to himself, to the connexions of all the unfortunate men, and to society, to collect and lay before the Public these extraordinary circumstances.

The sufferings of Captain Bligh and his companions in the boat, however severe they may have been, are perhaps but a small portion of the torments occasioned by this dreadful event: and whilst these prove the melancholy and extensive consequences of the crime of Mutiny, the crime itself in this instance may afford an awful lesson to the Navy, and to mankind, that there is a degree of pressure, beyond which the best formed and principled mind must either break or recoil. And though public justice and the public safety can allow no vindication of any species of Mutiny, yet reason and humanity will distinguish the sudden unpremeditated act of desperation and phrenzy, from the foul deliberate contempt of every religious duty and honourable sentiment; and will deplore the uncertainty of human prospects, when they reflect that a young man is condemned to perpetual infamy, who, if he had served on board any other ship, or had perhaps been absent from the *Bounty* a single day, or one ill-fated hour, might still have been an honour to his country, and a glory and comfort to his friends.

Glossary

allegory

A narrative that has a sustained parallel meaning; an extended metaphor in the form of a story. John Bunyan's *The Holy War* narrates the story of El-Shaddai and Diabolus, but simultaneously points to several parallel narratives, like the stories of God and the Devil, and of Cromwell and Charles I.

alliteration

An example of the patterning of sound in poetry, alliteration occurs when words that appear in close proximity to one another begin with the same letter or sound, as in Othello's line, 'Rough quarries, rocks, and hills whose heads touch heaven' (*Othello*, 1.3.141), which repeats the 'r' sound and, even more strikingly, the 'h' sound in 'hills whose heads touch heaven'.

alliterative

see **alliteration**.

antithesis (pl. antitheses)

Opposed or contrasting ideas juxtaposed in quick succession. Pope's line 'All partial evil, universal good' in *An Essay on Man* is an example of antithesis.

aside

A dramatic device that involves a character onstage expressing his or her thoughts to the audience but not to any other characters present onstage, to whom the aside is supposedly inaudible.

blank verse

Unrhymed lines of iambic pentameter. It is thought to be the verse form that most closely resembles the rhythms of spoken English, and became the standard metre for English Renaissance verse drama.

characterisation

The techniques a writer uses in creating a character in a dramatic or narrative work.

dumb show

A part of a play performed without words, in pantomime.

Chorus

In ancient Greek tragedies, the Chorus was a collection of people which commented on the action and characters, often expressing traditional moral and social values.

context

The word context derives from the Latin for 'connection' and has often been used to refer to the relationship between the different parts of a piece of writing or speech. So one can study a passage from a literary text 'in its context' by considering how its meaning is determined by the passages that come immediately before and after it. Nowadays, we tend to use the word more broadly, to denote the cultural/political/social circumstances or conditions in which a literary text was written and the way they affect its meaning.

couplet

A pair of rhymed lines, as in Iago's lines, 'I have't! It is engendered: Hell and Night / Must bring this monstrous birth to the world's light.' (*Othello*, 1.3.392–3). Early modern dramatists were fond of using a couplet to bring a scene to a close, as Iago's couplet does.

denouement

French for 'unknotting', denouement is the general term used for the final resolution of a play, novel or other narrative.

discourse

In linguistic theory, 'discourse' has a broad meaning, and refers to spoken utterances or written texts in their sociolinguistic contexts. In literary studies, 'discourse' generally has a narrower meaning: it refers to the forms of expression and vocabulary associated with a particular area of knowledge. On this narrower meaning, we might, for example, refer to 'legal discourse' to describe the modes of expression and vocabulary associated with the law. Alternately, we might also refer to 'racial discourse' to describe the modes of expression and vocabulary regarding race. Particular words used in one discourse might assume quite different meanings when used in another discourse.

dramatic irony

Dramatic irony occurs when an audience or reader is in possession of knowledge of which a character is ignorant.

exposition

The opening section of a play when characters are introduced and essential information imparted to the audience.

figurative language

Language used in a non-literal way with a view to achieving a particular effect. The most well-known examples of figurative language are **metaphor** and **simile**.

first-person narrator

A first-person narrative has 'I' or 'We' as the originator of the narrative. In some cases, the 'I' of the narrative might correspond with the historical figure of the author – as in the case of William Bligh – and in others, the 'I' might be a fictional invention of the author – as in the case of Robinson Crusoe. It is useful to think of the first-person narrator as one of the characters in the story, who is her/himself actually telling the story.

genre

The French word for 'kind', a genre is a category or type of art work with its own form and conventions. For example, in literary studies, tragedy is a distinct genre of drama characterised by (among other conventions) an unhappy ending.

hyperbole

Extravagant overstatement.

hyperbolic

see **hyperbole**.

iambic pentameter

A line of ten syllables that falls into five measures of two syllables each, in which one unstressed syllable is followed by one stressed syllable.

ideology

An ideology is a set of assumptions, ideas, representations and narratives that together promote or support a particular world view.

Close inspection might reveal contradictions and inconsistencies within an ideology, but the function of any ideology is to present its specific world view as 'natural' or as 'universal truth'. For example, 'capitalist ideology' presents competitive individualism and private property as universal truths; 'communist ideology' presents the common ownership of land and resources as a natural aspiration; and 'nationalist ideology' presents the promotion of national interest as self-evidently paramount.

idiom

A manner of expression, especially one peculiar to a person or language.

imagery

A general term for the images that appear in a poem or other literary text. Images tend to evoke strong sense impressions in readers and audiences; often these are visual, creating vivid pictures in the mind. Images can be figurative (e.g. **similes**, **metaphors**) or literal.

implied reader

The term 'implied reader' refers to the hypothetical figure of the person best equipped to respond fully to a particular literary text. Any text has an implied reader, whose attitudes (cultural, moral and so on) enable it to achieve its full effect.

irony

Generally speaking, irony involves implying something other than what is explicitly said; it requires readers to read between the lines and, often, to perceive more than a fictional or dramatic character does. *See* **dramatic irony**, **proleptic irony** and **verbal irony**.

metaphor

A type of figurative language that establishes an identity between two apparently dissimilar things. So when Bosola asks the Duchess of Malfi, 'and do these lice drop off now?' (*The Duchess of Malfi*, 3.2.232), he identifies the Duchess's officers with small, parasitic insects.

morality play

A kind of religious drama prevalent in the Middle Ages which sought to dramatise the battle between good and evil within the individual.

pastoral

A literary genre with a history dating back to classical times, pastoral describes poems, plays or novels set in the countryside. The conventional assumption of pastoral is of a rural innocence or purity that provides a moral reference point for the corruption, greed and decadence of cities.

persona

From the Latin for 'mask', a persona is sometimes used in literary studies to refer the person/the 'I' who speaks in a poem, novel or other literary work.

personifying

Attributing human qualities to an inanimate object or abstract concept. This is a kind of figurative language known as personification.

plot

A plot may conveniently be defined in opposition to a story. A story is a narrative of events told in the order in which they happened. A story turns into a plot when it is told in a particular way, with a stress on cause and effect (why things happened), and with any number of emphases and distortions: a plot need not be chronological, for example. A writer normally seeks to structure the plot in such a way as to arouse curiosity in the reader or spectator.

point of view

Point of view refers to the perspective from which a particular story is told. In first-person narratives the point of view tends to be that of the **first-person narrator**; in third-person narratives, the point of view may shift from one character to another, though **third-person narrators** normally privilege the points of view of one or a few of the principal characters.

proleptic irony

The foreshadowing of an event that will take place later in a play or other literary text.

protagonist

The chief character in a literary work.

pun

A play on words that sound identical or similar but have very different meanings, often with comic effect.

punning

see **pun**.

reception history

The reception history of literary texts refers to how they have been interpreted by different readers, audiences and critics over time. This might also include literary re-workings of the original text. Certain historical events written up in a particular way might also have a 'reception history', as they are re-written again and again at later historical moments.

register

A register is a particular type or style of language associated with a particular context. Thus, for example, we can talk about formal and informal registers, or registers associated with different professions (legal, medical, academic, and so on). They are often employed by writers as a technique of characterisation.

rhetoric

Language designed to persuade or impress.

satire

A work that seeks to diminish its subject through ridicule.

simile

A comparison of two apparently dissimilar things that uses either 'like' or 'as' to enforce the comparison.

soliloquy

A speech, usually of substantial length, in which a character gives voice to his or her thoughts and emotions while alone onstage. Early modern dramatists like Shakespeare and Webster employed the soliloquy often and to great dramatic effect.

sonnet

A 14-line lyric poem in iambic pentameter with a complex rhyme scheme.

sub-plot

A subsidiary plot in a play or narrative that may comment on the main plot in a number of ways.

third-person narrator

In contrast to the **first-person narrator** ('I'/'we'), who is a character in the story telling the story, the third-person narrator is not a character but tells the story from outside/above the characters and events. Whereas 'I'/'we' abound in first-person narration, in third-person narration all the characters are described in the third-person (she/he/they). Many third-person narrators are endowed with omniscience, that is, they know everything about the story they are telling.

tradition

In literary studies a tradition denotes a well-established literary practice; a mode or genre of writing with its own conventions which is part of a writer's literary inheritance.

tragedy

A tragedy is a play or other literary work dealing with matters considered to be serious and important and which culminates in a disastrous conclusion for the protagonist.

verbal irony

Verbal irony occurs when the actual meaning of a text is quite different from its ostensible meaning.

Acknowledgements

Grateful acknowledgement is made to the following sources:

Chapter 4

Mahon, D. (2000) 'Dirge', *Selected Poems*, London, Penguin, www.penguin.co.uk, pp. 196–7.

Reading 8.4

Nordoff, C. and Hall, J.N. (1934) *Men Against the Sea*, London, Chapman and Hall, pp. 47–54.

Index

Page references in **bold** refer to figures